TRAVELS IN NORTH AMERICA

in the Years 1780, 1781 and 1782

The Institute of Early American History and Culture is sponsored jointly by the College of William and Mary and Colonial Williamsburg, Incorporated. Publication of this book has been assisted by a grant from the Lilly Endowment, Inc.

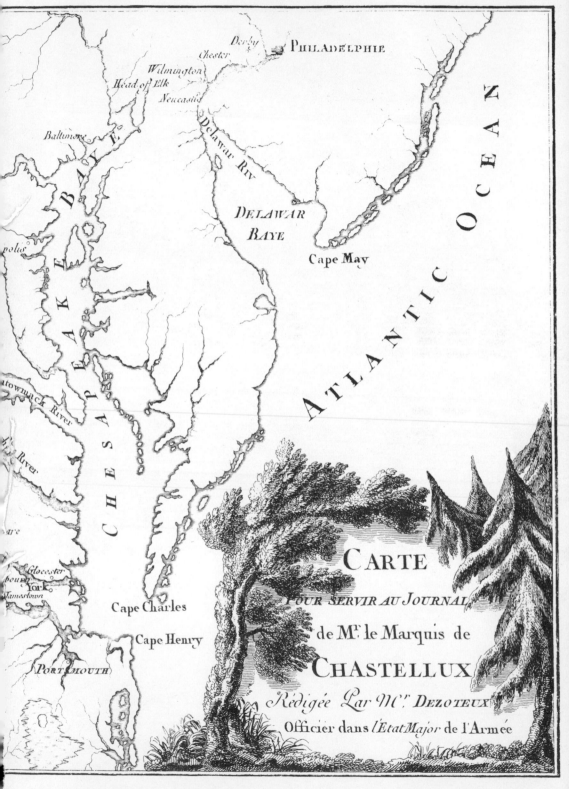

PHILADELPHIE

Derby

Chester

Wilmington

Head of Elk

Newcastle

Baltimore

Delawar Riv

DELAWAR BAYE

Cape May

ATLANTIC OCEAN

polis

CHESAPEAKE BAYE

towmack River

River

are

Gloecester

bourg

York

Jamestown

Cape Charles

Cape Henry

PORTSMOUTH

CARTE
POUR SERVIR AU JOURNAL
de M.^r le Marquis de
CHASTELLUX
Rédigée Par Mr DEZOTEUX
Officier dans l'Etat Major de l'Armée

GENERAL CHASTELLUX
at the age of forty-eight
by Charles Willson Peale, Philadelphia, 1782
(see p. vii)

TRAVELS IN NORTH AMERICA

in the Years 1780, 1781 and 1782

by the
MARQUIS DE CHASTELLUX

A REVISED TRANSLATION
with Introduction and Notes
by
HOWARD C. RICE, JR.

Volume 2

Published for the
Institute of Early American History and Culture
at Williamsburg, Virginia

by THE UNIVERSITY OF NORTH CAROLINA PRESS • CHAPEL HILL

CONTENTS

Volume 2

Illustrations   vii

Facsimile of title page of Paris, 1786, edition   xi

PART II: Journey into Upper Virginia, in the Appalachians and to the Natural Bridge, April 1782

Editor's Introduction: Interlude between Journeys, January 1781-March 1782   365

CHAPTER 1: Williamsburg to the Piedmont   377

CHAPTER 2: Visit to Mr. Jefferson at Monticello   389

CHAPTER 3: Across the Mountains to the Natural Bridge; and the Journey back to Powhatan Courthouse   397

CHAPTER 4: Petersburg, Richmond, Westover, and back to Williamsburg   419

CHAPTER 5: Notes on the State of Virginia   434

APPENDIX A: Description of the Natural Bridge   445

APPENDIX B: Notes on the Purple Martin and other American Birds   457

APPENDIX C: The Opossum   462

PART III: Journey into New Hampshire, the State of Massachusetts, and Upper Pennsylvania

Editor's Introduction: Interlude between Journeys, May-October 1782   471

CHAPTER 1: Hartford, Conn., to Portsmouth, N.H.   477

CHAPTER 2: Boston and Vicinity   490

CHAPTER 3: Providence, across Connecticut, and the Farewell to Washington at Newburgh   510

CHAPTER 4: The Moravian Settlements at Hope and Bethlehem; Return to Philadelphia   517

PART IV: Epilogue:

Letter from the Marquis de Chastellux to Mr. Madison, Professor of Philosophy at the University of Williamsburg, on the Progress of the Arts and Sciences in America

Editor's Introduction   529

List of Surviving Houses and other Sites mentioned by Chastellux   549

Note on Bibliographic and Cartographic Sources   556

Notes to Part II   563
Notes to Part III   614
Notes to Part IV   653

Index   661

Maps

Journey into Upper Virginia. 1782   376

Itinerary in New England. 1782   478

Boston and Vicinity. 1782   494

Itinerary from Newburgh on Hudson to Philadelphia. 1782   516

End Papers

Carte pour servir au Journal de Mr. le Mquis. de Chastellux. From Paris, 1786, edition. Virginia
                                                    End papers
                                                          front

Carte pour servir au Journal de Mr. le Mquis. de Chastellux. From Paris, 1786, edition. New England and the Middle Atlantic States
                                                    End papers
                                                          back

ILLUSTRATIONS

Volume 2

PORTRAIT OF CHASTELLUX,
By Charles Willson Peale   frontispiece

Peale's portrait of Chastellux, at the age of forty-eight, was painted
from life in Philadelphia, in August 1782, when Chastellux was on
his way north from Virginia, or perhaps the following December,
just before his return to France. It was subsequently displayed
among the other "celebrated personages" in Peale's gallery at the
corner of Third and Lombard Streets, and has remained a part of
this collection of the founders of the Republic, formerly on display
in Independence Hall and now shown in the Park Service museum
adjacent to it. C. C. Sellers, *Portraits by Charles Willson Peale*,
No. 140. (Courtesy of Independence National Historical Park
Collection.)

THE SURRENDER AT YORKTOWN,
By John Trumbull   between pp. 446-447

Although Trumbull's canvas is an idealized and formal arrangement
of the historic scene, rather than realistic on-the-spot reporting, the
portraits of individuals were in most cases drawn from life. Those
of the French officers, for example, were from studies made in Paris,
at Jefferson's residence there, during the winter of 1787-88. The
portrait of Chastellux, though commemorating his role at Yorktown, thus shows him as he appeared the year before his death at
the age of fifty-four. Trumbull's painting is of further significance
when seen in the light of Chastellux's exhortation, expressed in his
letter on the arts and sciences in America (see Part IV): "And your
public buildings, your *curiae*, why should they not display in sculptured relief and in painting the battles of Bunker's Hill, of Saratoga, . . . ? Thus would you perpetuate the memory of these glorious
deeds; thus would you maintain, even through a long peace, that
national pride, so necessary to the preservation of liberty." A large
replica of Trumbull's "Yorktown," together with others in his series
commemorating the events of the Revolution, hangs today in the
Rotunda of the Capitol at Washington; the "small oil" (reproduced
here) is in the Trumbull Gallery in New Haven. (Courtesy of the
Yale University Art Gallery.)

THE NATURAL BRIDGE IN VIRGINIA   between pp. 446-447

These three engravings of the Natural Bridge, reproduced from Chastellux's *Voyages* (Paris, 1786), were designed to accompany his own description of it (Pt. II, Appendix A). As explained in his text, they are from drawings made by Baron de Turpin, of the Royal Engineer Corps, who visited the Natural Bridge in May 1782 at Chastellux's instigation and Rochambeau's orders. "The General thought that he could render another service to the Americans by making known one of the natural wonders which shed lustre upon their country, and that it would even be rather droll for people to see that the French had been the first to describe it with precision and publish a correct plan of it." The engravings based on Turpin's surveys were indeed the first published pictures of the Natural Bridge, and served as the unacknowledged prototypes of many later prints and paintings. For further notes on the engravings see Vol. I, Introduction, "Check-list of the Different Editions of Chastellux's Travels," Nos. 10-14.

BOSTON IN THE AUTUMN OF 1778   between pp. 510-511

As indicated in the legend at the top of the picture, this pen and wash drawing, attributed to Pierre Ozanne, is one of a series recording the campaign of Admiral d'Estaing, whose squadron sailed from Toulon in April 1778. After a violent storm upset plans for a joint Franco-American land and sea attack on Rhode Island, then held by the English, D'Estaing's squadron put in for repairs at Boston, where it remained from late August to early November 1778. Although the view thus depicts Boston four years prior to Chastellux's visit there in November 1782 (Pt. III, chap. 2)—when another French squadron under Vaudreuil was waiting in the harbor to transport Rochambeau's victorious troops to the West Indies and eventually home to France—the general appearance of the city had not changed: the skyline and the landmarks were the same. The French artist's pleasant designation of Boston as capital of the United States no doubt reflects the interest aroused by events in America among his compatriots, who enthusiastically, albeit somewhat uncritically, referred to all American insurgents as *les Bostoniens* or *les Bostonnais*, while they played a card game called *le wisk bostonien* (or plain *boston*) in some provincial *Café de Boston*. (Courtesy of the Metropolitan Museum of Art, Prints Division, gift of William H. Huntington.)

CAMBRIDGE, MASSACHUSETTS, *ca.* 1783-1784   between pp. 510-511

Cambridge, according to Chastellux, who visited it on November 18, 1782, was then "a little town inhabited only by students, professors, and the small number of servants and workmen they employ." This watercolor from the mathematical notebook of a Harvard student, Samuel Griffin, '84, shows Harvard Hall (the second large building from the right, with belfry), which Chastellux describes in his journal—as well as the other college buildings which he fails to mention, or perhaps failed to notice during his hurried visit late on a winter afternoon. Overshadowed and almost hidden by the First Church (towards the left of the picture, with tall spire—no longer standing today) is the still extant "Wadsworth House," where Chastellux took tea with President Willard and met several professors and students. See Pt. III, chap. 2, nn. 37, 40. (Courtesy of the Harvard University Archives.)

MORAVIAN SETTLEMENT AT HOPE, NEW JERSEY

between pp. 510-511

The Moravian town of Hope—which Chastellux visited on December 9, 1782—is here viewed from Jenny Jump Mountain, looking northwest, with the Delaware Water Gap on the horizon to the far left. The oil painting by Gustavus Grünewald (1805-78), although done in the mid-nineteenth century, was intended to show Hope in 1809, that is, the year it ceased to be a Moravian community. The gristmill and millrace that Chastellux admired may be distinguished on the right edge of the town; further to the left is the Gemeinhaus (with belfry), which had been dedicated only a few weeks before his visit. Many of these stone buildings survive today; the present town is in fact closer in general pattern and size to Chastellux's time than almost any of the others mentioned in his *Travels*. See Pt. III, chap. 4, nn. 6-14. (Courtesy of the Moravian Historical Society, Whitefield House, Nazareth, Pennsylvania.)

BETHLEHEM, PENNSYLVANIA, 1784

between pp. 510-511

This view of Bethlehem shows the Moravian community substantially as it appeared at the time of Chastellux's visit, with all the landmarks as he describes them. The drawing from which J. Spilsbury's engraving was taken is, in part at least, the work of Nicholas Garrison, Jr., the retired seaman and drawing master who served as Chastellux's guide on the morning of December 11, 1782, and who is perhaps the figure seated on the heights above the Lehigh in the lower left-hand corner of the picture. Many of the buildings here depicted survive today, still serving their original purpose, in the "Old Bethlehem" enclave of the modern industrial city. See Pt. III, chap. 4, especially nn. 29, 33, 34. (Courtesy of the Archives of the Moravian Church, Bethlehem, Pennsylvania.)

VOYAGES

DE M. LE MARQUIS

DE CHASTELLUX

DANS L'AMÉRIQUE

SEPTENTRIONALE

Dans les années 1780, 1781 & 1782.

Πολλῶν δ' ἀνδρώπων ἴδεν ἄςεα, καὶ νόον ἔγνω.

Multorumque hominum vidit urbes, & mores cognovit.

ODISSÉE, Liv. I.

TOME SECOND.

A PARIS,

CHEZ PRAULT, IMPRIMEUR DU ROI,

Quai des Auguſtins, à l'Immortalité.

———

1786.

Title Page, First Trade Edition of Chastellux's Travels

PART II

Journey into Upper Virginia, in the Appalachians and to the Natural Bridge

April 1782

EDITOR'S INTRODUCTION

Interlude between Journeys
January 1781—March 1782

CHASTELLUX's two months' tour from Newport to Philadelphia and back, which produced Part I of his *Travels*, also bore fruit of more immediate practical importance. During this philosophical tour he had not forgotten that he was a soldier of his King, nor were his hosts along the route unmindful of the fact. The journey was thus a liaison or goodwill mission, for in the course of it Chastellux not only familiarized himself with the terrain of past battles and future operations, but had occasion to observe American troops and meet many of the American officers (including several of his own compatriots serving with the Americans) with whom he was soon to cooperate in active warfare. Not the least of these was the Commander in Chief, General Washington, who was in fact Chastellux's own commander in chief, for it must not be forgotten that the French expeditionary force had been sent by the King to serve under Washington's command. One of the first letters that Chastellux wrote upon his return to Newport was a word of thanks for Washington's hospitality. The Commander in Chief straightway replied in a letter that began: "Dear Sir, Accept my congratulations on your safe arrival at New Port in good health, after traversing so much of the American theatre of war," and ended on a still warmer note: "I wish I had expression equal to my feelings, that I might declare to you the high sense I have of, and the value I set upon, your approbation and friendship; it will be the wish and happiness of my life to merit a continuance of them, and to assure you upon all occasions of my admiration of your character and virtues." [1]

Washington's letter, written from his New Windsor headquarters, January 28, 1781—the first in a correspondence that continued until Chastellux's death in 1788—was more than a well-phrased compliment to a high-ranking brother officer and ally. As subsequent

365

events indicate, Washington placed considerable confidence in Chastellux, in part perhaps because the latter's knowledge of English facilitated an easy and frank exchange of views. During the months that followed, Chastellux was not merely present on the scene, but had an important share in planning the campaign that culminated happily at Yorktown in October 1781.

At the beginning of the year 1781 British forces under Generals Phillips and Benedict Arnold invaded Virginia, soon to be followed by Cornwallis. In March, when Washington visited the French army at Newport, a French squadron under Destouches was dispatched to the Chesapeake in an attempt to effect a junction with American land forces sent south to Virginia under Lafayette. This attempt failed, but it nevertheless foreshadowed, and set the pattern for, the similar operation, on a much larger scale, that was to be successfully completed before the end of the year. During Washington's visit to Newport Chastellux was among those who "heaped civilities" upon him.[2] A fortnight or so after the Commander in Chief's return to New Windsor, when he had important secret information to send to Rochambeau, he instructed Major Benjamin Tallmadge, his emissary: "As the Count de Rochambeau does not understand English, it may be well to communicate your business to the Chevalier de Chattelus in the first instance and thro' him to the Count, lest it should by accident get abroad in the Communication."[3] Tallmadge returned from his mission with the incidental news—which caused Washington genuine concern—that Chastellux was seriously ill. Thanks to the skill of Dr. Coste, chief physician of the French army, he recovered rapidly and in a few weeks was able to resume his accustomed activity.[4]

At the end of April Chastellux privately informed Washington, in advance of official notification, of the departure of Admiral de Grasse's fleet from Brest for the West Indies. In acknowledging the receipt of this highly important news, Washington confided: "I am impressed with too high a sense of the abilities and candor of the Chevr. Chastellus, to conceive that he is capable of creating false hopes; his communication therefore of the West India intelligence, comes with merited force and I would to God it were in my power to make the proper advantages of it! But if you can recollect a private conversation which I had with you in the Count de Rochambeau's chamber, you will be perswaded it is not; especially when I add that the want of which I then complained exists in much greater force than it did at that moment; but such preparations as can be made, I will make for the event you allude to." [5] Upon the heels of this "West India intelligence" came the crucial Franco-American conference held at Wethersfield, Connecticut, on May 21-22, 1781.

General Washington arrived at Wethersfield from New Windsor on Sunday the 20th with General Knox and General Duportail. The French engineer, who had been serving so effectively with the Americans since 1777, had been taken prisoner at the capitulation of Charleston the previous year, but had been exchanged and was now back again with the Continental Army. General Rochambeau and General Chastellux arrived from Newport on Monday the 21st, thus missing the long sermon preached the previous day by the Reverend John Marsh on Matthew 5 : 3: "Blessed are the poor in spirit, for their's is the kingdom of heaven." Admiral de Barras, who had succeeded Destouches as the ranking French naval officer at Newport, was detained in Rhode Island by the appearance of a British fleet off Block Island; his absence placed an added burden on Chastellux's diplomatic skill. Washington and his suite were lodged in the house of Joseph Webb; the French generals stayed nearby at Stillman's Tavern.[6] Upon this occasion Chastellux again saw his friend Col. Jeremiah Wadsworth, a key man in the important business of supplies for the French army, and again had the pleasure of dining with the good, methodical Governor Trumbull ("supra public expence," as the latter duly noted in his diary). On Wednesday the 23rd Rochambeau and Chastellux set out on their return journey to Newport. The concentration of French and American forces on the Hudson was now decided upon, and plans for an attack against New York had been outlined—it being hoped at this time (at least by Washington) that De Grasse's fleet would soon sail from the West Indies for Sandy Hook.

Not long after the conference at Wethersfield Washington again demonstrated his confidence in Chastellux's "goodness and candor" by requesting him to smooth over a misunderstanding that had arisen with Rochambeau concerning his views on the safest location for De Barras's squadron.[7] Indeed there is some reason to believe that certain of the French officers thought Washington placed too much confidence in Chastellux, who was in their eyes rather *trop Américain*. The episode of "the burned letter" is a case in point. In a confidential communication to the Chevalier de La Luzerne, the French Minister in Philadelphia, written at the end of May,

Chastellux had occasion to review the proceedings at Wethersfield and to speak rather querulously and indiscreetly of Rochambeau and his "incredible ignorance" of everything concerning America. The letter did not reach its intended destination. It was intercepted by the British who straightway had it conveyed to Rochambeau, with the obvious intent of stirring up inter-allied and intra-staff discord. Rochambeau thereupon showed the letter to Chastellux, then magnanimously threw it into the fire, and left his embarrassed subordinate "a prey to his remorse." [8] At the time, nothing of the incident transpired beyond Rochambeau's chamber. Surface harmony was preserved, and, remorseful or not, Chastellux continued to play his role in the councils of war.

On June 10, 1781 the French army, consisting of nearly five thousand men, began to move northward to Providence; most of the troops were ferried up the bay, and the rest took the land route. While at Providence Chastellux was lodged in town at the residence of Joseph Russell on Main Street, not far from the Market House. Then, on the 18th, commenced the three weeks' march that took the army westward across Connecticut, according to the plan determined at Wethersfield, to join the American forces on the Hudson.[9] The Bourbonnais Regiment, with Generals Rochambeau and Chastellux, led off from Providence, followed on successive days by the Deux-Ponts, the Soissonnais, and the Saintonge. The route went to Waterman's Tavern, then through "Voluntown," Plainfield, Windham, Bolton, and Hartford to Farmington—over roads that Chastellux had reconnoitered the previous November. After Farmington (where Chastellux was lodged in the house of the Reverend Timothy Pitkin), the army swung to the southwest, instead of continuing on the upper road to Fishkill, as he had done during his own earlier journey. Southington, Newton, Danbury, and Ridgebury were soon left behind. Then, entering New York State, came North Castle [Mount Kisco] and finally, on July 5 and 6, the long-wished-for junction with the Americans was made at Phillipsburg, to the rear of Dobbs Ferry on the Hudson.

For a month and a half the combined Franco-American armies remained in their encampment on the heights between the Bronx and Sawmill Rivers, some fifteen miles north of Manhattan Island, while daily expecting to launch an attack against the British bridgehead there. Chastellux met again the American officers whose acquaintance he had made during his tour. This time, however, there was more pressing professional business to discuss, even though occasional "civilities" were not wholly banished. General Chastellux, with his "family," had his own headquarters, not far from those of General Rochambeau, in a house belonging to Frederick Philipse, a Tory absentee.[10] It was from these quarters, on July 18, that he dispatched to the Commander in Chief, who was established less than two miles away, a cask of claret, with the following note, couched in his most elegant English:

Dear General, Your excellency knows very well that it is an old precept to offer the tithes of all earthly goods to the ministers of God. I think in my opinion that the true ministers of God are those who at the risk of their life employ their virtues and abilities to promote the happiness of mankind which consists for the greatest part in freedom and liberty. Accordingly I believe I am bound in duty to present your excellency with one of *ten* barrils of claret that I have just received. If you was, dear general, unkind enough not to accept of it, I should be apt to think that you want to prevent the blessings of heaven to fall upon me, or, as I was saying yesterday, that you are an enemy to the French produce and have a little of the tory in your composition.—Whatsoever be the high opinion that I entertain of your excellency, I wish to judge by that criterion and to guess by it your dispositions for the French troops and for myself. I have the honor to be with all respect and attachment, dear general, your most humble and obedient servant, le chr. de Chastellux.[11]

Washington rose to the occasion. "You have taken a most effectual method of obliging me to accept your Cask of Claret," he replied, "as I find, by your ingenious manner of stating the case, that I shall, by a refusal, bring my patriotism into question, and incur a suspicion of want of attachment to the French Nation, and of regard to you. . . . In short, my dear sir, my only scruple arises from a fear of depriving you of an Article that you cannot conveniently replace in this Country. You can only relieve me by promising to partake very often of that hilarity which a Glass of good Claret seldom fails to produce." [12]

The "Cask of Claret" came on the eve of another crucial interallied conference, held at Dobbs Ferry on July 19. In urgently requesting the meeting, for the purpose of determining upon a plan of operations to be communicated to De Grasse upon his arrival in North American waters, Rochambeau had informed Washington that he was bringing the Chevalier de Chastellux with him as an interpreter and suggested that Washington employ Duportail in the same capacity. At the conference Washington still held to the "Wethersfield plan" and gave his preference to an operation against New York, but nevertheless accepted conditionally, should De Grasse not find it possible to force a passage through Sandy Hook, the alternative of a transfer of the army to Virginia and a combined land and sea operation against Cornwallis.

Two days after the Dobbs Ferry conference, Chastellux for the first time since his arrival in America had a taste of active warfare. This was a reconnaissance in force in the direction of British-held New York.[13] On the evening of July 21, Major General Chastellux commanded a French detachment of some 2,500 men, which, with an American detachment under Gen. Benjamin Lincoln on his right, made a night march from the Phillipsburg cantonments to Kingsbridge and Morrisania. The troops remained in position during the 22nd and returned northward on the following day. During this time Washington, Rochambeau, and their engineers made a careful reconnaissance of the British fortifications on the opposite shore, at the northern end of Manhattan Island. The chief casualty was the Count de Damas's horse, which was shot from beneath him by a Tory sharpshooter's bullet, and indeed, the purpose of this display of force was somewhat of a mystery to most of the participants. By convincing Washington of the strength of the British positions the reconnaissance no doubt served as further proof of the infeasibility of an attack on New York and as another argument in favor of a march southward to Virginia.

Three weeks later, on August 14, news of the impending arrival of the French fleet off Chesapeake Bay—not at New York—removed all reasons for indecision and determined the plan of the subsequent campaign. On August 19 the French and American armies began preparations for crossing the Hudson and by the 24th they had started on their rapid southward march to Virginia. On the 29th Chastellux dined in Princeton with Washington, Rochambeau, and their entourage. On the 30th the cavalcade of generals reached Philadelphia, where the French Minister, La Luzerne, among others, offered the appropriate civilities. On September 5 Washington and Rochambeau parted company briefly—the former to take the land route to Head of Elk, and the latter to proceed by barge down the Delaware to Chester in order to view the river forts (as Chastellux had done the previous December). A few miles beyond Chester a dispatch-rider brought to the Commander in Chief the long-awaited information that De Grasse's fleet, with reinforcements aboard, was in Chesapeake Bay. Washington thereupon retraced his footsteps to Chester, where he joyfully greeted Rochambeau and his staff with the great news. On September 8, Chastellux rode into Baltimore. On the 11th he rested at Mount Vernon as Washington's guest. On the 12th he set out again in the company of Washington and Rochambeau, in advance of the troops, which were now being transported down Chesapeake Bay. By forced riding across Virginia, via Fredericksburg, Dumfries, Newcastle, and New Kent Courthouse, the three generals reached Williamsburg on the York peninsula in the afternoon of September 14. Saint-Simon's French reinforcements, brought by De Grasse's ships from the West Indies, were already established there, alongside Lafayette's American infantry. At 4 P.M. twenty-one guns from the American artillery park fired a resounding salute to greet the new arrivals. Then the two armies turned out on their battalion parades to pay them honor.

On September 17, Chastellux set out with Rochambeau, Washington, Knox, and Duportail—the same who met together at Wethersfield—for another decisive staff conference. This time it was with Admiral de Grasse, aboard his flagship, *Ville de Paris*, anchored off Cape Henry. Appropriately, a captured English corvette, *Queen Charlotte*, took the generals to their rendezvous, where they beheld, as Washington wrote, "the most powerful fleet that ever appeared in these Seas." At the conference on the 18th plans for naval participation in the siege of Yorktown were decided upon. Due to contrary winds the conferees had a longer cruise than planned, and did not return to Williamsburg until the 22nd.

The trap was now set. On September 28, the allied armies began their march "for the investiture of the enemy at York," as Washington phrased it in his diary. On the 30th the enemy abandoned the exterior works and retired within the town. Preparations for the siege then began. This was war according to the book, as the French officers knew it, not border warfare or forest skirmishes. Washington was the first to recognize the importance of his Allies' contribution: "The experience of many of those Gentlemen [the French officers of every denomination] in the business before us," he wrote to Congress while the siege was still in progress, "is of the utmost advantage in the present operation." [14] Nor was he unmindful of the French fleet and the fact that "whatever efforts are made by the Land Armies, the Navy must have the casting vote in the present contest." [15]

The siege of Yorktown is fully described elsewhere; it is sufficient to recall here that Chastellux took an active and not insignificant part in the operation. The command of the French besiegers devolved by rotation upon Baron de Vioménil, Chastellux, the Marquis de St. Simon, and the Comte de Vioménil. Chastellux's turn came on October 7-8, on the 11-12, and again on the 15-16. The official French "journal" of the siege [16] records that on this latter date: "The trench was relieved by the Bourbonnais and Soissonnais regiments commanded by the Chevalier de Chastellux. Bourbonnais took over twelve hours in advance to assure the attack and was itself relieved by the Agenois regiment at nightfall. The enemy made a sortie with six hundred of the best of his infantry; he met with resistance at all the redoubts, and then attacked a battery in the second parallel where four pieces of artillery had just arrived but were not yet in position. The Chevalier de Chastellux marched the Agenois pickets to the right and left, and his reserve directly against the attackers. Several of the latter were either killed or wounded, six prisoners were taken, and the rest fled. Six hours later the four spiked guns were firing [thanks to the efforts of D'Aboville, commander of the artillery]. Thirty-nine of our men were killed or wounded during this night." Before Chastellux's tour of duty came round again, the enemy began overtures for a cessation of hostilities. On October 18, the guns were silent.

The siege was over. On October 19, 1781, Cornwallis, yielding at length to the combined pressures of the Franco-American armies and the French navy, formally surrendered. "After Orders" congratulating the army upon the "glorious event," issued the following day under Washington's signature, included due recognition of His Most Christian Majesty's contribution: "The General upon this occasion intreats his Excellency Count de Rochambeau to accept his most grateful acknowledgements for his Counsels and assistance at all times. He presents his warmest thanks to the Generals Baron Vioménil, Chevalier Chastellux, Marquis de St. Simon and Count Vioménil and to Brigadier General de Choisy . . . for the illustrious manner in which they have advanced the interest of the common cause." [17]

Chastellux is present, too, in the formal commemorative canvas of the Surrender at Yorktown, painted a few years after the event by the young American artist, John Trumbull. On the "French side" of the scene, as Trumbull reconstituted it in the grand manner, Rochambeau and the French officers sit astride their steeds, balancing Washington and the Americans. At Rochambeau's right hand we see the two admirals, De Grasse and De Barras, then the Baron de Vioménil, and next the alert and well-formed face of the Chevalier de Chastellux. Trumbull sketched this portrait from life in Paris in December 1787 or January 1788 (less than a year before Chastellux's death), as he did those of the other French officers represented in the "Surrender." As he sat for this portrait, in the salon of Jefferson's Paris residence on the Champs-Elysées, recalling no doubt the stirring scene in which he had been one of the principal actors, Chastellux also recalled perhaps the words he had written to an American correspondent not long after the surrender: [18] "My love for philosophy must not lead me to forget that I am a soldier. . . . I have written against war, but I have loved it when it humiliated the satellites of despotism and the incendiaries of your fair provinces. The end of this campaign has been most sweet to me.—*Cette fin de campagne a été bien douce pour moi.*"

Winter at Williamsburg

News of the successful ending of the Virginia campaign spread at once throughout the United States and was speedily borne across the seas by Rochambeau's messengers. The Duc de Lauzun, who crossed the Atlantic on the frigate *Surveillante* in twenty-two days, reached Paris with the glad tidings on November 21. Yorktown did not, however, mark the end of the war. "I will candidly confess," General Washington wrote at this time, "that my only apprehension (which I wish may be groundless) is, lest the late important success, instead of exciting our exertions, as it ought to do, should produce such a relaxation in the prosecution of the War, as will prolong the calamities of it . . . our only sound policy is to keep a well-appointed, formidable Army in the field, as long as the War shall continue." [19] The great concentration of forces in Virginia was soon dispersed. On November 4, De Grasse's fleet, as previously agreed, sailed out of Chesapeake Bay for the West Indies, leaving behind only a small light squadron commanded by M. de La Villebrune. On the 5th and 6th the Virginia Line departed southward, as did the Maryland and the Pennsylvania Lines, while the rest of the American troops embarked for Head of Elk and thence marched to the north. Only Rochambeau's army remained in Virginia for its winter quarters.

General Headquarters was in Williamsburg. The Bourbonnais and Deux-Ponts Regiments were likewise stationed there; Soissonnais and Saintonge were quartered in Yorktown, the Duc de Lauzun's Legion in Hampton, and the artillery at West Point at the head of York River. A chain of hussars was established to assure rapid communications between the different units of the French army, as well as with Philadelphia and with the American army. Certain of the French officers—including Baron de Vioménil and Chastellux's aide-de-camp, Baron de Montesquieu—obtained leave to return temporarily to France, but Chastellux himself spent the winter on duty with the army at Williamsburg. With Baron de Vioménil's departure, he was indeed the second in command, and when Rochambeau was absent, the ranking general.

During the winter quarters at Williamsburg, General Rochambeau maintained his headquarters in the Wythe House on the Palace Green. No detailed documents concerning the lodgings of the other French officers have as yet been found. It is not unreasonable, therefore, to suppose that Chastellux, too, had his residence in the Wythe House with Rochambeau. On the other hand, his rank was such that he may have been billeted with his "family" in a house of his own, as he had been at Newport and at Phillipsburg.[20] The administrative problems of a large army did not prevent the time from passing agreeably. As part of the public celebrations ordered by Congress for the Yorktown victory, a *Te Deum* was sung on December 15, 1781. That evening General Rochambeau gave a dinner, followed by a ball, for the leading residents of Williamsburg. Dancing was indeed one of the chief distractions of the younger French officers. Nelsons and Byrds, Randolphs and Taliaferros, all flocked into town from their plantations, with their daughters in tow. Hunting was another favorite diversion. Rochambeau himself could often be seen riding through the woods with a pack of hounds and a score of enthusiastic followers. Horse races and cockfights had their adepts. There were even two notable fires to enliven the scene. On November 23, one wing of the College of William and Mary, then being used as a hospital by the French, was destroyed, resulting in the loss of part of President Madison's library and scientific instruments. A generous settlement of 12,000 *livres* was made by Rochambeau—a negotiation in which Chastellux, as the chief diplomat and English-speaking general of the French army, no doubt had a major share. A month after this disaster, on December 22, the former Governor's Palace, used as a hospital for the American wounded, was burned to the ground (to rise again only in the twentieth century).

The rest of the winter elapsed with no other major disasters. While the younger officers were riding to hounds or calling on the ladies, Chastellux found leisure for occupations befitting a philosopher. He initiated experiments in natural history—notably the one concerning the gestation of the opossum, as recorded below in his book. He spent long hours in conversation with President Madison and the other professors at William and Mary, George Wythe and Carlo Bellini, discussing his favorite subject of "public happiness." Early in March 1782 he had the satisfaction of receiving from these same professors the honorary degree of Doctor of Civil Law. Later that month His Most Christian Majesty's Minister in Philadelphia, the Chevalier de La Luzerne, paid a visit to army headquarters at Williamsburg. Then, at the beginning of April, Chastellux set out on the three weeks' journey into Upper Virginia which is the subject of Part II of his *Travels*.

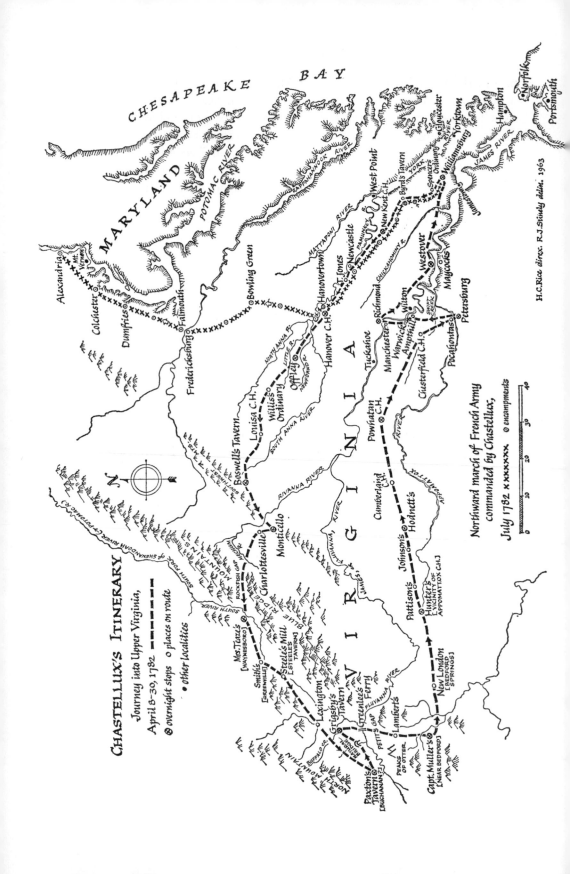

CHESAPEAKE BAY

MARYLAND

VIRGINIA

CHASTELLUX'S ITINERARY
Journey into Upper Virginia,
April 8–30, 1782 ▬ ▬ ▬
⊗ overnight stops ○ places on route
• other localities

Northward march of French Army
commanded by Chastellux,
July 1782 ××××××× ⊙ encampments

H.C. Rice direx. R.J. Stinely delin. 1963

Chapter

1

WILLIAMSBURG TO THE PIEDMONT

As soon as the French troops were established in the quarters they occupied in Virginia, I planned to make a journey into the upper part of that state. I had been assured that I should find there objects worthy of exciting a foreigner's curiosity and, faithful to the principle which I had adopted in my youth of never neglecting an opportunity to see as many countries as possible, I burned with impatience to set out. However, the season was not favorable and rendered traveling difficult and laborious. Experience furthermore has taught me that traveling in winter never offers the greatest satisfaction we can enjoy, that of seeing Nature as she ought to be and of forming a correct idea of the appearance of a country. It is easier for the imagination to strip a landscape of the charms of spring than it is to clothe the hideous skeleton of winter with them; as it is easier to imagine what a beauty at eighteen may be at eighty than to conceive what eighty was at eighteen.[1] Besides, as Monsieur de Rochambeau was absent during the month of February and as the Chevalier de La Luzerne [French Minister in Philadelphia] chose the month of March to pay us a visit, both politeness and duty obliged me to wait until April before beginning my journey.

April 8, 1782: Williamsburg—Byrd's Tavern—New Kent Courthouse

I therefore set out on the 8th of April with M. Lynch, then my aide-de-camp and now [i.e., 1786] *aide-major général;* M. Frank Dillon, my second aide-de-camp; and the Chevalier d'Oyré of the Engineers.[2] Six servants and an extra horse composed our train, so that our little caravan consisted of four masters, six servants, and eleven horses. I had given spring due warning and plenty of time to meet me. In the 37th degree of latitude she might be expected in the month of April, but she was not to be found in the woods through which I passed. I could barely discern a few thornbushes beginning to leaf. The sun was nevertheless very warm, and I regretted finding summer in the heavens, while the earth presented no appearance of spring. The eighteen miles that we traveled before stopping to feed our horses at Byrd's Tavern [3] were familiar to me, for this was the same route I had taken last summer when coming to Williamsburg. The remaining sixteen miles, which completed my day's journey and brought us to New Kent Courthouse,[4] offered nothing curious. All that I learned from my conversation with Mr. Byrd was that he had been plundered by the English when they were passing by his house on their march to Westover in pursuit of Monsieur de La Fayette, and again when they were returning to Williamsburg after unsuccessfully trying to engage him.[5] It was comparatively nothing to see fruit, fowl, and cattle carried away by the light troops which formed the vanguard, to see the army gather up what the vanguard had left, and even the officers seize the rum and all kinds of provisions without paying a farthing for them.[6] This hurricane, which destroyed everything in its path, was followed by a scourge yet more terrible: a numerous rabble, under the names of Refugees and Loyalists, followed the army, not to assist in the field, but to share the plunder.[7] The furniture and clothing of the inhabitants was in general the only booty left to satisfy their avidity; after they had emptied the houses, they stripped the owners; and Mr. Byrd still recalled with distress that they had forcibly taken the very boots from off his feet. I must not forget to mention that before reaching Mr. Byrd's I had had occasion to recall the first punishment inflicted on these robbers. This was six miles from Williamsburg when I passed near a place where there is an open space in the woods at the intersection of two roads, one of which leads to Williamsburg and the other to Jamestown.[8] Here, on June 25 [1781], Monsieur de La Fayette ordered his vanguard to attack Lord Cornwallis's vanguard. Simcoe, who commanded the latter, had remained behind to collect some cattle, while Lord Cornwallis was encamped at Williamsburg, where he had arrived the preceding evening. Monsieur de La Fayette's cavalry with some infantry mounted behind them arrived soon enough to force Simcoe to stop and fight. The rest of the American light infantry soon joined them. Simcoe fought at a disadvantage until Lord Cornwallis marched to his assistance. Then the Americans retired, after having killed or wounded nearly 150 men, with a loss of only seven or eight.[9] Colonel [Richard] Butler, an American officer who commanded a battalion of light infantry, and Colonel Galvan,[10] a French officer, who commanded another, greatly distinguished themselves on this occasion. The recollection of this event, which foreshadowed the success which crowned our campaign, employed my thoughts all the more agreeably during the whole evening, as I was lodged in a rather good inn, where we were served an excellent supper, composed chiefly of sturgeon and shad, two kinds of fish which are at least as good in Virginia as in Europe, but which make their appearance only in the spring.

April 9, 1782: New Kent Courthouse—Newcastle—Hanover Court-house

The next morning I experienced a pleasure of another kind. I rose with the sun, and while breakfast was preparing, took a walk around the house. The birds were heard on every side, but my attention was chiefly attracted by a very agreeable song, which appeared to proceed from a neighboring tree. I approached softly and perceived that I owed it to a mockingbird who was greeting the rising sun.[11] At first I was afraid of frightening it, but my presence on the contrary gave it pleasure, for apparently delighted at having an audience, it sang better than before, and its emulation seemed to increase, when it saw two dogs which were following me approach the tree on which it was perched. It kept hopping incessantly from branch to branch, still continuing its song, for this extraordinary bird, no less remarkable for its agility than for its warbling, continually rises and sinks, so that it appears as much the favorite of Terpsichore as of Polyhymnia. This bird can certainly not be reproached with tiring its auditors, for nothing can be more varied than its song, of which it is impossible to give an imitation or even any adequate idea. As it had every reason to be pleased with my attention, it concealed from me no one of its talents; and you would have thought, that after having delighted me with a concert, it was desirous of still further entertaining me with a comedy. So it began to counterfeit different birds; those which it imitated the most recognizably, at least to a stranger, were the jay, the crow, the cardinal, and the lapwing.[12] It appeared desirous of retaining me near it, and when, after having listened to it for a quarter of an hour, I was about to return to the house, it followed me, flying from tree to tree, always singing, sometimes its natural song, and at others, those which it had learned in Virginia or during its travels; for this bird is one of those which change climate, although it is sometimes seen here during the winter.

As this day's journey was to be longer than that of the day before, I left New Kent Courthouse before eight o'clock and rode twenty miles to Newcastle, where I resolved to give my horses an hour or two of rest. The road was not so level as it had been the day before: a few hills break the monotony of it. From the top of them you can see for a distance of some miles, and now and then you catch a glimpse of the Pamunkey River, which flows in a deep, wood-covered valley. As you approach Newcastle, the country opens up. This little Capital of a little County contains twenty-five or thirty houses, some of which are pretty enough.[13] When my horses were rested and the heat, already rather strong in the middle of the day, was a little abated, I continued on my way in order to reach Hanover Courthouse, which was still sixteen miles away, before dark. The country through which I passed is one of the most agreeable of lower Virginia. One sees many well-cultivated estates and handsome houses, among others, one belonging to Mr. [Thomas] Jones, situated near the road, two miles from Newcastle. It had a fine appearance from the outside, and we were assured that it was furnished with much refinement, and, what is more uncommon in America, that it was further embellished with a garden laid out in the English style. It is even said that this kind of a park, which is bounded in part by the river, yields not in beauty to those English models which we [in France] are now imitating with much success.[14]

Three miles before reaching Hanover, there are two roads; the one that I was to take turns a bit towards the north and brings you closer to the Pamunkey. I arrived before sunset and alighted at a rather good inn.[15] A very large hall and a covered portico are used to receive the people who assemble every three months at the courthouse, either for private or public business. This asylum is the more necessary as there are no other houses in the neighborhood. Travelers make use of these establishments, which are indispensable in a country so thinly inhabited that the houses are often at a distance of two or three miles from each other. Care has been taken to place the courthouse in the center of the county. As there are a great many counties in Virginia, they are seldom more than six or seven leagues in diameter, thus every man can return home after he has finished his business.

Hanover County, like that of New Kent, still remembered the passage of the English. Mr. [Paul] Thilman, my landlord, though he lamented his misfortune in having lodged and boarded Lord Cornwallis and his retinue, without his Lordship's having made any payment, could still not help laughing at the fright which the unexpected arrival of Tarleton spread amongst a considerable number of gentlemen who had come to hear the news and were assembled at the courthouse. A Negro on horseback came full gallop to warn them that Tarleton was no more than three miles off. They resolved without delay to retreat, but the alarm was so sudden and the confusion so great, that everyone jumped on the first horse he could find, so that only a few of those curious gentlemen returned home on their own horses. The English were at the time coming from Westover, they had crossed the Chickahominy at Bottom's Bridge and were heading towards the South Anna, which M. de La Fayette had put between them and himself.[16]

Mr. Thilman having had time to restock his larder since the retreat of Lord Cornwallis, we supped very well, and had the company of Mr. [Charles] Lee, brother of the Colonel Henry Lee who has long commanded a legion and often distinguished himself, particularly in Carolina.[17]

April 10-11, 1782: Hanover Courthouse—Offley

We set out at nine the next morning, after having breakfasted much better than our horses, for they had had nothing but oats, the country being so destitute of forage, that we could not find a truss of hay or even leaves of Indian corn, though we had scoured the country for more than two miles round. Three miles and a half beyond Hanover we crossed over the South Anna on a wooden bridge. I observed that the river was deeply embanked, and from the nature of the country concluded that it must be the same for a great part of its course. It seemed to me therefore that it could have been made a good defense if Monsieur de La Fayette, who had crossed it higher up, had had time to reach the bridge and destroy it.[18] On the left bank of this river the ground rises and you go up a fairly good hill. The country is barren, and I traveled in the woods most of the time until one o'clock, when I arrived at Offley, the

liver" [Taliaferro] who sang some airs, the words of which were English, but the music Italian. Her charming voice and the artless simplicity of her singing were her substitute for cultivated taste. Indeed, these in themselves showed real taste, that shy, natural taste which is always sure when it is held within proper limits and when it has not yet been spoiled by false precepts and bad models.

Miss Tolliver had come to Offley with her sister, Mrs. William Nelson, who had just had a miscarriage and remained in bed. She was brought up in the middle of the woods by her father, a great fox hunter, and consequently could learn singing only from the birds in the neighborhood, when the howling of the dogs permitted her to listen to them. She is of a pleasing appearance, as is Mrs. Nelson her sister, although less pretty than a third sister who had remained with her father. These young ladies often came to Williamsburg to attend the balls there; they were as well dressed as those of the town and always behaved with becoming modesty. The young men of our army, on the other hand, had taken a great liking to Mr. Tolliver, the young ladies' father, and often took the trouble to ride over to breakfast and talk hunting with him.[25] The young ladies, who appeared from time to time, never interrupted the conversation. These pretty nymphs more timid and gentle than those of Diana, though they did not lead the chase, inspired a taste for it; they knew how to defend themselves from the hunters, but did not crush with their arrows those who dared look at them.

After this little digression, which will doubtless be viewed indulgently, it is difficult for me to find a proper transition leading to an old magistrate, whose white locks, noble figure, and lofty stature command respect and veneration. Secretary Nelson, who is now my concern, owes this title to the office he held under the English government.[26] In Virginia the Secretary, responsible for preserving the records of all public acts, was an ex officio member of the Council, of which the Governor was the chief. Mr. Nelson, who held this office for thirty years, saw the morning of that bright day which began to shine upon his country; he saw too the storms arise which threatened its destruction, though he attempted neither to provoke nor to avert them. Too far advanced in age to desire a revolution, too prudent to check it if it was necessary, and too faithful to his countrymen to separate his interests from theirs, he chose this time of crisis to retire from public affairs. Thus, leaving the stage when new dramas demanded other actors, he took his seat among the spectators, content to offer up his wishes for the success of the play, and to applaud those who acted their parts well. But in the last campaign, chance brought him again on the stage, and conferred fatal celebrity upon him. He lived at York, where he had built a very handsome house, from which neither European taste nor luxury was excluded; a chimney piece and some bas-reliefs of very fine marble, exquisitely sculptured, were particularly admired, when fate conducted Lord Cornwallis to this town to be disarmed, together with his hitherto victorious troops. Secretary Nelson did not judge it necessary to flee from the English, in whom he could inspire neither odium nor suspicion. He was well treated by the General [Cornwallis], who established his headquarters in his house, which was built on an eminence, near the most important fortifications, and in the most agreeable situation in the town.[27] It was the first object which struck the eye when approaching the town. Soon, however, instead of travelers, it attracted the attention of our bombardiers and cannoniers; and soon it was almost entirely destroyed. Mr. Nelson was still occupying it when our batteries, trying their first shots, killed one of his Negroes at a very short distance from him. Lord Cornwallis himself was obliged to seek another shelter. But what refuge could be found for an old man, deprived of the use of his legs by the gout? But what, above all, could shelter him from the cruel anguish a father must feel at being besieged by his own children—for two of his own sons were in the American army. Thus, every shot, whether fired from the town, or from the trenches, might prove equally fatal to him. I was witness to the cruel anxiety of one of these unfortunate young men, when after a "flag" [28] was sent to request his father, he kept his eyes fixed upon the gate of the town, by which "the flag" was to come out, and seemed to expect his own sentence in the answer. Lord Cornwallis had too much humanity to refuse so just a request. I cannot recall without emotion having seen this old gentleman just after he arrived at General Washington's headquarters: he was seated, the attack of the gout still troubling him, and while we stood around him, he related to us, with a serene countenance, what had been the effect of our batteries, and how much his house had suffered from the first shots.

The tranquillity which has succeeded these unhappy times, by giving him leisure to reflect upon his losses, has not embittered the recollection; he lives happily in one of his plantations, where, in less than six hours, he can assemble thirty of his children or grand-children, nephews or nieces, who number seventy in all, and all of whom live in Virginia. The rapid increase of his own family justi-fies what he told me of the population in general, of which, from the offices he has held all his life, he must have it in his power to form a very accurate judgment. In 1742 the people subject to pay taxes in the state of Virginia, that is to say, the white males above sixteen, and the male and female blacks of the same age, amounted only to the number of 63,000; by his account they now exceed 160,000.[29]

April 12, 1782: Offley—Willis's Ordinary—Louisa Courthouse—Boswell's Tavern

After passing two days very agreeably with this interesting fam-ily, I left on the 12th at ten in the morning, accompanied by the Secretary, and five or six other Nelsons, who conducted me to the bridge over Little River, a small "creek" which was on my route, about five miles from Offley. There we separated, and riding eleven miles further through woods and over rather barren country, I arrived at one o'clock at Willis's Ordinary, for the inns which in the other provinces of America are known by the name of taverns, or public houses, are in Virginia called "ordinaries." This one con-sists of a small house placed in a solitary situation in the middle of the woods, notwithstanding which I found a good many people assembled there.[30] As soon as I alighted, I inquired what might be the reason of this numerous assembly in such a deserted spot, and learned that it was a cockfight. This diversion is much in fashion in Virginia, where English customs are more in evidence than in the rest of America. When the principal promoters of this diversion propose to match their champions, they take care to announce it to the public, and although there are neither posts nor regular con-veyances, this important news spreads with such facility that plant-ers come from thirty or forty miles around, some with cocks, but all with money for betting, which is sometimes very considerable. They are obliged to bring their own provisions, as so many people with good appetites could not possibly be fed at the inn. As for lodgings, one large room for the whole company, with a blanket for each individual, is sufficient for such countrymen, who are no more particular about the conveniences of life than they are in the choice of their amusements.

While my horses were feeding, I had an opportunity of seeing a fight. The preparation took up a great deal of time; they arm the cocks with long steel spurs, very sharp, and cut off a part of their feathers, as if they meant to deprive them of their armor. At last they fought and one of them remained dead on the battlefield. The stakes were very considerable; the money of the parties was deposited in the hands of one of the principal persons, and I took pleasure in pointing out to them that it was chiefly French money.[31] I know not which is most astonishing, the insipidity of such diversion, or the stupid interest with which it animates the parties. This passion appears almost innate among the English, for the Virginians are still English in many respects. While the bettors urged the cocks on to battle, a child of fifteen, who was near me, leaped for joy and cried, "Oh! it is a charming diversion!"

I still had twenty-seven or eight miles to ride to the only inn where it was possible to stop before reaching Mr. Jefferson's; for M. de Rochambeau, who had traveled the same road two months before, had strongly advised me not to sleep at the tavern at Louisa Courthouse, the worst lodging he had found in America.[32] This public house is sixteen miles from Willis's Ordinary. As he had given me a very forcible description not only of the house, but of the landlord, I was curious to judge with my own eyes. Under the pretence of inquiring for the road, I went in, and saw that there was no other lodging for travelers than the landlord's own room. This man, called Mr. Johnson,[33] has become so monstrously fat that he can no longer move out of his armchair. He is a good humored fellow, whose manners are not very strict, who has loved good cheer and all sorts of pleasures to such an extent that at the age of fifty he has so augmented his bulk and diminished his fortune, that by two opposite principles he is near seeing the termination of both; but all this does not in the least affect his gaiety. I found him stretched out in his armchair, which serves him for a bed; for it would be difficult for him to lie down, and impossible to rise. A stool supported his enormous legs, in which were large fissures on each side, a prelude to what must soon happen to his belly. A large ham and a "bowl of grog" served him for company, like a man resolved to die surrounded by his friends. He reminded me in short of that country mentioned by Rabelais, where men had their bellies hooped to prolong their lives, and especially of the Abbé, who having exhausted every possible resource, resolved at last to finish his days by a great feast, and invited all the neighborhood to his *bursting*.[34]

It was already dark when I arrived at Colonel Boswell's;[35] he is a tall, stout Scotsman, about sixty years of age, and who has been about forty years settled in America, where he was a colonel of militia under the English government. Although he keeps a sort of tavern, he appeared ill prepared to receive strangers. It was indeed late, and besides, this road, which leads only to the mountains, is very little frequented. He was quietly seated near the fire, by the side of his wife, as old, and almost as tall as himself, whom he called "honey," which is the equivalent in French of *mon petit coeur*. These good people received us admirably, and soon called up their servants, who were already in bed. While they were preparing supper, we often heard them call, "Rose, Rose," which at length brought to view the most hideous Negress I have ever beheld. Our supper was rather frugal. Our breakfast the next morning was better; we had ham, butter, fresh eggs, and coffee with milk for drink; for the "whiskey," or corn spirits, that we had had the evening before mixed with water, was very bad; besides, we were perfectly accustomed to the American habit of drinking coffee as a beverage with meat, vegetables, or other food.

Chapter

2

VISIT TO MR. JEFFERSON AT MONTICELLO

April 13, 1782: Boswell's Tavern—Monticello

I SET out the next morning at eight o'clock, having learned nothing in this house worthy of remark, except that notwithstanding the hale and robust appearance of Mr. and Mrs. Boswell, not one of their fourteen children had attained the age of two. We were now approaching a chain of mountains of considerable height, called the South-west Mountains, because they are the first you meet in traveling westward before reaching the chain known in France as the Appalachians and in Virginia as the Blue Ridge, North Ridge [North Mountain], and Alleghany Mountains. As the country is heavily wooded, we seldom had a view of them. I traveled a long time without seeing any habitation, and was at a loss to know which of the many crossroads to take.[1] At last I overtook a traveler who had preceded us and he not only served as my guide, but also made the journey seem less long by his company. He was an Irishman,[2] who though but lately arrived in America, had served in several campaigns and had received a considerable wound in his thigh. He told me that they had never been able to extract the bullet, but he was none the less in good health and spirits. I got him to tell me about his military exploits, and particularly asked him for details about the country where he now lives, for he had told me that he was settled in North Carolina, upwards of eighty miles from Catawba and more than 300 from the seacoast. These new settlements are of special interest as they are remote from all trade and thus wholly dependent on agriculture; I mean that patriarchal agriculture which consists in producing only what is sufficient for the owner's consumption, without hope of either sale or barter. These settlers must therefore be self-sufficient. It is easy to conceive that there is soon no deficiency of food, but it is also necessary that their own flocks and their own fields supply them with clothing; they must manufacture their own wool and flax into cloth and linen, they must prepare the hides to make shoes, etc., etc. As for drink, they are obliged to content themselves with milk and water, until their apple trees are large enough to bear fruit, or until they have been able to procure themselves stills, to distill their grain. It would be difficult in Europe to imagine that the article which the new settlers are most in need of, in these difficult days, is nails, for the axe and saw can supply every other want. They contrive however to erect fences and to construct roofs without nails, but the work thus takes much longer and it is obvious what this costs in time and labor. It was a natural question to ask this farmer what could take him four hundred miles from home, and I learned that he was carrying on the only trade possible in his country [3] and by which the people who are the best off seek to increase their income—that of selling horses. Indeed, these animals multiply very fast in regions where there is abundant pasturage; and as they can be driven with no expense, by letting them graze along the way, they are the most convenient article of exportation for localities distant from the main roads and from the trading centers.

The conversation continued between us and brought us imperceptibly to the foot of the mountains. We had no difficulty in recognizing on one of the summits the house of Mr. Jefferson, for it may be said that "it shines alone in this secluded spot." [4] He himself built it and chose the site, for although he already owned fairly extensive lands in the neighborhood, there was nothing, in such an unsettled country, to prevent him from fixing his residence wherever he wanted to. But Nature so contrived it, that a Sage and a man of taste should find on his own estate the spot where he might best study and enjoy Her. He called this house *Monticello* (in Italian, Little Mountain), a very modest name indeed, for it is situated upon a very high mountain, but a name which bespeaks the owner's attachment to the language of Italy and above all to the Fine Arts, of which Italy was the cradle and is still the resort.

As I had no further occasion for a guide, I parted ways with my Irishman, and after continuing uphill for more than half an hour by a rather good road, I arrived at Monticello. This house, of which Mr. Jefferson was the architect, and often the builder, is constructed in an Italian style, and is quite tasteful, although not however without some faults; it consists of a large square pavilion, into which one enters through two porticoes ornamented with columns.[5] The ground floor consists chiefly of a large and lofty *salon*, or drawing room, which is to be decorated entirely in the antique style; above the *salon* is a library of the same form; two small wings, with only a ground floor and attic, are joined to this pavilion, and are intended to communicate with the kitchen, offices, etc. which will form on either side a kind of basement topped by a terrace. My object in giving these details is not to describe the house, but to prove that it resembles none of the others seen in this country; so that it may be said that Mr. Jefferson is the first American who has consulted the Fine Arts to know how he should shelter himself from the weather. But it is with him alone that I should concern myself.

Let me then describe to you a man, not yet forty, tall, and with a mild and pleasing countenance, but whose mind and attainments could serve in lieu of all outward graces; an American, who, without ever having quitted his own country, is Musician, Draftsman, Surveyor, Astronomer, Natural Philosopher, Jurist, and Statesman; a Senator of America, who sat for two years in that famous Congress which brought about the Revolution and which is never spoken of here without respect—though with a respect unfortunately mingled with too many misgivings; a Governor of Virginia, who filled this difficult station during the invasions of Arnold, Phillips, and Cornwallis; and finally a Philosopher, retired from the world and public business, because he loves the world only insofar as he can feel that he is useful, and because the temper of his fellow citizens is not as yet prepared either to face the truth or to suffer contradiction. A gentle and amiable wife, charming children whose education is his special care,[6] a house to embellish, extensive estates to improve, the arts and sciences to cultivate—these are what remain to Mr. Jefferson, after having played a distinguished role on the stage of the New World, and what he has preferred to the honorable commission of Minister Plenipotentiary in Europe.[7]

April 14-16, 1782: At Monticello

The visit which I made Mr. Jefferson was not unexpected, for he had long since invited me to come and spend a few days in his company, that is, amid the mountains. Nevertheless I at first found his manner grave and even cold; but I had no sooner spent two hours with him than I felt as if we had spent our whole lives together. Walking, the library—and above all, conversation which was always varied, always interesting, always sustained by that sweet satisfaction experienced by two persons who in communicating their feelings and opinions invariably find themselves in agreement and who understand each other at the first hint—all these made my four days spent at Monticello seem like four minutes.

This conformity of feelings and opinions, on which I dwell because it was a source of satisfaction to me and because egotism must now and then appear, this conformity, I repeat, was so perfect that not only our tastes were similar, but our predilections also—those predilections or partialities which cold and methodical minds hold up to ridicule as mere "enthusiasm," but which men of spirit and feeling take pride in calling by this very name of "enthusiasm." I recall with pleasure that as we were conversing one evening over a "bowl of punch," after Mrs. Jefferson had retired, we happened to speak of the poetry of Ossian.[8] It was a spark of electricity which passed rapidly from one to the other; we recalled the passages of those sublime poems which had particularly struck us, and we recited them for the benefit of my traveling companions, who fortunately knew English well and could appreciate them, even though they had never read the poems. Soon the book was called for, to share in our "toasts": it was brought forth and placed beside the bowl of punch. And, before we realized it, book and bowl had carried us far into the night. At other times, natural philosophy was the subject of our conversations, and at still others, politics or the arts, for no object has escaped Mr. Jefferson; and it seems indeed as though, ever since his youth, he had placed his mind, like his house, on a lofty height, whence he might contemplate the whole universe.

The only stranger who visited us during our stay at Monticello was Colonel Armand whom I have mentioned in my first journal.[9] As my friends know, he went to France last year [1781] with Colonel [John] Laurens, but returned in time to be present at the siege of Yorktown, where he marched as a volunteer in the attack on the redoubts. His object in going to France was to purchase clothing and complete equipment for a legion that he had already commanded, but which had been broken up in the southern campaigns, so that it was necessary to form it anew. He himself advanced the necessary funds to Congress, which agreed to provide the men and the horses. Charlottesville, a rising little town situated in a valley two leagues from Monticello, is the headquarters assigned for assembling this legion. Colonel Armand invited me to dine with him the next day; I went there with Mr. Jefferson, and found the legion under arms.[10] It is to be composed of 200 horse and 150 foot. The cavalry was almost complete and fairly well mounted; the infantry was still much below full strength, but the whole was well clothed, well armed, and made a very good appearance. We dined at Colonel Armand's with all the officers of his regiment, and with his wolf, for he has made a pastime of raising a wolf, which is now ten months old, and is as familiar, mild, and gay as a young dog. The wolf never leaves his master, and even has the privilege of sharing his bed. I hope that he will still reflect his good upbringing and not revert to his natural character when he has come to wolf's estate. He is not quite of the same kind as ours, for his coat is almost black and very smooth; so that there is nothing fierce about his head, and were it not for his upright ears and pendant tail, one might easily take him for a dog. Perhaps he owes the singular advantage of not exhaling a bad smell to the care which is taken of his toilet, for I noticed that the dogs were not in the least afraid of him and that when they crossed his track they paid no attention to it.[11] Now it is difficult for me to believe that all the cleanliness possible can deceive the instinct of these animals, which have such a dread of wolves, that they have been observed at the *Jardin du Roi* in Paris to bristle up and howl at the mere smell of two mongrels born of a dog and a she-wolf. I am inclined therefore to believe that this peculiarity belongs only to the species of black wolf, for you also see in America species similar to ours. It may be that we also have in Europe something like the American black kind; one might at least so conclude from the common saying, "*il a peur de moi comme du loup gris* (he is as much afraid of me as of a grey wolf)," which would imply that there were also black wolves.

Since I am on the subject of animals, I shall mention here some observations which Mr. Jefferson enabled me to make upon the only wild animals which are common in this country. I was long in doubt whether they should be called *chevreuils* (roe deer), *cerfs* (hart), or *daims* (deer), for in Canada they are known by the first name, in the eastern provinces by the second, and in the south by the third. Besides, in America, nomenclatures are so inexact, and observations so rare, that no information can be acquired by querying the people of the country. Mr. Jefferson having amused himself by raising a score of these animals in a park, they soon become very tame, which happens to all American animals, which are in general much more easily tamed than those of Europe. He enjoys feeding them with Indian corn, of which they are very fond, and which they eat out of his hand. I followed him one evening into a deep valley where they are accustomed to assemble towards the close of the day. I watched them walk, run, and bound; and the more I examined their paces, the less I was inclined to annex them to any European species: they are of absolutely the same color as the *chevreuil*, and this color never varies from one individual to another, even when they are tamed, as often happens with our *daims*. Their horns, which are never more than a foot and a half long, and never have more than three or four branches on each side, are more open and broader than those of the *chevreuil* and slant forward; their tail is from eight to ten inches long, and when they leap they carry it almost upright like our *daims*, which they further resemble not only in their proportions, but in the form of their head, which is longer and less frizzled than that of the *chevreuil*. They differ also from the *chevreuil* in that they never go in pairs, but gather in herds as do our *cerfs* and *daims*. From my own observations, in short, and from all I have been able to collect on the subject, I am convinced that this species is peculiar to America, and that it may be considered as somewhere in between the *daim* and the *chevreuil*.[12]

Mr. Jefferson being no sportsman, and never having crossed the seas, could have no definite opinion on this point of natural history; but he has not neglected the other branches. I saw with pleasure that he had applied himself in particular to meteorological observation, which, in fact, of all the branches of natural philosophy, is the most appropriate for Americans to cultivate, because the extent of their country and the variety of sites give them in this particular a great advantage over us, who in other respects have so many over them. Mr. Jefferson has made, with Mr. Madison [president of the College of William and Mary], a well-informed professor of mathematics, some corresponding observations on the prevailing winds at Williamsburg and at Monticello; and although these two places are only fifty leagues distant from each other and are not separated by any chain of mountains, the difference between the results was that for 127 observations of the northeast wind at Williamsburg there were only 32 at Monticello, where the northwest wind in general took the place of the northeast. This latter appears to be a seawind, easily counteracted by the slightest obstacle, insomuch that twenty years ago it was scarcely ever felt beyond West Point, that is, beyond the confluence of the Pamunkey and the Mattaponi which unite to form the York River about thirty-five miles from its mouth.[13] Since the progress of population and agriculture has considerably cleared the woods, this northeast wind penetrates as far as Richmond, which is thirty miles further inland.[14] It may thus be observed, first, that the winds vary greatly in their obliquity and in the height of their regions; and, secondly, that nothing is more important than the manner in which the clearing of a country is undertaken, for the salubrity of the air, even the order of the seasons, may depend on the access allowed to the winds and the direction given to them. It is a generally accepted opinion in Rome that the air there is less healthy since the cutting of a large forest which used to be situated between that city and Ostia and which protected it from the winds known in Italy as the *Scirocco* and the *Libico*. It is also believed in Spain that the excessive droughts, of which the Castilians complain more and more, are occasioned by the cutting down of the woods, which used to stop and break up the clouds. There is still another very important consideration upon which I thought fit to call to the attention of the learned in this country, whatever diffidence I may have of my own knowledge in natural philosophy, as in every other subject. The greatest part of Virginia is very low and flat, and so divided by creeks and great rivers, that it appears in fact redeemed from the sea and entirely of very recent creation; it is therefore swampy, and can be dried only by cutting down many woods; but as on the other hand it can never be so drained as not still to abound in mephitic exhalations; and of whatever nature these exhalations may be, whether partaking of fixed or inflammable air, it is certain that vegetation absorbs them equally, and that trees are the most proper to accomplish this object.[15] It therefore appears equally dangerous either to cut down or to preserve a great quantity of wood; so that the best manner of proceeding to clear the country would be to disperse the settlements as much as possible, and always to leave some groves of trees standing between them. In this manner the ground inhabited would always be made healthy; and as there will still remain considerable marshes which cannot be drained, there will be no risk of admitting too easily the winds which blow the exhalations from them.

April 17, 1782: Departure from Monticello

But I perceive that my journal is something like the conversation I had with Mr. Jefferson. I pass from one object to another, and forget myself as I write, as it happened not unfrequently in his society. I must now take leave of the Friend of Nature, but not of Nature herself, for she expects me in all her splendor at the goal of my journey—I refer to that famous "rock bridge" which joins two mountains, the greatest curiosity that I have ever beheld, because it is the one most difficult to account for. Mr. Jefferson would most willingly have taken me there, although this wonder with which he is perfectly acquainted is more than eighty miles from his home; but his wife was expecting her confinement at any moment,[16] and he is as good a husband as he is a philosopher and citizen. He therefore only acted as my guide for about sixteen miles, as far as the crossing of the little Mechum River. Here we parted, and I presume to believe that it was with mutual regret.[17]

Chapter

3

ACROSS THE MOUNTAINS TO THE NATURAL BRIDGE; AND THE JOURNEY BACK TO POWHATAN COURTHOUSE

April 17, 1782 (continued): Mechum River (beyond Charlottesville)—Rockfish Gap—Mrs. Teaze's [Waynesboro]

I CONTINUED on for seventeen miles more, the whole way in the defiles of the Western Mountains, before finding a place where I could rest my horses. At last I stopped at a lonely house, belonging to an Irishman by the name of Macdonald [*Gr.:* MacDonnell], where I found eggs, ham, chicken, and whiskey, and where I had an excellent dinner. He was an honest and obliging man, and his wife, who had a very agreeable and mild countenance, had nothing rustic either in her bearing or manners. For, in the midst of the woods and rustic tasks, a Virginian never resembles a European peasant: he is always a free man, who has a share in the government, and the command of a few Negroes. Thus he unites in himself the two distinct qualities of citizen and master, and in this respect clearly resembles the majority of the individuals who formed what were called *the people* in the ancient republics; a people very different from the people of our day, though the two are very improperly confused in the frivolous declamations of our half-philosophers, who, in comparing ancient with modern times, have invariably mistaken *the people* for mankind in general, and have praised the oppressors of humanity, thinking that they were defending its cause.[1] How many ideas need to be rectified! How many words, whose meanings are still vague and indeterminate! The "dignity of man" has been urged a hundred times, and this expression has enjoyed great favor. The "dignity of man," however, is a comparative matter. If taken as applying to individuals, dignity increases as a man considers his relationship to the classes beneath him. It is the plebeian who makes the dignity of the noble, the slave that of the free man, and the Negro that of the white. If the term is taken to apply to men in general, it can further inspire them with sentiments of tyranny and cruelty in relation to animals; and by thus destroying general benevolence, can go against the order and the design of Nature. What then is the principle on which Reason, freed from Sophists and Rhetoricians, can finally rely? It is equality of rights, the general interest which rules all, private interest linked to the general good, social order as necessary as the symmetry of the beehive, etc., etc. If all this does not lend itself easily to eloquence, we must console ourselves, and prefer sound, to high-sounding, morality.[2]

I had reason to be pleased with the sound morality of Mr. Macdonald; he served me with the best he had, did not make me pay too dear, and gave me all the information I needed to continue on my way; but not being able to set out until half past four o'clock, and having twelve miles to go before crossing over the "Blue Ridges," I was glad to meet on the road with an honest traveler, who served as my guide, and with whom I struck up a conversation. He was an inhabitant of Augusta County, who had served in Carolina as a common "rifleman," [3] notwithstanding which, he was well mounted, and appeared well off. For, in America, the militia is composed indiscriminately of all citizens, and the officers are elected by the militiamen themselves without regard either to years of service or experience.

My "Rifleman" had been at the battle of the Cowpens, where General [Daniel] Morgan, with 800 militia, completely defeated the famous [Banastre] Tarleton, then at the head of his own legion, of a regiment of regulars, and of different pickets drawn from the army, forming in all nearly 1200 men, of whom upwards of 800 were killed or made prisoners.[4] This event, the most extraordinary of the whole war, had always excited my curiosity. The modesty and simplicity of General Morgan's report on it have been generally admired.[5] But one circumstance in this account had always astonished me. Morgan had drawn up his troops in order of battle in an open wood, and had divided his riflemen on the two wings, so as to form, with the line, a kind of pincer (*tenaille*), which focused the whole fire, both directly and obliquely, on the English center. But after the first discharge, he made so dangerous a movement, that had he commanded the best-disciplined troops in the world, I should be at a loss to account for it. He ordered the whole line to wheel to the right, and after retreating thirty or forty paces, made them halt, face about, and recommence the fire. So I asked this witness, whose deposition could not be suspect, to tell me what he had seen, and I found that his account agreed perfectly with Morgan's own report. I then asked him the reason for this retrograde movement they had been ordered to make; he told me that he could give no reason. I persisted and inquired if the ground behind the first position was not more elevated and advantageous. He assured me it was absolutely the same, so that if it was this action which tempted the English (whose attack is not quick and generally consists of a brisk fire rather than in closing with the enemy) to break their line and advance rashly into the kind of focus of shots which were aimed at them from the center as well as the wings, then General Morgan had only to claim credit for it, and to boast of having employed one of the boldest stratagems used in warfare. This, however, is a merit that he has never claimed, and the account of this rifleman would lead me to conclude that his general, alarmed at the superiority of the English, had at first intended to yield the field of battle to them bit by bit, until he had found a more wooded spot and one more advantageous for an inferior force; but then, finding himself closely pressed, he had felt that time was short and that he had no other resource but to risk everything and give battle on the spot.[6] Whatever the motive for this unusual maneuver, it still resulted in the defeat of Tarleton, whose troops gave way on all sides, without a possibility of rallying them. Fatigued by a very long march, they were soon overtaken by the American militia, who, assisted by sixty horse under Colonel [William] Washington, took more than 500 prisoners, and captured two flags and two pieces of cannon. It was natural to ask what Tarleton's cavalry was doing during and after the engagement: during the fight this cavalry had tried to turn General Morgan's flanks, but had been held in check by some riflemen and by the American cavalry, which Colonel Washington had divided into two troops and sent to the flanks; after the battle it had fled at full gallop, with no thought of the infantry, and without taking any measures to cover their retreat. As for the English general, the Lord only knows what became of him. And this is that Tarleton who with Cornwallis was expected to complete the conquest of America, who with Cornwallis has received the thanks of the House of Commons, and whom all England admires as the hero of the army and the honor of the nation! [7]

Now, let us reflect on the fortunes of war, and recall that two months after this victory won by 800 militia [8] over 1200 veteran troops, General [Nathanael] Greene—after having collected nearly 5000 men, half militia and half Continentals, chosen an excellent position [Guilford Courthouse, North Carolina], and employed all the resources of military art—was beaten [March 15, 1781] by 1800 men, abandoned by his militia, and forced to limit all his glory to making the English pay dearly for the field of battle, which the rest of his troops defended foot by foot and yielded only with reluctance. [9]

While talking of war and battles I reached the foot of Rockfish Gap, which, for an extent of more than fifty miles, is the only passage through the Blue Ridge, at least in a carriage. We ascended rather easily, for a distance of about two miles. On reaching the top of the mountain, I was surprised to find there a newly built cabin inhabited by white people. I inquired of my fellow traveler what could have led them to settle in so barren and deserted a place; he told me they were poor people who expected to get some assistance from passers-by. I expected this answer, but I was sorry to find in an absolutely new country, where the land wants only inhabitants and agriculture hands, that white people should thus be obliged to beg. I stopped for a moment to look at the view—more wild than attractive—of the western mountains as seen from the summit of the Blue Ridge. But as the sun was near setting, I hastened on to reach the only inn where lodgings could be had, on the other side of the mountains. Notwithstanding which, I stopped once more, nor had I reason to regret it. As I was always followed by a servant with a fowling piece, and as I frequently got down from my horse to shoot partridge or some other game, conversation did not prevent me from keeping my eyes peeled (*les yeux alertes*). I now noticed a large bird which was crossing the road, and my sportsman's instinct told me that it must be what the inhabitants of these mountains call a "pheasant," which much more nearly resembles

our *gelinotte,* or hazel hen. Dismounting, calling my dog, and taking my gun, was the work of a moment; but, as I was preparing to
follow my *gelinotte* into the brush, one of my servants pointed out
to me two others, perched upon a tree behind him, and which were
calmly watching me. I fired at the one nearest to me, nor did it
require much skill to bring it down. Except that it was perhaps a
little bigger, it resembled those I had seen at Newport, where the
Americans sometimes brought them to market, but only in winter,
the season when they come down from the mountains and when
they are easier to kill. This one, before it was plucked, was of the
size of a capon; its plumage on the back and wings resembled that
of a hen pheasant, and, on the belly and thighs, our large winter
thrush. It was booted like the rough-footed pigeon, and the plumage
came down to its feet; the feathers on the head formed a sort of
tuft. Altogether, it is a fine bird and excellent eating, but when
stripped of its feathers, it is not larger than our *perdrix rouge* (red-
legged partridge), or our *bartavelle* (rock partridge).[10] After carefully instructing my servant to keep this bird for my supper, I attempted to find the first one that I had seen run into the underbrush.
I raised it once, but although I ran after it immediately and had an
excellent dog, it was impossible to find it again, for these birds run
very fast, like pheasants and rails. The way the inhabitants of the
mountains go about killing them is to walk in the woods at sunrise
or sunset, and to listen for the noise they make when beating their
sides with their wings; this noise is such that it can be heard more
than a mile away; they then approach softly and find them sitting
upon old trunks of fallen trees.

It was perhaps lucky that my shooting did not continue with
more success, for it was almost night when I reached the ford over
the South River, and the waters, considerably swollen by the recent
rains, were rather high. I was full of pride to be *fording* the famous
Potomac here, when it had taken me an hour to cross it at the Alexandria ferry.[11] The South River is indeed only a branch of the
Potomac, the source of which is in these mountains, and which like
all other rivers is of humble origins; but it may be considered the
most ostentatious of parvenus, for after thirty leagues it is over a
mile wide and more like an arm of the sea than a river.

Two hundred paces beyond the ford, but more than forty miles
from the place which I had set out from, I found the inn that Mr.
Jefferson had indicated to me; it is one of the worst lodging places

in all America.[12] Mrs. Teaze, the mistress of the house, was some time ago bereft by the death of her husband, and I verily believe that she was also bereft of all her furniture, for I have never seen a more badly furnished house. A poor tin vessel was the only "bowl" used for the family, our servants, and ourselves; I dare not say for what other use it was offered to us when we went to bed.[13] As we were four masters, without counting the rifleman, who had followed us and whom I had invited to supper, the hostess and her family were obliged to give up their bed to us. Just as we were deciding to make use of it, a tall young man entered the room where we were assembled, opened a closet, and took out a little bottle. I asked him what it was. "It's a drug," he said, "which our Doctor hereabouts has ordered me to take every day." "And what's your trouble?" I added. "Oh! not much," he replied, "only a 'little itch.' " I found this admission appealing in its candor, but I was by no means sorry that I had sheets in my portmanteau. It may easily be imagined that I was not tempted to breakfast in this house next morning.

April 18, 1782: Mrs. Teaze's [Waynesboro]—Steel's Mill—Paxton's Tavern

I set out therefore very early on the 18th, in hopes that we should find (as we had been told) a better inn, at the distance of ten miles, but these hopes were vain. Mr. Smith, a rather poor farmer to whom I was recommended, had neither forage for our horses, nor food for ourselves.[14] He merely assured us that eight miles further along we would find a mill, the owner of which was also an innkeeper. We found accordingly the mill and the miller.[15] He was a young man, twenty-two years of age, whose charming face, fine teeth, red lips, and rosy cheeks called to mind Marmontel's attractive portrayal of Lubin.[16] His walk and carriage did not however correspond to the freshness of his looks, for he appeared sluggish and inactive. I inquired the reason, and he told me he had been in a languishing state ever since the battle of Guilford Courthouse, where he had received fifteen or sixteen sword wounds. He had not, like the Romans, a crown to attest his valor; nor, like the French, either pension or certificate of honor; instead of these, he had a piece of his own skull, which his wife brought out to show me. I certainly little expected to find here in the American wilderness such deplorable traces of European steel; but I was the most touched to learn that it was after he had received his first wound, and was made prisoner, that he had been thus cruelly slashed. This unfortunate young man related to me how, when beaten down and bathed in blood, he had still had presence of mind enough to think that his cruel enemies would not want to leave any witness or victim of their barbarity, and that there remained to him no other way of saving his life than to pretend to have lost it. Oh, for the all-seeing eye of Divine Justice to discover and recognize the authors of such a crime!! Oh, for the voice of Stentor and for Fame's trumpet to consign them to the abhorrence of present and future ages! And to proclaim to sovereigns, generals, and all chiefs that the atrocities which they tolerate or leave unpunished will one day accumulate upon their heads, and that they will be held in execration by a posterity more touched by feeling and more enlightened than we yet are!

Even had Mr. [David] Steel—for that was my landlord's name —been more active, and his wife, who was young and pretty, more industrious, both together could not have made up for the total lack of bread and any kind of drink that they were then experiencing. The bread was just kneaded, but not yet put into the oven. And as for liquors, the house made use of none, and the same brook which turned the mill quenched the young couple's thirst, so that we might apply to Mrs. Steel those verses of Guarini:

> Quel fonte ond'ella beve,
> Quel solo anco la bagna, e la consiglia.[17]

But these pastoral manners ill suit the convenience of travelers. A few cakes, however, baked over the coals, excellent butter, good milk, and above all, the interest with which Mr. Steel inspired us, made us pass agreeably the time needed to put our horses in condition to complete a long and hard day's journey.

About five o'clock in the evening, after we had traveled thirty-eight miles, we found some houses, where we learned that we were still six miles from Paxton's Tavern, where we were to spend the night; [18] that we had two fords to cross, the last of which had become impassable because of the late rains; but that we should not be stopped, as we should find a boat to take us across, and our horses would swim behind. Approaching darkness and a black storm which was brewing made us hasten our steps. However, as we were obliged to mount and descend a very high mountain, scarcely a glimmer of twilight remained when we reached the second river, which is none other than the James, but near its source and at the place where it flows out of the mountains under the name of the Fluvanna. The difficulty was to get ten men and as many horses across with nothing but a single Indian canoe, which could hold four or five persons at most, and a single Negro, armed with a paddle for an oar. We put our saddles and baggage in the boat, made several trips, and each time took two horses by the bridle and made them swim across behind. Night closed in and it was pitch dark before this business was finished. Then, after laboriously resaddling and reloading our horses, we had the problem of reaching the inn, which was still half a mile from our landing place. As the river flows between two very steep banks, and as the canoe had not been able to land us at the ford, nor consequently at the road, we were obliged to climb up the mountain by a little-used path, very difficult even by daylight. We should never have found our way had I not got the boatman to guide us. So we clambered up as best we could, each of us leading his horse among the trees and the branches, which we could not see, so dark it was, even when they struck us in the face.

At last we arrived at Paxton's Tavern. It was now ten o'clock, and the house was closed, or rather the houses, for there were two. I approached the first of them and knocked at the door. It was opened, and I saw five or six little Negroes lying upon a mat before a large fire. I then went to the other house, and there found five or six white children lying in the same manner on a mat before a large fire. Two or three grown-up Negroes presided over each of these little troops.[19] They told me that Mr. Paxton, his wife, and his whole family, were invited to a wedding, but not far off, and that they would go and fetch them. I was also being invited to supper— by hunger resulting from a long journey and much fatigue—but found myself in a less favorable situation than the newlyweds and their guests. And I was further chilled by the expectation of seeing our host and hostess come home completely drunk. But I was mistaken; they arrived perfectly sober, were polite and solicitous, and at about midnight we had an excellent supper. Although the rooms and beds were not all we might have wished for, they were better than at Mrs. Teaze's, and we had no right to complain. Besides, we enjoyed the satisfaction of having reached the goal of our journey; the Natural Bridge was not more than eight miles distant, and we had obtained all the necessary directions for finding the way there.

April 19, 1782: Paxton's Tavern—Natural Bridge—Grigsby's Tavern

Next morning our breakfast was ready betimes, and served by Captain Paxton's daughters. The evening before they had not appeared entirely to their advantage; nevertheless, as far as the dim light of the room where we were supping, our own appetites, and the immense bonnets in which they were decked out for the wedding, had permitted us to judge, we had found them fairly pretty; but when we saw them by daylight, with no other headdress than their own brushed locks, with the night's rest as their only adornment, and their natural simplicity for every grace, we were confirmed in the opinion we had already formed, that the mountain people are in general handsomer and healthier than those on the seacoast.[20] There was also a young man in the house, rather well dressed, and of an agreeable countenance, whom I concluded to be an intended match for one of our young hostesses. But I soon discovered that he had come for matches of another kind. My traveling companions having asked me to come and look at a very fine horse, which stood alone in a little stable, I was told that it was a stallion which this young man had brought upwards of eighty miles, to dispose of his favors to the mares of the country.[21] His price was twenty shillings,[22] or eighteen *livres* of our money, for each visit, or the double for a connection of longer duration: which is much less than is paid in the other parts of Virginia. These details, which may appear trifling, will however serve to make the reader acquainted with a country, the inhabitants of which, dispersed in the woods, are separated only for the purposes of domestic comfort, which renders them independent of each other, but who readily communicate when mutual events or the general interest require it. But I am too near the Natural Bridge to linger over other subjects.

We set out at nine o'clock in the morning, and—to be truthful— a bit aimlessly; for in these mountains, where there are either too many or too few roads, people always think they have given sufficient directions to travelers, who seldom fail to go astray. This is the common fault of those who teach what they know too well, nor are the roads of learning exempt from this inconvenience. Fortunately, after proceeding for less than two miles, I met a man who had just had his horse shod at a nearby smithy, and was returning home followed by five or six hounds.[23] We soon struck up conversation and, what seldom happens in America, he was curious to know who I was and where I was going.[24] The fact that I was a French general officer and my curiosity about the wonders of his country aroused his interest. He offered to be my guide, and led me now over little paths, and now through the woods, uphill and down, so that without a guide, I should have needed to be a magician to find the way. Finally, after two hours, we went down a steep slope, and then climbed up another; during which time he endeavored to converse more briskly than ever. At last, he urged his horse forward, and then, stopping short, he said to me: "You want to see the Natural Bridge, don't you? Well, you are on it now! Get down from your horse, go twenty steps to your right or your left, and you will see this wonder!"

I had indeed noticed that there was on either side a fairly considerable drop, but the trees had prevented me from forming any idea of the depth, or paying much attention to it. Now, approaching the precipice, I at first saw two great masses or chains of rocks which formed the walls of a ravine, or rather of an immense abyss; but when standing, very cautiously, on the very brink of the cliff, I saw that these two walls came together under my feet, to form an arch, only the height of which I could as yet perceive. After enjoying this magnificent spectacle, but so awesome that some people can scarcely bear it, I went to the western side, which presents as imposing a sight, and one which is even more picturesque. This deep solitude, these ancient pines, these masses of rocks, the more astonishing as they appear to possess a wild symmetry and rough design, this whole display of rude and formless Nature striving to achieve art's forms—all this besets the senses and the mind, and excites a gloomy and melancholy admiration. But it is at the foot of these crags, on the edge of a little stream which flows under this immense arch, that one must judge of its astonishing structure; from there one can distinguish the buttresses, the rear-vaults, and the outlines which architecture might have given it. The arch is not a perfect one, the eastern part of the span not being as large as the western, because the mountain is higher on the western than on the eastern side. It is quite extraordinary that no considerable debris is to be seen at the bottom of the stream, no trace of the rending which must have destroyed the core of the rock and left only the upper part standing; for that is the only hypothesis that can account for such a prodigy. No recourse is possible to the theory of a volcano or of an alluvium; for there is no trace either of a sudden conflagration or of the slow and laborious work of the waters.[25] The rock is of a calcareous kind, and its strata are horizontal, a circumstance which further excludes the idea of an earthquake or of an underground crevasse. But it is not for a small number of travelers to give a general verdict concerning this natural wonder; it is for the learned of the Old World and the New to decide the question, and they will now be in a position to do so. The necessary steps have been taken to give it the publicity it deserves. An officer of the Engineers, Baron de Turpin, an excellent mathematician and draftsman, has gone to make measured drawings of its main features. His labors will make up for the imperfect description that I could give of it.[26] Let us then recognize the limits of our own powers, even though we cannot know the powers of Nature—and leave to more able hands the task of completing this picture of which I have given but an imperfect sketch. And let me continue the account of our journey. Its goal has been reached, but its end is not yet, for the Natural Bridge is more than two hundred and fifty miles from Williamsburg.

While I was examining the Natural Bridge from all sides, and trying to draw some of its aspects, my traveling companions had learned that their guide and mine was an innkeeper whose house was no more than seven or eight miles from the place where we were, and not more than two from the road which we would have to take next day to leave the mountains. Mr. Grigsby (the name of our guide) had shown some desire to receive us, assuring us we should be as well lodged as at the tavern recommended by Mr. Paxton. Even had this been otherwise, I had too many obligations to Mr. Grigsby not to give him the preference.[27] We therefore resumed our journey under his guidance, through woods which were very lofty. Strong robust oaks and immense pines sufficient for all the fleets of Europe here grow old and perish on their native soil, undisturbed by the hand of industry.[28] One is surprised to find everywhere in these unsettled forests the traces of several fires. These accidents are sometimes caused by the carelessness of travelers, who light a fire when they go to sleep and neglect afterwards to extinguish it. Little attention is paid them when the woods alone are the victims, but as there are always some cultivated parts, the fire often reaches the fences which surround fields, and sometimes the houses themselves, which is the ruin of the settlers. I recall that during my stay at Monticello, whence one can discern an extent of thirty or forty leagues of forest, I saw several fires three or four leagues apart; they continued to burn until a heavy rain fortunately extinguished them.[29]

I arrived at Mr. Grigsby's a little before five o'clock, having met with nothing on the road but a wild turkey, which rose so far off that it was impossible for me to find it again. The house was not large, but neat and convenient. We found it already occupied by other travelers, to whom we assuredly owed every token of respect, if rank among travelers be measured by the distances they still have to cover. These other guests were a healthy good-natured young man of twenty-eight, who had set out from Philadelphia with a pretty wife of twenty and a babe in arms, to settle five hundred miles beyond the mountains in a recently settled country bordering on the Ohio, called the county of "Kentucket." His whole retinue consisted of one horse, which carried his wife and child. We were astonished at the offhand manner in which he proceeded on his expedition, and took the liberty of mentioning our surprise to him. He told us that good lands in Pennsylvania were too expensive to get, that provisions were too dear and inhabitants too numerous, and that he had consequently deemed it better to purchase for about fifty *louis* a grant of a thousand acres of land in Kentucky. This grant had formerly been made to a militia colonel, at the time when the King of England thought proper to order the distribution of these immense tracts of land, part of which were sold and the rest set aside as compensation to American troops who had served in Canada.[30] But, I asked him, where are the cattle and the farming tools with which you must begin the clearing of your land?

In the region itself, he replied. I am taking nothing with me, but I have money in my pocket, and shall want for nothing. I began to understand the resolution of this young man, who was active, vigorous, and free from care; but I still imagined this pretty woman, only twenty, in despair at the sacrifice she had made. I thought to detect in her features and looks the secret sentiments of her soul. Though she had retired into a little chamber, to make room for us, she came several times into the one where we were, and I saw, not without astonishment, that her natural charms were even embellished by the serenity of her mind. She often caressed her husband and her child, and appeared to me very willing to fulfill the first object of every infant colony—"to increase and multiply."

While supper was being prepared, and we were talking of travels and finding on the map the road our emigrants were to follow, I remembered that an hour of daylight still remained, that this was precisely the time I had seen the *gelinottes,* and that I had been assured that there were some in the neighborhood. Nor was I unmindful that the gloaming is an auspicious moment for lovers as well as for hunters. So I took my gun and proceeded to the woods. Instead of wood hens, I found only a rabbit, which I wounded, but it rolled down into a hollow, where I lost sight of it. Luckily for me, Mr. Grigsby's dogs came running at the sound of the shot and found me my rabbit, which had got into the hollow of a tree, up which it would have climbed had its leg not been broken. The rabbits of America differ from those of Europe in that they do not burrow, but take refuge in hollow trees, which they climb like cats, and often to a very considerable height [!]. Content with my victory, I returned to the house, but stopped for a time to hear, at sunset, two thrushes or *grives rousses,* who seemed to have challenged each other to song, like the shepherds of Theocritus. This bird ought, in my opinion, to be considered as the nightingale of America. It resembles our European nightingale in its form, color, and habits, but is twice as large. Its song is similar to that of our thrush, but is so varied and so accomplished that, except for the uniform plaintive notes of the European nightingale, it might be taken for one. It is a bird of passage, like the mockingbird, and like it sometimes remains through the winter.

Upon my return to the house supper was henceforth my sole object; Mr. and Mrs. Grigsby were taking great pains with it, while their daughters, about sixteen or seventeen, and pretty as pictures, were setting the table. I asked Mr. Grigsby to sit down to supper with us, but he would not do so because he still had to wait on us. Nor was the trouble he took useless, for we had an excellent supper, although "wheyski" was our only drink, as it was on the three days following. We managed however to make tolerable "towdy" of it.

April 20, 1782: Grigsby's Tavern—Greenlee's Ferry—across the
Blue Ridge—Lambert's—Capt. Muller's

Breakfast was ready early the next morning, and was as good as
our supper had been. Mr. Grigsby, who had nothing more to do,
sat down at the table with us. He had a horse saddled, because he
wanted to be our guide again, as far as Greenlee's Ferry, where we
were to recross the Fluvanna [James]; but I was informed that one
of my servants' horses was so much wounded in the withers that
it was impossible to mount him. This accident was the more incon-
venient, as I had already been obliged to leave one at Mr. Jefferson's, so that I had no fresh horse to substitute. When I put the
matter up to my friend Mr. Grigsby, he told me that the only one
of his horses that could answer my purpose was the one he generally rode and which he was about to use, but that he would willingly oblige me with it, and take mine in its place. On my assuring
him that I would give him anything he thought proper in return,
he went to look at my horse, and when he came back told me that
when cured, he thought it might be worth his own, and that I could
give him whatever I wanted for it. As either of them might be
worth ten or twelve *louis,* I gave him two in exchange, and he was
perfectly contented. A moment earlier I had asked him for the bill
for our food and lodgings, but as he had been unwilling to present
it and kept saying that he left it up to me, I gave him four guineas.
He accepted them, although assuring me that it was twice what
I had cost him. At last we were obliged to take our leave of this
good house, but not of Mr. Grigsby, who had taken another
horse to accompany us. On the road he showed me two plantations which he had successively owned, before he settled on the
one he at present cultivates. He had left them in rather good
shape, and had sold them at the rate of twelve or thirteen shillings
an acre, which makes about ten *livres* of our money.[31] We saw several other settlements in the woods, all of which were situated on
the banks of some stream, whose source was not far distant. The
peach trees, which they take care to plant there, and the Judas trees
which grow naturally at the water's edge, were both in flower, and
made a charming contrast to the immense firs and oaks in the midst
of which these new clearings were situated.

It was nearly ten o'clock when we arrived at the ferry. As we
were approaching and already following along the river bank, I

saw an unfamiliar animal coming up from the bank and trying to reach the woods. I pushed my horse in his direction, hoping to frighten him and make him climb a tree, for I took it for a raccoon. It did in fact climb the nearest tree, but rather slowly and awkwardly. I had no great difficulty in killing it, for it did not even try to hide itself behind some large branches, as squirrels do. When I had taken it away from my dogs, among whom it was struggling and whom it had even bitten rather sharply, I examined it more carefully and recognized it as the *"monax,"* or marmot [woodchuck] of America. In its form, fur, and color it very much resembles the muskrat; but it is larger and differs especially in the tail, which is short and bushy. Like the muskrat, however, its ribs are so short and flexible that they might be taken for mere cartilages, so that though it is much bulkier than a hare, it could pass through a hole of not more than two inches in diameter.

Greenlee's Ferry derives its name from the owner, and is situated between two steep banks.[32] We crossed in three trips, and having taken leave of Mr. Grigsby, we were now left to our own devices to find the road to a very steep and little frequented "gap," the only passageway by which we could get out of the mountains.[33] We had been told at the ferry that we would find only one house three miles from there and at the very foot of the mountain we had to climb. A little path led us to this house: after having obtained further instructions there, we followed another path and began to ascend, not without difficulty, for in general the acclivity was so rapid that we were obliged to stop our horses to let them get their breath. The incline which forms the road is at least three miles long, by which you may judge of the height of this mountain, which is, however, over a distance of a hundred miles, the least steep of those which comprise the Blue Ridge. Having reached the summit, we enjoyed the reward generally bestowed on such labors: a magnificent, but wild, spectacle presented itself to our view; we saw the mountains which form the North Ridge [North Mountain], and those which, crossing from one chain to the other, sometimes unite with the Blue Ridge. It is in one of these transversal chains that the Natural Bridge is situated. It is to be noted that I am speaking here only of the view to the north, for we could not enjoy the view in both directions, as nearby summits and the height of the trees prevented us from extending our gaze to the southward.

The descent was not less steep than the ascent; its length was also three miles. We judged it necessary, for the relief of our horses and our own safety, to alight and walk, although the stones which rolled under our feet made it rather uncomfortable. My dogs, who were not so concerned with this inconvenience as I was, roamed the woods while I walked slowly on. Two hundred paces from the road they raised five wild turkeys, but as these birds directed their flight toward a steep hill that I had just come down, I decided not to go after them. We were already near the foot of the mountain when we began to perceive the horizon, but on this horizon we saw only more woods and mountains much less elevated than those we were leaving, with the exception of three [two] summits known by the name of the Peaks of Otter, which are very lofty and advance from the Blue Ridge like a kind of counterguard.[34] In general the whole country from the Blue Ridge to the sources of the Appomattox may be considered as a *glacis* composed of little mountains beginning at the foot of the Blue Ridge and diminishing in height as they extend forward. Of this the best maps of Virginia give no indication, so that it is impossible, by looking at them, to form an accurate idea of the nature of this country.

It was half past one, and we had gone sixteen miles over very difficult roads, when we reached the first house at the foot of the "gap"; but as it was only a rather poor hut, we were obliged to proceed two miles further to the house of a farmer named Lambert, who received us with every mark of politeness.[35] He gave us cakes and milk, for he had neither bread nor biscuit; and while our horses were feeding on a little grain he kept us good and merry company. This Mr. Lambert is something of a phenomenon in America, where longevity is not common; he is eighty-three years old but appears to be scarcely more than fifty-five; he is very well known in his region, for there is hardly a trade he has not followed, nor a part of the country he has not lived in. Now he is a farmer and lives on a very fine plantation which he has cleared at the foot of the mountains. His wife, who is only sixty-five, looked much older than he did. His sons are still young; one is now a captain in the Virginia Line and formed his own company at the beginning of the war. It was then composed of sixty-three men, all recruited in the neighborhood, and after six campaigns all sixty-three are still alive, only a few of them having been wounded. At five we set out again to proceed ten miles further to the house of a Captain Muller, who, like Mr. Lambert, does not keep a public house, but willingly receives the few travelers who pass along this unfrequented road. Although we had been assured that we could not miss the road, it could more properly have been said that we could not fail to miss it. We were lucky to have lost our way but twice, and at length, after dark, we reached Captain Muller's.[36] He is a man of sixty, about six feet tall and proportionately big, very talkative, but a good-natured sort, attached to his country and curious for news. He told me he would do his best to give us something for supper, but that he could offer us no other lodging than the room in which he received us, where he would have beds set up. This room was spacious and clean, but it was already occupied by a sick person whom he could not disturb, and whom he begged us to leave in the little corner he occupied. This was an unfortunate old man of eighty who, two days before, when traveling in the neighborhood, had been half devoured by a great bitch, whose puppies he had imprudently approached; she had torn one of his arms and thighs. Mr. Muller bestowed on him every possible care, and Mrs. Muller herself dressed his wounds. This poor man slept all the evening, but during the night he complained a great deal and sometimes awakened us. On my asking him, the next morning, how he was, he answered: "Oh, mighty weak!" For the adverb "mighty," *puissamment,* is very much in fashion in this country, and its use is sometimes ridiculous, as in this instance. Before leaving I asked for the "bill," but was told that Mr. Muller did not want to present one. I called him and gave him two *louis,* asking if this was enough. "Much too much," he replied, "you've come from France to my country to aid and defend it; I ought to receive you better and take nothing, but I am a poor countryman, and not in a position to express my gratitude. If I were not ill (and indeed he was asthmatic), I would mount my horse and go off to battle with you."

*April 21, 1782: Capt. Muller's—New London [Bedford Springs]—
    Hunter's*

The scanty resources I had found in his house, and the necessity of breaking up the long journey we had to make next day, made me decide to set out early and breakfast at New London, a little town ten miles away. Finding the road was again a problem; a man I met in the yard, ready to mount, as I was, fortunately solved the question for me. He was a former captain of the Virginia Line, whom I had seen arrive the evening before in the company of two tall young ladies, in huge gauze bonnets, covered with ribbons, and dressed in a manner that contrasted sharply with the simplicity of the house where I was staying.[37] These, I learned, were Mr. Muller's daughters, returned from supping in the neighborhood; but I was careful not to speak to them, as I suspected that we had taken possession of the beds intended for these fine ladies and their company, and was mortally afraid that French gallantry might compel me to give them back to them. I know not how they managed, but they appeared again in the morning and did not look pretty.

As for the Captain, he had spent the night a mile away, at the house of one of Mr. Muller's sisters, and had come back in the morning to get his horse to return to New London. He offered to take me there and to give me breakfast, as he kept a tavern. I accepted both his proposals, and we traveled the distance of ten miles very agreeably, this country, like that through which we had passed the evening before, being diversified with very pretty plantations.[38] New London, which I reached at ten in the morning, is an infant town, but already rather considerable, for there are at least sixty or eighty houses.[39] It has been made a depot for military stores. There are even different workshops for repairing arms. Its situation, in the middle of the woods, far distant from the seat of war, as well as trade, does not require it to be fortified, but Nature has contrived everything in such a way as to make a fortress of it. Situated on a little plateau, surrounded by a *glacis,* the slope of which is exactly what could be wished, this little town might be fortified at a small expense and defended by a trifling garrison. We left it about noon and had twenty-four miles to go to the only house where we could find a decent lodging. This was not a tavern, but the owner, Mr. Hunter, willingly received strangers. This distinction between a real tavern and private hospitality for which you pay is greatly to the advantage of travelers, for in America, as in England, innkeepers pay heavy taxes and indemnify themselves by their exorbitant charges. Mr. Hunter received us well, and in a very clean house.

April 22, 1782: Hunter's—Pattison's—Johnson's—Hodnett's [40]

We set out early the next morning, and after riding eight miles, through dry arid woods all the way, we stopped to breakfast at Mr. Pattison's. He is a fat man, about forty-five, disabled in his legs since he was two years old, and so helpless that he can transport himself from one place to another only by hitching about in his chair. One would hardly think that a man afflicted with such an infirmity would choose to live in the midst of the woods, where he has no company but one white manservant and Negroes of both sexes. I believe him impotent in more respects than one, for he has remained a bachelor, and his infirmity alone would have been no obstacle in a country where everybody marries.

After proceeding twenty miles farther, I stopped at four o'clock at a Scotsman's of the name of Johnson, who is the most ridiculous personage imaginable. He pronounced English in so unintelligible a manner that M. Dillon innocently asked him what language he was speaking. As Mr. Johnson was in a rather bad humor, and even a little drunk, I foresaw that this question would not be very successful, and would even turn to our disadvantage when we came to leave this tavern of sorts. And I was right, for after stopping three-quarters of an hour and when we were ready to remount he had no shame asking seven dollars for about twenty pounds of corn leaves for our horses and two bowls of toddy for our servants. I consoled myself, like Molière's Monsieur de Pourceaugnac; I paid him, but I told him what I thought of him, and went twelve miles further to seek hospitality from another Scotsman, at whose house we arrived at nightfall. But this was a very different character from the other. He was an old man of seventy-two, called Hodnett, who came to America forty years ago, though he has but recently settled on the farm where he offered me shelter. He was eager to please, polite, and even a bit obsequious, but proud of having been born in Europe and of having spent some time at Cork, where he missed, he told me, a fine opportunity of learning French; for he had lived there with several French merchants, whose names he still remembered, although it was more than fifty years ago. He asked me at least twenty times if I knew them, and then brought me an old book, the only one he had in the house, which was a bad geography book. There was a bookmark at the article on Cork, and you could see that he often read this chapter, as the paper was more thumbed there than elsewhere. While he was showing me this book, he informed me with an air of importance that in his opinion it was the best geographical work in existence. I was quite certain that he had never read any others, but I amused myself by telling him that he had a real treasure there, and that he ought to preserve it carefully. So he immediately went to lock it up, and soon returned with a scrap of illuminated paper, which represented the arms and mottoes of the family of Hodnett. I made him happy by declaring that the Hodnetts were known throughout Europe, and surely this was not paying too much for a good supper and good beds, for the next morning he would not give us any "bill." I thought proper, however, to pay him decently, hoping that the family of the Hodnetts would know nothing of it, nor think themselves under the necessity of adding the sign of an alehouse to their armorial bearings.

April 23, 1782: Hodnett's—Cumberland Courthouse—Powhatan Courthouse

It was only the 23rd of April, but the heat was already very troublesome at nine in the morning when I reached Cumberland Courthouse, where I stopped for breakfast.[41] This is the shire town of a fairly extensive county; it is situated in a little plain a mile in diameter, about sixteen miles from Hodnett's house. Besides the courthouse and a large tavern which is its necessary appendage, there are seven or eight houses inhabited by gentlemen of property. I found the tavern full of people, and learned that the county judges were assembled to hold a "Court of Claims," that is to say, to hear and register the claims of sundry persons who had furnished supplies to the army. It is a well-known fact that in general, but especially in the event of an unexpected invasion, the American troops have no established supply depots, and as they have to be fed, provisions and forage are taken wherever they can be found, and are paid for only by a receipt called a "certificate." As long as the enemy is close at hand, as long as the fighting continues, little attention is paid to these certificates (a loan of a sort), which accumulate without the sum total being known, or without any measures being taken to establish their validity. However, the country is now loaded with these certificates, and, soon or later, a liquidation must be resorted to. The last Assembly of the state of Virginia accordingly thought proper to pass a "bill" authorizing the judges in each county to call in all these certificates, to verify their validity, and to register them, specifying the value of the provisions in money, according to an established rate. I had the curiosity to go to the courthouse to see how this business was transacted, and found that it was performed with great order and simplicity. The judges wore their ordinary clothes, but were seated on an elevated tribunal, as at the Court of King's Bench or Common Pleas in London. One of them seeing me standing at the door of the hall, came down from

the bench and invited me to go and take some refreshment at his house, where his family would entertain me until the sitting was over. I told him I was obliged to proceed on my journey, and indeed I had no time to lose, for I still had twenty-eight miles to travel, and over a road so lacking in every resource for travelers that though I intended giving our horses another stop for food and rest along the way, I could find no forage nearer than twenty miles away, at a blacksmith's shop. As I therefore expected to stop at Cumberland Courthouse for only half an hour at most, I seated myself under some trees; but Monsieur d'Oyré having gone into the house, returned to tell me that there was a company of four or five young girls, all pretty and very well dressed. I was curious to see them, and my attention was at once attracted by a young woman of eighteen suckling her child. Her features were so fine and so regular, there was such decency and modesty in her bearing, that she recalled to my mind those beautiful Virgins of Raphael, the model or example of ideal beauty. As it is now permitted me to consider beauty only as a Philosopher,[42] I may here record an observation that I have often made in foreign countries, and particularly in England and America. I have noticed that beauty of forms and of features—beauty independent of the graces, of movements, and of expression—is more commonly found among the peoples of the North, or among the races descending from them, than in France and towards the South. If I were to assign the cause for this, I should say that for some unaccountable reason, probably unrelated to the temperature of the climate, youth is with them more forward and premature, from which it results that in young people, even in girls of twelve or thirteen, roundness of form is united with freshness of complexion and with that more perfect regularity that features have when they have not yet been modified by passions and habits.

In France it is quite different; children there are very pretty up to the age of seven or eight; but it is seldom that girls preserve their beauty to the age when they approach puberty. One must therefore divine, so to speak, what they will one day be like, and such prognostications are often misleading. This age is a kind of chrysalis, during which the pretty become ugly, and the ugly pretty. It is only when the age of twenty to twenty-five is reached that features develop and declare themselves, and that Nature completes her work, if not disturbed by sickness, or especially by the moral and

physical consequences of marriage. On the other hand, our women, this danger once over, retain their beauty much longer than anywhere else. It seems as if their souls have become identified with their features and watch over their preservation; not a movement without grace, no grace without expression; the desire to please improves and perpetuates the means of pleasing; and Nature, helped rather than hindered by Art, is not surrendered to the indulgence of domestic life, nor lavished on unrestrained fecundity.[43] Thus useful trees may serve to decorate our gardens, if the too great abundance of fruit does not prevent the flowers from reblossoming. From these reflections we may conclude that French women have nothing to envy those of other lands; that their beauty, indeed, though less precocious and less perfect, is more bewitching and more lasting; that though others may supply better models for the painter, they are better to behold; and that, in short, though they are not always those who are most admired, they are certainly the most—and the longest—loved.

But let me return from this dangerous excursion, and resume my journey. I had already ridden forty-four miles, and it was already dark, when I reached Powhatan Courthouse. This is a more recent, and more rustic settlement than Cumberland.[44] It consists of a plain wooden structure that serves as a courthouse, and another which does for an inn, but which was barely ready for travelers. It was kept by a young man who had just settled here; his wife was a tall and pretty woman, his sister-in-law not quite so pretty. We had a good supper and good beds, but our horses were obliged to do without forage. The county of Powhatan takes its name from an Indian King, famous in the history of Virginia, who reigned at the beginning of the last century when the first settlement in the colony was made at Jamestown. It was often necessary to treat with him, and sometimes to wage war against him. He is represented as a profound, but perfidious, politician. He had conquered the whole country between the Appomattox and Chesapeake Bay, and was dreaded by all the neighboring nations.

Chapter

====== 4 ======

PETERSBURG, RICHMOND, WESTOVER, AND BACK TO WILLIAMSBURG

April 24, 1782: Powhatan Courthouse—Chesterfield Courthouse—Petersburg

I LEFT Powhatan rather early on the 24th, and after having stopped twice—first to breakfast in a fairly poor little house eight miles from Powhatan, and then twenty-four miles further at a place called Chesterfield Courthouse, where I saw the ruins of the barracks formerly occupied by Baron Steuben and since burned by the English [1]—arrived at Petersburg at nightfall. This day's journey was again forty-four miles. The town of Petersburg is situated on the right bank of the Appomattox; there are some houses on the opposite shore, but this kind of suburb is a district independent of Petersburg, called "Pocahunta." [2] I crossed the river on a "ferry-boat," and was conducted to a little inn about thirty paces thence, which had an indifferent appearance. But on entering I found a very neatly furnished room. I saw a tall, well-dressed, and attractive woman, who was giving the necessary orders for our reception, and a no less tall and most elegant young lady busy with her sewing. I inquired their names, which I found no less imposing than their appearance. The mistress of the house, already twice a widow, was called Mrs. Spencer, and her daughter, by her first husband, Miss Saunders. I was shown my bedchamber, and the first thing which struck my eye was a large and magnificent harpsichord, on which lay also a guitar. These musical instruments belonged to Miss Saunders, who knew very well how to use them; but as I stood more

in need of a good supper than a concert, I was apprehensive at first of finding our landladies too good company, and feared that I should have fewer orders to give than compliments to pay. Mrs. Spencer, however, happened to be the best woman in the world. She was gay and even fond of laughter—no common disposition in America—while her daughter, with all the elegance of her appearance, was mild, polite, and easy in conversation. But to hungry travelers all this could, at best, be considered but a good omen for the supper. It was not long in coming, for scarcely had we time to admire the cleanliness and beauty of the tablecloth, before it was covered with plenty of good dishes, particularly some monstrous-large and excellent fish. We were very good friends with our landladies before we went to bed, and breakfasted with them next morning.

April 25, 1782: Petersburg—Visit to Mrs. Bolling's

I was ready to go out for a walk, when I received a call from a certain Mr. Victor, whom I had seen at Williamsburg; he is a Prussian, formerly an army officer, who after traveling widely in Europe, came to settle in this country, where he first made his way by his skills, and ended up, like everybody else, by becoming a farmer. He is an excellent musician and plays every kind of instrument, which makes him in great demand throughout the neighborhood. He told me he had come to spend a few days with Mrs. [Robert] Bolling, one of the richest landholders in Virginia, and the owner of half the town of Petersburg. He added that she had heard of my arrival and expected me to come and dine with her. I accepted the invitation and put myself under the guidance of Mr. Victor, who first took me to the tobacco warehouses. These warehouses, of which there are a great number in Virginia, though unfortunately some of them have been burned by the English, are under the direction of public authority. There are inspectors appointed to verify the quality of the tobacco brought in by the planters, and if found good, they give a receipt for the quantity. The tobacco may then be considered as sold, for these "receipts" circulate as money in this part of the country. For example, suppose I have deposited twenty "hogsheads," or *boucaux*, of tobacco at Petersburg, I may go fifty leagues thence to Alexandria or Fredericksburg, and if I want to buy horses, cloth, or any other article, I can pay for them with these receipts, which will perhaps circulate

through a number of hands before they reach the merchants who purchase the tobacco for export. As a result, tobacco is not only bank credit, but also cash. You often hear people say, "This watch cost me ten hogsheads of tobacco, this horse fifteen hogsheads, I've been offered twenty, etc." It is true that the price of this commodity, which seldom varies in time of peace, is subject to fluctuations in time of war; but then he who receives it in payment, making a free bargain, calculates the risks and expectations. In short, we may consider this as a very useful establishment, since it gives to commodities value and circulation, as soon as they are gathered, and in some measure renders the planter independent of the merchant.

The warehouses at Petersburg belong to Mrs. Bolling. They were spared by the English, either because Generals Phillips and [Benedict] Arnold, who lodged with her, had some respect for her property, or because they wished to preserve the tobacco in expectation of selling it to their profit. Phillips died in Mrs. Bolling's house [May 15, 1781], by which event the command devolved upon Arnold. I have heard it said that Lord Cornwallis, on his arrival, found Arnold at great variance with the navy, who pretended that the booty all belonged to them. Lord Cornwallis terminated the quarrel by having the tobacco burned; but Mrs. Bolling had had time enough and enough influence to get hers moved out of her warehouses. She was equally fortunate in saving a superb piece of property in the same town. This is a mill, which turns such a number of millstones, bolting machines, cribbles, etc. and, in so simple and easy a manner, that it brings her an income of more than twenty thousand *livres* a year.[3] I spent nearly an hour in examining its various parts, and admiring the carpenter's work and the construction. It is turned by the waters of the Appomattox, which are conveyed to it by a canal excavated in the rock.

After having continued my walk into the town, where I saw a number of shops, several of which were rather well stocked, I thought it was time to pay my respects to Mrs. Bolling and asked Mr. Victor to take me there. Her house, or rather houses, for she has two symmetrical houses on the same axis, which she intends to join together by a connecting building, are situated on the summit of a fairly considerable slope, which rises from the level of the town of Petersburg and corresponds so exactly to the course of the river that there is no doubt of its having formerly formed one of its banks.[4] This slope and the extensive plateau on which Mrs. Bolling's house is built are covered with grass and form an excellent pasture, which is also her property. It was formerly fenced in and she raised fine horses there; but the English burned the fences and carried off most of the horses. Upon arriving I was first greeted by Miss [Anne?] Bolling, a young lady of fifteen, possessing all the freshness of her age; she was followed by her mother, brother, and sister-in-law. The mother, a lady of fifty, has but little resemblance to her countrywomen; she is lively, active, and intelligent; knows perfectly well how to manage her immense fortune, and what is yet more rare, knows how to make good use of it. Her son [Robert, Jr.] and daughter-in-law I had already seen at Williamsburg. The young gentleman appears mild and polite, but his wife, only seventeen years old, is a most interesting acquaintance, not only from her face and figure, which are exquisitely delicate and quite European, but from her being, despite this appearance, descended from the Indian Princess, "Pocahunta" [Pocahontas] daughter of King Powhatan, whom I have already mentioned. We must suppose that it is the character of that amiable American, rather than her physical appearance, that young Mrs. Bolling has inherited.

Perhaps those who are not particularly acquainted with the history of Virginia do not know that Pocahontas was the protectress of the English and often screened them from the cruelty of her father. She was but twelve years old when Captain Smith, the bravest, the most intelligent, and the most humane of the first colonists, fell into the hands of the savages. He had already succeeded in learning their language, had often had dealings with them, and had often appeased the quarrels which arose between the Europeans and them; he had often, too, been obliged to fight with them and punish their perfidy. One day, under the pretext of trading, he was drawn into an ambush, and his two companions fell before his eyes; but, though alone, he managed to extricate himself from the band which surrounded him. Unfortunately, imagining he could save himself by crossing a swamp, he stuck fast, so that the Indians, against whom he had no further means of defense, at last captured him, bound him and took him to Powhatan. The King was so proud of having Captain Smith in his power that he sent him in triumph to all the tributary princes, ordering them to feast him splendidly until he returned to suffer the fate which was prepared for him.[5]

The fatal moment at last arrived. Captain Smith was laid upon the hearth of the savage King, his head placed upon a large stone to receive the stroke of death, when Pocahontas, the youngest and darling daughter of Powhatan, threw herself upon his body, and clasped him in her arms, and declared that if the cruel sentence were executed the first blows should fall on her. All savages, including sovereigns and tyrants, are more affected by the tears of a child than by the voice of humanity. Powhatan could not resist the tears and prayers of his daughter. Captain Smith thus obtained his life, on condition of paying his ransom. But how was he to obtain the quantity of muskets, powder, and iron tools demanded? They would neither permit him to return to Jamestown nor let the English know where he was, lest they should demand his return sword in hand. Captain Smith, who was as sensible as he was courageous, told King Powhatan that if he would permit one of his subjects to carry to Jamestown a little board which he would give him, he should find under a tree, at the day and hour appointed, all the articles demanded for his ransom. Powhatan consented, but without having much faith in these promises, believing it to be only a trick of the Captain to prolong his life. But Smith had written on the board a few lines sufficient to give an account of his situation. The messenger returned. The King sent to the appointed place, and was greatly astonished to find everything which had been demanded. Powhatan could not conceive that there could be such a means of transmitting thoughts, and Captain Smith was henceforth looked upon as a great magician, to whom they could not show too much respect. He let the savages believe this, and hastened to leave them. Two or three years later, when some fresh differences arose between them and the English, Powhatan, who no longer thought them sorcerers, but still feared their power, hatched a horrid plot to get rid of them. His plan was to attack them in the midst of peace, and cut the throats of the whole colony. The very night when the plot was to be carried out, Pocahontas took advantage of the darkness and of a terrible storm which kept the savages in their huts, escaped from her father's house, warned the English to be on their guard, but begged them to spare her family, to appear ignorant of what she had told them, and to terminate all their differences by a new treaty.

It would be tedious to relate all the services which this angel of peace rendered to both nations. I shall only add that the English, I know not from what motives, but certainly against all good faith and equity, decided to kidnap her from her father. Long and bitterly did she deplore her fate, but her consolation was Captain Smith, in whom she found a second father. She was treated with great respect and was married to a colonist by the name of "Roll" [Rolfe] who soon after took her to England. This was in the reign of James I. It is said that this monarch, pedantic and ridiculous in every respect, was so infatuated with the prerogatives of royalty that he expressed his displeasure that one of his subjects should dare marry the daughter of a savage King. It will perhaps not be difficult to decide whether, in this instance, it was the savage King who was honored in finding himself placed upon a level with the European prince, or the English monarch who, by his pride and prejudices, reduced himself to the level of a savage. Be that as it may, Captain Smith, who had returned to London before the arrival of Pocahontas, was extremely happy to see her again, but dared not to treat her with the same familiarity as at Jamestown. As soon as she saw him she threw herself into his arms, calling him her father; but finding that he neither responded to her caresses, nor called her his daughter, she turned aside her head, wept bitterly, and it was a long time before they could obtain a single word from her. Captain Smith inquired several times what could be the cause of her affliction.

"What!" said she, "did I not save thy life in America? When I was torn from the bosom of my family, and taken among thy brothers, didst thou not promise to be a father to me? Didst thou not tell me that if I went into thy country thou wouldst be my father and I thy daughter? Thou hast deceived me, and behold me here, a stranger and an orphan." It is easy to imagine that it was not difficult for the Captain to make his peace with this charming creature whom he loved tenderly. He presented her to several people of the first quality, but dared not take her to court, from which however she received several favors. After a residence of several years in England, an example of virtue, piety, and attachment to her husband, she died as she was about to embark on her return to America. She left an only son, who was married, and left only daughters; these daughters, others; and thus it is, through the female line, that the blood of the fair Pocahontas now flows in the veins of the young and fair Mrs. Bolling.[6]

I hope I shall be pardoned this long digression, which may be pleasing to some readers. My call on Mrs. Bolling and her family having convinced me that I should spend part of the day with them agreeably, I continued my walk, with a promise of returning at two o'clock. Mr. Victor, who was still my guide, took me to the camp formerly occupied by the enemy. He expressed regret that I could not get a closer view of Mr. Banister's handsome country house, which I could see from where we were. There being no other obstacle however than the distance, about half a league, and the noonday heat, we determined that this should not stop us; and, walking slowly, we easily reached this house, which is really worth seeing, as it is decorated in more Italian, than English or American taste, having three porticoes at the three principal entrances, each of them supported by four columns.[7] It was then occupied by an inhabitant of Carolina, called Nelson. War had driven him from his country, and war had caught up with him at Petersburg. He invited me to walk in, and while he was having me drink a glass of wine, according to custom, another Carolinian, of the name of Mr. [Stephen] Bull, happened in to dine with him. The latter was a brigadier general of the militia and he had just left General [Nathanael] Greene's army, where he had served his time. The story of Mr. Bull, which will be very brief, will give an idea of the state of the southern provinces. The owner of a great number of Negroes, considerable personal property, particularly in plate, before and during the war, he did not think proper, after the capture of Charleston, to expose his wealth to the rapacity of the English. He set off therefore with two hundred Negroes, followed by a great number of wagons laden with his effects and provisions for his little army, and traveled in this manner through South and North Carolina, and part of Virginia, pitching his camp every evening in the most convenient situations. At length he arrived at "Tukakoe" [Tuckahoe] on the James River, the seat of his old friend Mr. [Thomas Mann] Randolph, a wealthy inhabitant of Virginia.[8] His friend gave him a piece of land near his house, on which Mr. Bull straightway had his Negroes build one for himself. Here he lived in tranquillity, surrounded by his slaves and his flocks, until Arnold and Phillips invaded Virginia, and approached his new asylum. Mr. Bull once more departed with his treasures, his flocks and his Negroes, to retire into the upper country near Fredericksburg. On my asking him what he would have done, had we not opportunely arrived to expel the English, who intended to complete the conquest of Virginia, he replied: "I should have retired to Maryland." —And if they had gone thither?—"I should have proceeded to Pennsylvania, and so on, even to New England." Does not this recall to mind the ancient patriarchs emigrating with their family and flocks, sure of finding everywhere a land which will receive and feed them? [9] General Bull was now making ready to return to his home in Carolina in hopes, henceforth, of passing happier days; and I, after putting many questions to him respecting affairs in the South, which he answered with great frankness and good sense, made ready to return to Mrs. Bolling's, where I was not disappointed in finding a good dinner, the honors of which she did with much cordiality, without restraint or ceremony. After dinner Miss Bolling played on the harpsichord, and sang like an adept in music, although her voice was not agreeable. The descendant of Pocahontas touched her guitar and sang like a person unskilled in music, but with a charming voice. At length I returned home, where I had still another concert, Miss Saunders having consented to sing me some airs, accompanying herself, now on the harpsichord, now on the guitar.

April 26, 1782: Petersburg–Richmond

Next day we were obliged to leave this good house and agreeable company; but before I left Petersburg I noted that it was already a flourishing town and that it will become more so, as its situation is very favorable for trade. First, because it is placed immediately below the "falls," or rapids, of the Appomattox, and the river can here float vessels of fifty or sixty tons. Secondly, because all the products from the southern part of Virginia have no other outlet, and even those of North Carolina are gradually taking this route, the navigation of the Roanoke and of Albemarle Sound being by no means as convenient as that of the Appomattox and James Rivers. These advantages are unfortunately offset by the unhealthiness of the climate; I have been assured that of all the inhabitants of the three little boroughs of Pocahontas, Blandford, and Petersburg, which may be considered as forming one town, not two persons are to be found who are natives of the country. Nevertheless, commerce and navigation continue to attract newcomers. The site, moreover, is agreeable, and perhaps the climate will eventually be rendered more salubrious by draining some of the swamps in the vicinity.

Five miles from Petersburg, we crossed over the little Randolph River [Swift Creek] on a stone bridge; and still traveling through a rich and well populated country arrived at a fork in the road, where we of course managed to take exactly the one not leading to Richmond, where we wanted to go. But we had no reason to regret our error, as we went only two miles out of our way, and skirted the James River to a charming place called Warwick.[10] A group of several pretty houses forms a sort of village here; but some really superb ones may be seen in the neighborhood, among others, that of Colonel Cary, on the right [south] bank of the river,[11] and Mr. Randolph's on the opposite shore.[12] When traveling in Virginia, you must be prepared to hear the name of Randolph frequently mentioned. This is one of the first families of the country, since a Randolph was among the first settlers, but it is also one of the most numerous and wealthiest. It is divided into seven or eight branches, and I am not afraid of exaggerating when I say that this family possesses an income of upwards of a million.[13] From Petersburg to Richmond is only twenty-five miles, but as I had gone out of my way and traveled rather slowly, it was nearly three o'clock when I reached Manchester, a sort of suburb to Richmond, on the right bank of the river, at the place where you take the ferry. The crossing was short, there being two boats for the accommodation of travelers. Although Richmond is already an old town and well situated for trade, being built on the spot where the James River begins to be navigable, that is, just below the rapids, it was before the war one of the least considerable towns in Virginia, where they all are generally very small; but the seat of government having been removed here from Williamsburg, it has become a real capital and is growing every day. It was no doubt necessary to place the legislative body at some distance from the seacoast, where it was exposed to the sudden and unexpected incursions of the English. But Williamsburg had the further disadvantage of being situated at the far end of Virginia, which obliged most of the delegates to make a long journey to the state Assembly; besides, being placed between the James and York Rivers, it has no port nor communication with them but by small creeks very difficult for navigation, whereas vessels of 200 tons can come up river to Richmond. This new capital is divided into three parts: one of them is on the edge of the river and may be considered as the port; the two others are built on two heights separated by a little valley. I was taken to the western hill to a very good inn, where I had no trouble finding lodgings and ordering my dinner, for I had sent a servant ahead, with a lame horse, two days earlier.[14] We were therefore served immediately, but with such magnificence and profusion that there would have been more than enough for twenty persons. Each new dish placed before us was greeted with bursts of laughter, but not without considerable anxiety for the next day's bill; for I had been warned that the inns at Richmond were very dear. I escaped, however, for seven or eight *louis*, which was not enormous considering what we had. Some time previously M. de Rochambeau had paid twenty-five *louis* at another inn, merely for having some horses there for four or five days and without having himself dined or slept there. Mr. Formicola, my landlord, was more honest than this; his only error was his exalted idea of how French general officers should be treated. He is a Neapolitan who came to Virginia with Lord Dunmore, as the latter's *maître d'hôtel;* but he had not come by the shortest route, for he had previously been in Russia. Now he has a fine house, furniture, and slaves, and will soon become a man of consequence in his new country. He still, however, recollects his native land with pleasure, and I have no doubt that my mark of attention in speaking to him only in Italian saved me a few *louis*.

As soon as I had finished dinner I went to call on Mr. [Benjamin] Harrison, who is now Governor of the state. I found him settled in a very plain, but spacious enough house, which had just been fitted up for him.[15] As the Assembly was not then sitting, there was nothing to distinguish him from other citizens. One of his brothers [Charles Harrison], who is an artillery colonel, and one of his sons [Carter Bassett Harrison], who acts as his secretary, were with him. The conversation was unrestrained and agreeable, which he was even desirous of prolonging, for upon my rising after half an hour, fearing that he might have some business to attend to, he assured me that the day's work was done and begged me to resume my seat.

We talked a great deal of the first Congress assembled in America, in which he had sat for two years, and which, as I have already said, was composed of those most distinguished for virtue and talent of the time. This subject led us naturally to the topic on which the Americans most willingly converse, the origin and beginning of the present revolution. What particularly distinguished it in Virginia was that the people in this colony were certainly the best off of all the colonists under the English government. The Virginians were planters rather than merchants, and their agriculture was more profitable than it was painstaking. They were the almost exclusive possessors of a privileged commodity—tobacco. The English came in quest of it into the very heart of the country, bringing in exchange every article of utility, and even of luxury. They had a particular regard and predilection for Virginia, and accordingly favored the peculiar disposition of that country, where cupidity and indolence go hand-in-hand and serve only to limit each other. It was doubtless no easy matter to persuade this people to take up arms, simply because the town of Boston, three hundred leagues away, did not choose to pay a duty upon tea, and was in open rupture with England. To produce this effect, activity had to be substituted for indolence, and foresight for indifference. People had to be awakened to that idea, which makes every man educated in the principles of the English constitution shudder—the idea of submitting to a tax to which he has not consented. Matters had not reached this stage and only the best informed foresaw that a resort to arms was the aim and the inevitable consequence of the first measures. But how were the people to be convinced of this? By what other motive could they be brought to a decision, if not by the confidence they placed in their leaders? Mr. Harrison told me that when he was setting out with Mr. Jefferson and Mr. [Richard Henry] Lee to attend the first Congress at Philadelphia, a number of respectable but uninformed inhabitants waited upon them and said: "You assert that there is a fixed intention to invade our rights and privileges; we own that we do not see this clearly, but since you assure us that it is so, we believe it. We are about to take a very dangerous step, but we have confidence in you and will do anything you think proper." Mr. Harrison added that he was greatly relieved by a speech made by Lord North soon after, in which the latter could not avoid revealing the plan of the British government.[16] Lord North's speech was printed in the newspapers, and all America rang with its contents. Returning afterwards to Virginia, Mr. Harrison saw the same persons who had thus addressed him on his departure, who now confessed that he had not deceived them and that henceforward they were resolutely determined upon war.

These particular details cannot but be useful to such Europeans as are desirous of forming a just idea of those great events in which they have taken so deep an interest. They would indeed be greatly mistaken were they to believe that all the thirteen states of America had invariably been animated by the same spirit, and imbued with the same feelings. They would commit a still greater error were they to imagine that these people all resemble each other in their forms of government, their manners, and opinions. One must be in the country itself, one must be acquainted with the language, and enjoy conversing and listening, to be able to arrive, even slowly, at one's own opinion and verdict.[17] After this reflection, the reader will not be surprised at the pleasure I took in conversing with Mr. Harrison. I was furthermore particularly happy to form an acquaintance with a man of so estimable a character in every respect, and who needs no other praise than for me to say that he is the intimate friend of Dr. Franklin.[18] He urged me to dine with him next day and to spend another day at Richmond, but there was nothing to excite my curiosity in this town, and I still wanted to stop at Westover before returning to Williamsburg, where I was anxious to arrive.

April 27, 1782: Richmond—Westover

So I set out on the 27th at eight in the morning, under the escort of Colonel Harrison, who accompanied me to a road from which it was impossible to go astray. I traveled twenty-six miles without halting, in very hot weather, but over a very agreeable road, with magnificent houses in view all the way, for the banks of the James River form the garden of Virginia. Mrs. Byrd's, where I was going, surpasses them all in the magnificence of the buildings, the beauty of its situation, and the pleasures of the society to be found there.[19]

Mrs. Byrd [Mrs. William Byrd III, née Mary Willing] is the widow of a colonel who served in the last war [Seven Years' War] and was afterwards a member of the King's Council. His talents, his personal qualities, and his riches—for he possessed immense tracts of land—made him one of the principal personages of the country; but being a spendthrift and a gambler, he left his affairs, at his death, in very great disorder. He had four children by his first wife, who were already settled in the world, and has left eight by his second, of whom the widow takes care. She has preserved his beautiful house situated on the James River, rich furnishings, a considerable number of slaves, and some plantations which she has exploited. She is about forty-two, with an agreeable countenance, and great wit. Four [five] of her eight children are daughters; two of them are nearly twenty, and all are amiable and accomplished. Her care and activity have in some measure repaired the effects of her husband's dissipation, and her house is still the most renowned and agreeable in the region. She has nevertheless experienced fresh misfortunes. The English raided Westover three times under the leadership of Arnold and General Cornwallis, and although these visits cost her dear, her husband's former attachment to England, where his eldest son is still serving in the army, her relationship with Arnold, whose cousin she is, and perhaps too, the jealousy of her neighbors, have given place to suspicions that war alone was not the object which induced the English to make their descents at her house. She has even been accused of some connivance with them, and the government at one time put the seal on her papers; but she has braved the tempest, defended herself with firmness, and although this affair is not yet terminated, it appears unlikely that she will suffer any other inconvenience than that of having been disturbed and suspected.[20] Her two eldest daughters came last winter to Williamsburg, where they were much entertained by M. de Rochambeau and the whole army.[21] I had also received them in the best manner I could, and had received the thanks of Mrs. Byrd, who had extended a pressing invitation to come and see her. So I now found myself among friends. I also found my previous acquaintance, young Mrs. Bolling; she was visiting at Mr. Meade's, a friend and neighbor of Mrs. Byrd's, who had invited them all to dinner. I therefore spent this day very agreeably. Mr. and Mrs. Meade, whom I had also known at Williamsburg, engaged the company to dine with them the next day.

April 28, 1782: Westover—Visit to Maycocks

Only the river separates the two houses, which are nevertheless more than a mile distant from each other; but as there is very little current, the breadth of water between them does not prevent crossing over very quickly. Mr. Meade's house is by no means so handsome as Westover, but it is extremely well fitted up within and is charmingly situated, for it is directly opposite Mrs. Byrd's, which, with its different annexes, has the appearance of a small town and forms a most delightful prospect.[22] Mr. Meade's garden, like the one at Westover, forms a terrace along the bank of the river. It can become still more beautiful if Mr. Meade keeps his house and gives some attention to it; for he is a philosopher of a very amiable but singular turn of mind, especially for Virginia, since he rarely attends to business and cannot prevail upon himself to make his Negroes work.[23] He is even so disgusted with a form of agriculture that requires the use of slaves, that he is tempted to sell all he owns in Virginia and move to New England. Mrs. Byrd, who has a numerous family to provide for, cannot carry her philosophy so far; but she takes great care of her Negroes, makes them as happy as their situation will admit, and serves as their doctor when they are sick. She has even made some interesting discoveries about their sicknesses, and has found a very salutary method of treating a sort of putrid fever which commonly carries them off in a few days, and against which the local physicians have exerted themselves with no success.

April 29, 1782: Westover

The 29th, the whole of which day I spent at Westover, supplies nothing interesting for this journal, except some information I had the opportunity of acquiring respecting two sorts of animals of very different species, the *sturgeon* and the *hummingbird*.

As I was walking by the riverside, I saw two Negroes carrying an immense sturgeon, and on my asking them how they had caught it, they told me that at this season sturgeon were so common that they could easily be taken with a seine, and that as many as fifteen or twenty were sometimes found in the net. But, they said, there was a much simpler method of catching them, which they had just been using. These monstrous fish, which are so active in the evening as to be seen perpetually leaping to a great height above the surface of the water, usually sleep deep down at midday.[24] Two or three Negroes then proceed in a little boat; they have a long rope, at the end of which is a sharp hook, which they trail along like a sounding line. As soon as they feel this line stopped by some obstacle they pull it sharply towards them, so as to hook the sturgeon, which they either drag out of the water, or which, after some struggling and losing all its blood, finally floats to the surface, where it is easily taken.

As for the hummingbirds, I was seeing them for the first time here, and never tired of watching them. The walls of the garden and the house were covered with honeysuckle, which afforded an ample harvest for these charming little animals. I saw them perpetually fluttering about the flowers, from which they take their food, without ever alighting; for it is while maintaining themselves with their wings that they insinuate their beaks into the calices of these flowers. Sometimes they perch, but never for more than an instant. Then only can you admire the beauty of their plumage, especially when they are in the sunlight and when, as they move their heads, they display the brilliant glaze of their red throats, which have all the brilliance of rubies or diamonds. It is not true that they are naturally irascible and tear to shreds the flowers in which they find no honey. I myself observed no such thing either at Westover, or subsequently at Williamsburg, and furthermore the inhabitants of the country assured me that they had never observed it either.[25] These birds put in their appearance only with the flowers, and disappear when the flowers do, without anyone knowing what becomes of them. Some are of the opinion that they hide themselves and remain torpid for the remainder of the year. It is indeed difficult to conceive how their wings, which are so slight and slender as to be perceptible only when in motion, could possibly resist the winds and carry them to distant climates. They are not shy, for I saw one, which had been caught a few days before, in nowise frightened by people looking at it; it flew about the room, as in a garden, and came to suck the flowers held out to it—but it lived only a week. These birds are so fond of motion that it is impossible for them to live without the enjoyment of the most unrestrained liberty. It is even difficult to catch them unless they happen, as was the case with the one that I have just mentioned, to fly accidentally into the room, or to be driven there by the wind. An inhabitant of the country, who was fond of stuffing them for his "cabinet," has discovered a very ingenious method of killing them without disfiguring them. This is a very difficult undertaking, for a single grain of small shot is like a cannon ball with so small a creature. The method he devised was to load his gun with a bladder filled with water. The explosion of this water is sufficient to knock down the hummingbird and deprive it of motion.

My readers can certainly not accuse me of playing the orator and reserving objects of the greatest magnitude for the end of my discourse; for I shall now bring my journal to a close.

April 30, 1782: Westover—Williamsburg

It is unnecessary to speak of my return to Williamsburg, unless it be worthy of remark that the Chickahominy, which is only a secondary river flowing into the James, is nevertheless so wide, six miles from its conflux, that I was three-quarters of an hour crossing it. But if my readers will still favor me with their attention, I shall conclude this long narrative of my short journey with some general remarks on a country that I have traveled through and inhabited long enough to know well.

Chapter

5

NOTES ON THE STATE OF VIRGINIA

THE Virginians differ essentially from the inhabitants to the north and eastward of the Bay [Chesapeake], not only in the nature of their climate, soil, and agriculture, but also in that indelible character which every nation acquires at the moment of its origin, and which by perpetuating itself from generation to generation, justifies this great principle, that *every thing which is partakes of that which has been.* The discovery of Virginia dates from the end of the sixteenth century, and the settlement of the colony took place at the commencement of the seventeenth. These events took place in the reigns of Elizabeth and James I. At that time the republican and democratic spirit was not common in England; that of commerce and navigation was only in its infancy; and the long wars with France and Spain had perpetuated, under another form, the same military spirit given to the nation by William the Conqueror, Richard *Coeur de Lion*, Edward III, and the Black Prince. There were no longer any knights, as in the time of the Crusades, but in their place arose a number of adventurers who served indiscriminately their own country or foreign powers, and gentlemen who disdained agriculture and commerce and had no other profession than arms; for at that period the military spirit maintained the prejudices favorable to the nobility, from which it was long inseparable; furthermore, nobility through elevation to the peerage being then less common in England than it is now, hereditary rank had kept more glamour and consideration. The first colonists of Virginia were composed, for the most part, of such soldiers and such gentlemen, some of whom went in search of fortune and others of adventures. And indeed, if the establishment of a colony requires all the industry of the merchant and the husbandman, the discovery and

434

conquest of new lands seems more peculiarly suited to warlike and romantic ideas. Accordingly the first company which obtained the exclusive property of Virginia was principally composed of men most distinguished by rank or birth; and although all of these illustrious stockholders did not themselves become colonists, several of them were not afraid to cross the seas; and a Lord Delaware was among the first governors of Virginia. It was natural therefore that these new colonists, imbued with military principles and the prejudices of nobility, should carry them into the very midst of the savages whose lands they were coming to usurp; and of all our European ideas these were the most readily understood by these rude nations. I know that there now remain but a small number of these old families, but they have retained great standing, and the first impulse once given, it is not in the power of any legislator, or of time itself, to destroy its effect. The government may become democratic, as it is at the present moment; but the national character, the very spirit of the government, will always be aristocratic. Nor can this be doubted when one considers that another cause is still operating to produce the same result. I am referring to slavery, not because it is a mark of distinction or special privilege to possess Negroes, but because the sway held over them nourishes vanity and sloth, two vices which accord wonderfully with established prejudices. It will doubtless be asked how these prejudices have been reconciled with the present revolution, founded on such different principles. I shall answer that they have perhaps contributed to it; that while New England revolted through reason and calculation, Virginia revolted through pride. I shall add, as I have hinted at above, that in theory the very indolence of this people may have been useful to them, as it obliged them to rely upon a small number of virtuous and enlightened citizens, who led them further than they would have gone had they proceeded with no guide and consulted only their own dispositions. For it must be admitted that Virginia, at the beginning of the disturbances, stepped forth willingly; that she was the first to offer assistance to the Bostonians, and the first also to set on foot a considerable body of troops. But it may likewise be observed that as soon as the new legislature was established, and when, instead of leaders, she had a government in which the citizens had a share, then the national character prevailed, and everything went from bad to worse. Thus, States, like individuals, are born with a temperament of their own, the bad effects of which may be corrected by the régime of government and by habits, but which can never be entirely changed. Thus, legislators, like doctors, ought never presume to believe that they can bestow, at will, a particular temperament on bodies politic, but should attempt to understand the temper they already have, while striving to combat the disadvantages and increase the advantages resulting from it. A general glance at the different states of America will serve to substantiate this opinion.

The peoples of New England had no other motive for settling in the New World than to escape from the arbitrary power of their monarchs, who were both the sovereigns of the State and the heads of the Church, and who were at that time exercising the double tyranny of despotism and intolerance. They were not adventurers, they were men who wished to live in peace, and who labored to live. Their doctrine taught equality and enjoined work and industry. The soil, naturally barren, affording but scanty resources, they resorted to fishing and navigation; and at this hour, they are still friends to equality and industry; they are fishermen and navigators.

The states of New York and the Jerseys were settled by necessitous Dutchmen who lacked land in their own country, and who concerned themselves much more with domestic economy than with public government. These people have kept this same spirit: their interests and their efforts are, so to speak, individual; their views are centered on their families, and it is only from necessity that these families form a state. Accordingly, when General Burgoyne marched on Albany, it was the New Englanders who contributed most to stop his progress; and, if the inhabitants of the state of New York and of the Jerseys have often taken up arms and displayed courage, this is because the former were animated by an inveterate hatred against the Indians, whom the English always sent ahead of their own armies,[1] and because the latter were impelled to take personal vengeance for the excesses committed by the troops of the enemy, when they overran their country.[2]

If you go farther to the south, and cross the Delaware, you will find that the government of Pennsylvania, in its origin, was founded on two very opposite principles; it was a government of property, in itself a feudal, or if you will, a patriarchal government, but whose spirit was characterized by the greatest tolerance and the most complete liberty. Penn's family at first formed the vain idea of establishing a sort of Utopia, a perfect government, and then of

deriving the greatest possible advantage from their immense property by attracting foreigners from all parts. As a result of this the
people of Pennsylvania has no identity of its own, it is mixed and
confused, and more attached to individual than to public liberty,
more inclined to anarchy than to democracy.[3]

Maryland, subjected at first to proprietary government, and considered only as a private domain, long remained in a state of the
most absolute dependence. Now for the first time it deserves being
regarded as a state; but this state seems to be taking shape under
good auspices. It may become important after the present revolution, because it was nothing before.

There remain the two Carolinas and Georgia, but I am not sufficiently acquainted with these three states to subject them to my
observations, which may not be as correct as they appear to me,
but which are in any case delicate and require more than a super-
ficial examination. I know only that North Carolina, peopled for
the most part by Scotsmen, brought thither by poverty rather than
by industry, is a prey to brigandage and to internal dissensions; [4]
and that South Carolina, whose only commerce is the export trade,
owes its existence to its seaports, especially to the city of Charleston, which rapidly increased and became a commercial town, where
foreigners have abounded, as at Marseilles and Amsterdam,[5] so that
the manners there are polished and easy, that the inhabitants love
pleasure, the arts, and society—and that this country is in general
more European than the rest of America.

Now if there be any accuracy in this sketch, let my readers compare the spirit of the states of America with their present government. I ask them to make the comparison at the present moment,
twenty years hence, fifty years hence, and I am persuaded that
although these governments resemble each other in that they are all
democratic, there will always be found the traces of their former
character, of that spirit which has presided over the formation of
peoples and the establishment of nations.

Virginia will retain its distinctive character longer than the other
states; either because prejudices are the more durable, the more
absurd and frivolous they are, or because those which injure only
a part of the human race are more noticeable than those which
affect all mankind. In the present revolution the old families have
with pain seen new men occupying distinguished situations in the
army and in the magistracy. The Tories have even taken advan-

tage of this circumstance to cool the ardor of the less zealous of the
Whigs. But the popular party has maintained its ground, and one
can only regret that it is not displaying as much activity in fighting
the English as it does in quarreling over questions of precedence.
It is to be feared, however, that when circumstances become less
favorable to it, with the coming of peace, the popular party may
be obliged either to give way entirely, or to maintain itself in power
through factions, which would necessarily disturb the order of
society. But if Reason must blush at beholding such prejudices so
strongly established among new peoples, Humanity has still more
to suffer from the state of poverty in which a great number of
white people live in Virginia. It is in this state, for the first time
since I crossed the sea, that I have seen poor people. For, among
these rich plantations where the Negro alone is wretched, one often
finds miserable huts inhabited by whites, whose wane looks and
ragged garments bespeak poverty. At first I found it hard to understand how, in a country where there is still so much land to
clear, men who do not refuse to work could remain in misery; but
I have since learned that all these useless lands and those immense
estates, with which Virginia is still covered, have their proprietors.
Nothing is more common than to see some of them possessing five
or six thousand acres of land, but exploiting only as much of it as
their Negroes can cultivate. Yet they will not give away, or even
sell the smallest portion of it, because they are attached to their
possessions and always hope to increase eventually the number of
their Negroes. These whites, without means and often too without
ambition, are thus restrained on all sides and are reduced to the
small number of acres they have been able to acquire. As land is
not generally good in America,[6] especially in Virginia, it takes a
good deal of it to make cultivation profitable, as well as cattle to
assist in gaining a livelihood. In the eastern states one sees many
cleared farms, but the tracts of land which can be easily and very
cheaply purchased there are always of at least two hundred acres.
Besides, in the South, the climate is less healthy, and the new settlers,
without sharing the wealth of Virginia, share all the disadvantages
of the climate and even the indolence it inspires.[7]

Beneath this class of inhabitants we must place the Negroes,
whose situation would be even more lamentable than theirs, did
not natural insensibility extenuate in some degree the sufferings

attached to slavery.[8] On seeing them ill lodged, ill clothed, and often overwhelmed with work, I concluded that their treatment was as rigorous as everywhere else. I was assured, however, that it was extremely mild in comparison to what they experience in the sugar colonies. You do not, indeed, generally hear, as in Santo Domingo and in Jamaica, the sound of whips and the cries of the unhappy wretches whose bodies are being lashed.[9] This is because the people of Virginia are in general milder than the inhabitants of the sugar islands, who consist wholly of avid men, eager to make their fortune and return to Europe. Another reason is that the yield of agriculture in Virginia not being of so great a value, labor is not urged on the Negroes with so much severity. In fairness to all it should be added that the Negroes in Virginia for their part are not so much addicted to cheating and stealing as in the islands, because, since the propagation of the black species is very rapid and very considerable here, most of the Negroes are born in this country, and it is a known fact that they are generally less depraved than those imported directly from Africa. I must likewise do the Virginians the justice to declare that many of them treat their Negroes with great humanity. I must further add a still more honorable testimonial in their favor, that in general they seem grieved at having slaves, and are constantly talking of abolishing slavery and of seeking other means of exploiting their lands. It is true that this opinion, which is almost universally accepted, is inspired by different motives. The philosophers, and the young men who are for the most part educated in the principles of sound philosophy,[10] consider only justice and the rights of humanity. The fathers of families, and those who are principally concerned with their interests, complain that the maintenance of their Negroes is very expensive, that their labor is neither so productive nor so cheap as that of day laborers or white servants, and, lastly, that epidemical disorders, which are very common, render both their property and their income extremely precarious. However this may be, it is fortunate that different motives concur in disgusting men with that tyranny which they exercise over those who may at least be described as of their own species, even though they cannot be called, in the strict sense of the term, their likes; for the more we observe the Negroes, the more must we be persuaded that the difference distinguishing them from us does not consist in color alone. Moreover, one cannot conceal the fact that the abolition of slavery in America is an extremely delicate question. The Negroes in Virginia amount to two hundred thousand. They at least equal, if they do not exceed, the number of white men. Necessarily united by a common interest deriving from their situation, and brought together by the distinguishing badge of their color, they would doubtless form a distinct people, from whom neither succor, virtue, nor labor could be expected. Sufficient attention has not been paid to the difference between slavery, such as we have kept it in our colonies, and slavery as it was generally established among the ancients. A white slave, in ancient times, had no other cause of humiliation than his present lot; if he was freed, he could mix straightway with free men and become their equal. Hence that emulation among the slaves to obtain their liberty, either as a favor or to purchase it with the fruit of their labor. Two advantages resulted from this: the possibility of enfranchising them without danger, and that ambition generally prevalent among them, which turned to the advantage of morals and of industry. But in the present case, it is not only the slave who is beneath his master; it is the Negro who is beneath the white man. No act of enfranchisement can efface this unfortunate distinction; accordingly the Negroes do not seem very anxious to obtain their freedom, nor much pleased when they have obtained it. The free Negroes continue to live with the Negro slaves, and never with the white men, so that only when they have some special work or trade, and want to turn it to their profit, does their interest make them wish to leave the state of bondage. It appears, therefore, that there is no other method of abolishing slavery than by getting rid of the Negroes, and such a measure can only be carried out gradually. The best means would be to export a great number of males, and then to encourage the marriage of white men with the Negresses. For this purpose it would be necessary to abrogate the law according to which slavery is transmitted through the mothers; or at least to decree that any slave would become free by marrying a free man. Out of respect to property, it might perhaps be just to require of the latter a compensation to be fixed by law, to be paid either in labor or in money, as an indemnity to the owner of the Negresses thus freed; but it is certain, at all events, that such a law, aided by the less licit but already well-established commerce between the white men and Negresses, would give rise to a race of mulattoes, which would in turn produce a race of quadroons, and so on, until the color would be totally changed.

But enough has been said on this subject, which the political thinkers and philosophers of our day have by no means neglected. I have only to apologize for having treated it without declamatory flourishes; but I have always believed that eloquent oratory can influence only the decisions of the moment, and that anything which requires time to achieve can be accomplished only through reason. It would be easy, in fact, to add ten or a dozen pages to these few reflections, which are to be considered merely as the main themes of a symphony which may be elaborated upon at will—*con corni ad libitum.*

We have seen the ill effects in Virginia of slavery and of too extensive estates: let us now examine the few good effects resulting from them. The Virginians have the reputation, and rightly so, of living nobly in their homes and of being hospitable; they receive strangers both willingly and well. This is because, on the one hand, having no large towns where they can gather, they know society only through the visits they make to each other; and, on the other hand, because their lands and their Negroes supplying them with the products and labor they need, this renowned hospitality is no burden to them. Their houses are spacious and well ornamented, but living quarters are not conveniently arranged; they think little of putting three or four persons in the same room; [11] nor do people have any objection to finding themselves thus crowded in, because they experience no need to read and write, and all they want in a house is a bed, a dining room, and a drawing room for company. The chief magnificence of the Virginians consists in furniture, linen, and silver plate; in which they resemble our own forefathers who had no private apartments in their castles, but only a well-stored wine cellar and handsome sideboards. If they sometimes dissipate their fortunes, this is through gaming, hunting, and horse races; [12] but the latter are of some utility, inasmuch as they encourage the training of horses, which are really of a very fine breed in Virginia. It will be seen that women have little share in the amusements of the men; beauty here serves only to find husbands; for the wealthiest among them give but a trifling dowry to their daughters and it is in general the young ladies' faces that determine their fortunes. The consequence of this is that they are often co-

quettish and prudish before marriage, and dull and tiresome afterwards. The convenience of being served by slaves still further
increases their natural indolence; they always have a great number
of slaves at hand to wait on them and on their children; they themselves suckle their infants, but that is all. The women, as well as
their husbands, pay attention to the children as long as they are
little, but neglect them when they are older. We may in general say
of the Americans, as of the English, that they are very fond of their
little ones, and care much less for their *children*. It would perhaps
be untactful to inquire whether this sentiment is not really the natural one, and whether our efforts in France to counteract it are not
the result of self-esteem or ambition. But we can always confidently
affirm that the care we take of our children is a means of attaching
ourselves to them and them to us—the nobility and utility of which
cannot be denied.[13]

I wanted to speak of the virtues peculiar to the Virginians, but
in spite of my wishes, I have found only magnificence and hospitality to mention. I have been unable to add generosity to these; for
they are strongly attached to their interests,[14] and their great wealth,
joined to their pretensions, further distorts this vice.

I should have begun these remarks by considering the subject of
religion; but there is nothing noteworthy about it in this country,
save for the way they manage to dispense with it. The predominant
one before the Revolution was the Anglican religion, which, as is
well known, requires episcopacy and that every priest must be ordained by a bishop. Before the war people went to England to study
and to be ordained. It is therefore impossible, under the present
circumstances, to fill the pastorates that have become vacant. What
has been the consequence of this? The churches have remained
shut; people have done without a minister, and have not even
thought of any future arrangements for establishing an Anglican
church independent of England.[15] The most complete tolerance has
been established; nor have the other communions made any gains
from the losses of the former; each sect has remained as it was, and
this sort of religious interregnum has caused no disorder. The
clergy, furthermore, have received a severe setback in the new constitution, which forbids them any share in the government, even
the right of voting at elections. It is true that the judges and lawyers
have been subjected to the same exclusion, but this was from another motive, that of keeping public affairs free from competition

with private affairs. The legislator feared the effects of such a conflict of interests; an attempt was made, in short, to form within the state a sort of separate body known as the judiciary. These views are perhaps good in themselves; but they have become a doubtful blessing in the present circumstances; for the lawyers, who are certainly the most enlightened part of the community, are removed from the civil councils, and the administration is entrusted either to the ignorant, or at least to the unskilled. This is the principal objection made here to the present form of government, which, I should add, appears to me good in many respects. The Virginia constitution is readily available in print, and anyone can easily obtain it for himself. However if an outline is here desired, I can say in a few words that the government is composed of: 1st. The Assembly of Deputies, named by the towns and counties, a body corresponding to the House of Commons. 2nd. A Senate, the members of which are elected by several counties grouped together, with the number of members varying according to the population of the counties—which corresponds to the House of Peers. 3d. An Executive Council, presided over by the Governor, and the members of which are chosen by the two Chambers, which takes the place of the executive power exercised by the King in England.[16]

It is not mere chance that has led me to postpone to the end of these notes matters respecting the progress of the arts and sciences in Virginia. I have done so expressly because the mind, after bestowing its attention on the variety of human institutions, lingers with pleasure over those which tend to the perfection of understanding and to the progress of knowledge; and above all, because, since I have found myself under the necessity of speaking less advantageously of this state than I should have liked, I wish to conclude with a subject which is wholly to its credit. I shall therefore state that the College of William and Mary—the name alone denotes its founders—is a magnificent establishment which adorns Williamsburg and does honor to Virginia. The beauty of the building is surpassed by the richness of the library, and the worth of this library by several of the distinguished professors, such as Doctors [Rev. James] Madison, [George] Wythe, [Carlo] Bellini, etc., etc., who may be looked upon as living books, in which both precepts and examples are to be found. I must likewise add that the zeal of these professors has already been crowned with very marked success, and that they have already formed many distinguished characters, now ready to serve their country in different capacities. Among these, I am pleased to mention Mr. [William] Short, with whom I was particularly well acquainted. And now, having done justice to the labors of the University at Williamsburg (for the College of William and Mary is in fact a university), I might add, if miracles need be cited to enhance her fame, that she has made *me* a Doctor of Law! [17]

Williamsburg, May 1, 1782

Appendix

A

DESCRIPTION OF THE
NATURAL BRIDGE

Editor's Introduction

WHEN recording in his journal (April 12, 1782) that Mr. Jefferson was "well acquainted" with the Natural Bridge and would willingly have accompanied him there had Mrs. Jefferson's approaching confinement not prevented, Chastellux might have added that Jefferson was also the owner of this wonder of the New World. It was on July 5, 1774, by a deed drawn in the name of King George III, that Jefferson acquired title to a tract of 157 acres of land in what was then Botetourt County—a tract "including the natural Bridge on Cedar Creek." It remained his property and that of his heirs until sold by the latter in 1833. A rough diagram of the Bridge and some descriptive notes survive on the flyleaf of one of Jefferson's early account books.

The Rock Bridge—or "Rocky Bridge" as Chastellux insisted on calling it—was obviously one of the subjects touched upon in the conversations at Monticello just before Chastellux's journey over the Blue Ridge. Both he and Jefferson were intent upon finding a plausible hypothesis that would explain this "curiosity of Nature." Jefferson thought that it must have been "cloven" by "some great convulsion." When Chastellux observed the Bridge on the spot, he, too, thought that this was "the only hypothesis" that could account for it, while rejecting both the idea of a volcano and that of the slow action of the waters. Nevertheless, after his return to Williamsburg and eventually to France—after Baron de Turpin had made a careful survey for him, and after he had discussed the prob-

445

lem with his master, Buffon, author of the *Époques de la Nature*—Chastellux arrived at the conclusion that the formation of the Natural Bridge could only be attributed to "the action of the waters." This is essentially the explanation still put forth, with refinements, by twentieth-century geologists. Thus, Chastellux's journal (April 19, 1782) records his first inconclusive gropings, whereas the "Description" printed below (which he wrote in France before publishing his book) presents his mature opinion.

Meanwhile, Jefferson clung to his own idea of a "great convulsion," which he recorded in his *Notes on the State of Virginia*, privately printed in Paris in 1785 (see below, n. 2). The passage remained unchanged in the trade edition of the book, published in London in 1787, and in subsequent editions. Eventually, it would seem, Jefferson was persuaded to abandon this idea, probably by his young protégé, Francis William Gilmer, with whom he visited the Natural Bridge in the autumn of 1815. Gilmer's paper "On the Geological Formation of the Natural Bridge of Virginia" was read before the American Philosophical Society in Philadelphia on February 16, 1816, and was subsequently printed in the Society's *Transactions*, New Ser., 1 (1818), 187-92. After paying homage to Mr. Jefferson as well as to the Marquis de Chastellux (thanks to whom "both Europe and America were supplied with plates"), and after effectively refuting Jefferson's hypothesis of a sudden convulsion, Gilmer outlined succinctly and in elegant language the theory of an arch formed by "the chemical and mechanical action" of the waters—which is basically the same idea expressed here by Chastellux in his "Description." "It is possible," Gilmer wrote, "that the water of Cedar Creek originally found a subterranean passage beneath the arch of the present bridge, then only the continuation of the transverse ridge of hills. The stream has gradually widened, and deepened this ravine to its present situation. Fragments of its sides also yielding to the expansion and contraction of heat and cold, tumbled down even above the height of the water. Or, if there was no subterraneous outlet, the waters opposed by the hill flowed back, and formed a lake, whose contact dissolved the resistance where it was least, wore away the channel through which it now flows, and left the earth standing above its surface. I incline, however, rather to the first hypothesis, because the ravine has the appearance, from its narrow banks, of having been the channel of

THE SURRENDER OF CORNWALLIS AT YORKTOWN,
BY TRUMBULL

Left to right: GEN. CHASTELLUX, GEN. BARON DE VIOMÉNIL,
ADMIRAL DE BARRAS, ADMIRAL DE GRASSE

(see p. vii)

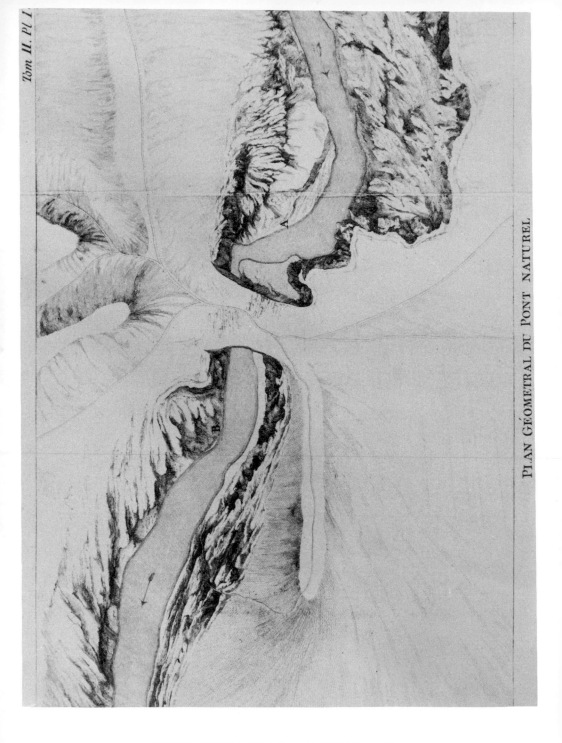

PLAN GÉOMÉTRAL DU PONT NATUREL

BIRD'S-EYE VIEW OF THE NATURAL BRIDGE
Engraved for Chastellux's *Voyages* (1786) from surveys by Baron de Turpin, May 1782
Cf. Chastellux's Description, II, Appendix A (see p. viii)

PERSPECTIVE PRISE DU POINT A.

NATURAL BRIDGE, FROM UPSTREAM, OR WESTERN SIDE
Cf. Point "A" in preceding plate (see p. viii)

PERSPECTIVE PRISE DU POINT B.

NATURAL BRIDGE, FROM DOWNSTREAM, OR EASTERN SIDE

Cf. Point "B" on birds-eye view, preceding (see p. viii)

a stream in all time, and had it been the bed of a lake, the continual action of the water would have widened it into a basin. The stone and earth composing the arch of the bridge, remained there and no where else; because, the hill being of rock, the depth of rock was greatest above the surface of the water where the hill was highest, and this part being very thick, and the strata horizontal, the arch was strong enough to rest on such a base."

Modern geologists still accept the general validity of Gilmer's explanation (although they appear not to have noted its similarity to Chastellux's earlier "Description"). Clyde A. Malott and Robert R. Shrock, for example, in their study of the "Origin and Development of Natural Bridge, Virginia" (*American Journal of Science*, New Ser., 19 [1930], 257-73) assert: "Cedar Creek did find a subterranean passage beneath the ridge (spur), and this passage was developed into a cavern tunnel. The roof-rock, especially at the ends and more particularly at the upper end, weakened and, lacking sufficient support, gradually fell into the deepening tunnel and was dissolved and washed away. A remnant of the roof-rock, however, still remains over this much shortened tunnel and forms the magnificent natural span over the steep-walled, cavern-born canyon." More recently, Frank J. Wright ("The Natural Bridge of Virginia," *Virginia Geological Survey*, Bulletin 46-G [Richmond, 1936]) has proposed the "limestone sink piracy theory," according to which "the diversion of Cedar Creek from its ancestral course across Sallings Mountain to its present position under Natural Bridge" was accomplished by "the headward growth of a stream gnawing back into the escarpment, combined with the effects of sink hole drainage."

Although Jefferson and Chastellux diverged in their geological theorizing about the Natural Bridge, they were in perfect communion—as they had been when reading Ossian's poems—when considering it as an "awesome spectacle" and "the most sublime of Nature's works." Indeed, writing in a playful vein, Chastellux even maintained that he had found in Virginia two things worth traveling far to see: one was the Natural Bridge and the other ... Mr. Jefferson! (Chastellux to T.J., June 10, 1782). Ever since Chastellux's time thousands of tourists, famous and humble, have traveled far to see the Natural Bridge. Thousands more daily pass over it (on U.S. Route 11), but without seeing it. Jefferson, while he was still the owner, once wrote: "I view it in some degree as a public trust, and would on no consideration permit the bridge to be injured, defaced or masked from the public view." (T.J. to William Caruthers, of Lexington, Va., March 15, 1815.) Although it has unfortunately never become public property, the Natural Bridge has nevertheless been preserved as a public attraction. Circumstances permitting, it can still present an "awesome spectacle" and excite "a gloomy and melancholy admiration."

Description of the Natural Bridge, called Rocky Bridge in Virginia

On my return from my journey in Upper Virginia, I still regretted not having been able to take proper measurements of the Natural Bridge. I was anxious that some person, who was both a draftsman and a surveyor, should make the journey to the Appalachians for this sole purpose, and that he should be provided with the instruments necessary for doing it accurately. No one was more capable of this than Baron de Turpin, Captain in the Royal Engineer Corps (*Corps Royal du Génie*), for he possesses all that theoretical knowledge, which is carried to such a high degree in the Corps to which he belongs, combined with the skill of drawing with as much facility as precision; [1] he was furthermore well enough acquainted with the English language to dispense with an interpreter. I therefore proposed to the Comte de Rochambeau to entrust him with this errand, which I was sure he would undertake with pleasure. The General thought that he could render another service to the Americans by making known one of the natural wonders which shed luster upon their country, and that it would even be rather droll for people to see that the French had been the first to describe it with precision and publish a correct plan of it. [2] Baron de Turpin set out, therefore, at the beginning of May, and in three weeks brought me back five plans, three of which have been engraved and are annexed to this book. [3] Two of these plans give perspectives, taken from the two sides of the Natural Bridge and from the bottom of the valley whence it rises. The third is a bird's-eye view, and shows a part of the surrounding country. The two others being only imaginary sections of this bridge at the spots where it holds to the bank and which may be considered its abutments, I have not seen fit to have them engraved, in order not to increase the number of plates that have to be added to this work. As for the measurements, here are those given me by M. de Turpin:

The Natural Bridge forms a vault fifteen *toises* long,[4] of the type known as a *corne de vache* (cow's horn). The chord of this vault is seventeen *toises* on the upstream side, and nine on the downstream side, and the arc is a semi-ellipse so flattened that its minor axis is only a twelfth of the major axis. The solid mass of rock and stone which loads this vault is 49 feet high on the crown of the big arch, and 37 on the small one; and as about the same difference is found in the slope of the hill, it may be supposed that the roof of the vault itself is on a level the whole length of the crown. It is worth noting that the living rock extends over the whole span of the vault, which is only 25 feet wide at its greatest width and gradually becomes narrower.

The whole vault seems to form but a single stone, for the sort of seams which one notices on the upstream face are the result of lightning which struck this part in 1779; the other face has not the least vein, while the intrados is so smooth that the martins, which flutter about in great numbers, can get no hold on it.[5] The abutments, which have a slight talus, are quite entire, and without being absolutely smooth, have all the polish which a current of water would give to rough stone after a certain time. The four cliffs adjacent to the abutments seem to be perfectly homogeneous and to have very little rock debris at their base. The two cliffs on the right bank of the stream rise 200 feet above the water; the two on the left bank, 180 feet; the intrados of the vault is 150 feet above the stream.

If we consider this bridge simply as a picturesque object, we are struck by the majesty with which it towers in the valley. The white oaks which grow on its soil seem to rear their lofty tops to the clouds, while the same trees growing along the stream appear but as shrubs. As for the Naturalist, he must content himself with such observations as may guide a bolder Philosopher to form some conjecture on the probable origin of this extraordinary mass.

From all parts of the vault and from its supporting piers, cubic pieces of rock measuring three or four lines were taken; these were placed successively in the same aqua fortis. The first ones dissolved in less than half an hour; the others required more time, but this difference must be attributed to the weakening of the acid, which lost its activity as it became progressively saturated.

It will be seen that these rocks, being of a calcareous nature, exclude any idea of a volcano, which furthermore could not be reconciled with the form of the Bridge and all its adjacent parts. If one wants to believe that this astonishing arch is the result of a current of water, it must then be supposed that this current had enough force to take with it and carry to a great distance a mass of 5000 cubic *toises*, for there remains close by no trace of such an operation. The blocks found beneath the vault and a little below it have their former places still visible on the overhanging walls on the downstream side, and come from no other demolition than that of the Bridge itself, which is said to have been a third wider than it is now.

The depression of eight or ten inches hollowed out at the foot of the arch on the left bank of the stream extends this base into the form of a *bec de corbin*, or claw. This wearing away, and some other parts which are flaking off, give reason to believe that this surprising edifice will one day become the victim of time, which has destroyed so many others.

Such are the observations that Baron de Turpin brought back and which he was pleased to favor me with. As their accuracy may be relied on, it would perhaps be sufficient to transcribe them here and let the reader form his own opinions about the causes which could have produced this sort of prodigy. This was in fact what I had intended when, abandoned to my own powers, which I quite properly mistrusted, I was writing up for myself alone, at Williamsburg, the journal of my recent excursion. But it was then that a Spanish work, which fell into my hands, confirmed me in the opinion that I had at first entertained, that it was to the action of the waters alone that we owed the magnificent construction of the Natural Bridge.[6] The opinion of Comte de Buffon, whom I have since consulted, has left me no further doubt. His sublime ideas on the different Epochs of Nature should have been sufficient to put me on the right path; but the disciple who is aware of his own limitations is timid, even in applying his master's principles. Nevertheless, anyone who has traveled in America becomes a witness entitled to depose in favor of that genius whose oracles too frequently find contradictors. If it were necessary to justify what the Montesquieus, the Humes, the Voltaires have said about the baleful effects heretofore produced by superstition, ignorance, and prejudice, we might still, in surveying Europe, find peoples which could display to us the picture of what we were like 300 years ago, nations which are, so to speak, the contemporaries of past ages, and thus the truth of historical facts could be confirmed by those which we might ourselves witness. The same holds true for America, as far as the Epochs of Nature and all documents of natural history are concerned. In traveling through this part of the world, you might think yourself carried backwards in time for a whole epoch: the lowlands and the plains are watered by such large rivers and so intersected by creeks, the coasts are so frequently indented by gulfs and arms of the sea—which seem to carry the ocean into the very heart of the land and to the very foot of the mountains—that it is impossible not to be persuaded that all this part of the continent is of recent creation, and is simply the product of successive alluviums. On the other hand, if we observe that all the high mountains form long chains parallel to each other, and almost always in a north-south direction; that most of the rivers which flow into the ocean have their source in the narrow valleys which separate these mountains, and that after following the direction of the valleys for a considerable distance, they suddenly turn towards the east, pierce the mountains, and at length reach the sea, acquiring magnitude as they proceed—we shall believe ourselves, if not coeval with, at least not far removed from that Epoch of Nature when the waters, collected to an extraordinary height and confined in the valleys, were seeking to break through their dikes, still uncertain of the means they would take to make their escape. We shall further be inclined to believe that the motion of the earth on its axis, or the westerly winds, which in North America correspond to the trade winds of the tropics, and are perhaps a result of them, have at length determined the motion of the waters towards the east. In which case, one of two things happened: either the waters, having exceeded the height of the least lofty summits which opposed their passage, formed some sort of gutters, through which the surplus escaped; or being unable to reach the height of these mountains, they found some softer parts in the greater mass itself, which they first undermined, and then entirely pierced. In the first case, if the declivity was very steep, and the rock which served as the bed was very hard, the waters would have formed a cataract, but where the slope was less steep, and the soil less compact, the waters would not only have formed the gutter which served as a passage, but would have loosened and carried along with them the lands, forming them into long slopes, which would finally merge into the plains. Thus the Hudson River, the Delaware, the Potomac, the James River, and many others, have opened channels for themselves to the sea by piercing the mountains at more or less right angles, and forming more or less spacious valleys. In the second case, the waters unable to pierce the mountains except below the summits, must have left above them a sort of *calotte*, or roof, similar to that of the Natural Bridge. But how many chances there were that these arches would eventually crumble, especially when, as the river-beds gradually deepened, the load became too heavy, and they thus lost their support! [7]

If we still doubt the probability of this hypothesis and still want more striking tokens, more obvious traces of the action of the waters, let us continue our travels in America; let us go to the vicinity of the Ohio, to the banks of the "Kentucke River." Here is what we may observe there, or rather what the recent historian of that region has written:

Amongst the natural curiosities of this country, the winding banks, or rather precipices of Kentucke, and Dick's Rivers, deserve the first place. The astonished eye there beholds almost every where three or four hundred feet of a solid perpendicular lime-stone rock; in some parts a fine white marble, either curiously arched, pillared or blocked up into fine building stones. These precipices, as was observed before, are like the sides of a deep trench, or canal; the land above being level, except where creeks set in, and crowned with fine groves of red cedar. It is only at particular places that this river can be crossed, one of which is worthy of admiration; a great road large enough for waggons made by buffaloes, sloping with an easy descent from the top to the bottom of a very large steep hill, at or near the river above Lees-town [Frankfort].[8]

Or let us consult Don Joseph [Antonio] de Ulloa, already so famous for his travels; he is the author of the Spanish book which I have mentioned above, a book entitled *Noticias Americanas*, in which he gives very curious and detailed descriptions of all Spanish America.[9] In the article I am about to translate, he begins by pointing out a very noticeable difference between the mountains in America situated below the torrid zone, and those we observe in other parts of the world; for although the height of the latter is often very considerable, nevertheless, as the ground rises gradually and as their combined summits cover immense expanses, those who inhabit them may be ignorant of their elevation in relation to sea level; whereas these American mountains being separated, and, so to speak, cloven through their whole height, continually give evidence, and even the measure of their prodigious altitudes. De Ulloa then continues:

[9]. In these high regions the land is dissected by deep gorges or *quebradas,* as they are called, of considerable width; they form the boundary between the plains and mountains on either side, and some are more than two leagues across when seen from above. They are broader where they are deepest. The rivers flow through the middle and deepest parts of these valleys, leaving plains of about the same width on either side. What is remarkable is that the angles and bends made by the rivers correspond exactly to those of the two walls, so that if these could be fitted together they would match perfectly and form a solid mass with no breaks. The rivers continue their courses through these canyons until they reach the low country, and thence to the sea. But the channels they cut in the latter part of their courses are not very deep nor much above sea level. Thus it may in general be said that the higher the mountain ranges, the deeper the gorges of the rivers....

[10]. Among the many natural wonders to be found in the province of Angaraez, and which are more varied and remarkable here than in larger and more extensive countries, there is one of unique interest. This province, which is a dependency of the government of Guancavelica [Huancavelica], is divided into several *doctrinas* or departments,[10] in one of which, called Conaica, there is a little village called Viñas. The distance between it and Conaica, the capital, is nine leagues; at a distance of five of these leagues there is a hill called Corosunta. Below it there is an opening through which flows the river called the Chapllancas. For a distance of about a half a league this river flows through a canyon about 6 to 8 *varas* wide [approx. 20 feet; 1 *vara,* or yard, equivalent now to 2.8 feet] and more than 40 *varas* high, the width being not perceptibly more at the upper than at the lower part. By this route, where the stream in the narrow parts fills the whole width, goes the road leading from Viñas to the town of Conaica. The river can only be followed through the places where the opening is 8 *varas* wide, as has been said, and it must be crossed nine times, at those spots, generally at the bends, where it flows away from the banks a bit, for when it flows straight it completely fills the gap. This canyon is cut through the bedrock with such precision that the recesses or indentures on one side correspond to the projections on the other, as if the mountain had parted on purpose, with its windings and turnings, to make a passage for the waters between the two high walls. They are so

similar that if they were joined they would fit exactly together with no space in between. There is no danger in traveling this road, for the rock is too solid to crumble and the river is not so swift as to be dangerous. Nevertheless, one is seized with fear and trembling when entering into this narrow gorge with its high and perpendicular sides, so perfectly matched that they seem ready at any moment to snap back together again.

[11]. This opening is an example in miniature of what the great *quebradas* were originally like, when their depth was no greater than this one and when their banks, which now slope away, were perpendicular, or nearly so, as in this instance. It was only after the waters had cut the channels deeper that there were landslides above and that the upper walls, unable to maintain themselves perpendicular, gradually crumbled to their present shape. In the same manner the passage of time and the effects of rain, frost, and sun are abrading the Chapllancas canyon, so that it too will eventually lose the even width from top to bottom that it now has, and which it has retained more than others because the rock is hard and not interbedded with easily eroded veins of earth. Everything thus leads us to believe that the waters alone have worn away this channel to its present form and that the waters will by the same process continue to widen it in its upper part, inasmuch as time suffices to reduce the hardest and most solid rocks to sand, and as evidences of this are already apparent in the fragments of stone in the river-bed here and where it leaves the canyon in the mountain and broadens out on to the plain.

[12]. But whether we attribute the origin of this deep channel to the action of the waters which have worn it down to its present state, or whether we suppose that an earthquake rent asunder the mountain to give a new course to the river which had previously taken another direction, there can be no doubt that this opening was formed at some time after the Deluge had receded, and from this example, that the *quebradas* frequently met with throughout the higher parts of South America were formed by the gradual wearing of the waters, for it can be observed, on the one hand, that the force of their current is capable of wrenching off rocks of extraordinary size, and, on the other hand we have manifest proofs of the continuing effort of the waters to deepen their bed, traces of which are seen in the huge blocks shaped like dice or cubes which they have formed wherever the rocks have offered too great an obstacle to allow them to split them and clear away the whole extent of the channel. In the Iscuchaca River, near the place of the same name, there is one such rock which looks exactly like a die, about

12 *varas* square and rising out of low water to a distance of 7 or 8 *varas*. Such large formations and the smaller ones found in the river beds must have been left standing there after the waters had eaten away the surrounding rocks and sand, but they will remain only until such time as the deepening rivers find some soluble material at their bases, penetrate it, destroy it, and weaken its substance. Put in motion by great floods, these masses of rock will go crashing against others, and be broken into smaller pieces which will roll more easily. Such is doubtless the origin of all the stones seen beneath the waters or along the banks, some very small and others so enormous that human strength could not move them. To give some idea of the depth of these *quebradas* or valleys in relation to the habitable areas of South America certain experiments may be cited as evidence. The town of Huancavelica was founded in one of the valleys among the various chains of mountains. Here the mercury in the barometer tube remains at 18 *pulgadas* (inches), 1½ *líneas* (lines), this being the average between the two extremes of 1¼ and 1¾ lines. The elevation above sea level is accordingly 1949 *toesas* or 4536⅔ *varas*. At the summit of the mountain where the mercury mine is located—which is still habitable and which is surrounded by other mountains as high again as this one is above Huancavelica—the barometer marks exactly 16 inches, which makes its altitude above sea level 2337⅔ *toesas* or 5448 *varas*, and its height above Huancavelica 912⅔ *varas*. This latter figure thus represents the depth to which the Huancavelica valley has been cut since the time of the Deluge by the action of the different rivers which take their rise in another region called Icho and join to form the Huancavelica River.

After so many observations concerning the extraordinary action of the waters and the astonishing effects resulting from it, are we not justified in supposing that the Natural Bridge is also the work of the waters, and should we not regard it as a sort of *quebrada?* [11] When the valleys of the Appalachians were only great lakes, in which the waters were imprisoned, the little valley now spanned by the Bridge may have formed a special reservoir in which the waters remained even after they had escaped from the larger valleys. The mass of the rock out of which the Natural Bridge was hollowed may have served as a barrier to them; but whether the height of the waters did not reach the summit of this rock, or whether they more easily succeeded in undermining its lower part, they would in either case have left subsisting the immense *calotte*, or roof, which forms the arch of the Bridge as we now see it. It would be useless, and perhaps rash, to attempt to explain in detail how the curve of this vault was so regularly drawn; but once the cause is known, all the effects, however varied, and however astonishing they may appear, must be attributed to it. We may further observe that the largest arc of this vault bears a relation to the angle formed by the valley at this place, inasmuch as the rock seems to have been most hollowed out there where the force of the waters was greatest. However this may be, I leave every one free to form any conjecture he pleases, and as I have said above, my design has been less to explain this prodigy of Nature than to describe it with enough accuracy to enable the learned to form an opinion about it.[12]

NOTES ON THE PURPLE MARTIN AND OTHER AMERICAN BIRDS

ALTHOUGH the spring was already well advanced when I reached the Natural Bridge, since it was then the 20th of April, I do not recall having seen swallows of any kind there. Baron de Turpin did not visit the Bridge until about the 15th of May, by which time the martins, which appear later than the swallows, had indeed had time to arrive; but I have reason to think that the bird he mentions [in his description of the Bridge, above] is no other than the *hirondelle à croupion blanc* (white-rumped swallow) which is improperly called a *martinet* (martin) in some provinces of the kingdom [of France].

I shall take this opportunity to point out that the bird called in America a "martin" (*martinet*) is a particular species, which is unknown in Europe, and which has been nowhere well described, not even in Catesby,[13] at least if this is the bird he has in mind when speaking of a Carolina martin which he calls the "purple martin." [14] Unfortunately I am not in a position to supply this deficiency. Several reasons have prevented me from taking advantage of my residence in America to devote myself to such observations as the trifling knowledge I have gained of natural history might have allowed me to take. For one thing, the little room left to officers, and even to general officers, for transporting their effects, at the time of our departure from Europe, did not allow me to take with me any other books than those I needed for political and military knowledge of the continent where I was going to wage war. It was beyond my powers to work from memory and after my own ideas; and furthermore I had conceived the erroneous notion that everything was already known and written about a country as well known and as frequently visited as North America then was. I found, too late, that I was mistaken. Indeed, the small success attending my subsequent efforts to derive some advantage either from my own curiosity or from the information of people I employed, has convinced me that it would even now be a very useful thing to send to America a little caravan composed of naturalists, geographers, and draftsmen. Meanwhile, until such a plan—which has already been proposed—can be carried out,[15] I shall here submit a few observations that I have made on the "martin" or *martinet* of America.

This bird [*Progne subis subis*] differs from our European martin in its form, its color, and its behavior. In form: its body is fairly large and similar to that of several other birds of different species, such as the *merle* (blackbird) and the *sansonnet* (starling). In color: although the male is wholly black like other martins, the female is of a cindery gray, a little lighter than our female blackbird, while its breast is a dingy and mixed white. In behavior: instead of being wild like our martin, it is even more tame and domestic, if that be possible, than our chimney swallow. The Americans have an almost superstitious respect for these birds; not only do they prepare for them, at the beginning of spring, earthen pots like those we affix to our walls to attract sparrows, but they hang under the eaves of the roof little cages for them to nest in. The more credulous of the Americans say that these birds bring good luck to the houses that they visit; the most sensible think they are useful, not only because they destroy the flies which are very troublesome in summer, but also because by their boldness and their cries they drive away the birds of prey when they come to attack the poultry. These birds are so familiar that with a little adroitness one might catch them in one's hand. Their song is far removed from the disagreeable cry of our martin; it is more like that of the chimney swallow, but is much more melodious. I have only seen them at liberty, for I confess that having a hundred times resolved to kill at least one or two of them, in order to examine them more closely, I never had the courage to do so, so much did I respect the kind hospitality which is proffered them and which they as trustfully accept.

I do not know why Catesby calls this bird the "purple" martin, for I have never observed the slightest shade of that color in their plumage; the male is the most beautiful black, and as I have already said, the female is cindery gray on the back and white mixed with gray on the belly. If this martin were not a bird of passage and a bird which, like all those of its species, must travel very rapidly, it would seem fairly likely that it might take on a purple color nearer the tropics. For perceptible differences in the coloration of birds of the same species are to be found according to their distance from the tropics, or the equator. The hummingbirds seen in Virginia, and which range as far north as Pennsylvania and the Jerseys, are of a gray color, and only their throat glistens with the color of the ruby —while those of Guiana and Brazil display in their whole plumage that brilliancy which Nature has bestowed only partially upon the others. No species would furnish more examples of this progression in brilliancy and intensity of colors than the starlings, were these not migratory birds and were it possible to know exactly from what country come the different flocks that are seen arriving in the spring. The most beautiful variety of this species is the black starling, called the "blackbird" [red-winged blackbird, *Agelaius phoeniceus*] in America: when perching he appears wholly black, but in the folds of his wings he has several feathers of a very bright, but shaded, red, which can only be compared to the carbuncle; so that, when he flies off, his brilliant colors produce an effect which is the more agreeable for being unexpected. Following immediately after this one, another variety arrives; this is the grayish-colored starling, which also has several red feathers, but fewer in number, and of a less brilliant red. A third variety is of a brown color inclining to red, something like the hen pheasant; it also has in the fold of its wings three wholly red feathers, but of a dull and lusterless red. Lastly, a fourth variety, which would be absolutely similar to our European starling, had it not, like the others, in the fold of its wings three or four reddish feathers, which seem to attest its American origin and which might be regarded as the facings of an incomplete uniform, sufficient, however, to indicate to what army this legion belongs. There is every reason to believe that if we could know where these birds come from—they appear throughout North America and even in Virginia and Carolina only at the beginning of spring—we could then ascertain that the degree of brilliancy of their plumage is due to the degree of latitude of the regions they inhabit during the winter. We read in [Buffon's] *Histoire Naturelle* that the starling is not a bird of passage: this may be true of European starlings, but I can affirm that from Boston to Chesapeake Bay I have seen them arrive only at the end of winter.

I have not spoken of a sort of starling which is not mentioned in the *Histoire Naturelle*, but which is to be seen in the King's Cabinet [at the Jardin du Roi in Paris] and which is described by Catesby; indeed, I should have begun with this species, as it is the bird which has led me into this long digression. It is called in America the *étourneau corneille* or "starling crow" [*Sturnus vulgaris vulgaris*]. This bird is a great deal larger than the other starlings, and when one considers its beak, one is tempted to confuse it with the *choucas* or jackdaw; but there is no doubt of its being a real starling, for it has the cry and behavior of a starling, it dwells in marshes, and mixes with all the other varieties of starlings that I have mentioned. Its color is of a mixed and changeable black, which shows, according to the way the light falls on it, bluish and purplish shades. Now it would seem plausible to suppose that birds, whose color is originally black, might acquire from living in sunny climes those blue or purplish shades which can be seen in the starling crow; and in this case it is possible that the "purple" martin mentioned by Catesby may exist in South Carolina, though I have never seen it in Virginia. But it would still be difficult to explain why such a martin, of more southerly origin, should not extend its migration as far as Virginia and Pennsylvania, for though we have said that starlings are birds of passage in America, their migrations must be clearly distinguished from those of the swallows and the martins. There is every reason to think that the starlings merely retire during the winter to the neighborhood of the lakes and rivers which abound between the [Atlantic] Ocean and the Pacific, from 35 to 33 degrees of latitude, for it is enough for them to avoid the frost which would hinder them from finding subsistence in the marshes. On the other hand, swallows must go to countries where winged insects still fill the air during the winter. However, as evidence to the contrary, we have the following observation, which deserves all possible confidence: Mr. [William] Fleming, Judge of the General Court in Virginia, a trustworthy and highly respectable man,[16] assured Mr. Jefferson that on a winter's day, as he was superintending the cutting of some trees on land that he intended to sow, he was greatly surprised to see fall, with an old cleft oak, a great number of martins, who had taken refuge and become torpid in the hollows of this tree, as bats do in caves and caverns. Does this fact, which it is difficult to contest, prove that martins do not migrate like quail and storks? Or does it only mean that a lazy flock of those birds, having delayed their departure too long, were surprised by the cold weather and compelled to seek a shelter where they could spend the winter? [17]

Appendix

C

THE OPOSSUM

Editor's Introduction

THE opossum is the first pouch-bearer with which Western civilization came into contact. Born a veritable embryo and incubated in the abdominal pouch, the opossum has been a source of wonderment and conjecture ever since the year 1500. In that year the explorer Pinzón picked up, in newly discovered Brazil, a female opossum with young in her pouch ... brought her to Spain. ... With the settlement of Virginia ... it was Captain John Smith who wrote the first description in English of the 'Virginia' opossum [*Didelphis virginiana*] and bestowed upon it the Indian name, *opossum,* by which it is now known." (Carl G. Hartman, *Possums* [Austin, Texas, 1952], 1.) In the mid-eighteenth century the French naturalist Buffon summed up in his *Histoire Naturelle* the already extensive literature on opossums that had accumulated during the preceding two centuries and a half. Buffon also invited those who might have an opportunity to study the opossum in its native haunts to find answers to some of the unanswered questions about this curious animal.

Chastellux's investigation of the subject—undertaken during the winter of 1781-82 while in winter quarters at Williamsburg, and in which his brother officer, the Chevalier d'Aboville, had a major share—was an attempt to answer some of the questions outlined by Buffon. D'Aboville, by his careful observations, was able to determine the span of pregnancy of the opossum (thirteen days), and the period of incubation of the young in the mother's pouch (two months). Many more questions remained for future investigators (how the newborn possums are transferred from the uterus to the pouch, for example), but, as far as he went, D'Aboville reached conclusions that can still bear the scrutiny of scientists today. Only his final surmise (concerning the nipples of the female) is in error. For a survey of the subject by a modern authority the reader is referred to Carl G. Hartman's well-illustrated book, *Possums*. In dealing with the earlier writings on the subject Hartman refers (pp. 73, 92) to the Chastellux-D'Aboville study, but his citations are unfortunately secondhand (via Bewick) and he appears to be unacquainted with the original text. In the present Editor's opinion, he does not give to this Chastellux-D'Aboville "paper" the place it would seem to deserve in the history of possum literature.

The Opossum

Since I have allowed myself to be led into the discussion of subjects relative to natural history, I shall not terminate this long appendix without adding one more note. I can throw no new light on this subject, as it has already been treated by Count de Buffon; but I shall at least have the satisfaction of confirming, by irrefragable proofs, what his genius alone revealed to him. I am happy, too, to find this opportunity to render my personal homage to the most illustrious man of our age, and to boast of the long-standing friendship that unites us—a friendship that dates from my early admiration for his immortal works.

Readers of Buffon all know that one of the most interesting chapters in his *History of the Quadrupeds* is the one dealing with the *sarigue*, or opossum.[18] Observation had taught that the female of this animal had under her belly a sort of pouch in which she carried her young, that they were never to be seen outside this pouch before they were able to run about and seek their food, and that until that period they always remained attached to their mother's teats; but ignorance and credulity had adopted all sorts of ridiculous tales respecting the manner in which generation takes place in this species. For example, I found the opinion established in Virginia, even among physicians, that the young of the opossum came out of their mother's belly through the teats.[19] Only their extreme smallness at the moment of their birth could accredit such an opinion, which anatomy would so easily have disproven, had it but been consulted.

My first concern during the winter of 1781 to 1782 was to procure some of these animals and have them dissected. M. Robillard, first surgeon to our army, and one of the most skillful surgeons in France, was pleased to undertake this.[20] Having dissected a male and a female, he found the organs of generation similar to those of other quadrupeds, the only difference being that he observed a bifurcation in the glans penis of the male and in the clitoris of the female, and that he discovered in the uterus of the latter a sort of partition or mediastinum which divided it into two compartments, but which was not continuous enough to make these two cavities entirely separate from each other. This was sufficient to confirm and clarify the most essential points of a description which M. Daubenton had been able to make only from a specimen preserved in alcohol.[21] But M. de Buffon went further and concluded with truly admirable sagacity that Nature in forming this animal had proceeded in a special manner and given it a faculty of reproducing itself which was intermediary, so to speak, between that of quadrupeds and that of birds, in order that the brevity of gestation might correspond to the long incubation they receive in the pouch where they are kept. M. de Buffon then added:

Nobody has observed the length of the gestation of these animals, which we presume to be much shorter than in others; and as this premature exclusion is an exceptional example in Nature, we exhort those who have the opportunity of seeing opossums alive in their native country to endeavor to discover how long the females bear them, and how much longer, after their birth, the young remain attached to the teats before they separate from them. Such an observation, curious in itself, might also become useful by pointing out to us perhaps some means of preserving the lives of prematurely born children.

In this instance the interpreter of Nature, as often happens to the dragomans of Asia, had been obliged to *divine* his master's thought before attempting to express it in language intelligible to others. But when the interpreter (as was the case with me) already knows his master's thought and can transmit it without resorting to divination, then it matters little whether he translates or speaks of his own accord. Thus, as the minister and confidant of M. de Buffon, my only apprehension was not being able to procure the means necessary to prove to the Americans a truth which I had already accepted.

To attain my object opossums had to be tamed and then persuaded to copulate in this state of domestication, or rather of slavery; this union would have to prove fruitful, and we would have to observe its successive results. Now nobody in this country had thought of raising opossums, and the only ones we could get were those that the soldiers caught for us in the woods. I had one at my house, which had already become very tame, but I had taken advantage of the sailing of the *Hermione* to send it to M. de Buffon. Comte de La Touche, who commanded this frigate, had kindly consented to take with him several animals and other objects of natural history that I wished to send to Europe.[22] Fortunately chance served me better than my own repeated attempts could have done. It so happened that the Chevalier d'Aboville, *Brigadier des Armées du Roi* and commander of our artillery, availed himself of the repose we were enjoying and employed his leisure to increase his knowledge of physics and natural history, with the same talents and activity that had been so useful to us during the campaign.[23] He raised several animals, including a female opossum, which he had the good fortune to see conceive, become a mother, and bring up her young, in his own house, and even in his own bedroom. I can do no better than to transcribe here the following observations that he [M. d'Aboville] has written down and that he has been pleased to commit to me:

The opossum is more timid than shy, and very quickly becomes tame. I had had a female for some time, when a male was brought to me. At first she appeared to be afraid of him, and so, to avoid any quarrel, I tied up the newcomer in a box near my fireplace. The female enjoyed the freedom of my room, where she likewise had a box, which she came out of only at night to eat, drink, and void herself. The evening of the second day after the arrival of the male, while I was writing before my fire, I saw the female advance slowly towards the box the male was in, then go back under my bed, come out again, repeating the movement until she finally became so bold as to enter the box of the male, who instantly threw himself upon her with such precipitation, that having hitherto observed him very indifferent, I concluded that he was impelled by anger. I pulled her out, and beat him. A few minutes later she renewed the attempt, and the male hearing her approach, came out of his box, and the length of the cord allowing him to join her on the middle of the hearth, he fell upon her with the same impetuosity, and I soon perceived that since the female was not frightened by this, I ought not to meddle with her affairs. She was crouched down; the male was upon her, with his four feet resting on the ground, and both of them in a state of perfect immobility. I watched them in this position for nearly half an hour; I then passed my finger between them, and could perceive that there was no intromission. My presence did not seem to bother them in the least, but lest any movement of mine distract them, I got into bed. The fire before which I left them gave light enough for me to observe them. I continued to watch them from my bed for more than half an hour, during which time they still remained motionless. My own state of immobility made me drowsy: I had closed my eyes for a few moments, when the female climbed up onto my bed. I caressed her, and passing my hand towards her posterior parts, found them wet. This led me to believe that in spite of appearances the act of copulation had been completed. The next morning I found spots on the floor, which were further evidence of it. But what completed the proof for me was the change I soon perceived in the pouch of this female.

The mating had taken place on the 7th of February [1782]; ten days later I noticed that the edge of the orifice of the pouch was somewhat thickened. This was even more noticeable on the following days, and I also observed that the pouch was becoming larger and that the opening was wider than before.

The night of the 20th to the 21st, that is to say, thirteen days after the copulation, the female did not leave the box until the night was far advanced, and then only to eat, drink, and void herself, after which she returned immediately to her box, so that I failed that day to continue to observe the progress of the changes taking place in her pouch.

The fourteenth day, towards evening, seeing that she did not come out of her box, I put in my hand, which she greatly caressed, licking it, and gnawing it very gently; she grasped my fingers with her little hands, trying to retain mine when I attempted to withdraw it. I gave her some pieces of meat, which she ate, continuing to caress my hand, and seeing that she could not retain it, she determined to follow it, and came out of her box still keeping hold of my finger. I was most eager to feel inside the pouch: for the change I perceived in it made me realize that I had lost much by having missed a day in observing it and that I had let slip the most interesting moment. This pouch, the opening of which had been gradually widening during the preceding days, was now almost closed, showing only a small round opening in the middle of a depression similar to a navel. The orifice of it was rather moist, and the hair round the orifice was wetted with a glairy humour common to the anus and the vagina. It seemed to me that I might still have been able to introduce one of my fingers into the pouch, but I thought that this could not be done without forcing the passage, thus risking hurting it and perhaps destroying the delicate embryos it contained—for I now no longer doubted that they were there.[24]

The fifteenth day—whether it was because my impatience got the better of my fear of hurting the embryos, or because the orifice of the pouch was really more open than on the previous day—I introduced my finger, and felt, at the bottom of the pouch, a little round body, which I judged to be about the size of a pea. The mother, who had previously allowed me without much difficulty to put my fingers in her pouch, now became very uneasy and tried to escape, which prevented me from exploring enough to be sure whether this body was spherical, whether it was adherent, and if there were several of them; but it seemed to me adherent, and placed on one side of the pouch, from which I concluded that there was a second on the other side.

The sixteenth night she came out only to eat, and returned immediately. The seventeenth day in the evening she came out; I reached into her pouch, I felt two bodies placed at the bottom, one beside the other, clinging to the body of the mother. Their volume did not exceed that of a pea, and as far as I could judge by touch, their shape seemed to me to approximate that of a fig whose stem had been implanted in a rounded base which presented some unevenness to the finger. Although I had felt only two bodies, I had no doubt that this pouch contained a greater number.

The twenty-fifth day after the mating, consequently the twelfth of the sojourn of the young in the pouch, I began to feel them move under the finger, and one month after the beginning of their residence in the pouch, they could be seen when the pouch was partly opened with the finger. A fortnight later, it remained naturally open enough so that the young could be seen easily; and at the end of two months, when the female was lying down and the opening of the pouch was in a more lax position than when she was walking, the young ones were part in and part out of the pouch, and could easily be counted. They were to the number of six, all holding to the mother by a canal which enters the mouth of the young ones, and which can be pulled out only with some effort, and, if this happens at an early period, at the risk of causing the young one to die, for it is then unable to take hold of the teat again. But when about six weeks old, it is able to take hold again, although it manages to do this only by a strong sucking movement, the opening at the end of the muzzle being only large enough to receive the nipple, which is about two lines [⅙ inch] in length and the size of the second or third string of a violin. The opossum has however a very wide mouth, but for as long as it has to remain attached to the mother, Nature has joined the two jaws with a membrane, which dries up and disappears when the young one has reached the age of about three months, at which time it begins to eat and to walk.

The number of the young varies greatly. I have seen females who had ten or eleven, others who had only five or six. There are never more teats than young, and when the latter are weaned, the nipples of the mother dry up and fall off, just as the umbilical cord does from the young of other animals; with this difference, that other animals preserve the mark of the place where the umbilical cord was, whereas the female opossum retains no trace of the points where her nipples have been, and which are not, as in other animals, placed in two parallel lines, but irregularly and as if by accident.[25] It seems that the nipples are formed at those places where the embryos happen to touch the mother's belly after she has put them into her pouch, one by one, as she *lays* them—for that is the most appropriate expression, immature embryos being comparable only to eggs.

PART III

A Journey into New Hampshire, the State of Massachusetts, and Upper Pennsylvania

November—December 1782

EDITOR'S INTRODUCTION

Interlude between Journeys
May—October 1782

THE month of May found Chastellux back again in his comfort-able quarters at Williamsburg, busy writing up the journal of his recent trip, while pondering with the other staff officers the army's next move. The war was not yet over, the English were still in possession of New York, Charleston, and Savannah; indeed, America was but one theater of a war which extended to any part of the world where the French, the English, the Spanish, or the Dutch, had colonies. Rochambeau planned, with Washington's ap-proval, to march his army north again, join forces with the Ameri-cans, and attack New York—that is, if naval superiority were assured. Once again, the whereabouts of the French navy would be the deciding factor. Early in May disturbing rumors reached Wil-liamsburg concerning De Grasse's West Indian fleet. By the end of the month the worst was confirmed. De Grasse himself was a prisoner of the English and his fleet had been badly defeated by Admiral Rodney on April 9 and 12, in two successive engagements known as the "Battles of the Saints" (from the name of the small islands off Guadeloupe where the two forces met). The English could henceforth count on superiority at sea. The Marquis de Vaudreuil had assumed command of the remnants of the French fleet and would presumably be sailing for North American waters. Washington now advised Rochambeau to remain in Virginia, pre-pared to march north or south, according to the movements of Vaudreuil's squadron. But plans were already made for the north-ward march; Rochambeau hoped that a threat against New York would prevent the British from sending troops to the West Indies to further endanger French possessions there, and he still hoped for effective aid from the navy. Furthermore, the season for campaigning was fast progressing, and tidewater Virginia was hot and ill-suited for a summer sojourn.

Relations between the French army and the civilian population appear to have been generally harmonious. At the end of May Governor Harrison could report that civilians claiming damages had been paid their money by the French, thanks to the efforts of the claims agent, Col. Dudley Digges, who had "finished the business much to the satisfaction of the people." [1] The satisfaction was doubtless increased by the sight of the good "hard money" received in settlement. One problem did, however, trouble certain of the Virginian planters. Governor Harrison felt obliged to inform General Rochambeau of complaints of Negroes being concealed in York and Williamsburg among the French troops, and the fears of the owners that they would thus be unable to recover their property. [2] The British policy during the recent invasion of emancipating such slaves as came to their lines had obviously set a disquieting precedent.

It was Chastellux who attempted to allay the fears. In a letter drafted in Rochambeau's absence, when the army was already bound northward, he wrote: "I know well the intentions of the General, and can assure you that I have not less attention than he has to preserve with the greatest care the property of the inhabitants of Virginia. . . . I know that all the officers have been forbid, under the most severe penalties, to take any Negro into their service, or even to receive them into camp. These precautions are not only dictated by justice, but also by reciprocal interest. Your Excellency having taken the same steps to have our deserters apprehended that we have taken to prevent the desertion of your Negroes." [3]

The closing weeks of the French army's sojourn in Virginia were also marked by an international incident of somewhat less grave implications—the affair of Chastellux's claret. On the night of May 10, 1782, the sloop *William and John*, bound for Head of Elk with a cargo of tar, turpentine, and four boxes of claret addressed to Chastellux, was boarded and captured in Hampton Roads by "pirates" identified as five men from the crew of the British "flag" brig *Maria*. In reply to his protests against this violation of the flag of truce, Governor Harrison received assurances from the English commander in New York, Sir Guy Carleton, that satisfactory compensation would be made. Harrison, eager to show his esteem for Chastellux and feeling that his own honor was in some manner engaged, thereupon undertook to see that the Frenchman's claim was settled to his satisfaction. But the negotiations became complicated, for the pirated sloop had been in turn captured by American privateers and condemned by a New Jersey admiralty court as a prize cargo. Thus this "trifling subject" eventually involved Governor Harrison in a long-drawnout and troublesome correspondence in Chastellux's behalf. It is not entirely clear from the extant documents whether Chastellux finally got his money, but it may at least be stated that his baggage on his northward journey was the lighter by four cases of claret.[4]

There was no mention, however, of fugitive slaves or wine casks errant in the formal compliments exchanged at the time the French departed. The General Assembly congratulated General Rochambeau both on the birth of an heir to the crown of France and on the excellent discipline of the French troops during their stay in Virginia. In reply the "gentlemen of the General Assembly of the State of Virginia" received a gracious communication in English, dated at Williamsburg, June 28, 1782. It bore the signature of Rochambeau, but one suspects that Chastellux may have been his ghost writer.

The marks of the interest which you are pleased to show upon the birth of an heir to the crown of France [the message ran] cannot but be exceeding agreeable to the King my master. The sentiments which you share with us towards our August Sovereigns, strengthen the ties that unite us. The hope which you entertain that this young Prince will inherit of his royal father's affection towards his good and faithful allies, makes me foresee with great satisfaction the continuation of our alliance with America as being eternal.

If the French troops have been happy enough to cooperate under General Washington's command to the brilliant succès which has ended the last campaign and the calamities of this State, they have been well rewarded by the good harmony and good reception which they have met with this winter in this country in the general and private walks of life.

I am overjoyed that you have been pleased with the discipline of the troops. I likewise with pleasure transmit their sincere thanks for the good treatment they have experienced from the inhabitants of Virginia.[5]

By July 1, 1782, the French army had begun its march to the north—its ultimate destination still a matter of uncertainty.[6] Lauzun's Legion (the Duke himself was still absent in France) went ahead as the vanguard. Then came, a day apart, the Bourbonnais, Deux-Ponts, Soissonnais, and Saintonge Regiments. Chastellux started out at the head of Bourbonnais. Then, when Rochambeau went on to confer with Washington at Philadelphia, he was in command of the entire army. The heat was excessive, the marches were in striking contrast to the speed of the southward movement the previous year. Slowly the army made its way up through Virginia, averaging less than ten miles a day. The route led through Drinking Spring, Byrd's Tavern, Newcastle, Hanovertown, Bowling Green, Dumfries, Colchester (where Chastellux had the pleasure of meeting General Daniel Morgan and refighting the Battle of Cowpens with him), to Alexandria.

Early in August the army reached Baltimore. During its three weeks' sojourn, there were reviews, balls, and other festivities in which the whole city participated. There were also rumors of preliminary peace negotiations in Paris and London. But Washington advised Rochambeau that such rumors might be a mere ruse, urged him to proceed to the Hudson, as planned, and suggested that if orders came from the French Court for the withdrawal of the troops, the embarkation could take place as well from there as from the Delaware or Chesapeake. The army thus resumed its march on August 23, the vanguard reaching Philadelphia on the 30th. There was a few days' pause here, with more festivities, and an opportunity for Chastellux to resume his acquaintance with old friends. (It was perhaps at this time—if not during his subsequent visit to Philadelphia the following December—that he sat to Charles Willson Peale for his portrait.) Then, at the beginning of September the army proceeded north through New Jersey, over roads that Chastellux was already familiar with: Trenton, Princeton, Middle Brook, Bullion's Tavern, Morristown, Whippany, Pompton, Suffern, Kakiat, and thence to Joshua Hett Smith's abandoned house at Haverstraw. This part of the march was by brigades of two regiments each. The First Brigade crossed the Hudson at King's Ferry on September 17, followed the next day by the Second. On the 20th General Washington—still their Commander in Chief—reviewed the whole army near Peekskill. Once again, for another month, the combined French and American armies were encamped on the Hudson, as they had been in the summer of 1781. This time the positions were considerably farther north, near the entrance to the Highlands: the Americans at Verplanck's Point and the French ten miles or so away at Crompond (now Yorktown Heights, Westchester County, N.Y.).

While the French were settling into their camp, officers fresh from France—newcomers as well as old troopers—arrived bringing dispatches and the latest instructions from Versailles, as well as first-hand news of friends and relatives at home. Baron de Vioménil, the Marquis de Laval, the Duc de Lauzun, and Chastellux's aide-de-camp, Baron de Montesquieu, now rejoined their posts. Two months earlier, when Baron de Vioménil's return had still been uncertain, Rochambeau, when soliciting leave for himself, had proposed leaving Chastellux in command of the army: "I may inform you," he wrote to the Minister of War, "that this general officer is infinitely agreeable to General Washington and to the Americans, whose politics and customs he knows perfectly, that he is the intimate friend of the Chevalier de La Luzerne, and that I will thus have full confidence in his manner of corresponding with both of them." [7] However, Chastellux was not called upon to assume the command, for the arrival of Baron de Vioménil at Crompond meant that he could soon relinquish his own responsibilities and expect home leave for himself. In the contingent of newcomers, avid for action and eager to see strange sights, were the Comte de Ségur (son of the Minister of War), the Prince de Broglie, the Vicomte de Vaudreuil, and Boson de Talleyrand-Périgord.[8] The last two were soon to serve as aides-de-camp to Chastellux on his journey to Portsmouth and Boston.

Plans for the future—for the army as well as for individuals—could now be made. The dispatches received from France instructed Rochambeau, in the event that the British should evacuate either Charleston or New York, to take his army to Santo Domingo and there await further orders. New York was still firmly in the enemy's grasp, but the evacuation of Charleston appeared imminent and eventually materialized in December. Furthermore, the Marquis de Vaudreuil had brought the crippled French fleet to Boston in August, and was refitting his ships there and at Portsmouth. Rochambeau could thus make arrangements with him for transporting the army to the West Indies, and for his own return to France with several of his staff (including Chastellux). Such plans, however, could not yet be divulged to the rank and file. On October 19, 1782, the anniversary of the Yorktown victory, Rochambeau, Chastellux, and the other French generals were present at a drill presented in their honor by the entire American army. Three days later the allied armies parted ways, for the last time. On October 22 the First Brigade of the French army, commanded by Chastellux, left Crompond on its march through Salem, N.Y., Danbury, Connecticut, Newtown, Waterbury, and Farmington, to Hartford, where it arrived on October 29. Rochambeau now spoke openly of the approaching embarkation of the troops from Boston, under the command of Baron de Vioménil, and of his own imminent return to France. Here at Hartford Chastellux relinquished his command, and set forth on the journey through New England described in Part III of his *Travels*.

═══════════ **1** ═══════════

HARTFORD, CONNECTICUT, TO
PORTSMOUTH, NEW HAMPSHIRE

As the Baron de Vioménil returned to the army at the beginning of October, I should normally have handed back to him the command of the first division, and would have then had no further necessary duties, unless I had chosen to take the command of the second division, in which case I would have taken it away from the Comte de Vioménil, which was far from my intention. I myself was therefore free to go back to Philadelphia to wait for M. de Rochambeau, who was to return there after marching his troops to the eastward; but my departure would have too plainly signified our intention of embarking the troops which it was wished to keep a secret, at least until they had reached Hartford. On the other hand, as the Comte de Vioménil wanted to visit Saratoga, the Baron de Vioménil requested me to retain the command of the first division, while he marched with the second. I consented, therefore, to sacrifice another tiresome and fatiguing fortnight, and marched with the troops as far as Hartford.[1] I also reluctantly agreed not to return to the southward until the Comte de Rochambeau could do so, after the troops had been embarked. But I at least wished to avail myself of these circumstances to visit the upper part of the state of Massachusetts and New Hampshire, which I had not yet had time to see.

November 4, 1782: Hartford, Conn.—Coventry

I therefore set out from Hartford on the 4th of November, the same day that the Comte de Rochambeau marched with the first division to encamp at Bolton. It was two in the afternoon when I got on horseback; my traveling companions were Messieurs Lynch,

Chandler's. Our journey this day was thirty-three miles, it being seventeen from Clark's to Chandler's Tavern. This inn is kept by a widow, who was from home, and M. Lynch, who had preceded us, was very ill received by an old servant maid. I found him in great distress, because she would make no preparations, not even kill any chickens, before she received the orders of her mistress. Fortunately, however, the latter arrived in a quarter of an hour, in a sort of one-horse chaise, and I found her very polite and obliging. She gave us a tolerable supper, and we were very neatly lodged.[6]

November 6, 1782: Woodstock, Conn.—Oxford, Mass.—Sutton

The 6th we set out from Chandler's Tavern at about ten o'clock. I had been warned that on reaching Oxford it would be necessary to inquire the road at an innkeeper's called Mr. [Joseph] Lord. His house was only twelve miles from the one I had left, but the weather was so bad when we got there, that I decided to stop a couple of hours until the driving rain, which had continued the whole morning, ceased.[7] I had two roads to choose from: the one that goes through Shrewsbury would have taken me more directly to Portsmouth; but I preferred the one by way of Sutton and Grafton, which would take me through Concord, that celebrated spot where the first blood was shed and the civil war began. The rain seeming to abate a little, I resumed my journey at two, and proceeded through the town of Sutton, a pretty enough place, where there are several well-built houses; but the rain redoubling, I was obliged to halt there—seven miles from Oxford—at "Baron's" [LeBaron's] Tavern, where we were very well received.[8] We dried ourselves by a good fire, in a very pretty room, adorned with good prints and handsome mahogany furniture; and finding that the useful corresponded to the agreeable in this house, we were reconciled with the bad weather, which had brought us to such a good refuge.

November 7, 1782: Sutton—Grafton—Westborough—Marlborough
    —Concord

I left this place at nine the next morning; my route took me through Grafton. I there crossed the Blackstone River and then arrived at Gale's Tavern, fifteen miles from LeBaron's, after a journey through very pleasant country.[9] I noticed that the meadows, of which there are a great number, were in general intersected and watered by little ditches in which the waters were held along the hillsides. I asked Mr. [Abijah] Gale how much these meadows might be worth; he informed me that they sold for ten, twelve, and as much as twenty dollars an acre; he owned one which yielded four tons of hay in a single harvest. The after-grass is fed to the cattle, to produce butter and cheese, one of the chief articles of trade in this region. The price of meat here is usually five *sols* [10] for a pound of fourteen ounces. After feeding our horses we continued our journey through Marlborough, where there are handsome houses which are grouped closer together than in the other towns or townships.

I then entered woods, which took me to the Concord River [i.e., Sudbury River, branch of the Concord], otherwise known as the Billerica, which we crossed on a bridge [the South Bridge] about a mile from the meetinghouse, and at the same distance from Mr. "John's" [Ephraim Jones] inn, which I did not reach until nearly nine o'clock. This is an excellent inn, kept by a most determined Whig, who even played his part in the affair of Concord. [11] Major Pitcairn, who commanded the English on this occasion, had lodged several times at Jones's house, when traveling through the country, usually in disguise; a method he had sometimes taken, though very dangerous, of getting information to communicate to General Gage. The day on which he headed the English troops to Concord, he arrived at seven in the morning, followed by a company of grenadiers; he went immediately to Mr. Jones's tavern, the door of which being shut, he knocked several times, and on the refusal to open it, ordered his grenadiers to force it. Entering it himself the first, he pushed Mr. Jones so roughly that he knocked him down; he then kept him prisoner behind the counter and asked him several times to tell him where the rebels' storehouses were. The Americans had in fact collected some cannon and war supplies at Concord, but having received warning during the night, they had had time to remove everything into the woods, except three twenty-four pounders, which had remained in the prison yard, of which Mr. Jones was the keeper. Major Pitcairn carried his violence so far as to clap a pistol to his throat. Mr. Jones, who had himself at first been in a passion, grew calm, and tried in turn to pacify the English commander. He assured him that there were only the above three pieces of cannon at Concord, and that he would show them to him, if he would follow him. He conducted him to the prison, where the English, he says, fell in a great rage at seeing the "Yankees" so expert in mounting cannon, and in providing themselves with everything necessary for the service of artillery, such as sponges, rammers, etc. Major Pitcairn made his men destroy the carriages and break the trunnions; then ordered the prison opened, where he found two prisoners, one of whom, being a Tory, he released.

These first moments of agitation and ill temper being over, Major Pitcairn returned to Mr. Jones's, asked for breakfast, and punctiliously paid for it. The latter resumed his station of innkeeper; numbers of the English came to ask for rum, which he measured out as usual, and made them all pay exactly. In the meantime, the Americans, who had crossed over the river as they retreated, began to rally and to unite with those, who, apprised by the alarm bells and by various messengers, were coming to their assistance. The measures that Major Pitcairn had to take for his security, while he was searching for and destroying the munitions were by no means difficult; it was only necessary to place strong guards at the two bridges, the North Bridge and the South, which he had done. Towards ten o'clock in the morning, the firing of musketry was heard at the North Bridge; the English immediately rallied at the place appointed, on a height, in a cemetery situated to the right of the road, and opposite the town house. Three hundred Americans had assembled on the other side of the river; they descended from the heights by a winding road which leads obliquely to the bridge, but which, at sixty paces from the river, turns to the left, and comes straight upon it. Until they had reached this turn, they had their flank covered by a small stone wall. When they reached this point, they marched boldly up to the bridge and found the enemy trying to break it down. The latter fired the first shot, but the Americans fell upon them and easily made them give way, which must appear rather surprising. Mr. Jones affirms that the English at first imagined the Americans had no ammunition, but that they soon found out their error on seeing several of their soldiers wounded. They even tell of an officer who informed his men that they had nothing to fear, for "the Americans fired only with powder"; a drummer who was near him and who at that moment received a musket shot, replied, "Watch out for that powder, Captain." The English had three men shot dead here, and several wounded, two of them officers. The Americans now crossed over the bridge, and formed immediately on a small eminence to the left of the road, as they were situated, and at short cannon range from the height on which the English were collected. There they remained some time watching each other; but the sight of some houses which had been set on fire irritated the Americans and determined them to march against the English, who thereupon retreated by the main Lexington road; but as this road makes a bend, the Americans, who knew the country, took the string of the bow, and caught up with them [at Meriam's Corner] before they had advanced a mile. This was the beginning of that long retreating fight, accounts of which are everywhere available, and which ended only at Lexington, where the English were joined by the reinforcements brought to them by Lord Percy.

November 8, 1782: Concord—Billerica—Andover [West Andover] —Haverhill

It was on the morning of the 8th that I reconnoitered the field of battle at Concord, which took me until half past ten, when I resumed my journey. Ten miles from Concord is Billerica, a rather large township; the country here was less fertile, and the road rather more stony. We halted at South Andover, five miles beyond Billerica, at a bad inn, kept by one "Forster" [Capt. Asa Foster]; his wife had some beautiful children, but she seemed to me rather mad, and I think she was a bit drunk.[12] She showed me with considerable vanity a book that her eldest daughter was reading, and I found it, to my no small surprise, to be a book of prayers in Italian. This daughter, who was about seventeen, also recited to me a prayer in the Indian language, of which she understood not a word, having by chance learned it from an Indian servant; but her mother thought all this was admirable. We contented ourselves with feeding our horses in this wretched alehouse, and set out at half past one. We went through South and North Andover. North Parish, or North Andover, is a charming place, where there are a great number of very handsome houses, many meadows, and cattle of the handsomest species. Almost as you leave this long township, you enter Bradford, where night overtook us, and we traveled two or three miles in the dark before we reached Haverhill ferry. It was half past six before we had crossed it and got to Mr. "Harward's" [Joseph Harrod] inn, where we had a good supper and good lodgings.[13] At Haverhill the Merrimack is only fit for vessels of thirty tons, but much larger ones are built here, which are floated down empty to Newbury. Three miles above Haverhill are "falls," [14] and higher up the river is only navigable for boats. The trade of this town formerly consisted in timber for shipbuilding, but it has been interrupted since the war. The town is fairly considerable and rather well built; and its situation, in the form of an amphitheater on the left bank of the Merrimack, gives it many agreeable aspects.

November 9, 1782: Haverhill, Mass.—Plaistow, N.H.—Exeter—Portsmouth

We left Haverhill the 9th, at nine in the morning; my route took me first to Plaistow, a rather sizable township, after which we met with woods and a wild and arid country. We saw here a great number of pines and spruces; there are also several fairly large ponds, some of which are marked on the map. Ever since we left the confines of Connecticut I have in general observed a great number of these ponds, and this is one of the things which makes this country look like Bourbonnais and Nivernais.[15] Twelve miles from Haverhill is Kingston, a township smaller than most of those I saw along the route; and finally at eighteen miles is Exeter, which is now the capital of New Hampshire, that is to say, the place where the president or governor resides and the legislature meets. It is rather a handsome town and something of a port, for vessels of seventy tons can come up this far, while others as large as three or four hundred tons are built here, and are floated down the Exeter River into the bay of that name [Great Bay], and thence into the Piscataqua. I stopped at a very fine inn kept by a Mr. "Ruspert."[16] I left at half past two, and although we rode very fast, night was coming on when we reached Portsmouth. The road from Exeter is very hilly. We passed through Greenland, a very populous township, composed of well-built houses. Cattle here are abundant, but not so handsome as in Connecticut and Massachusetts. They are dispersed over fine meadows, and it is a pleasant sight to see them gather near the barns in the evening. This country presents, in every respect, the picture of abundance and of happiness. The road from Greenland to Portsmouth is wide and beautiful, dotted with habitations, so that these two towns are almost continuous. I alighted at Mr. Brewster's, where I was very well lodged; he seemed to me a true gentleman and much attached to his country.[17]

November 10, 1782: Portsmouth

On the 10th I went at about ten o'clock in the morning to pay a visit to M. d'Albert de Rions, Captain of the *Pluton*,[18] who had a house on shore, where he resided for reasons of health; he invited me to dinner, which he advised me to accept, as the Comte de

Vaudreuil [19] was in great confusion on board his ship, because five days before [November 8] lightning had severed the mizzen mast and penetrated the vessel to the first battery. He furthermore offered me his boat to take me on board the *Auguste*. I went back home to get my coat, but as I happened to pass by the meeting, precisely at the time of the service, I had the curiosity to enter, and remained there for a good half hour, so as not to interrupt the preacher and also to show my respect for this assembly. The audience was not numerous on account of the severe cold, but I saw several very pretty and elegantly dressed women. Mr. Buckminster, a young minister, spoke with a great deal of grace, and reasonably enough for a preacher.[20] I especially noted the skillful manner in which he introduced politics into his sermon by comparing Christians redeemed by the blood of Jesus Christ, but still compelled to fight against the flesh and sin, to the thirteen United States, who have acquired liberty and independence, but are still obliged to employ all their strength to combat a formidable power and preserve the treasure they have gained. It was nearly noon when I embarked in M. d'Albert's boat. I saw on the left, near the little island of Rising Castle,[21] the *America*, the vessel which had been launched a week earlier, and which appeared to me a fine ship.[22] I left on my right Washington Island, on which stands a fort of that name.[23] Fort Washington is built in the form of a star, the parapets of which are supported by stakes; it was not finished. Then leaving Newcastle on the right, and Kittery on the left, we arrived at the anchoring ground, this side of the first pass. This is not the anchorage they would have taken in case of attack; but would then have taken a position near the *America*. I found the Comte de Vaudreuil on board, who presented me to the officers of his ship, and afterwards to the officers of the army detachment with him, among whom I found three officers of my former regiment of Guyenne, at present called the Viennois.[24] He then took me to see the damage done to the ship by lightning. Here is how M. de Biré, who was then commanding the ship (M. de Vaudreuil having slept on shore) related this unfortunate event to me. It was half past two in the morning [November 8] and it was raining very violently: suddenly a dreadful explosion was heard; the sentinel, who was in the gallery, came in a panic into the council chamber, where he met M. de Biré, who had leaped out of his bed; they were both struck by the smell of sulphur which surrounded them. They immediately rang the bell and went to examine the ship: it was found that the mizzen mast was cut in two, four feet above the deck, that it had been lifted in the air and then fallen perpendicularly on the quarterdeck, which it had penetrated, as it had the second battery. Two sailors had been crushed by its fall, two others, who could not be found, had doubtless been thrown into the sea by the commotion, and several were wounded.[25]

At one o'clock we returned on shore to dine with M. d'Albert de Rions:[26] our table companions were M. de Biré, who was acting as flag captain on the *Auguste*, although he was only a lieutenant; M. de "Marteques" [MacCarthy-Martaigue] who had hitherto commanded the *Magnifique* and was appointed to the command of the *America*; M. de Siber, *Lieutenant en pied* of the *Pluton*; M. d'Hizeures, captain in the Viennois Regiment, etc.

After dinner we went to take tea with Colonel [John] Langdon.[27] He is a large handsome man, and of a very noble bearing; he has been a member of Congress, and is still one of the leading men of his region; his house is attractive and well furnished, and the apartments admirably well wainscotted; he has a rather good manuscript chart of the harbor of Portsmouth. Mrs. Langdon, his wife, is young, fair, and rather pretty, but I conversed less with her than with her husband, in whose favor I was prejudiced, from knowing that he had displayed great courage and patriotism at the time of Burgoyne's expedition. He repaired at that time to the chamber of the Council, of which he was a member, and perceiving that they were about to discuss some affairs of little consequence, he said: "Gentlemen, you may talk as long as you please, but I know that the enemy is on our frontiers, and that I am going to take my pistols and mount my horse to fight beside my fellow citizens." The majority of the members of the Council and of the Assembly followed him, and they joined General Gates at Saratoga. As he was marching day and night, resting only in the woods, a favorite Negro servant who had followed him said to him, "Master, you are giving yourself a heap of trouble, but no matter, you are going to fight for Liberty; I should also suffer patiently if I had Liberty to defend." "Don't let that stop you," replied Mr. Langdon, "from this moment you are free." The Negro followed him, behaved with courage, and has never left him since. On leaving Mr. Langdon's, we went to pay a visit to Colonel [Joshua] Wentworth: he is respected by his countrymen not only because he is of the same family as Lord Rockingham, but because his probity and ability are generally acknowledged. He was business agent for our navy at Portsmouth, and our officers were unstinting in their praise of him.[28] From Mr. Wentworth's, the Comte de Vaudreuil and M. d'Albert de Rions took me to Mrs. Whipple's, a widow, who is, I believe, sister-in-law to General [William] Whipple; she is neither young nor pretty but appeared to me to have wit and gaiety.[29] She is bringing up one of her nieces, who is only fourteen years old, but already charming. Mrs. Whipple's house, as well as Mr. Wentworth's, and all those I saw at Portsmouth, are very handsome and very well furnished.

November 11, 1782: Portsmouth

I proposed, on the morning of the 11th, to make a tour among the islands in the harbor, but some snow having fallen and the weather being by no means inviting, I therefore contented myself with paying visits to the officers of the navy, among others the Comte de Vaudreuil, who had slept on shore the preceding night. We again met for dinner at M. d'Albert de Rions', a meeting place which was always most agreeable. M. d'Hizeures had ordered the Viennois regimental band to attend; I saw with pleasure that the taste for music which I had inspired in this corps, had been maintained, and that the former musicians had been well replaced.[30] After dinner we again drank tea at Mr. Langdon's and then paid a visit to Dr. [Joshua] Brackett,[31] a physician much respected in this region, and afterwards to Mr. [Thomas] Thompson.[32] The latter was born in England; he is a good seaman, and a good builder; he also seemed to me a sensible man and greatly attached to his new country, which he nevertheless adopted only fifteen years ago. His wife [Margaret] is an American, and pleases by her countenance, but still more by her amiable and polite behavior. We finished the evening at Mr. [Joshua] Wentworth's, where the Comte de Vaudreuil lodged; he gave us a very nice supper, without formality, during which the conversation was gay and agreeable.

A General View of Portsmouth

The following are the ideas which I had an opportunity of acquiring relative to the town of Portsmouth. It was in a pretty flourishing state before the war, and carried on trade in ship timber and salt fish. It is easy to conceive that this commerce has greatly suffered since the beginning of the disturbances, but notwithstanding, Portsmouth is, perhaps, of all the American towns, the one which will gain the most from the present war. There is every appearance of its becoming to *New* England, what the other Portsmouth is to the *Old;* that is to say, that this place will be chosen as the depôt of the Continental Navy.[33] The access to the harbor is easy, the road immense, and there are seven fathoms of water as far up as two miles above the town; add to this, that notwithstanding its northern situation, the harbor of Portsmouth never freezes, an advantage arising from the rapidity of the current. This circumstance, joined to its proximity to the timber for shipbuilding, especially for masts, which can only be balanced by the harbor of Rhode Island, will doubtless determine the choice of Congress. But if a naval establishment be thought necessary at Portsmouth, the quays, the ropewalks, the arsenals, etc. must be placed on the islands, and not on the mainland; for it would be easy for an enemy's army to land there and take possession of the town, the local situation of which would require too considerable a development of fortifications to protect it from insult. I imagine, however, that a good entrenched camp might be formed between the two creeks, but I am only able to judge of that from slight observation, and from maps.

It has happened in New Hampshire, as in the state of Massachusetts, that the losses of commerce have turned to the advantage of agriculture; the capital of the rich and the industry of the people having flowed back from the coasts towards the interior of the country, which has profited rapidly by this reflux. It is certain that this country has a very flourishing appearance, and that new houses are being built and new farms being settled every day.

New Hampshire has no permanent constitution as yet, and its present government is only a simple convention; it much resembles that of Pennsylvania, for it consists of a single legislative body, the Assembly, composed of the representatives of the people, and the Executive Council, which has for its chief a President, instead of a Governor. But during my stay at Portsmouth I learned that there was an assembly at Exeter for the purpose of establishing a constitution, the principal articles of which were already agreed on. This constitution will greatly resemble those of New York and Massachusetts. There will be, as in the former, an executive power vested in the hands of the Governor, the Chancellor, and the Chief Justices, the latter of whom will be perpetual, at least "during good behavior"; but the members of the Senate will be annually changed, and the property qualification necessary to be elected Senator will be very inconsiderable, which I think is a great disadvantage.[34] Mr. Langdon observes, and perhaps with reason, that the country is as yet too young, and the materials wanting to give this Senate all the weight and consistency it ought to have, as in Maryland, where the Senators are elected for three years and must possess at least five hundred pounds.

At Portsmouth I was told of a new sect, which has not failed to make some noise in the country. An individual, I think, of the name of "André" [John Murray] has thought proper to preach a doctrine called that of the Universalists.[35] He pretends that Jesus Christ having redeemed all men, no man can be damned; for were it otherwise, his mission would be useless, at least in a great measure. If this opinion be not novel, it is at least very convenient; but it forms rather a subject of conversation, and even of pleasantry, than a matter of dispute.

When I was at Portsmouth the necessaries of life were very dear, owing to the great drought of the preceding summer. Wheat cost two dollars a bushel (of sixty pounds weight), oats almost as much, and Indian corn was extremely scarce. I shall hardly be believed when I say that I paid eight *livres* ten *sols* [36] a day for food for my horses. Only butcher's meat was cheap, selling at from four to five *sols* a pound.[37] That part of New Hampshire bordering on the coast is not very fertile; there are very good lands at forty or fifty miles from the sea, but the expense of carriage greatly increases the price of provisions when they are sold in the more inhabited parts. As for the value of landed property it is dear enough for such a new country. Mr. "Ruspert" [Brewster?], my landlord, rented the inn where I lodged at seventy pounds a year (the pound being worth eighteen [French] *livres*).[38] Lands are sold at from ten to sixteen dollars an acre. The country produces little fruit, and the cider is very mediocre.

Chapter

2

BOSTON AND VICINITY

November 12, 1782: Portsmouth, N.H.—Newburyport, Mass.

I SET out on the 12th, after taking leave of the Comte de Vaudreuil, whom I met as he was coming to call on me, and it was
certainly in all sincerity that I testified to him my sense of the
polite manner in which I had been received by him and by the
officers under his command.

The road from Portsmouth to Newbury passes through a barren country. Hampton is the only township you meet with, and
there are not such handsome houses here as at Greenland. As I had
only twenty miles to go, I was unwilling to stop, and I merely
requested the Vicomte de Vaudreuil to go on ahead to get dinner
prepared for me. It was two o'clock when I reached the ferry over
the Merrimack, and from the shore I saw the opening of the harbor, the channel of which passes near the northern extremity of
Plum Island, on which is a small fort, with a few cannon and some
mortars. Its situation appears to me well chosen, at least as far as I
was capable of judging from a distance. At the entrance of the
harbor is a bar, on which there is only eighteen feet of water at the
highest tides, so that although there is much trade here, the port
has always been respected by the English. Several frigates have
been built here; among others, the *Charlestown* and the *Alliance*.[1]
The harbor is extensive and well sheltered. After crossing the ferry
in little flat boats which held only five horses each, I went to Mr.
Davenport's inn, where I found a good dinner ready.[2] I had letters
from Mr. Wentworth to Mr. John Tracy, the most considerable
merchant in the place; but, before I had time to send them, he had
heard of my arrival, and, as I was leaving the table, entered my

room and very politely invited me to spend the evening with him.[3] He was accompanied by a colonel, whose name is difficult for me to write, having never been able to catch the manner in which it was pronounced to me; but it was something like "Wigsleps." [4] This colonel remained with me while Mr. Tracy finished his business. The latter came back with two handsome carriages, well equipped, and conducted me and my aides-de-camp to his country house. This house stands a mile from the town in a very beautiful situation; but of this I could myself form no judgment, as it was already night. I went however, by moonlight, to see the garden, which is composed of different terraces. There is likewise a hothouse, and a number of young trees. The house is very handsome and perfectly furnished, and everything breathes that air of magnificence accompanied with simplicity, which is only to be found among merchants. The evening passed rapidly with the help of agreeable conversation and a few glasses of punch. The ladies we found assembled were Mrs. Tracy, her two sisters, and their cousin, Miss Lee. Mrs. Tracy has an agreeable and a sensible countenance, and her manners are in keeping with her appearance. At ten o'clock an excellent supper was served; we drank some very good wine, Miss Lee sang, and prevailed upon Messieurs de Vaudreuil and Talleyrand to sing also: towards midnight the ladies withdrew, but we continued drinking Madeira and sherry. Mr. Tracy, according to the custom of the country, offered us pipes, which were accepted by M. de Talleyrand and M. de Montesquieu, the consequence of which was that they became intoxicated, lost their supper, and were led home, where they were very happy to get into bed. As for myself, I kept a clear head, and continued to converse on trade and politics with Mr. Tracy, who interested me greatly with an account of all the vicissitudes of his fortune since the beginning of the war. At the end of 1777, his brother [Nathaniel Tracy] and he had lost forty-one ships, and as for himself, John Tracy, he had not a ray of hope but in a single "letter of marque" of eight guns, of which he had received no news. As he was walking one day with his brother, and they were reasoning together on the means of supporting their families (for they were both married) they perceived a sail making for the harbor. He immediately interrupted the conversation, saying to his brother, "Perhaps it is a prize for me." The latter laughed at him, but he immediately took a boat, went to meet the ship, and found that it was in fact a prize belonging to him, worth twenty-five thousand pounds sterling.[5] Since that period, he has nearly always been lucky, and he is at present thought to be worth nearly two millions.[6] He has my warmest wishes for his prosperity, for he is a sensible, polite man, and a good patriot. He has always assisted his country in time of need. In 1781 he lent five thousand pounds (nearly one hundred thousand *livres*) to the state of Massachusetts for the clothing of their troops, and this on the mere receipt of the Treasurer. Yet his quota of taxes in that very year amounted to six thousand pounds. It is difficult to imagine that a single individual can be taxed so much; but it must be realized that besides the duty of 5 per cent on importations, required by Congress, the state imposed another tax of the same value on the sale of every article, in the form of an excise on rum, sugar, coffee, etc. These taxes are very strictly levied: a merchant who receives a vessel is obliged to declare the cargo, and nothing can go out of the ship or warehouse without paying the duty. The consequence of this restraint is that the merchants, in order to obtain free use of their property, are obliged themselves to turn retailers, and pay the whole duty, the value of which they must recover from those to whom they sell. Without this, they could neither draw from their stores what is necessary for their own consumption, nor the small articles which they are able to sell at first hand; they are consequently obliged to take out "licenses," like tavernkeepers and retailers, thus supporting the whole weight of the impost both as merchants and as shopkeepers. Patriot that he is, Mr. Tracy cannot help blaming the rigor with which commerce is treated. This rigor arises from the preponderance of the farmers or landholders, and also from the necessity which the government is under of finding money where it can, for the farmers easily evade the taxes—"certificates," "receipts," alleged "grievances," reduce them almost to nothing. Thus has a state, still in its infancy, all the infirmities of old age, and taxation attaches itself to the very source of wealth, at the risk of drying up its channels.[7]

November 13, 1782: Newburyport—Ipswich—Beverly—Salem

I left Newburyport the 13th at ten in the morning, and often stopped before I lost sight of this pretty little town, for I had great pleasure in enjoying the different aspects it presents. It is in general well built, and is daily increasing in new buildings. The warehouses of the merchants, which are near their own houses, serve to ornament them, and in point of architecture resemble not a little our large greenhouses (*orangeries*). You cannot see the ocean from the road which leads to Ipswich, and the country to the eastward is dry and rocky. Towards the west it is more fertile; but in general the land throughout the country, bordering on the sea, is not fruitful. After going twelve miles I came to Ipswich, where we stopped to bait our horses, and I was surprised to find a town between Newburyport and Salem, at least as populous as these two seaports, though indeed much less opulent. But going up on a height of land near the tavern, where I had stopped, I saw that Ipswich was also a seaport; I was told however that the entrance was difficult and that at some times of the year there were not five feet of water upon the bar. From this height you see Cape Anne, and the southern end of Plum Island, as well as a part of the north coast. The bearing of the coast, which trends to the eastward, seemed to me badly figured on the maps; this coast trends more southerly above Ipswich, and forms a sort of bay. Ipswich at present has but little trade, and its fishery is also on the decline; but the land in the neighborhood is pretty good, and abounds in pasturage, so that the seamen having turned farmers, they have been in no want of subsistence,[8] which may account likewise for the very considerable population of this place, where you see upwards of four hundred houses in about two square miles. Before reaching Salem, there is a handsome rising town called Beverly. This is a new establishment produced by commerce, on the left shore of the "creek" which borders the town of Salem on its northern side. One cannot but be astonished to see beautiful houses, large warehouses, etc., springing up in great numbers, at so small a distance from a commercial town, the prosperity of which is not diminished by it.[9] The rain had overtaken us as we were passing near a pond which is three miles from Beverly. We crossed the creek [Beverly Harbor] in two flat-bottomed boats, each of which held six horses. It is nearly a mile wide; and in crossing, we could very plainly distinguish the opening of the harbor and a castle situated on the farthest point of the "neck," [10] which defends the entrance. This "neck" is a tongue of land running to the eastward and connected with Salem only by a very narrow sort of causeway. On the far side of the neck and the causeway is the creek that forms the true port of Salem, which has no other defense than the extreme difficulty of entering without a good practical pilot. The view of these

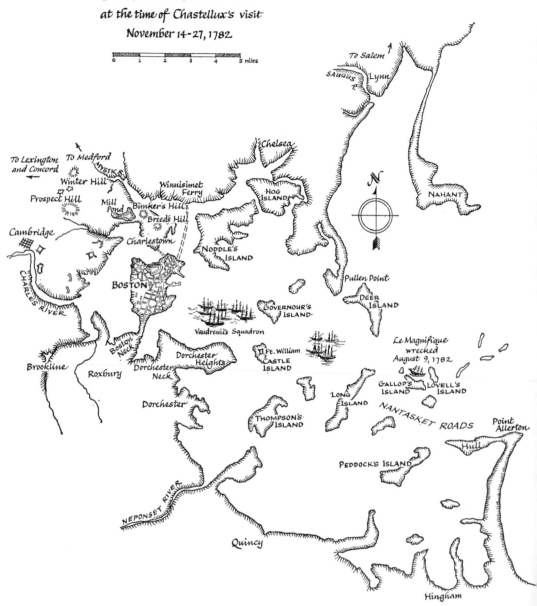

BOSTON & VICINITY

at the time of Chastellux's visit

November 14-27, 1782

0 1 2 3 4 5 miles

To Salem

To Lexington and Concord

To Medford

SAUGUS R.

Lynn

NAHANT

N

Chelsea

MYSTIC R.

Winter Hill

Winnisimet Ferry

Prospect Hill

Hog Island

Mill Pond

Bunker's Hill

Breed's Hill

Cambridge

Charlestown

Noddle's Island

Pullen Point

CHARLES RIVER

BOSTON

Deer Island

Governour's Island

Vaudreuil's Squadron

Le Magnifique wrecked August 9, 1782

Boston Neck

Dorchester Heights

Ft. William Castle Island

Brookline

Roxbury

Dorchester Neck

Gallop's Island

Lovell's Island

Long Island

NANTASKET ROADS

Point Allerton

Dorchester

Thompson's Island

Peddock's Island

Hull

NEPONSET RIVER

Quincy

Hingham

H. C. Rice direx. R. J. Stinely delin. 1963

two ports, which appear as one—that of the town of Salem, which is embraced by two creeks, or rather arms of the sea; the ships and edifices which appear intermingled—all form a very beautiful picture, which I regret not having seen at a better season of the year. As I had no letters for any inhabitant of Salem, I alighted at Goodhue's Tavern, now kept by Mr. Robinson; I found it very good, and was soon served with an excellent supper.[11] In this inn was a sort of club of merchants, two or three of whom came to visit me; and among others, Mr. de la Fille, a merchant of Bordeaux, who had been established five years at Boston; he appeared to me a sensible man, and rather well informed respecting the commerce of this country, the language of which he speaks very well.[12]

November 14, 1782: Salem—Lynn—Boston

The 14th in the morning, Mr. de la Fille called to take me to see the port and some of the warehouses. I found the harbor well suited for trade, as all vessels may unload and take in their lading at the quays; there were about twenty in the port, several of which were ready to sail, and others which had just arrived. In general, this place has a rich and animated appearance. On my return to the inn I found several merchants who came to testify their regret at not having been informed earlier of my arrival, and at not having been able to do me the honors of the town. At eleven, I got on horseback, and taking the road to Boston, was surprised to see that the town, or suburb of Salem, extended nearly a mile in length to the westward. On the whole it is difficult to conceive the growth and the state of prosperity of this country after so long and so disastrous a war. The road from Salem to Boston passes through an arid and rocky country, always within three or four miles of the sea, but without a sight of it. At length however, after passing Lynn,[13] and Lynn Creek, you get a view of it, and find yourself in a bay formed by Nahant Point and Pullen Point. I got upon the rocks to the right of the road, in order to get a wider view and form a better judgment of the country. I could distinguish not only the whole bay but several of the islands in Boston roads, and part of the peninsula of Nantasket, near which I discerned the masts of our warships. From hence to the Winnisimmet ferry, you travel over rather disagreeable roads, sometimes at the foot of the rocks, at others across salt marshes. It is just eighteen miles from Salem to this ferry, where we embarked on a large "scow" which could take twenty horses; the wind, which was rather contrary, becoming more so, we made seven tacks and were nearly an hour in crossing. The landing is to the north of the harbor and to the east of Charlestown ferry. Although I knew that M. [Mathieu] Dumas had prepared me a lodging, I found it more convenient to alight at Mr. [Joshua] Brackett's inn, the Cromwell's Head, where I dined.[14] After dinner I went to the lodgings prepared for me in "Main Street," at Mr. Colson's, a merchant at the sign of the glove.[15] As I was dressing to wait on the Marquis de Vaudreuil,[16] he called upon me, and after permitting me to change my traveling clothes, we went together to Dr. [Samuel] Cooper's,[17] and thence to the association ball, where I was received by my old acquaintance Mr. [Samuel] Breck, who was one of the managers. Here I remained until ten o'clock. The Marquis de Vaudreuil opened the ball with Mrs. Temple.[18] M. de L'Eguille the elder, and M. Truguet each danced a minuet, and did honor to the French nation, by their noble and easy manner; [19] but I am sorry to say that the contrast was considerable between them and the Americans, who are in general very awkward, particularly in the minuet. The prettiest women dancers were Mrs. [Charles?] Jarvis, her sister, Miss Betsy Broome, and Mrs. Whitmore. I found the ladies were all well dressed, but with less elegance and refinement than at Philadelphia.[20] The Assembly room is superb, in a good style of architecture, well decorated, and well lighted; for as far as the general *coup d'oeil*, good order, and refreshments are concerned, this assembly is much superior to that of the City Tavern at Philadelphia.

November 15, 1782: Boston

The 15th, in the morning, M. de Vaudreuil, and M. de Létombe, the French consul,[21] called on me just as I was going out to visit them. After some conversation, we first went to wait on Mr. [John] Hancock,[22] who was ill of the gout and unable to receive us; thence we went to Mr. [James] Bowdoin's, Mr. [Samuel] Breck's, and Mr. [Thomas] Cushing's, the Deputy Governor.[23] I dined with the Marquis de Vaudreuil, and after dinner drank tea at Mr. Bowdoin's, who invited us to supper, only allowing M. de Vaudreuil and myself half an hour to pay a visit to Mrs. Cushing. The evening was spent agreeably, in a company of about twenty persons, among whom were the pretty Mrs. Whitmore and the younger Mrs. Bowdoin, who was a new acquaintance for me, not having seen her at Boston when I was there the preceding year.[24] She has a mild and agreeable countenance, and a character corresponding with her appearance.

November 16, 1782: Boston

The next morning I went to see the Marquis de Vaudreuil and made some more calls: I dined with him at Mr. [Samuel] Breck's,[25] where were upwards of thirty persons, and among others Mrs. [William] Tudor, Mrs. [Perez] Morton, Mrs. [James] Swan, etc. The two former know French; Mrs. Tudor in particular knows it perfectly and speaks it fairly well. I was very intimate with her during my stay at Boston, and found her possessed, not only of understanding, but of grace and delicacy in her mind and manners. After dinner tea was served, and when it was over, Mr. Breck insisted, but very politely, on our staying to supper. This supper was served exactly four hours after we had risen from dinner; it may be easily imagined therefore that we scarcely touched it, but the Americans toyed with it a bit; for, in general, they eat less than we do at their meals, but they eat as often as they are so inclined, which is in my opinion a very bad method. Their food behaves in respect to their stomachs, as we do in France when making calls; it leaves only when newcomers enter. In short, we passed the day very agreeably. Mr. Breck is an amiable man, and does the honors of his house extremely well; and there reigned in this society a *ton* of ease and freedom, which is pretty general at Boston, and cannot fail of being pleasing to the French.

November 17, 1782: Boston

The day following I waited at home for the Marquis de Vaudreuil, who called on me to take me to dinner on board the *Souverain*. This ship, as well as the *Hercule*, was at anchor about a mile from the port. M. de Glandevès who commanded the ship, gave us a large and excellent dinner, the honors of which he did, both to the French and Americans, with that noble and benevolent politeness which characterizes him. Among the Americans was a young man of eighteen, named Barrell, who had been two months on board, so that by living continually with the French, he might accustom himself to speak their language, which cannot fail of being one day useful to him.[26] For such training is far from being common in America, nor can it be conceived to what extent it has hitherto been neglected; its importance is at least beginning to be appreciated, and indeed it cannot be too much encouraged for the benefit of both nations. It is said, and certainly with great truth, that individuals, and even nations, quarrel only because they do not understand each other; it may be affirmed in a more exact and positive sense, that men in general are not disposed to love those to whom they cannot easily communicate their ideas and their impressions. Not only does vivacity suffer, and impatience become exasperated, but self-esteem is offended whenever a person speaks without being understood; instead of which, a man experiences a real satisfaction in enjoying an advantage not possessed by others, and of which he is authorized constantly to avail himself. I have noticed during my residence in America, that those among our officers who spoke English were much more disposed to like the inhabitants of the country than the others who had not been able to familiarize themselves with the language. Such is in fact the procedure of the human mind, always to impute to others the contrarieties it experiences, and such is perhaps the true origin of that disposition we call *humeur*, which must be considered as a discontent of which we cannot complain, an interior dissatisfaction which torments us, without our being able to blame anyone else for it. *Humeur*, or peevishness, seems to bear the same relationship to anger as melancholy does to grief; both are more enduring because they have no fixed object and do not, so to speak, carry their own cure; so that never attaining that excess, that maximum of sensibility, after which nature has willed that there always be a rest or change of situation, they can neither be wholly satisfied nor entirely released. As for the Americans, they showed more surprise than peevishness when meeting with a foreigner who did not understand English. At first they thought that this language was universal in Europe, but if they owed this opinion to a prejudice of education, to a sort of national pride, that pride suffered not a little when they recalled, which frequently occurred, that the language of their country was that of their oppressors. Accordingly they avoided the expressions, "you speak good English" or "you understand English well." I have often heard them say, "you speak good American," or "American is not difficult to learn." They have even gone further, and have seriously proposed introducing a new language; and some people, for the convenience of the public, wanted Hebrew to take the place of English; it would have been taught in the schools, and made use of for all public documents. It may readily be imagined that this proposal had no sequel; but we may conclude from the mere suggestion that the Americans could not express in a more energetic manner their aversion for the English.[27]

This digression has led me far from the *Souverain;* I would return there with pleasure, were it not to take leave of Captain de Glandevès, and to experience the annoyance of a fog so thick that it compelled me to give up the excursion I wanted to take in the harbor, and to return at once to Boston without having seen Castle Island and Fort William. On landing, the Marquis de Vaudreuil and I went to drink tea at Mr. [Thomas] Cushing's, who is Lieutenant Governor of the state; and from there went to Mr. [William] Tudor's where we spent the rest of the evening very agreeably.[28] M. de Parois, nephew of the Marquis de Vaudreuil, had brought his harp; he sang to its accompaniment with great taste and skill. This was the first time in three years that I had heard vocal music, which was also music of my native land. It was the first time that my ear had been struck with those airs, and those words, which reminded me of the many pleasures and agreeable sentiments which had filled the happiest period of my life. I thought myself in Heaven, or, which is the same thing, I thought myself back in my own country, and once more surrounded by all the objects of my affection.

November 18, 1782: Boston–Cambridge

On the 18th I breakfasted at home with several artillery officers, who had arrived with their troops, that corps having greatly preceded the rest of the infantry, in order to have time to embark their cannon and other stores.[29] At eleven I mounted my horse and went to Cambridge to pay a visit to Mr. [Joseph] Willard, who is now the president of [Harvard] University. My route, though short, it being scarce two leagues from Boston to Cambridge, required me to travel both by land and by sea, and to pass through a field of battle and an entrenched camp. It has long been said that the road to Parnassus is difficult, but the obstacles to be encountered there are rarely of the same nature with those which were in my way. A glance at the map of the harbor and town of Boston will explain this better than the most elaborate description. It will be seen that this town, one of the oldest in America, and which contains perhaps from twenty to twenty-five thousand inhabitants, was built upon a peninsula in the bottom of a large bay, the entrance of which is difficult, and in which lie dispersed a number of islands which serve still further for its defense; it is only accessible one way on the land side, by a long "neck" or tongue of land, surrounded by the sea on each side, and forming a sort of causeway.[30] To the northward of the town is another peninsula, which is attached to the opposite shore by a very short "neck," and on this peninsula is a height called Bunker's Hill, at the foot of which are now the remains of the little town of Charlestown. Cambridge is situated to the northwest, a short league from Boston, but to go there in a straight line, you would have to cross a fairly wide arm of the sea, in which there would be dangerous shoals, and, along the shore, marshes difficult to cross, so that the only communications between the whole northern part of the mainland and the town of Boston, are by the ferries of Charlestown and of Winnisimmet. The road to Cambridge lies through the battlefield of Bunker's Hill. After an attentive examination of this position, I could find nothing formidable about it; [31] the Americans had scarcely time to construct what they call a "breastwork," that is, a slight retrenchment without a ditch, which shelters the men from musket shot, only as high as the breast. To their valor alone, therefore, must be attributed the obstinate resistance and the enormous loss sustained by the English on this occasion. The British troops had been repulsed on all sides, and put in such disorder, that General Howe, it is said, found himself for a moment alone on the field of battle, when General Clinton arrived with a reinforcement and turned the left of the American position, which was weaker and more accessible on that side. It was then that their general—Doctor [Joseph] Warren, who had formerly been a physician—was killed and that the Americans quitted the field, less perhaps from the superiority of the enemy, than from knowing that they had another position as good, behind the neck which leads to Cambridge. Indeed, the Bunker's Hill position was useful only because it commanded the Charlestown ferry,[32] and allowed them to raise batteries which could reach the town of Boston. But should they have risked destroying their own houses and killing their fellow citizens merely in order to harass the English in an asylum which the latter must sooner or later abandon? Furthermore, the Americans could occupy only the height of Bunker's Hill, for the sloops and frigates of the enemy would take them in flank the instant they descended from it. Such, however, was the effect of this battle, honorable in every respect to our allies, that it is impossible to calculate the consequences of a complete victory.[33] The English, who had upwards of eleven hundred men killed and wounded, in which number were seventy officers, might possibly have lost as many more in their retreat, for they were under the necessity of embarking to return to Boston; which would have been almost impossible, without the protection of their ships; the little army of Boston would in that case have been almost totally destroyed, and the town must soon have been evacuated. But then what would have happened? Independence was not yet declared, and the road to negotiation was still open; an accommodation might have taken place between the mother country and her colonies; animosities might have subsided; the separation would not have been completed; England would not have expended one hundred millions; she would have preserved Minorca and Florida; the balance of power in Europe and the liberty of the seas would not have been restored. For it must in general be admitted that England alone has reason to complain of the manner in which the fate of arms has decided this long quarrel.

Scarcely have you passed the "neck" which joins the peninsula to the mainland, and which is hemmed in on one side by the mouth of the Mystic and on the other by a bay called the Mill Pond, than you see the ground rising before you, and you distinguish on several eminences the principal forts which defended the entrenched camp of Cambridge. The left [north] of this camp was bounded by the [Mystic] River, and the right extended towards the sea, covering this town which lay in the rear. I examined several of these forts, particularly that of Prospect Hill.[34] All these entrenchments seemed to me to be executed with intelligence; nor was I surprised that the English respected them during the whole winter of 1776. The American troops, who guarded this position, passed the winter more or less at their ease, in good barracks, well roofed and floored; they had at that time an abundance of provisions, while the English, notwithstanding their communication with the sea, were in want of various essential articles, particularly firewood and fresh meat. The English government, not expecting to find the Americans so bold and obstinate, provided too late for the supply of the little army at Boston. This negligence, however, they endeavored to repair, and spared nothing for that purpose, by freight-

ing a great number of vessels, in which they crowded a vast number of sheep, oxen, hogs, and poultry of every kind; but these
ships, sailing at a bad season of the year, met with gales of wind in
going out of port, and were obliged to throw their cargoes into
the sea. It is said that the seas adjoining the coast of Ireland were
for some time covered with herds, which, unlike those of Proteus,
were neither able to live amidst the waves nor gain the shore. The
Americans, on the contrary, who had the whole continent at their
disposal, and had not yet exhausted their resources or their credit,
lived happy and tranquil in their barracks, awaiting the assistance
promised them in the spring. This aid was offered and furnished
with much generosity by the southern provinces; provinces with
which, under the English government, they had no connection
whatever, and which were more foreign to them than the mother
country. It was already, therefore, a proof of great trust on their
part to count upon this aid which had been offered through generosity alone: [35] but who could foresee that a citizen of Virginia who,
for the first time, visited these northern countries, should not only
become their liberator, but would even be able to erect trophies
which would serve as a foundation for the great edifice of Liberty?
Who could foresee that the enterprise—which could not be
achieved at Bunker's Hill, even at the cost of the blood of the
brave Warren and of a thousand English sacrificed to his valor—
would, when attempted from another side and conducted by General Washington, be the work of a single night, the fruit of a simple
maneuver, of a single combination? Who could foresee, in short,
that the English would be compelled to evacuate Boston, and to
abandon their whole artillery and all their ammunition, without its
costing the life of a single soldier?

To attain this important object, it was only necessary to occupy
the heights of Dorchester, which formed still another peninsula,
the extremity of which is within cannon shot of Boston and commands most of the port; but it required the eye of General Washington to appreciate the importance of this post; it required his
activity and resolution to undertake to steal a march upon the English, who surrounded it with their ships, and who could transport
troops thither with the greatest facility. But it required still more:
nothing short of the power, or rather the great credit he had already
acquired in the army, and the discipline he had established, were
requisite to effect a general movement of the troops encamped at

both Cambridge and Roxbury, and carry his plan into execution, in one night, with such rapidity and silence, that the English should only be apprised of it, on seeing, at the break of day, entrenchments already thrown up, and batteries ready to open fire upon them. Indeed he had carried his precautions so far as to take the whips from the wagoners, lest their impatience and the difficulty of the roads might induce them to make use of them, and occasion an alarm. It is not easy to add to the astonishment naturally excited by the principal, and above all, by the early events of this war; but I must still mention, that while General Washington was blockading the English in Boston, his army was in such want of powder as not to have three rounds a man; and that if a bomb-ketch had not chanced to run aground in Boston harbor, containing several tons of powder, which fell into the hands of the Americans, it would have been impossible to attempt the affair of Dorchester, as without it, they would not have had the powder to serve the batteries they proposed erecting there.

I apprehend that nobody will be displeased at this digression; but should it be otherwise, I must plead this excuse, that during a very short excursion I had made to Boston, eighteen months earlier,[36] I had visited all the retrenchments at Roxbury and Dorchester, so that I thought it unnecessary to return there again, and I was the less disposed to repeat this tour as the season was very rigorous and I had very few days to spend in Boston. But how is it possible to enter into a few details concerning this so justly celebrated town, without recalling the principal events which have given it renown? But how, above all, resist the pleasure of retracing here anything which may contribute to the glory of the Americans and to the reputation of their illustrious Chief? Nor is it straying from the temple of the Muses, to consider objects which must long continue to constitute their theme. Cambridge is an asylum truly worthy of them; it is a little town inhabited only by students, professors, and the small number of servants and workmen whom they employ. The building assigned to the university is noble and imposing, although it is not completely finished;[37] it already contains very fine rooms for classes, a cabinet of natural philosophy and instruments of every kind, both for astronomy and for mathematical sciences, a vast gallery in which the library has been placed, and finally, a chapel in keeping with the size and magnificence of the other parts of this edifice. The library, which is already extensive and which contains very handsome editions of the best authors, and very well-bound books, owes its wealth only to the zeal of several citizens, who, shortly before the war, formed a subscription, by means of which they began to send for books from England. But as the funds they had raised were very moderate, they availed themselves of their connections with the mother country, and, above all, of that generosity which the English have invariably displayed whenever the object has been to propagate useful knowledge in any part of the world. These zealous citizens not only wrote to England, but made several voyages thither in search of assistance, which they readily obtained. One individual alone, made them a present which was worth more than 12,000 *livres* in our money.[38] I wish I had remembered his name, but it is easy to find out,[39] for it may be seen inscribed in letters of gold over the bay where the books which he gave are assembled and form a special library; for such is the custom at Cambridge, that each donation of this sort to the university shall remain as it was received, and occupy a place apart; a practice better adapted to encourage the generosity of benefactors and to express the gratitude they inspire than to facilitate the work of the librarians or the students. It is probable, therefore, that, as the collection is augmenting daily, a more convenient and didactic arrangement will eventually be adopted.

The professors of the university live in their own houses, and the students board with different persons in the town for a moderate price. Mr. [Joseph] Willard, who had just been elected president of the university, is also a member of the Academy of Boston, for which he acts as secretary for foreign correspondence.[40] We had already been in touch with each other, but I was delighted to have the opportunity of forming a more particular acquaintance with him; he unites to great understanding and literary merit, a knowledge of the exact sciences, and particularly astronomy. I must here repeat, what I have observed elsewhere, that in comparing our universities and our studies in general, with those of the Americans, it would not be in our interest to call for a decision of the question, which of the two nations should be considered as an infant people.

The short time I remained at Cambridge allowed me to see only two or three of the professors, and as many students, whom I either met with, or who came to visit me at Mr. Willard's. I was expected to dine with our consul, Mr. de Létombe, and I was obliged to set full sail in order to get there in time, for they dine much earlier in Boston than in Philadelphia.

I found upwards of twenty persons assembled, both French officers and Americans; among the latter was Doctor [Samuel] Cooper, a man justly celebrated, and no less distinguished by the graces of his mind and the amenity of his character, than by his uncommon eloquence and patriotic zeal. He has always lived on terms of great intimacy with Mr. Hancock, and has been useful to him on more than one occasion. Among the Americans attached by political interest to France none has displayed a more marked attention to the French, and none has received from Nature a character more analogous to theirs. But it was in the sermon he delivered, at the solemn inauguration of the new constitution of Massachusetts, that he seemed to pour forth his whole soul, and develop at once all the resources of his genius and every sentiment of his heart. The French nation, and the monarch who governs it, are there characterized and celebrated with as much grace as delicacy. Never was there so happy, and so poignant a mixture of religion, politics, philosophy, morality, and even of literature.[41] This discourse should be known in Paris, where I have sent several copies, which I have no doubt will be eagerly translated. I only hope that it will escape the avidity of those hasty writers who have appropriated the present revolution as their special domain; nothing, in fact, is more dangerous than these traders in literary novelty, who pluck the fruit the moment they have any hopes of selling it, thus depriving us of the pleasure of enjoying it in its ripeness. It behooves none but the Sallusts and Tacituses to record in their works the actions and speeches of their contemporaries; nor did *they* write till after a great change in affairs had placed an immense interval between the epoch whose history they transmitted and that in which they composed it; the art of printing too, being then unknown, they were able to measure and to moderate at will the publicity they gave to their writings.

Doctor Cooper, whom I never quitted without regret, proposed that I come and drink tea with him, and had no difficulty in persuading me. He received me in a very small house, furnished in the simplest manner: [42] everything in it bore the appearance of a modesty which proved the feeble foundation of those calumnies so industriously propagated by the English, who lost no occasion of insinuating that his zeal for Congress and for its allies had another motive than patriotism and the love of liberty.[43] A visit to Mrs. Tudor, where M. de Vaudreuil and I again had the pleasure of an agreeable conversation, interrupted from time to time by pleasing music, rapidly brought round the hour for repairing to the club. This assembly is held every Tuesday, in "rotation," at the houses of the different members who compose it; this was the day for Mr. [Thomas] Russell,[44] an honest merchant, who gave us an excellent reception. The laws of the club are not strict; only the number of dishes for supper has been limited, and there must be only two of meat, for supper is not the meal of the Americans. Vegetables, "pies," and especially good wine, are not spared. The hour of assembling is after tea, when the company play cards, converse, and read the public papers, and then sit down to table between nine and ten. The supper was as free as if there had been no strangers, songs were given at table, and a Mr. Stewart sang some rather merry ones, with a tolerable good voice.

November 19, 1782: Boston

The 19th the weather was very bad; I went to breakfast with Mr. Broome, where I remained some time, the conversation being always agreeable and unrestrained.[45] Some officers who called upon me having taken up the rest of the morning, I at length joined the Marquis de Vaudreuil to go and dine with Mr. Cushing.[46] The Lieutenant Governor, on this occasion, perfectly supported the justly acquired reputation of the inhabitants of Boston, of being friends to good wine, good cheer, and hospitality. After dinner he conducted us into the apartment of his son [Thomas Cushing, Jr.] and his daughter-in-law, with whom we were invited to drink tea. For although they inhabited the same house with their father, they had a separate household, according to the custom in America, where it is very rare for young people to live with their parents, when they are once settled in the world. In a nation which is in a perpetual state of growth, everything favors this general tendency; everything divides and multiplies. The sensible and amiable Mrs. Tudor was once more our rallying point during the evening, which ended with an informal and very agreeable supper at young Mrs. Bowdoin's. M. de Parois and M. Dumas sang different airs and duets, and Mrs. Whitmore undertook the pleasure of the eyes, while they supplied the gratification of our ears.

November 20, 1782: Boston

The 20th was wholly devoted to society. Mr. Broome gave me an excellent dinner, the honors of which were performed by Mrs. Jarvis and her sister with as much politeness and attention as if they had been old and ugly. I supped with Mr. Bowdoin, where I again found many pretty women assembled. If I do not include Mrs. Temple, Mr. Bowdoin's daughter, among these, it is not from want of respect, but because her face is so distinguished that it may be said that she is not merely pretty, but truly beautiful. Nor was Mrs. Temple outshone by her daughter, who, though only twelve, was nevertheless made to attract attention.[47] This daughter is neither a handsome child nor a pretty woman, but rather an angel in the guise of a young girl: for I am at a loss how otherwise to express the idea conveyed in England and America by young persons of this age, which, as I have already said, is not, among us, the age of beauty and the graces.

For the first time since my arrival in America I was made to play whist. The cards were English, that is, much handsomer and dearer than ours, and we marked our points with either *louis* or *portugaises* [*Gr.*—six-and-thirties]; when the party was finished, the losses were not difficult to settle, for the company was still faithful to that voluntary law established in society from the beginning of the disturbances, which prohibited playing for money for the duration of the war. This law was not scrupulously observed in the clubs and the games played by the men among themselves. The inhabitants of Boston are fond of high play,[48] and it is fortunate, perhaps, that the war happened when it did, to moderate this passion which began to be attended with dangerous consequences.

November 21, 1782: Boston

On Thursday the 21st so much snow fell that I decided to defer my departure. Mr. Breck, who was giving a big dinner for M. d'Aboville and the French artillery officers,[49] having learned that I had not yet left, invited me to be present at this dinner; I went there in a carriage with M. de Vaudreuil. Mr. Barrell had also come to invite me to tea at his house; we went there immediately after dinner, and as soon as we were free, we hastened to return to Mrs. Tudor's. Her husband,[50] after frequently whispering to her, at length revealed to us the secret of a very pretty piece of pleasantry of her invention; this was a petition to the Queen, written in French, wherein, under the pretext of complaining of the Marquis de Vaudreuil and his squadron, she bestowed on them the most delicate and most charming eulogium.[51] We passed the remainder of the evening with Mr. Breck, who had again invited us to supper, where we enjoyed all the pleasures inseparable from his society. I had a great deal of conversation with Doctor [Charles] Jarvis, a young physician and even a surgeon, but what was better still, a good Whig with excellent views in politics. When M. d'Estaing left Boston, Dr. Jarvis was entrusted with the care of the sick and wounded left behind.[52] He told me that these sick, who were all recovering fast, in general relapsed, when the hospital was removed from the town of Boston, where they enjoyed good air, to Roxbury, which is an unhealthy spot, surrounded with marshes. The physicians in America pay much more attention than ours to the qualities of the atmosphere, and frequently employ change of air as a remedy.

November 22, 1782: Boston—Wrentham

The 22nd I set out at ten o'clock, after taking leave of the Marquis de Vaudreuil, and having had reason to be satisfied both with him and the town of Boston. It is unbelievable how much the stay of the squadron has contributed to bring the two nations together, and to strengthen the ties which unite them.[53] The virtue of the Marquis de Vaudreuil, his splendid example of good morals, as well as the simplicity and kindness of his manners—an example followed, beyond all hope, by the officers of his squadron—have captivated the hearts of a people, who, though the most outspoken enemies of the English, had not hitherto been the greatest friends of the French. I have heard it repeated a hundred times at Boston that even at the time of the closest union with the mother country an English ship of war never anchored in this port without there being some violent quarrels between the people and the sailors; but that the French squadron had been there three months without the slightest dispute arising. The officers of our navy were everywhere received, not only as allies, but as brothers; they were admitted by the ladies of Boston to the greatest familiarity, without a single indiscretion, not even the least pretense or slightest appearance of impertinence ever having troubled the confidence and the innocent harmony of this pleasing intercourse.

The observations I have already made on the commerce of New

England render it unnecessary for me to enter into any particular details concerning the town of Boston. I shall only mention a vexation exercised towards the merchants; a vexation still more odious than that I have spoken of in connection with Mr. Tracy, and which I had not yet suspected until Mr. Breck gave me a particular account of it.[54] Besides the "excise" and "license" duties mentioned above, the merchants are subjected to a sort of tax on wealth (*taxe d'aisés*), which is arbitrarily levied by twelve assessors, named indeed by the inhabitants of the town; but as the most considerable merchant has the same vote as the smallest shopkeeper, it may be imagined to what extent the interests of the rich are respected by this committee. These twelve assessors having full power to tax the people according to their ability to pay, they estimate, at a glance, the business transacted by each merchant and his probable profits. Mr. Breck, for example, being agent for the French navy, and interested besides in several branches of commerce, among others in that of insurance, they calculate how much business he may be supposed to do, of which they judge by the bills of exchange he endorses and by the policies he underwrites, and according to their valuation, in which neither losses nor expenses are reckoned, they suppose him to earn so much a day; and he is consequently subjected to a proportionate daily tax. During the year 1781 Mr. Breck paid a tax of no less than three guineas and a half per day. It is evident that nothing short of patriotism, and above all, the hope of a speedy conclusion to the war, could induce men to submit to so odious and arbitrary a tax; nor can the patience with which the commercial interest in general, and Mr. Breck in particular, bear this burden, be too much commended.

Chapter

─────────── 3 ───────────

PROVIDENCE, ACROSS CONNECTICUT, AND THE FAREWELL TO WASHINGTON AT NEWBURGH

November 22-29, 1782: Boston—Wrentham, Mass.—Providence, R.I.

THE 22nd I went without stopping to Wrentham, where I slept, and reached Providence for dinner on the 23rd. Here I found our infantry assembled, and waiting until the vessels [at Boston] were ready to receive them.[1] I remained at Providence six days, during which time I nevertheless made an excursion of twenty-four hours to visit my old friends at Newport.

November 30, 1782: Providence, R.I.—Voluntown [Sterling Hill], Conn.

The 30th I left Providence with Messrs. Lynch, Montesquieu, and de Vaudreuil, and slept at Voluntown.[2]

December 1, 1782: Voluntown [Sterling Hill]—Windham—Bolton

The next day M. Lynch returned to Providence, and we separated with mutual regret.[3] The same day, the 1st of December, I stopped at Windham to rest my horses, and slept at "Whit's Tavern" near Bolton.[4]

December 2, 1782: Bolton—Hartford—Farmington

The 2nd I reached Hartford for breakfast. I spent two or three hours there, in order to arrange several details relative to the departure of my baggage, as well as to pay a visit to Mrs. [Jeremiah] Wadsworth. M. Frank Dillon, who had come to meet me at Provi-

"Old North
Church"

King's Chapel

"Old South
Church"

Fort Hill

BOSTON, IN THE AUTUMN OF 1778
Chastellux: November 1782 (see p. viii)

Hollis Hall

Harvard Hall

Massachusetts Hall

Christ Church

President Willard's House

CAMBRIDGE, MASSACHUSETTS, *ca.* 1783-1784
Chastellux: November 18, 1782 (see pp. viii-ix)

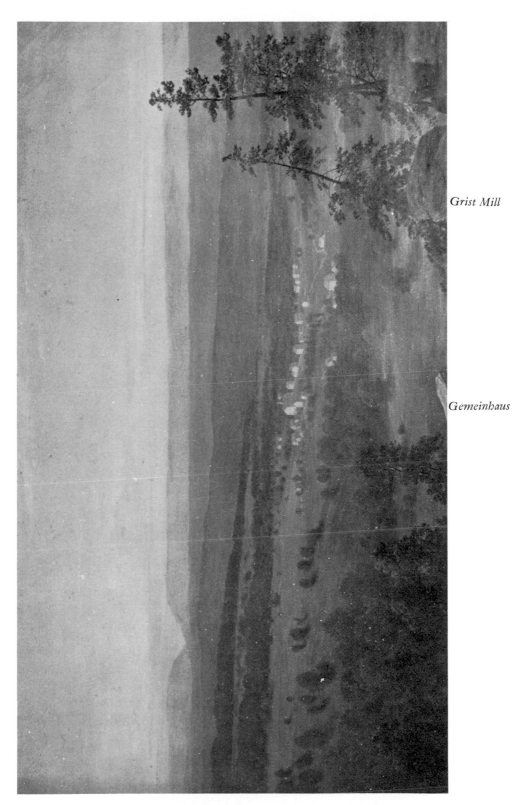

Grist Mill

Gemeinhaus

MORAVIAN SETTLEMENT AT HOPE, NEW JERSEY
by Gustavus Grünewald
Chastellux: December 9, 1782 (see p. ix)

A View of BETHLEHEM in North America.

1784

BETHLEHEM, PENNSYLVANIA, 1784
Chastellux: December 10-11, 1782 (see p. ix)

dence, where he remained a day longer than I did, joined me here at Hartford.[5] From hence we went to Farmington, where we arrived as night was coming on, and alighted at an inn kept by a Mr. [Asahel] Wadsworth, who is no relation of the Colonel's [i.e., Jeremiah W.], but with whom I had lodged a month before, when on the march with my division.[6] Mrs. [Phinehas] Lewis,[7] hearing of my arrival, sent her son to offer me a bed at her home, which I declined with a promise of breakfasting with her before leaving the next morning; but, in a quarter of an hour she called on me herself, accompanied by a militia colonel, whose name I have forgotten, and supped with me.

December 3, 1782: Farmington—Litchfield

The 3rd, in the morning, I visited Mr. [Timothy] Pitkin the minister, with whom I had lodged the preceding year, when the French army was on its march to join General Washington on the North River.[8] He is a man of a merry turn of mind and something of a character, who lacks neither literature nor learning. His father was formerly Governor of Connecticut; he professes a great regard for the French, and charged me, half joking and half in earnest, to present his compliments to the King and tell him that there was one Presbyterian minister in America on whose prayers he might reckon. I went from there to breakfast with Mrs. Lewis. At ten I set out for Litchfield. The roads were very bad, but the country is embellished by new settlements and a considerable number of newly built houses, several of which were taverns. It was four when we arrived at Litchfield and took up our quarters at [Samuel] Sheldon's Tavern,[9] a new inn, large, spacious, and neat, but rather badly supplied. I was struck with melancholy on seeing Mr. Sheldon send a Negro on horseback into the neighborhood to get something for our supper, for which however we did not wait long, and it was rather good.

December 4, 1782: Litchfield—Washington [New Preston Hill]— Bull's Bridge, Conn.—Morehouse's Tavern [Wingdale], N.Y.

The 4th I set out at half past eight. I stopped at Washington [New Preston Hill], after admiring once again the picturesque prospect of the two "falls" and two mills located halfway between Litchfield and Washington.[10] Nor was it without pleasure that I observed the great change two years had produced in a hitherto wild and deserted country. When I passed through it two years before there was only one miserable alehouse; at present we had the choice of four or five inns, all clean and fit to lodge in. Morgan's now passes for the best, but through mistake we alighted at another, which I think is not inferior to it.[11] Thus has the war, by stopping the progress of commerce, proved useful to the interior of the country; for it has not only obliged several merchants to quit the coasts, in search of peaceful habitations in the mountains, but it has compelled commerce to have recourse to land transportation and to use roads which were formerly but little used. It was five in the afternoon when I arrived at Morehouse Tavern; this time I crossed the river [Housatonic] at Bull's Works, and having again stopped to admire the beauty of the landscape, I had an opportunity of convincing myself that I had not too highly praised it in my first journal.[12] The river, which was swollen by the thaw, was even more impressive in its cataract; but a coal shed, which had tumbled down, made the appearance of the furnaces less picturesque. On this occasion I had not much reason to boast of Morehouse's Tavern.[13] The colonel, after whom it was named, no longer kept it, but had sold it to his son, who was absent, so that there were none but women in the house. M. Dillon, who had gone on a little before, had the greatest difficulty in the world to persuade them to kill some chickens; our supper was but indifferent, and as soon as it was over, and we had got near the fire, we saw these women, to the number of four, take our place at table, and eat the remains of our supper with an American dragoon who was stationed there—which gave us some uneasiness for our servants' supper. We learned in fact that they left them but a very trifling portion. On asking one of these women, a girl of sixteen, and rather pretty, some questions the next morning, I learned that she, as well as her sister, who was a bit older, did not belong to the family, but that having been driven by the Indians from the neighborhood of Wyoming [on the east branch of the Susquehanna, Pennsylvania], where they lived, they had taken refuge in this part of the country, where they worked for a livelihood, and that being intimate with Mrs. Morehouse, they took pleasure in helping her when there were many travelers; for this road is at present much frequented. Observing this poor girl's eyes filled with tears in relating her misfortune, I became more interested, and on asking her for more particulars, she told me that her brother had been murdered almost before her eyes, and that she herself had barely had time to escape on foot by running as fast as she could; that she had traveled in this manner fifty miles, before finding a horse, and that by then her feet were raw and bleeding. In other respects she was not in want, nor did she feel the weight of poverty: that is a burden unknown in America. Strangers and fugitives, these two unfortunate sisters had found succor. Lodgings and food are things never wanting in this country; clothing is more difficult to procure, from the dearness of all sorts of stuffs; but for this they were striving to provide by their own labor. I gave them a *louis* to buy some little article of dress; my aides-de-camp, to whom I immediately related the story, made them a present likewise, and this little act of munificence being soon made known to the mistress of the house, obtained us her esteem, and she appeared very penitent for having shown so much repugnance to kill her chickens.

December 5, 1782: Morehouse's Tavern [Wingdale]—Fishkill—Newburgh

The 5th I set out at nine, and rode without stopping to Fishkill, where I arrived at half past two, after a twenty-four mile journey over very bad roads. I alighted at Mr. "Boerom's" Tavern, which I recognized as being the same where I had lodged two years before, when it was kept by Mrs. Egremont.[14] The house was changed for the better, and we had a very good dinner. We crossed the North River as night came on, and arrived at six o'clock at Newburgh, where I found Mr. and Mrs. Washington, Colonel [Tench] Tilghman, Colonel [David] Humphreys, and Major [Benjamin] Walker. The headquarters at Newburgh consists of a single house, neither spacious nor convenient, which is built in the Dutch fashion.[15] The largest room in it, which had served as the owner's family parlor and which General Washington has converted into his dining room, is in truth fairly spacious, but it has seven doors and only one window. The fireplace, or rather the fireback, is against the walls, so that there is in fact but one vent for the smoke, and the fire is in the room itself. I found the company assembled in a rather small room which served as the "parlour." At nine o'clock supper was served, and when the hour of bedtime came, I found that the chamber to which the General conducted me, was this very parlor, in which he had just had a campbed set up.

December 6, 1782: Newburgh

We assembled at breakfast the next morning at ten, during which interval my bed was folded up and my chamber became the sitting room for the whole afternoon; for American manners do not admit of a bed in the room in which company is received, especially when there are women. The smallness of the house and the difficulty to which I saw that Mr. and Mrs. Washington had put themselves to receive me, made me apprehensive lest M. de Rochambeau, who was to have set out [from Providence] the day after me, by traveling as fast, might arrive on the same day that I was remaining here.[16] I therefore took it upon myself to send someone to Fishkill to meet him and request him to stay there that night. Nor was my precaution superfluous, for my express found him already at the "landing." [17] He spent the night there and did not join us until the next morning just as I was setting out. The day I remained at headquarters was passed either at table or in conversation. General [Edward] Hand, Colonel Reed [Lt. Col. George Reid] of New Hampshire, and Major [John] Graham dined with us.

December 7, 1782: Newburgh—Chester—Warwick

On the 7th I took leave of General Washington; it will not be difficult to believe that this parting was painful for me; but I have too much pleasure in recollecting the real tenderness with which it affected him, not to make mention of it.[18] Colonel Tilghman got on horseback to show me, along the way, the barracks that serve as winter quarters for the American army; they were not yet quite finished, although the season was already far advanced and the cold very severe.[19] They are spacious, healthy, and well built, and consist in a row of "log-houses" containing two rooms, each inhabited by eight soldiers when full, which commonly means five or six men in actual fact; a second range of similar barracks is destined only for the noncommissioned officers. These barracks are placed in the middle of the woods, on the slope of the hills and within reach of water; as the great object is a healthy and decent situation, the army is on several lines, not exactly parallel with each other. But it will appear surprising in Europe, that these barracks should be built without a bit of iron, not even nails, which would render the work tedious and difficult were not the Americans very expert in working with wood. After viewing the barracks, I regained the high road; but passing before General Gates's house, the same in which General Knox lived in 1780,[20] I stopped long enough to make a courtesy call. The remainder of the day I had very fine weather. I had to stop to rest and feed my horses at an inn in the township called Chester. In this inn I found only a woman, who appeared kind and honest, and who had some charming children. This route is sparsely populated, but new settlements are being made there every day. Before reaching Chester I had crossed on a wooden bridge a creek called Murderer's River,[21] which flows into the North River above [below] New Windsor and beyond Chester; I still kept skirting the ridge of mountains which separates this country from "the Clove." Warwick, where I slept, a pretty large place for so wild a country, is twelve miles from Chester, and twenty-eight from Newburgh; I lodged there in a very good inn kept by Mr. Smith, the same at whose house I had slept two years before at "Cockeat" [Kakiat], where he kept an inn much inferior to this one.[22] The American army having, for the past two years, had their winter quarters near West Point, Mr. Smith imagined, with reason, that this road would be more frequented than the Paramus road, and he had rented this inn from a Mr. "Beard" [Francis Baird], at whose house we stopped next day to breakfast. The house had been rented to him with some furniture, and he had upwards of one hundred and fifty acres of land belonging to it, for the whole of which he paid seventy pounds a year, or about one hundred *pistoles*. I had every reason to be content both with my old acquaintance and the new establishment.

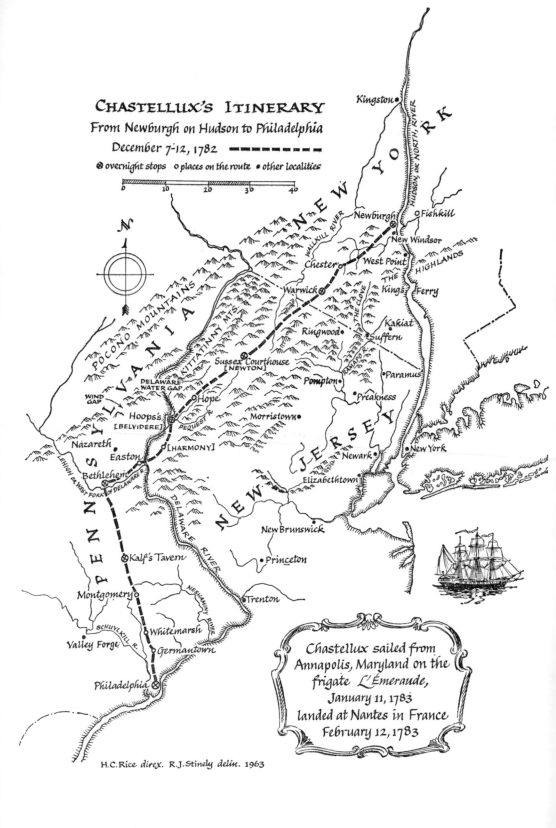

CHASTELLUX'S ITINERARY

From Newburgh on Hudson to Philadelphia

December 7-12, 1782 ▬ ▬ ▬ ▬ ▬

⊗ overnight stops ○ places on the route • other localities

0 10 20 30 40

Kingston •

NEW YORK

HUDSON OR NORTH RIVER

Newburgh ⊗ ○ Fishkill

New Windsor •

WALLKILL RIVER

Chester ○ West Point ○

THE HIGHLANDS

Warwick ⊗ King's Ferry

POCONO MOUNTAINS

KITTATINNY MTS.

Ringwood • Kakiat

THE CLOVE

Suffern ○

RAMAPO R.

PENNSYLVANIA

Sussex Courthouse [NEWTON] ○

Pompton •

Paramus •

DELAWARE WATER GAP

WIND GAP

○ Hope

Preakness •

Hoops's [BELVIDERE] ⊗

PEQUEST

Morristown •

Nazareth •

[HARMONY] ○

NEW JERSEY

Easton ○

Newark •

New York •

Bethlehem ⊗

LEHIGH OR WEST FORK OF DELAWARE R.

DELAWARE RIVER

Elizabethtown •

New Brunswick •

Kalf's Tavern ⊗

NESHAMINY RIVER

• Princeton

Montgomery ○

○ Trenton

SCHUYLKILL R.

Valley Forge •

○ Whitemarsh

○ Germantown

Philadelphia ⊗

Chastellux sailed from
Annapolis, Maryland on the
frigate L'Émeraude,
January 11, 1783
landed at Nantes in France
February 12, 1783

H.C. Rice direx. R.J. Stinely delin. 1963

4

THE MORAVIAN SETTLEMENTS
AT HOPE AND BETHLEHEM;
RETURN TO PHILADELPHIA

December 8, 1782: Warwick, N.Y.–Sussex [Newton], N.J.

THE next morning, the 8th, I set out before breakfast; the snow began to fall as soon as I got on horseback and did not cease until we got to Baird's Tavern.[1] This house was not nearly as good as the one I had left, but they were busy enlarging it. On inquiring of Mr. Baird, who is of Irish origin, why he had left his good house at Warwick to keep this inn, he answered me that it was a settlement he was forming for his son-in-law, and that as soon as he had put it in good shape, he would return to his house at Warwick. This Mr. [Francis] Baird had lived for a long time in New York, where he had been a merchant and had even sold books, which I learned from observing some good ones at his house, among others, *Human Prudence*, which I bought from him.[2] It ceased snowing at noon, and the weather became milder; but in the afternoon the snow returned in blasts, for which I had some compensation in the beautiful effect produced by the setting sun amidst the clouds, its rays being reflected in the east, and forming a sort of parhelion. Towards evening the weather became very cold. I reached Sussex an hour before dark, and lodged at Mr. [Jonathan] Willis's.[3] The fire being not well lighted in the room intended for me, I stepped into the parlor, where I found several people who appeared to be collected together upon business; they had, according to custom, drunk a good quantity of grog, and one of them, called Mr. Archibald Stewart, showed the effects of it a bit. We struck up a conversation, and Mr. [Robert] Hoops,[4] formerly aide-de-camp to General [Philemon] Dickinson, and at present a rich landholder in the Jerseys, having learned that I was going to Bethlehem,[5] or surmising so from the questions I asked about the roads, very obligingly invited me to come the next day and spend the night at his house. His house is on the banks of the Delaware, twenty-six miles from Sussex [Newton], thirteen from Easton, and twenty-four from Bethlehem. At first I had some hesitation about accepting his offer, due to the apprehension one always has in such cases, of inconveniencing others, or of being inconvenienced oneself. He insisted so strongly however, and assured me so often that I should find no inn, that I more or less promised to spend the following night at his house. These gentlemen, and he in particular, gave me all the information I needed; and, as I wanted to see the Moravian Mill,[6] a village situated on the way to Easton, fourteen miles beyond Sussex, he directed me to Mr. Culver, who keeps a sort of an inn there. The company set out, and I passed a very agreeable evening by a good fire, congratulating myself at not being exposed to the severe cold which one felt as soon as one stepped out of the house. I was also very well pleased with the supper and with my landlord, Mr. Willis, who seemed to me a gentleman, and a good conversationalist. He was born at Elizabethtown, but has been sixteen years settled at Sussex. Thus does population advance inland, ever seeking new lands.

December 9, 1782: Sussex [Newton], N.J.—Moravian Mill [Hope] —Hoops's House [Belvidere]

I set out the 9th a little before nine, the weather being extremely cold, and the roads covered with snow and ice; but on leaving the ridge to turn westward, and descending from the high mountains to lower hills, we found the temperature warmer and then the ground entirely free. I arrived at half past eleven at the Moravian Mill, and, on stopping at Mr. Culver's, found that Mr. Hoops had announced our coming and that breakfast was prepared for us.[7] This fresh attention on his part further encouraged me to accept his offer for the evening. As soon as we had breakfasted, Mr. Culver, who had treated us with demonstrative warmth and respect, which was more German than American, served as our guide and first took us to see the sawmill, which is the most beautiful and the best contrived I ever saw. One man only is all that is needed to direct the

work; the same wheels which keep the saws in motion, also serve
to convey the logs from the spot where they are deposited to the
mill, a distance of twenty-five or thirty *toises* [50 or 60 yards]; they
are placed on a sled, which sliding on a groove, is drawn by a rope
which rolls and unrolls on the axle of the mill wheel itself. Planks
are sold at six shillings (about four *livres* and ten *sols*) the hundred;[8] if you supply your own wood, it is only half the price, and
the plank in that case comes to a bit less than two *liards* per foot.[9]
This sawmill is near the fall of a pond which supplies it with water.[10]
A rather deep cut has been made through schist to form the race
for bringing the water to the gristmill, which has been built within
gunshot of the other;[11] this gristmill is very handsome and constructed on the same plan as Mrs. Bolling's mill at Petersburg,[12] but
not so large. From the mill I went to the church: it is a square
building, which also includes the minister's lodgings.[13] The unusual
thing about it is that the place where the services are held, and
which may properly be called the church, is on the first [i.e., sec-
ond] floor, and resembles the Presbyterian meetinghouses, except
that there are an organ and some religious paintings.[14] This house of
prayer, so singularly placed, reminds me of a rather good story I
heard told in Boston. Divine services used to be held there in a
church, where the faithful did not gather, to be sure, on the second
floor, but which, like this one, also contained the minister's house,
below which were cellars. The pastor, a very learned man furthermore, in addition to his spiritual functions, carried on trade; he sold
wine, that is to say, a great deal of it went out of his cellar, but not
a drop ever entered it. A simple Negro who worked for him used
to say that his master was a great saint, for he employed him every
year to roll into the cellar a number of casks of cider; and that after
the minister had preached and prayed *over* this cider for several
Sundays in a stretch, it was all changed into wine.

On coming out of the church I perceived Mr. Hoops, who had
taken the trouble to come and meet me; there was no turning back
now, but I had already made up my mind to accept his invitation.
We mounted on horseback together, and after passing through a
rather fertile valley, in which are to be seen beautiful farms, chiefly
Dutch, and very well-cultivated fields, we arrived about dusk at
his house.[15] It is a charming settlement, consisting of a thousand
acres of land, the greatest part of which is in tillage, with a fine
gristmill,[16] a sawmill, and a distillery. Obviously, the man who lives

here can have no time for idleness. The manor house is small, but neat and handsome. He led us into the parlor, where I found Mrs. Hoops, his wife; Mrs. Scotland, his mother-in-law; and Mr. Scotland, his brother-in-law. Mrs. Hoops has a pleasing countenance, although she is a bit faded from habitual bad health; her bearing is perfect and her conversation gracious. The evening was spent very agreeably, partly in conversation, and partly in games; for Mrs. Hoops gave me a lesson in "bagamon," and I gave her one in *trictrac*. I had some conversation also with Mr. Scotland, a young man, who though but twenty-six, has served in three campaigns, as an artillery captain, and who is now a lawyer with a considerable practice. I have already observed that this is the most respectable and most lucrative profession in America. He told me that he usually received, for a single consultation, four dollars, or even a "half joe" (42 *livres* in our money); [17] and furthermore, when the lawsuit is begun, as much again is paid for every "writ," or every "deed," for in America lawyers are also attorneys and notaries.[18] I also had much pleasure in conversing with Mr. Hoops, who is a man of good breeding, well informed, active, and who conducts with great intelligence a variety of business. He had been employed in the commissary's department when General [Nathanael] Greene [19] was Quartermaster General, and made extraordinary "exertions" [20] to supply the army, which rendered him so obnoxious to the Tories that he was for a long time obliged to remain armed in his house, which he barricaded every night. The supper was as agreeable as the preceding part of the evening; the ladies retired at eleven, and we remained at table until midnight. Mr. Hoops's brother arrived as we were at dessert; he also appeared to me a sensible man. He had married in Virginia a daughter of Colonel Syme who had married one of his sisters.[21] He is now a widower.

December 10, 1782: Hoops's House [Belvidere], N.J.–Easton, Pa.
* –Bethlehem*

The next day, the 10th of December, I breakfasted with the ladies, and set out at half past ten, Mr. Hoops accompanying me to Easton, where he had sent ahead to have dinner prepared for me. I should have preferred my usual custom of making my repast only at the end of my day's journey, but this little accommodation was the price I had to pay for all the civilities I had received. Two miles from the house of Mr. Hoops we forded a small river [Pequest], and then traveled through agreeable and well-cultivated country. Some miles before reaching Easton, we came on to a height [22] from which one can see a great expanse of country, including a range of mountains which Mr. Hoops pointed out to us: this forms a part of that great chain which traverses all America from south to north.[23] He pointed out to us two hiatuses,[24] resembling two large gateways or windows; one of these is an opening through which the Delaware flows as it breaks its way through the mountains; the other is a "gap" or pass leading to the other side of the mountains, and through which runs the road leading to Wyoming, made famous by General [John] Sullivan's march in 1779.[25] Before we got to Easton, we were ferried over the eastern branch of the Delaware, for this town is situated in the fork formed by two branches of the river.[26] It is a rather pretty, although not very sizable town; which will in all probability increase with the coming of peace, when the Americans can again, without fear of the Indians, cultivate the fertile lands between the Susquehanna, and the Delaware. Mr. Hoops took us to Mr. Smith's tavern: this Mr. Smith is both an innkeeper and a lawyer.[27] He has a handsome library, and his son, whom Mr. Hoops presented to me on my arrival, appeared to be a well-brought up and well-informed young man. I asked him to dine with us, as well as another youth who boarded with him, a native of Dominica, who had come to complete his studies among the Americans, to whom he seemed much more attached than to the English. He had chosen Easton as more healthy, and more tranquil than the other towns of America, and found all the necessary instruction in the lessons and the books of Mr. Smith. As I was expected, I did not have to wait long for dinner. At half past three I got back on my horse; Mr. Hoops again wanted to accompany me for another mile or two; and to gain my consent, he pretended that there was a crossroad where I might lose my way. At long last we parted, and he left me filled with gratitude for his numerous civilities. Before I wholly lost sight of Easton I stopped upon a hill, where I could admire, for some time, the picturesque *coup d'oeil* presented by the two branches of the Delaware,[28] and the confused and whimsical form of the mountains, through which they pursue their course. By the time I had had my fill of this spectacle, it was necessary to hurry on to reach Bethlehem before night; I traveled the eleven miles in two hours, but could not arrive by daylight.[29] I had no difficulty in finding the tavern, for it is right at the entrance of the town.

This tavern was built at the expense of the Society of Moravian Brethren, who formerly used it as their store, and is very handsome and spacious.[30] The person who keeps it is only the manager, and is responsible to the administrators. As I had already dined, I only asked for tea, but ordered a breakfast for the next morning at ten o'clock. The landlord telling me that he had a "growse," or "heath hen," I straightway had it brought to me, for I had long been very curious to see this bird. I found that it was neither the *poule de Pharaon,* nor the *coq de bruyère;* it is about the size of a pheasant, but has a short tail, and the head of a capon, which it also resembles in the form of its body; its feet are covered with down. This bird is remarkable for two large transversal feathers below its head; the plumage of its belly is a mixture of black and white, that of its wings a reddish gray, like our gray partridges. When this "growse" is roasted, its flesh is black like that of a *coq de bruyère,* but it is more delicate and has a higher flavor.[31]

I could not derive much enlightenment from my landlord on the origin, the opinions, and manners of the Society, but he informed me that I should next day see the minister and the administrators, who could satisfy my curiosity.

December 11, 1782: Bethlehem—Kalf's Tavern

The 11th, at half past eight, I went out with a Moravian, given me by the landlord. He was not much better informed and only served me as a guide.[32] This man is a seaman, who happens to have some talent for drawing; for, since the war, he has quitted the sea, although he has sent his son there. He subsists on a small estate he has at Reading, but lives at Bethlehem, where he and his wife board in a private family.[33] We went first to visit the house for "single women." [34] This edifice is spacious, and built of stone. It is divided into several large chambers, all heated with stoves; here the girls work, some at coarse tasks, such as spinning cotton, hemp, and wool, while others do more tasteful, and even very fine, fancywork, such as embroidery, either in silk or linen; they excel particularly in working ruffles, little pocketbooks, pincushions, etc., very much as our French nuns do. The superintendent of this house came to receive me. She is a woman of rank, born in Saxony, whose name is Madame von Gersdorf; but she does not presume upon her birth, and she even appeared surprised to see that I offered her my hand, whenever we went up and down stairs.[35] She took me to the first [second] floor, where she had me enter a large vaulted room, spotlessly clean, in which all the residents of the house sleep; each one has a separate bed, in which there is no lack of feathers.[36] There is never any fire in this room, and although it is high and very airy, they have built into the ceiling a ventilator like those in our playhouses. The kitchen is not large, but it is clean and well arranged; you see there immense kettles placed on stoves, as in our hospitals. The residents of the house dine in the refectory, and have meat and vegetables every day; the price they pay is three shillings and sixpence per week, about eight *sols* per day; they are not given supper, and I believe the house furnishes only bread for breakfast. After this expense and what they pay for heat and light are deducted, they enjoy the fruit of their labor, which is more than sufficient to maintain them. This house also has a place of worship [the Sisters' Chapel], which serves only for evening prayers, for they go to the church on Sundays. There is an organ in this chapel, and I saw several musical instruments hanging from hooks. I took leave of Madame von Gersdorf very well pleased with her reception, and then went to the church, which is simple and differs little from the one I had seen at Moravian Mill.[37] Here also several religious pictures can be seen.[38]

From the church I went to the house of the "Single men." [39] I entered the intendant's apartment, and found him busy copying music. He had in his room a rather indifferent *forte piano*, made in Germany. I talked music with him, and discovered that he was not only a performer, but a composer as well; so when we went into the chapel together, I asked him to play the organ. He played some improvisations, into which he introduced a great deal of harmony and chords in the base. This man, whose name I have forgotten, was born in New York, but resided seven years in Germany, whence he had recently arrived.[40] I found him better informed than the others, yet it was with some difficulty that I got from him the following details: The Moravian brethren, in whatever quarter of the world they live, are under the rule of their Metropolitans, who reside in Germany.[41] It is from there that the directors of the Society send out commissioners to manage their different settlements. These same Metropolitans advance the necessary funds, which are

repaid as the colonies prosper; thus the income from the mills I
have spoken of, as well as from the farms and manufactures of Bethlehem, are employed in the first instance to pay the expenses of the
community, and afterwards to reimburse the interest and principal
of the funds advanced from Europe. Bethlehem, for example, possesses lands purchased by the Moravians in Europe; this property
consists of fifteen hundred acres of land, forming a vast farm, which
is managed by a steward, who is responsible to the community. If
an individual wants a lot of land, he must purchase it from the
public, but under this restriction, that in case of defection from
the sect, or emigration from the place, he shall restore it to the
community, which will then reimburse him the original payment.
As to their opinions, this sect is closer to the Lutherans than to the
Calvinists; differing, however, from the latter, by admitting music,
pictures, etc. into their churches, and from the former, by having
no bishops, and being governed by a synod.[42] Their regulations
and discipline have something monastic about them, since they
recommend celibacy, although not requiring it, and keep the women
very much separated from the men. There is a special house, also,
for the widows, which I did not visit. The two sexes being thus
habitually separated, none of those familiar connections exist between them, which lead to marriage; it is even contrary to the
spirit of this sect to marry from inclination. If a young man finds
himself sufficiently at his ease to have a house of his own and to
maintain a wife and children, he presents himself to the commissioner and asks him for a girl; this official [43] proposes one to him,
whom he may, in fact, refuse to accept; but it is contrary to custom
to select or choose a wife for himself. Consequently the Moravian
colony has been far from multiplying in the same proportion as the
other American colonies. At Bethlehem there is a colony of about
six hundred persons, more than half of whom live in a state of
celibacy; nor does it appear to have increased for several years
past. Furthermore every precaution is taken to provide for the
livelihood of the brethren, and in the houses destined for the unmarried of both sexes, there are masters who teach them different
trades.[44]

The house of the single men which I saw in detail, does not
differ from that of the single women; I shall mention but one thing
which seems to me worthy of notice, that is a very convenient
method they have devised of being waked up at the hour they

want to arise: all the beds are numbered, and near the door is a slate, on which all the numbers are written. A man who wishes to be awakened early, at five o'clock in the morning for example, has only to write a figure 5 under his number; the servants who take care of the room are thus informed, and the next morning, at the time indicated, they go straight to the number of the bed without needing to know the sleeper's name.

Before I left this house, I went up on to the roof of the building, where they have built a belvedere. From there I could see the little town of Bethlehem and its surroundings: it is composed of seventy or eighty houses, and there are still a few others belonging to the colony a mile or two distant from the main town; most of them are quite handsome and built of stone.[45] Every house has a little garden cultivated with care. In returning home I was curious to see the farm, which I found rather well laid out, but the farmhouse was neither as clean nor as well kept as on the English farms, for the manners of the Moravians are still Teutonic like their language.[46] At length, at half past ten, I returned to the inn, where I was expected by my wood cock, two wood hens, and many other good things, so that I was even more pleased with my breakfast than with my walk.

At noon I set out to travel twenty miles farther on, to an inn called Kalf's Tavern; this is a rather poor and not very clean German house. We had crossed over the western branch of the Delaware [i.e., the Lehigh] a mile from Bethlehem; [47] there is neither town nor village along the road, but the townships to which the scattered houses we saw belong, are Socconock and Springfield.

December 12, 1782: Kalf's Tavern—Montgomery—Philadelphia

The 12th I breakfasted at Montgomery, twelve miles from Kalf's Tavern, and after passing through Whitemarsh and Germantown, I arrived at about five o'clock in Philadelphia.

Philadelphia, December 24, 1782

PART IV

EPILOGUE

Letter to Mr. Madison on the Progress
of the Arts and Sciences in America

EDITOR'S INTRODUCTION

C HASTELLUX's essay on "The Progress of the Arts and Sciences in America," in the form of a letter to the Reverend James Madison,[1] president of the College of William and Mary at Williamsburg, was completed in January 1783, on the eve of his homeward voyage to France, and was first printed as an appendix to the 1786 Paris edition of his *Voyages dans l'Amérique Septentrionale*. It forms an appropriate epilogue to the travel journals, for whereas these are chiefly concerned with day-to-day observations, the letter to Madison presents and sums up the author's general conclusions as an observer of the American scene. The essay might also be called a postscript or footnote to the author's treatise *De la Félicité Publique*, as he himself suggests here in a passing allusion to his earlier work. As the author of this investigation of "the State of Human Nature, under each of its Particular Appearances, through the Several Periods of History," Chastellux owed himself and owed his readers some further considerations on the progress of enlightenment in America.

Several of the American "literati" who made Chastellux's acquaintance during his sojourn in their country were familiar with his book *On Public Happiness*, and his reputation as a philosopher (a "Lover of Literature as well as everything tending to the Happiness of Society and the Aggrandizement of Republics," as Ezra Stiles described him) was such that they were prepared to treat with respect, and even to solicit, his expert opinion on the present state and future prospects of the United States.

During the winter and spring following the victorious conclusion of the Yorktown campaign, when the French army was established in winter quarters in Virginia, Chastellux again had time to cultivate "philosophy." His essay-letter to Madison reflects the many agreeable hours he must have spent in the company of the professors at the College of William and Mary discussing the state of America and of mankind. Other letters of the same period re-

veal similar preoccupations. In one of these, written from Williamsburg, February 18, 1782, to General Philip Schuyler,[2] he touched
more informally upon several of the topics of concern to him. To
Schuyler's praise of *De la Félicité Publique*, for example, Chastellux replied that he had merely pleaded the cause of humanity, which
Schuyler had actually served, and urged the American to look to
his own experience and judgment for guidance rather than to theoretical books on the subject. "It has seemed to me," he continued,
"that America abounds in *demi-philosophes* of two different sorts:
the older men, in matters political, look only to the Greeks and the
Romans, and the young men are satisfied with ready-made opinions
they have found in Locke and Montesquieu. Now I believe that
reading of the ancients and the moderns is no more capable of
suggesting the plan of a good government than Horace's Art of
Poetry is of bringing forth a good poem. I have said, and have
repeated, in my book that abstract ideas will never form the basis of
a reasonable constitution. Even experience is too brief and too
faulty. The times and the place must be consulted, as well as customs and even habits, for a people has always been something
before having any form of government established."

In the same vein Chastellux wrote from Williamsburg, June 5,
1782, to his compatriot De Létombe, French consul in Boston:[3]

The object of my treatise *De la Félicité Publique* can never be anything but a problem of approximation. If I had ever thought otherwise this country would supply me with the proof. America has all
the necessary conditions for being happy, and yet the idea of happiness that we ought to entertain would be incomplete were this
country to serve as its model or its measure. It will always be a
great deal that principles of tolerance, liberty, and equality of
rights remove the perceptible obstacles which work among us
against the happiness of Peoples. Hidden causes in the moral as in
the physical domain elude the régime and the remedies; but the
observer can always discover some of them. You, Sir, are in a position to find them out and if you care to share with me your reflections on these subjects, I shall be the gainer.

It was with this same desire to provoke reflection and exchange
ideas, rather than to offer abstract advice, that Chastellux composed
his letter for Madison. He hoped, too, that his correspondent would
share the little essay with others, and this indeed proved to be the

case. Thomas Jefferson, for example, was familiar with it even before its publication as an appendix to the *Voyages*. "Perhaps you would permit to be added [to the *Voyages*]," he wrote to Chastellux, "a translation of your letter to Mr. Madison on the probable influence of the revolution on our manners and laws, a work which I have read with great pleasure and wish it could be given to my countrymen." [4] Chastellux readily accepted Jefferson's suggestion: "As for the letter to Doctor Madison," he replied, ". . . I have no objection whatsoever to its being published in America." [5]

As a good Academician practiced in the ways of polite society, who had been honored with membership in the American Philosophical Society of Philadelphia and the American Academy of Arts and Sciences in Boston and received honorary degrees from both the College of William and Mary and the University of Pennsylvania, Chastellux no doubt conceived of his essay as a return courtesy for these honors, and as a sort of *discours de réception* to the infant academies of America. The essay is part of the author's continuing investigation of "Public Happiness" and has its place in the larger debate, then agitating the intellectuals of Europe, concerning the significance of the New World. Long after Chastellux's time the import of the American experiment was still being debated—and the end is not yet in sight. Many of the questions raised by Chastellux in his unpretentious letter to Madison were to be discussed again, in masterly fashion, a half-century later, by his compatriot Alexis de Tocqueville in the famous investigation of *Democracy in America*.

Letter from the Marquis de Chastellux to Mr. Madison, Professor of Philosophy at the University of Williamsburg, on the Progress of the Arts and Sciences in America.

I have not forgotten, Sir, the promises I made you on leaving Williamsburg; they remind me of the friendship with which you were pleased to honor me, and the flattering prejudices in my favor which were the consequences of it. But I fear that I promised more than I can now perform; I shall at least be acting in good faith, although I am like a bankrupt unable to honor his promises. By putting you in full possession of my feeble resources I may perhaps obtain a still further portion of that indulgence, to which you have so frequently accustomed me. The subjects on which I thought of asking information from you, rather than of offering you my ideas, would require long and tranquil meditation, and since I left Virginia, I have been continually traveling, sometimes on duty with the troops, and at others merely to gratify my curiosity, which has led me into the eastern parts of America, and as far as New Hampshire. But even had my time been subject to less interruption, I am not sure that I should have been more capable of accomplishing your wishes. My mind, aided and stimulated by yours, experienced an energy it has since lost; and if in our conversations, I chanced to express sentiments which merited your approbation, these belonged not so much to myself as to Mr. Madison's interlocutor. At present I must appear in all my weakness, and with this further disadvantage, that I lack both time and leisure not only to correct my thoughts, but even to record them on paper. Nevertheless, I shall launch forth, persuaded that you will easily supply my unavoidable omissions, and that the merit of this essay, if there be any, will be in your completion of it.

The most frequent subject of our conversations was the progress that the arts and sciences would make in America, and the influence that this progress would necessarily have on manners and opinions. It seems as if everything relative to government and legislation ought to be excluded from such discussions, and no doubt a foreigner should avoid as much as possible treating matters of which he cannot be a competent judge. But, in the moral as in the physical world, nothing stands isolated, no cause acts alone and independently. Whether we consider the fine arts and the enjoyments they produce as a delicious ambrosia that the Gods have thought proper to share with us, or whether we regard them as a dangerous poison, this liquor, whether beneficial or harmful, will always be modified by the vessel which receives it. It is necessary therefore to fix our attention for a moment on the political constitution of the American people, but in doing this, may I be permitted to recall a principle that I have established and developed elsewhere,[6] which is that the character, the genius of a people, is not solely the product of the government it has adopted, but of the circumstances in which it was formed. Locke, and Rousseau after him, have observed that man's education should begin in the cradle, that is to say, at the moment when he is contracting his first habits; it is the same with States. It was long possible to recognize in the rich and powerful Romans those same plunderers that Romulus had brought together to live by rapine; and in our day the French, who are docile and polished (perhaps possibly to excess), still preserve the traces of the feudal spirit, while the English, amid their clamors against royal authority, continue to manifest a respect for the Crown, which recalls the period of the Norman conquest and government. Thus *every thing that is, partakes of what has been;* and to attain a thorough knowledge of any people, it is as necessary to study its history as its legislation. If then we wish to form an idea of the American Republic, we must be careful not to confound the Virginians, who were brought to this continent by a spirit which was as warlike as it was mercantile and as ambitious as it was speculative, with the New Englanders who owe their origin to religious enthusiasm; we must not expect to find precisely the same men in Pennsylvania, where the first colonists thought only of populating and cultivating the wilderness, and in South Carolina where the growing of certain privileged crops fixes the general attention on the export trade and establishes unavoidable connections with the Old World. Let it be observed, too, that agriculture which was everywhere the occupation of the first settlers, was not enough to cast them all in one mold, since there are certain types of agriculture which tend to maintain equal wealth among individuals, and other types which tend to destroy it.

These are sufficient reasons to prove that the same principles, the same opinions, the same habits do not occur in all the thirteen United States, although they are all subject to more or less the same government, for, although their constitutions are not all alike, there is in all of them a democratic government and a government by *representation,* in which the people express their will through their delegates. But if we choose to overlook the shades which distinguish these confederated peoples one from another, if we consider the thirteen states only as one nation, we shall observe that she must long be marked by those circumstances which have led her to liberty. Any philosopher acquainted with mankind, and who has studied the springs of human action, must be convinced that, in the present revolution, the Americans have been guided by two principles, while they were perhaps imagining that they were following but one. He will distinguish in their legislation and in their opinions a *positive* and a *negative* principle. The positive principle I call everything that reason alone might dictate, in such an enlightened age as this, to peoples who were choosing the type of

government best suited to them; I call the negative principle everything that they have done out of opposition to the laws and usages
of a powerful enemy for whom they had conceived a well-founded
aversion. Struck by the example of the disadvantages offered by the
English government, they had turned to the opposite extreme, convinced that it was impossible to deviate from it too much. Thus a
child who has met with a serpent in his path, is not content to avoid
it, but flies far beyond the spot where he would be safe from its
bite. In England a septennial parliament invites the King to purchase a majority on which he may reckon for a long period; the
American assemblies *therefore* must be annual. On the other side
of the water, the executive power, too uncontrolled in its action,
frequently escapes the vigilance of legislative authority; on this
continent, every Official, every Minister of the people must therefore be under the immediate dependence of the assemblies, so that
his first care on attaining office will be to court popular favor in
view of the next election. Among the English employments confer
and procure rank and riches, and frequently elevate their possessors
to too great a height; so, among the Americans, where offices confer
neither wealth nor consideration, they will not, it is true, become
objects of intrigue or purchase, but they will be held in so little
esteem as to make them avoided, rather than sought after, by the
most enlightened citizens. Thus such public posts will fall into the
hands of new and untried men, the only persons who can expect
to find them advantageous.

Still considering the thirteen United States as a single whole, we
shall observe still other circumstances which have influenced the
principles of the government, as well as the national spirit. These
thirteen states were at first colonies; now the first necessity felt in
all rising colonies is population; I say in rising colonies, for I doubt
much whether that necessity exists at present as much as is generally imagined. Of this however I am very sure, that there will still
be a complaint of lack of population, long after the necessity has
ceased. America will long continue to reason as follows: we must
attract foreigners among us, to attract them we must offer them all
possible advantages; once within our midst they will therefore be
considered as members of the state, as real citizens. Thus one year's
residence in the same place will suffice to establish residence, and
every resident will have the right to vote, and will constitute a
part of the sovereign power; from whence it will result that this

sovereignty will spread and divide itself without requiring any pledge, any security from the person who is invested with it. This has arisen from not considering the possibility of other emigrants than those from Europe,[7] who are supposed to fix themselves in the first spot where they may form a settlement; we shall one day, however, see frequent emigrations from state to state; workmen will frequently transplant themselves, many of them will even be obliged to move about from the nature of their employments, in which case it may seem a bit surprising to see the elections in a district of Connecticut decided by inhabitants of Rhode Island or New York.

Some political writers, especially the more modern, have maintained that property alone should determine true citizenship. They are of the opinion that only he whose fortune is necessarily linked to the welfare of the state has a right to be a member of the state. In America a rather specious answer is given to this reasoning; among us, they say, landed property is so easily acquired that every workman who can use his hands may be looked upon as a person who will soon become a man of property. But can America long remain in this situation? And will the order of things appropriate to her infancy still be fitting now that she has attained manhood?

This, Sir, is a delicate question which I can propose only to a philosopher like yourself. In establishing among themselves a purely democratic government, had the Americans a real love of democracy? And if they have wished all men to be equal, is this not solely because, from the very nature of things, they were in fact equal, or nearly so? For to preserve a popular government in all its integrity, it is not sufficient not to admit either rank or nobility; wealth always creates marked differences, which are the greater because there exist no others. Now such is the present happiness of America that she has no poor, that every man there enjoys a certain ease and independence, and that if some individuals have been able to obtain a smaller portion than others, they are so surrounded by resources that their future status is considered more important than their present situation. Such is this general tendency to a state of equality that the same enjoyments which would be deemed superfluous in every other part of the world are here considered as necessities. Thus the wages of a workman must represent not only his subsistence and that of his family, but also neat and convenient furniture for his house, tea and coffee for his wife, and the silk gown she wears every time she goes from home; and this is one of the principal causes of the high cost of labor which is generally attributed to the want of hands. Now, Sir, suppose that the increase of population reduces your artisans to the status they have in France and England—do you then believe that your principles are democratic enough so that the landholders and the opulent would still continue to regard them as their equals?

I shall go still further, relying on the fairness of your judgment to rectify anything that you may find too subtle or too speculative in my idea. I shall ask you then, whether, while believing that you have the most perfect democracy, you would not have imperceptibly attained a point further removed from it than in any other Republic? You have only to recall that when the Roman Senate was compelled to renounce its principles of tyranny; the very traces of it were supposed to be effaced by making consular honors accessible to the plebeians. That numerous and long-oppressed class then found themselves exalted merely by the prospect which now lay open to a small number of their body. Most of them remained poor, but they consoled themselves by saying, *we may one day become Consuls.* Now observe, Sir, that in the present form of your government, you have not attached enough grandeur and dignity to any one position to render its possessor illustrious, still less the whole class from which he may be chosen. You have cast off all hereditary distinctions, but have you bestowed sufficient personal distinctions? Have you reflected that these distinctions, far from being less considerable than those which existed among the Greeks and Romans, ought rather to surpass them? The reason for this is very obvious: the effect of honors and distinctions is all the more marked when it operates on a greater number of men assembled together. When Gaius Duilius was conducted home on his return from supper to the sound of music, the whole city of Rome was witness to his triumph; grant the same honors to Governor Trumbull,[8] and three houses at most in Lebanon will hear the symphony. Men must be moved by some principle, and is it not better that this should be by vanity than interest? I have no doubt that love of country will always prove a powerful motive, but do not flatter yourself that it will long exist with its present intensity. The greatest efforts of the mind, like those of the body, are in resistance, and the same may happen with the state, as with opinions to which we cease to be attached when they cease to be contested.

Already, Sir, many objects have passed before our eyes. We have only glanced at them, but it would take more penetrating sight than mine to distinguish them more clearly. You hold the telescope; look through it with your own eyes and you will make good use of it. My task will be accomplished if I can but prove to you that such objects are not foreign to my subject. I shall observe then that to know at what precise point and on what principle you should admit the arts and sciences in your nation, it is first necessary to understand its natural tendency; for we may direct the course of rivers, but not turn them back to their sources. Now, to discover the natural tendency of a nation, we must not only examine its present legislation, but also the contradictions which may exist between the government and popular prejudices, between the laws and general habits; the reaction, in short, which these different motive forces may produce upon each other. In the present instance, for example, it is important to foresee to what degree democracy is likely to prevail in America, and whether the spirit of this democracy tends to equality of fortunes, or is confined to equality of ranks. It is sad to confess that it is to a very great inequality in the distribution of wealth that the fine arts are indebted for their most brilliant periods. In the time of Pericles, immense treasures were concentered in Athens, unappropriated to any particular purpose; under the reign of Augustus, Rome owed her acquisition of the fine arts to the spoils of the world, if indeed the fine arts were ever really naturalized at Rome; and under the Juliuses and Leo X, ecclesiastic pomp and riches, raised to the highest degree, gave birth to the prodigies of that famous age. But these epochs, so celebrated in the history of the arts, are either those of their birth, or of their revival, and similar circumstances are not necessary to maintain them in the flourishing and prosperous state they have attained. There is one circumstance, however, which we have not yet touched upon, and which seems indispensable, both for their preservation and for their establishment. The arts, there can be no doubt about it, can never flourish, except where a great number of men are assembled. They must have large cities, they must have capitals. America possesses five such which seem ready to receive them. You can yourself name them: Boston, New York, Philadelphia, Baltimore, and Charleston. But these are seaports, and commerce, it cannot be denied, has more magnificence than taste; it pays, rather than encourages artists.

There are thus two great questions to be answered: to know whether large towns are useful or harmful to America, and whether commercial towns are desirable capitals. Some may perhaps think that the first question can be answered by the mere reflection that rural life is best suited to mankind, contributing the most to their happiness and the maintenance of virtue, without which there can be no happiness. But it must be remembered, that this same virtue, those happy dispositions and peaceable amusements that we enjoy in the country, are not infrequently something acquired in towns. If Nature be nothing for him who has not learned to observe her, Retirement is sterile for the man without education. Now this education is best acquired in towns. Let us not confuse the man who has retired to the country with the man brought up in the country. The former is the most perfect of his species, and the latter frequently does not merit to belong to it. In a word, one must have education; I will even go further, and say that one must have lived with a certain number of men to know how to live well in one's own family. To be brief, shall I content myself with expressing to you my hopes? As far as possible I should like each state of America to have a capital which would be the seat of government, but not a commercial city. I should like to see this capital located in the center of the state, so that every citizen rich enough to provide for the education of his children and to taste the pleasures of society, might inhabit it for some months of the year, without making it his only residence and without giving up his precious country seat. I would like to see established at a small distance from the capital but farther away than Cambridge is from Boston, a university where civil and public law, and all the higher sciences, might be taught in a course of study to be begun only at the age of fourteen, and not to exceed three years' duration. I should like, furthermore, to see this capital and its annex preserve, like the sacred fire, the true national spirit, that is to say, that spirit which allies itself perfectly with liberty and public happiness. For we must not imagine that we can modify commercial towns to our taste. Commerce is more friendly to individual, than to public liberty; [9] it discriminates not between citizens and foreigners. A trading town is a common receptacle, where every man brings his own manners, opinions, and habits; and the best are not always those that prevail. English, French, Italian, all mix together, all lose a little of their distinctive character, and in turn communicate a portion of it; so that neither defects nor virtues appear in their genuine light; as, in the paintings of great artists, the different tints of light are so blended, as to leave no particular color in its primitive and natural state.

Though it seems impossible to conclude this topic without speaking of luxury, I am nevertheless somewhat reluctant to employ a term, the sense of which is not well defined. To avoid here all ambiguity, I shall consider it only *as an expense, abusive in its relation either to the wealth of individuals, or to their situation.* In the former case, the idea of luxury approaches that of dissipation, and in the latter, that of ostentation. Let us illustrate this thought by an example: if a Dutch merchant spends his fortune in flowers and shells, the sort of luxury into which he has fallen is only relative to his means, since his taste has led him further than his faculties would admit. But if, in a republic, a very wealthy citizen expends only a part of his fortune in building a noble palace, the luxury with which he is reproached is in that case proportional to his situation; it shocks the public, in the same manner as proud and arrogant behavior inspires estrangement and hatred.

We must do justice to commerce, it loves enjoyments more than luxury; and if we sometimes see the merchant exceeding the limits, this is rather from imitation than natural propensity. In France and England we see some ostentatious merchants, but the example is given them by the great lords. There is another more ridiculous, but less culpable abuse, from which commerce is not free, namely, fashion. This must doubtless prevail wherever there are a great number of foreigners; for what is mere custom at home becomes *fashion* when they transplant it abroad. On the other hand, the numerous connections, the very interest of the merchants, which consists in provoking, in exciting the taste of the consumers, tends to establish and assure the empire of fashion. What obstacle must be opposed to this?

I propose this question to myself with pleasure, because it leads me back to the fine arts by an indirect road. I shall ask what has heretofore been the remedy for those caprices of opinion which have begot so many errors, so many revolutions? Is it not Reason and Philosophy? Well then! the remedy against the caprices of fashion is the study of the arts, the knowledge of abstract beauty, the perfection of taste. But, you ask, do you hope really to fix that taste, hitherto so variable? How often has it changed? How often

will it not change? I shall continue to answer in the manner of
Socrates, by interrogating myself, and I shall say, What ridiculous
opinions have not prevailed in the world, from the time of the
Grecian sophists to the theologians of our own day? Has not
Reason, however, begun to resume her rights, and do you think
that when once recovered, she ever loses them? Why should you
expect that objects so frivolous as furniture and dress should attain
perfection before religion and legislation? Let us never cease repeating: that from every possible point of view, Ignorance is the
source of evil, and Knowledge that of good.

Do you not see that the Greeks, who had somehow acquired
very early such just notions of the arts and taste; do you not see,
I say, that they never varied in their fashions, as witness the statues
modeled at Rome by Grecian artists; as attest, too, the noble and
elegant mode of dress still retained by that people, though living
among the Turks. Erect altars, then, to the fine arts, if you would
destroy those of fashion and caprice. Taste and learn to relish
nectar and ambrosia, if you are afraid of becoming intoxicated with
common liquors.

Perhaps, Sir, what I am now about to say should only be whispered
in your ear. I am going to handle a delicate subject, I am venturing
to touch the *Ark.* But be assured, that during the three years I have
been in America, the progress of women's dress has not escaped
me. If I have enjoyed this as a man of feeling should, if the results of this progress have not been viewed by me with an indifferent eye, my age and character are a pledge to you that I have
observed them as a philosopher. Well, Sir, it is in this capacity that
I undertake their defense, but so long only as things are not carried
to excess. The virtue of women, which is more productive of happiness, even for men, than all the enjoyments of vice, if there be
any real pleasures arising from that source—the virtue of women,
I say, has two bucklers of defense. One is retirement, and distance
from all danger; this is the hidden treasure mentioned by La
Rochefoucauld, which is untouched, because it is undiscovered.
The other is pride, always a noble sentiment when it is equivalent
to self-respect. Let them learn to appreciate themselves; let them
rise in their own estimation, and rely on that estimable pride for
the preservation of their virtue as well as of their fair name. Men
who love only pleasure corrupt the opposite sex, whom they make
but an instrument of their own voluptuousness; those who truly
love women render them better by rendering them more lovable.

But, you will say, is it by dress, and by exterior charms, that they must establish their empire? Yes, Sir, every woman should seek to please; this is the weapon conferred on her by Nature to compensate for the weakness of her sex. Without this she is a slave, and can a slave have virtues? Remember the word *decus*, from which we have derived *decency;* its original meaning is *ornament*. A dirty and negligent woman is not *decent*, she cannot inspire respect. I have already allowed myself to give my opinions by expressing my hopes: I hope, then, that American women will be well dressed; but I should like their dress to be simple. They are not meant to represent the severity of the legislation, but neither should they form a contrast to the severity, and seem to convey a tacit insult to it. Gold, silver, and diamonds, then, shall be banished from American dress; what excuse can there be for a luxury which is not becoming? But this indulgence, Sir, which I have expressed for women's dress, I am far from allowing to the men. I am not afraid to say that I should have a very bad opinion of them, if in a country where there are neither etiquette nor titles, nor particular distinctions, they should ever indulge in the luxury of dress, a luxury, which even the French have laid aside, except for marriages and festivals, and which no longer exists anywhere but in Germany and Italy, where you will certainly not go in search of models.

Observe, Sir, that we have imperceptibly prepared the way for the fine arts, by removing the principal objections which might be raised against them; for, if, far from rendering nations vain and frivolous, they rather tend to preserve them from the excesses of luxury and the caprices of fashion, they can certainly not be considered either as dangerous or harmful. You will still, perhaps, have some hesitation on the subject of luxury; but recollect, please, the definition I have given of it, and if you reflect that every fortune which exceeds the necessary gradually produces some sort of personal wealth, such as valuable furniture, gold and silver jewelry, sumptuous services of plate, etc., you must perceive that such constant savings from annual income would be much better spent on painting, sculpture, and other productions of the arts. Luxury, we have said, is often an abusive use of wealth, in respect to the condition of the person who possesses it. Now, what ostentation is there in possessing a fine painting, or a handsome statue? Surely the parade of a magnificent sideboard will be more offensive to the sight of an unwealthy neighbor than an elegant apartment adorned

with paintings. I doubt, even, whether the man who keeps a musician in his pay be so much an object of envy as one who maintains
racehorses and a pack of hounds.

But let us go further: our concern is not only to make sure that
America possesses works of art; the fine arts themselves must be
planted in her midst. If I want her to purchase pictures, it is so that
she may have her own painters; [10] if I encourage her to send for
musicians, it is so that she may become musical in her turn. Let her
not apprehend the fate of the Romans, to whom she has the apparent pride, but the real humility to compare herself. The Romans, ferocious, unjust, grasping by nature, and ostentatious from
vanity, were able to purchase masterpieces of art, but not a taste
for the arts. The Americans proceeding in general from the most
polished countries of Europe, have no barbarous prejudices to cast
off. They ought rather to compare themselves to the Greek colonies; and certainly, Syracuse, Marseilles, Crotona, and Agrigentum
had no reason to envy their mother cities. There is one foundation
on which may safely rest the hopes of all those who, like yourself,
are equally attached to good taste and to your native land. Your
fellow citizens live, and will long continue to live, close to Nature;
she is continually at hand; she is always great and beautiful. Let
them then study and consult her, and they can never go astray.
Caution them only to trust in Nature more than in the pedantic
enactments of Cambridge, Oxford, and Edinburgh, which have
long established a sort of tyranny in the empire of Opinion, and
seem to have composed a vast "classic" Code for no other purpose
than to keep all mankind in "class," as if they were still children.

Thus, Sir, you will have the complete enjoyment of the fine
arts, since you will yourselves be artists. But is it not to be feared
that the powerful attraction which they exercise over sensitive
minds may divert a rising people from several more useful, though
less agreeable, occupations? I am far from being of this opinion; I
think, on the contrary, that the most distinctive and most peculiar
advantage of America is that her rapid advances are not laborious,
that they are not due to an excess of labor. Every American has
twice as much leisure in the day as a European. Need alone compels our painful efforts, and you are strangers to need. Furthermore, your winters are long and rigorous, and many hours may
be well spared for domestic society. This suggestion applies of
course only to the lower classes of the people, for you, who live in

Virginia, know too well how much time is sacrificed to gaming, to hunting, and the table—much more indeed than it would take to form a Phidias or a Polycletus.

You will perhaps object and ask me whether a taste for arts and letters will not soften your fellow citizens, whether it will not render them frivolous and vain? You may ask whether the national character and manners will not suffer, and even admitting their utility, you will perhaps wish to see the early progress of arts and letters at least directed and conducted with a certain measure? I think that you will find an answer to these questions in several of my preceding observations.

But it is time for me to establish a general principle, the extensive consequences of which you will develop better than I can: *as long as a taste for the Arts can be reconciled with rural and domestic life, it will always be advantageous to your country, and vice versa.* Public spectacles, gaudy assemblies, horse races, etc. drag both men and women from the country, and inspire them with a disgust for it. Music, drawing, painting, architecture, attach all persons to their homes. A harpsichord is a neighbor always at command, who answers all our questions and never speaks ill. Let three or four persons in the neighborhood gather to pass the evening together, and you already have the making of a concert. A young lady, in her long moments of idleness, amuses herself by drawing; once a wife and mother, she still draws, that she may instruct her children. This is indeed another important topic which I have not previously mentioned. Do you wish your children to remain long attached to you? Then be yourselves their teachers. Education increases and prolongs your relationship with them; it adds to the consideration and the respect they have for you. They must long be persuaded that we know more than they do, and that he who teaches always knows more than the person being taught. In America, as in England, parents spoil their children when they are little and abandon them to themselves as soon as they are grown; for, in these two nations, education is neither enough attended to, nor sufficiently prolonged. Indulgent to children when they are infants, it makes petty domestic tyrants of them; negligent of them when they reach adolescence, it makes strangers of them.

And now, Sir, it seems to me that there remains no good reason to hinder us from attracting the fine arts to America. Unfortunately the same does not apply to artists. I do not think I can better express my good opinion of the Americans, than by saying that they will always incur some risk when they receive a foreigner among them. The Europeans, it must be confessed, have vices from which you are exempt, and in general it is not the best of them who expatriate themselves, especially overseas. Let us however do this justice to painters and sculptors: their assiduous labors, and especially that feeling for the beautiful and that delicate taste which they have of necessity acquired, render them, generally speaking, better than other men. It is different with music and dancing; these arts are more common, and require less education. I even owe it to strict justice to distinguish between music and dancing. Custom has thought proper to place the latter among the fine arts, nor do I oppose this, since dancing serves to improve our exterior appearance, and to give us that decorum, the source of which is the respect of others and of ourselves. But this apology for dancing is not an apology for those who make it their profession. Distrust in general the dancing masters who come to you of their own accord from Europe; distrust even those who come at your own bidding. It will always be much safer not to trust to chance, but to take up subscriptions in each state, in each town, in order to induce artists to settle among you; but in this case apply only to correspondents in Europe on whom you may rely. The commission with which you entrust them ought to be sacred in their eyes, and the smallest negligence on their part would be highly criminal; yet even they are liable to be deceived, and as it is much better to defer, even for a long time, the progress of the arts, than to make the slightest step towards the corruption of your manners, I especially recommend to the Americans to naturalize all foreign artists as far as possible. Assimilate and identify them with the inhabitants of the country; to effect which I see no better method than to make them husbands and landowners. Induce them to marry, enable them to acquire lands, and let them become citizens. By thus assuring the dominion of morals, you will still further guard against the effect of those national prejudices and of that disdain which render foreigners so ridiculous and odious, and which, because of the disgust inspired by these artists, cast discredit on art itself.

Henceforward, Sir, let us enlarge our views. The Fine Arts are suited to America. They have already made progress there, they will make greater progress in the future. No obstacle, no reasonable objection, can stop them in their career. These are points on which you and I, at least, are agreed. Let us now see what use may be made of them by the Public, the State, and the Government. Here, a vast field opens to our speculation, but as it is exposed to every eye, I shall fix mine on the object which has most forcibly struck me. Recollect, Sir, what I have said above, concerning public offices and distinctions; I pointed out that jealousy, possibly well founded in itself, but carried to the extreme, had made honors too rare, and rewards too moderate among you.

Call the Fine Arts to the aid of timid legislation. The latter confers neither rank nor permanent distinction; so let it be generous with statues, monuments, and medals.[11] Astonished Europe, when admiring a *Washington*, a *Warren*, a *Greene*, or a *Montgomery*, seeks to know what rewards can repay their services. Here then are the rewards worthy of them and of you: let me behold in all the great towns of America statues of Washington, with this inscription, *Pater, Liberator, Defensor Patriae;* may I see, too, statues of the Hancocks and the Adamses, with only these two words, *Primi Proscripti;* and statues of Franklin, with the Latin verse inscribed in France below his portrait.[12] What glory America would derive from these! She would find that she has more heroes than she has marble and artists to commemorate them! [13] And your public buildings, your *curiae*, why should they not display in sculptured relief and in painting the battles of *Bunker's Hill*, of *Saratoga*, of *Trenton*, of *Princeton*, of *Monmouth*, of *Cowpens*, of *Eutaw Springs?* Thus would you perpetuate the memory of these glorious deeds; thus would you maintain, even through a long peace, that national pride, so necessary to the preservation of liberty; and you could, without offense to this liberty, lavish rewards equal to the sacrifices made in her name.[14]

It would be injurious, Sir, to both you and your country, to insist further on these reflections. Another subject now beckons to me, but I should again be guilty of offense were I to think for a moment that America needed to have her attention called to it. You yourself have wanted the progress of the sciences, as well as the arts, to form a part of these considerations. But indeed, cannot their progress be taken for granted in a country already celebrated for Academies and universities which rival those of the Old World? And for learned men—I will go further and say, for distinguished geniuses—whose names alone will mark famous epochs in the history of the human mind? [15] Doubt not, Sir, that America will render herself illustrious by the sciences, as well as by her arms and her government; and if the attention of the Philosopher be still needed to watch over their progress, it is less to hasten it than to remove the obstacles which might retard its forward march. Let the universities, which are always too dogmatic and too exclusive, be entrusted only with forming good scholars, and leave to unrestrained philosophy the care of forming good men. In England the universities have labored to destroy Skepticism, and from that period Philosophy has been visibly on the decline. It would seem indeed that the English, in all fields, want only half-liberty. Let the owls and bats flutter about in the murky dimness of a feeble twilight; the American eagle must be able to fix its eyes upon the sun! Nothing proves to me that it is not good to know the truth. And what, in fact, has error hitherto produced? The misfortunes of the world.

As for Academies, they will always be useful, as long as they are not too numerous. An Academician is a Senator of the Republic of Letters; he has taken an oath to advance nothing he cannot prove; he has dedicated his life to truth, and has promised to sacrifice even his own self-esteem to it. Such men cannot be numerous; such men ought not to be discredited by associates unworthy of them. But if academical principles tend to make science austere and scrupulous, encouragements held out to the public ought to excite every mind, and give a free rein to opinion. Such encouragements are the prizes proposed by the Academies; it is by means of these prizes that the activity of men's minds is directed towards the most useful objects; it is through them that first efforts acquire celebrity; it is such prizes, too, that spare a young man seeking glory too long a wait for her first favors. The more the sciences approach perfection, the more rare do discoveries become; but America has the same advantage in the learned world as in the world of daily living. The extent of her empire offers for her observation a large portion of heaven and earth. What observations may not be made from Penobscot to Savannah? From the lakes to the sea? Natural History and Astronomy are her particular provinces, and the first of these sciences at least is still susceptible of great improvement.

Morals form a branch of Philosophy lately in great repute.[16] As for myself, it seems to me that wherever legislation is good, morality is already achieved; and where legislation is lacking, I know not the use of morality. It is in general the same with morality as with health; little attention is paid to it until it be lost. Moralists too, are like doctors and apothecaries, whom a good diet would render useless, and who not infrequently serve only to arouse our anxiety and to divert our imagination. Preserve a good government, render the people mild and sensible, and they will make morals for themselves.

With respect to religion, its object and end conceal it from our observations. As it considers not the relations of men with each other, but their connection with God alone, its influence should be internal and personal; and whenever it extends further, it is invariably at the expense of public order. I can therefore only congratulate America on being the only country possessing true tolerance, that absolute tolerance, which has not only triumphed over superstition, but which makes even the enemies of superstition blush at the ignominious compromises they have made with her. But that none of those objects which interest you, Sir, may pass before our eyes without inducing some reflection, I shall allow myself to make just one, which, I trust, will find favor with a Philosopher.

All the religions established in America agree in one very important point: they proscribe all superstition, all dependence on any external power. But they agree also in a practice which seems to me to have no necessary connection with the dogmas of Protestantism. I mean the extreme strictness with which they observe Sunday. This day is consecrated to divine worship. Be it so, but it is also consecrated to rest, and what is this repose without gaiety, without relaxation? I venture to say that in America you know neither the pain of labor nor the pleasure of repose. What a gloomy silence reigns in all your towns on Sunday! One would imagine that some violent epidemic, or plague, had obliged everyone to shut himself up at home.[17]

Transport yourself to Europe, and especially to a Catholic country; behold, on the same day, when divine service is over, the people pouring into the squares and public walks, hurrying in crowds towards the suburbs, towards the neighboring villages, where a thousand taverns are open to receive them; everywhere you hear songs and the sound of music; everywhere your eye meets with gay and animated dances. It is a truly affecting spectacle to see the artisan pressing towards the *guinguettes*, or houses of entertainment; with one arm he holds his wife, dressed in her best array, the other serves to carry the youngest of his children, while another, who is able to walk, holds his mother's hand and tries to follow along; the whole family is going to make merry together. If the wine gives rise to quarrels, they are appeased by the women, who prevent that excess of drinking to which men are but too subject. The families drink and dance among themselves, and this happy day frequently encroaches on the night, and always terminates too soon. In America, it is just the reverse; as there is nothing but idleness without the resource of either sport or dance, the sexes separate, the women at a loss what to do with their fine dresses, which have shone only at the "meeting," fall into a state of dull listlessness, which is only to be diverted by frivolous discourse and scandal; while the men, wearied with reading the Bible to their children, assemble round a bowl, not prepared by joy, and at the bottom of which they find nothing but stupid intoxication.

I know not, Sir, whether the following principle be that of a Philosopher, or only of a Frenchman; but I believe that every amusement which separates men from women is contrary to the welfare of society, is calculated to render one of the sexes boorish and the other dull, and to destroy, in short, that sensibility, the source of which Nature has placed in interchange between the sexes.

Weigh these reflections, Sir, which are not perhaps as frivolous as they appear. Happiness is composed only of enjoyments; now Sundays make the seventh part of our lives, and if you deduct from the people their days of forced labor, you will see that they constitute more than half of our best time. Make happy days, then, of Sundays, give them to America, and you will have conferred on her an inestimable present.

These observations on the Sabbath, on the day of rest which follows the six days of work, seem to warn me that my own work is ended. May it not appear longer to you than it has to myself, and may you, after bestowing on me some moments of attention, not feel too sensibly the want of that dissipation that I have just been extolling. Recognize at least, Sir, in this feeble essay, my devotion to your wishes, and the sincere attachment with which I have the honor to be, etc., etc.

On board the frigate L'Émeraude,
in Chesapeake Bay, the 12th of January, 1783 [18]

LIST OF SURVIVING HOUSES
AND OTHER SITES MENTIONED
BY CHASTELLUX

THIS recapitulation includes only buildings still standing in some form in 1963 (sometimes well preserved or restored, but often radically transformed). A few related sites with visible remains have been added. Markers and monuments that merely recall vanished buildings are excluded. Dates refer to the entry in Chastellux's journals, above, where further information and annotations will be found, including references to local guides and booklets. The Federal Writers Project state guides, published in the 1930's and early 1940's, are still useful for locating many of these houses, and for suggesting related places worth visiting. Attention is also called to the booklets: *State Historical Markers of Virginia, Listing the Inscriptions on All Such Markers on the Principal Highways of Virginia*, issued by the Virginia Department of Conservation and Development, and *Guide to the Historical Markers of Pennsylvania*, issued by the Pennsylvania Historical and Museum Commission. Comparable lists have unfortunately not been published for roadside markers in the other states mentioned below. Places marked with an asterisk are maintained as historic museums or are otherwise "open to the public."

RHODE ISLAND
Newport:

*Mawdsley House. Chastellux's HQ during winter of 1780-1781, where he wrote Part I of his *Travels*. See Pt. I, chap. 1, n. 1.

Portsmouth:

*Remains of Butt's Hill fortifications. Nov. 11, 1780.

Providence:

*University Hall, Brown University. French Hospital. Nov. 12, 1780.

Joseph Russell House. Chastellux's HQ, June 1781. See Pt. I, chap. 1, n. 17.

Coventry:

Waterman's Tavern. June 1781. See Pt. I, chap. 1, n. 21, and also Pt. II, Introduction.

CONNECTICUT

Sterling Hill (Chastellux's "Voluntown"):

Dorrance's Tavern. Nov. 13-15, 1780; Jan. 7, 1781; Nov. 30, 1782.

Columbia:

Lebanon Crank Tavern (Hill's). Nov. 15, 1780.

Lebanon:

"Redwood," David Trumbull's House, Lauzun's HQ. Jan. 5-7, 1781.

*Governor Jonathan Trumbull's House. Jan. 5-7, 1781.

Ashford:

Benjamin Clark's Inn (Pompey Hollow Tavern), at Warrenville. Nov. 5, 1782.

Wethersfield:

*Webb House. Wethersfield Conference, May 22, 1781. See Pt. II, Introduction, n. 6.

Farmington:

*Congregational Meetinghouse. Nov. 17, 1780.
Phinehas Lewis's House (Elm Tree Apartment). Nov. 17, 1780.
Asahel Wadsworth's House. Dec. 2, 1782.

Litchfield:

Samuel Sheldon's Tavern. Dec. 3, 1782.

New Preston (Town of Washington):

Cogswell's Tavern (?). Dec. 4, 1782. See Pt. III, chap. 3, n. 11.

MASSACHUSETTS

Sheffield:

Dewey's Inn. Jan. 2, 1781.

Westborough:

Abijah Gale's Tavern. Nov. 7, 1782.

Concord:

*Battlefield at North Bridge. Nov. 7, 1782.
*"Cemetery opposite the town house" (The Hill Burying Ground).
　　Nov. 7, 1782.

Newburyport:

Lowell-Tracy-Johnson House. Nov. 12, 1782.

Cambridge:

*Harvard Hall. Nov. 18, 1782.
*President Willard's house (Wadsworth House). Nov. 18, 1782.

Boston:

[*Note:* There are of course buildings surviving from the time of
　Chastellux's visit, Nov. 14-22, 1782—such as the Old State
　House, King's Chapel, etc.—but none of the houses specifically
　mentioned by him are extant].

NEW HAMPSHIRE

Portsmouth:

Joshua Wentworth House, head of Fleet St. Nov. 10, 1782.
*Moffatt-Ladd House. Where Chastellux visited Mrs. William
　(Catharine Moffatt) Whipple, Nov. 10, 1782. See Pt. III,
　chap 1, n. 29.
*Remains of earthworks of Fort Washington, on Pierce's Island.
　Nov. 10, 1782.

NEW YORK

East Fishkill:

Col. Griffin's Tavern (on road from Hopewell to Fishkill).
　Nov. 20, 1780.

Fishkill:

*Trinity Church. American Hospital. Nov. 20, 1780.

West Point:
*Fort Putnam (restored). Nov. 21, 1780.

Bear Mountain Section, Palisades Interstate Park:
*Remains of redoubt of Fort Clinton. Nov. 22, 1780.

Stony Point:
*Remains of fortifications. Nov. 22, 1780.

Greenburgh (near Scarsdale, Westchester County):
Philipse House. Chastellux's HQ, July 1781. See Pt. II, Introduction, and n. 10.

New Windsor:
*Knox Headquarters. Knox HQ in 1780; Gates HQ in 1782. Dec. 20, 1780. Dec. 7, 1782.

Newburgh:
*Hasbrouck House. Washington's HQ. Dec. 5, 1782.

Albany:
*Schuyler Mansion. Dec. 24, 1780.

Cohoes:
*Cohoes Falls (Mohawk River). Dec. 25, 1780.

Waterford:
Remains of earthworks on Haver (Peoble's) Island. Dec. 25, 1780.

Saratoga National Historical Park:
*Saratoga Battlefields. Dec. 29, 1780.

Schuylerville (Old Saratoga):
*Schuyler Farmhouse. Dec. 29-30, 1780.

Glens Falls:
*Great Cataract of the Hudson. Dec. 30, 1780.

Warwick:
Francis Baird House. Dec. 7, 1782.

NEW JERSEY

Hawthorne:
Lafayette's HQ at Wagaraw (John Francis Ryerson, later Degray, house). Nov. 23, 1780.

Paterson:
*Totowa, or Passaic, Falls. Nov. 23, 1780.

Preakness (Wayne Township):
*Theunis Dey House, Washington's HQ. Nov. 23, 1780.

Morristown:
*American army's "winter quarters of 1779" (Morristown National Historical Park). Nov. 27, 1780.
Peter Kemble House. Gen. Wayne's HQ in 1780-1781. Dec. 18, 1780.

Bound Brook:
Van Horne House. Nov. 28, 1780.

Princeton:
*Nassau Hall. Nov. 29, 1780.
*Princeton Battlefield. Nov. 29, 1780.

Red Bank (on the Delaware, near Woodbridge):
*Whitall House. Dec. 8, 1780.
*Remains of earthworks of Fort Mercer, and salvaged river obstructions (Red Bank Battlefield Park). Dec. 8, 1780.

Ringwood:
*Mrs. Robert Erskine's manor, and iron mines. Dec. 19, 1780.

Hope:
Moravian gristmill, millrace, and pond. Dec. 9, 1782.
Moravian Church, i.e., *Gemeinhaus.* Dec. 9, 1782.

PENNSYLVANIA

Bristol:
*Bessonett's Inn (Ye Olde Delaware House). Nov. 29, 1780.

Philadelphia:
*State House (Independence Hall). Dec. 4, 1780.
*Carpenters' Hall. Meeting place of American Philosophical Society (in Library room), when Chastellux attended, Dec. 15, 1780.
*Pennsylvania Hospital. Nov. 30, 1780.
*Christ Church. Dec. 10, 1780.

*Powel House, South Third St. Dec. 1, 1780.
 Shippen-Wistar House, 4th and Locust Sts. Dec. 11, 1780.
*"Laurel Hill," or Randolph Mansion, East Fairmount Park. La
    Luzerne's country residence. Dec. 12, 1780.
*"Belmont," Fairmount Park West. Richard Peters' country resi-
    dence. See Pt. I, chap. 3, n. 100.
*"The Woodlands," Woodlands Cemetery, West Philadelphia.
    William Hamilton's house. See Pt. I, chap. 3, n. 100.
 Mud Island, remains of Fort Mifflin. Dec. 8, 1780.

Germantown:

"Cliveden," Chew House. The "stone house." Dec. 2, 1780.

Whitemarsh:

*Remains of redoubts. Dec. 11, 1780.

Brandywine Battlefield and vicinity:

*Benjamin Ring House, near Chadd's Ford. Washington's HQ in
    1777. Dec. 6, 1780.
*Gideon Gilpin House, near Chadd's Ford. See Pt. I, chap. 3, n. 65.
*Birmingham Friends Meeting House. Dec. 7, 1780.

Bethlehem:

*Tavern, i.e., the Sun Inn. Dec. 10, 1782.
*Moravian Church (the "Old Chapel"). Dec. 11, 1782.
*Brothers', or Single Brethren's House (Colonial Hall, Moravian
    College). Dec. 11, 1782.
 Sisters' House. Dec. 11, 1782.

VIRGINIA

*Mount Vernon:

Chastellux was Washington's guest here, Sept. 11, 1781. See Pt. II,
    Introduction; also Pt. II, chap. 4, Grieve's nn. 19, 24.

Williamsburg:

*College of William and Mary. See Pt. II, chap. 5 and n. 17.
*Wythe House. Chastellux's HQ during winter quarters, 1781-
    1782 (?). See Pt. II, Introduction, and n. 20.

Yorktown:

*Battlefield (Colonial National Historical Park). Sept. 28-Oct. 19, 1781. See Pt. II, Introduction, and n. 16.

Gov. Thomas Nelson House. Apr. 10-11, 1782. See Pt. II, chap. 1, nn. 23, 27.

Hanover Courthouse:

*Courthouse. Apr. 9, 1782.

Paul Thilman's Inn. Apr. 9, 1782.

Boswell's Tavern (Louisa County):

Apr. 12, 1782.

Charlottesville:

*Monticello, Jefferson's residence. Apr. 13-17, 1782.

Greenville (Augusta County):

Smith's Tavern (?). Apr. 18, 1782.

*Natural Bridge:

Apr. 19, 1782. See also Pt. II, Appendix A.

Powhatan Courthouse:

Inn. Apr. 23, 1782.

Petersburg:

"Battersea," John Banister's house. Apr. 25, 1782.

Richmond:

"Ampthill," Col. Archibald Cary's house. Moved from original site on James River below Richmond, near Warwick, where Chastellux noted it, Apr. 26, 1782.

*"Wilton," Randolph house. Moved from original site on James River below Richmond, where Chastellux noted it, Apr. 26, 1782.

Goochland County:

"Tuckahoe," Thomas Mann Randolph estate on James River, west of Richmond. Apr. 25, 1782.

Charles City County:

*"Westover," Mrs. Byrd's estate on James River, east of Richmond. Apr. 28-29, 1782.

NOTE ON BIBLIOGRAPHIC AND
CARTOGRAPHIC SOURCES

Since the Editor's footnotes provide a running bibliography, and since, from the nature of the work, the references concerning a given locality or subject generally fall together, a formal recapitulatory bibliography has not been deemed necessary. It may, however, be helpful to those interested in the other Frenchmen who participated in the American Revolution to summarize here the frequently cited works concerning them. For biographical information concerning these French participants the following older works are still useful: Edwin M. Stone, *Our French Allies...in the Great War of the American Revolution, from 1778 to 1782* (Providence, 1884); and Thomas Balch, *The French in America during the War of Independence of the United States, 1777-1783*, 2 vols. (Philadelphia, 1891-95). Balch's second volume is a brief biographical dictionary, alphabetically arranged. This has, however, been corrected and extended by later works. *Les Combattants Français de la Guerre Américaine, 1778-1783* (Paris, 1903), published under the auspices of the Ministère des Affaires Étrangères, provides a roster, by regiments or other units, of both officers and enlisted personnel, compiled from the official records of the French army and navy; the work lacks an index, is unwieldy, and is not necessarily complete or reliable.

A generally satisfactory biographical reference book is Ludovic de Contenson, *La Société des Cincinnati de France et la Guerre d'Amérique, 1778-1783* (Paris, 1934), which is illustrated with portraits of the French officers, drawn mainly from private family collections. Family portraits are also reproduced in the substantial but ill-organized *Catalogue illustré*, compiled by A.-Léo Leymarie, of the *Exposition Rétrospective des Colonies Françaises de l'Amérique du Nord* (Paris, 1929). By far the best of such works is André Lasseray, *Les Français sous les Treize Etoiles (1775-1783)*, 2 vols.

(Macon, 1935). It should be emphasized, however, that Lasseray's biographical sketches concern only the French volunteers who served in the American army, and not the army or navy officers who came to America with the French expeditionary forces subsequent to the Alliance of 1778; Lasseray's projected companion volume dealing with the latter has not been published, so that Balch or Contenson must be consulted.

Information on the later careers of such of the veterans of the American War as subsequently rose to the rank of general or admiral will be found in Georges Six, *Dictionnaire Biographique des Généraux et Amiraux Français de la Révolution et de l'Empire*, 2 vols. (Paris, 1934). Warrington Dawson, *Les 2112 Français Morts aux Etats Unis de 1777 à 1783 en combattant pour l'Indépendance Américaine* (Paris, 1936, reprinted from *Journal de la Société des Américanistes*, New Ser., 38 [1936]), provides a list, carefully compiled from official French records and other sources, of the French officers and enlisted men who lost their lives in America. Considerable information about the French engineers who served in the American army may be gleaned from the rather formless work of Elizabeth S. Kite, *Brigadier-General Louis Lebègue Duportail, Commandant of Engineers in the Continental Army, 1777-1783* (Baltimore, 1933). Good groundwork for the study of the French medical corps, hospitals, and related matters—generally overlooked in the other works mentioned—is provided by Maurice Bouvet, *Le Service de Santé français pendant la Guerre d'Indépendance des Etats-Unis (1777-1782)* (Paris, 1933, and reprint, 1934).

The incomplete *Guide to Materials for American History in the Libraries and Archives of Paris*, begun by the Carnegie Institution of Washington under the general editorship of Waldo G. Leland, is invaluable as far as it goes. Volume I, "Libraries," was published in 1932; Volume II, "Archives of the Ministry of Foreign Affairs," compiled by Waldo G. Leland, John J. Meng and Abel Doysié, in 1943; subsequent volumes, dealing notably with the War and Navy Archives, and for which material has long since been gathered, have regrettably not yet been published. Documents from French archives are printed in Henri Doniol, *Histoire de la Participation de la France à l'Etablissement des Etats-Unis d'Amérique, Correspondance Diplomatique et Documents*, 5 vols. (Paris, 1886-92).

Many of the French officers left diaries, journals, or memoirs treating of their experiences in America—some published during their lives, but most of them at a later period. Such works are conveniently listed in Frank Monaghan, *French Travellers in the United States, 1765-1932, A Bibliography* (New York, 1933, and reprint, with negligible additions, 1961); those concerning the Revolutionary period are grouped in a "Chronological List," p. 107. Dawson's work, cited above, has a useful bibliographical introduction, with a list of journals and diaries, mostly unpublished, supplementing Monaghan. Among the early published books cited from time to time in the Editor's notes to the present work are: *Mémoires militaires, historiques et politiques de Rochambeau*, 2 vols. (Paris, 1809); *Mémoires, Correspondance et Manuscrits du Général Lafayette, publiés par sa famille*, 6 vols. (Paris, 1837-38); Comte de Ségur, *Mémoires, ou Souvenirs et Anecdotes*, 3 vols. (Paris, 1824-26); Mathieu Dumas, *Souvenirs du lieutenant-général Mathieu Dumas, de 1770 à 1836*, 3 vols. (Paris, 1839), with an English translation, *Memoirs of His Own Time*, 2 vols. (Philadelphia, 1839)—the edition cited in notes to the present work. A later publication of special pertinence to Chastellux's *Travels* is *The Journal of Claude Blanchard, Commissary of the French Auxiliary Army sent to the United States during the American Revolution*, translated by William Duane, edited by Thomas Balch (Albany, 1876); the original text was subsequently published as *Guerre d'Amérique, Journal de campagne de Claude Blanchard* (Paris, 1881); references in the Editor's notes are to the English translation, but quotations have been checked against the original and in some instances corrected.

Other narratives include: "Journal du Voyage du Prince de Broglie," in Société des Bibliophiles Français, *Mélanges* (1903), 13-148; Louis-Alexandre Berthier, *Journal de la Campagne d'Amérique, 10 Mai 1780-26 Août 1781*, published from the Princeton manuscript by Gilbert Chinard (Washington, 1951); *The Revolutionary Journal of Baron Ludwig von Closen*, translated and edited by Evelyn M. Acomb (Chapel Hill, 1958). Miss Acomb's list of "Published Journals, Letters, Memoirs, and Papers," pp. 370-74, supplies a convenient recapitulation of still other French narratives. Finally, special mention must be made here of the Baron de Montesquieu, because he was Chastellux's aide-de-camp during his first and third journeys (Part I and Part III of the *Travels*). A few of his letters written from America have been published and are referred to at appropriate points in the present work. A series written to Montesquieu's former tutor, François de Paule Latapie (originals in family archives, Château de La Brède and elsewhere) is printed in Raymond Céleste, "Un Petit-fils de Montesquieu en Amérique (1780-1783)," *Revue Philomathique de Bordeaux et du Sud-Ouest*, 5 (1902), 529-56, and in the same author's "Charles-Louis de Montesquieu à l'Armée (1772 à 1782)," *ibid.*, 6 (1903), 504-24. Other letters written by Montesquieu to his friend the Vicomte Amand de Saint-Chamans, Baron de Rébénac (originals in Archives du Département de l'Aube, Saint-Chamans family papers) are printed in Octave Beuve, "Un Petit-fils de Montesquieu, Soldat de l'Indépendance Américaine," *Revue Historique de la Révolution Française et de l'Empire*, 5 (1914), 233-63; some of these letters to Saint-Chamans are also printed (but without indication of prior publication) in Emmanuel de Lévis Mirepoix, "Quelques Lettres du Baron de Montesquieu sur la Guerre de l'Indépendance Américaine," *Franco-American Review*, 2 (1938), 192-204. Montesquieu's long letter to Latapie, written from Newport, January 29, 1781 (Céleste, *Revue Philomathique*, 5 [1902], 544-50), is a summary of the journey made with Chastellux; although it shows the writer to be a dutiful, affectionate, and conscientious young man, it adds virtually nothing to Chastellux's account and lacks the concrete details about people and places that enliven the latter.

The emphasis given to French sources in the above brief survey —which has been prepared merely as an orientation chart for American readers who may not be familiar with them—should not be interpreted as neglect of the equally rich American sources. French historians in particular need to be reminded of the important materials concerning French participants in the American Revolution to be found in such documentary publications as, for example: Worthington Chauncey Ford, Gaillard Hunt, John C. Fitzpatrick, Roscoe R. Hill, eds., *Journals of the Continental Congress*, 34 vols. (Washington, 1904-37); John C. Fitzpatrick, ed., *The Writings of George Washington*, 39 vols. (Washington, 1931-44); Julian P. Boyd *et al.*, eds., *The Papers of Thomas Jefferson*, 16 vols. to date (Princeton, 1950———). Outstanding among the secondary works, and including valuable discussions of original sources, are: Douglas S. Freeman, *George Washington, A Biography*, 7 vols. (New York, 1948-57); and the four volumes published to date of Louis Gottschalk's biography of Lafayette: *Lafayette Comes to*

America, Lafayette Joins the American Army, Lafayette and the Close of the American Revolution, Lafayette between the American and the French Revolution, 1783-1789 (Chicago, 1935-50).

Cartographic Sources

Numerous maps contemporary with Chastellux's journeys are cited in the notes. Among these are the engraved maps of the battles of the Revolution published in England soon after the event by William Faden; others were published in the narratives of such English officers as Burgoyne, Tarleton, and Simcoe. Many of these were already available to Chastellux at the time he made his journeys. A valuable set is also found in Henry Cabot Lodge, ed., *Major André's Journal, 1777-1778 . . . with facsimile reproductions of original maps and plans*, 2 vols. (Boston, 1903). Still other manuscript maps of British origin are in the collections of the William L. Clements Library; see Christian Brun, *Guide to the Manuscript Maps in the William L. Clements Library* (Ann Arbor, 1959). The principal corpus of maps of American origin, by Robert Erskine, "geographer" to Washington, and his successor, Simeon Dewitt, is in the New-York Historical Society; for a list of the "Erskine-Dewitt maps," see Albert H. Heusser, *The Forgotten General, Robert Erskine, F.R.S. (1735-1780)* (Paterson, N.J., 1928).

Maps of French origin have, however, been emphasized in the notes, both because of their association with Chastellux and for their intrinsic merit, which reflects the high degree of cartographic skill cultivated in the French army and especially in the *Corps Royal du Génie*. Among the French maps is a series drawn for Lafayette, showing the engagements in which he participated, by his aide, Major Michel Capitaine du Chesnoy; scattered examples of these (of which there were several sets) are in various American collections. The maps by Louis-Alexandre Berthier (later known as Marshal Berthier, Napoleon's chief of staff) and his brother Charles-Louis, now in the Princeton University Library, record the camp sites and marches of Rochambeau's army in 1781 and 1782. A similar series, with numerous other maps, is in the Rochambeau Collection, Library of Congress; a third series is in the private library of Paul Mellon. A somewhat less skillfully drawn series, also depicting the movements of Rochambeau's army, illustrates the manuscript journal of Cromot du Bourg, now in the Historical Society of Pennsylvania; facsimiles of these are published in the *Magazine of American History*, vols. 4 and 5 (1880). Photographic copies of maps in French archives, obtained in 1926-27 by Louis C. Karpinski, are available in such American libraries as the New York Public, John Carter Brown, William L. Clements, and Library of Congress; see Henry P. Beers, *The French in North America, A Bibliographical Guide* (Baton Rouge, La., 1957), 121-23. Still others, in French collections, are incidentally described in the catalogue of the Société des Amis du Musée National de Blérancourt exhibition, *Les Etats-Unis et la France au XVIIIe siècle*, comp. André Girodie (Paris, 1929); and in the catalogue of the exhibition at the Archives Nationales, *La Fayette* (Paris, 1957).

In determining locations of the sites mentioned by Chastellux, eighteenth-century maps, such as those just mentioned, have been used, in conjunction with modern roadmaps, the U.S. Geological Survey quadrangles, and also—as a midway point of reference—nineteenth-century maps like those in the county atlases edited by F. W. Beers and others, and in Benson J. Lossing's *Pictorial Field-Book of the Revolution*, 2 vols. (New York, 1851-52, and later editions). Page references to Lossing in the Editor's notes are to the 1859 edition.

NOTES

Notes by Chastellux are preceded by the symbol: *Ch*. Notes by the eighteenth-century translator, George Grieve, are preceded by the symbol: *Gr*. All other notes are by the present Editor, and are preceded by the symbol *Ed*. only when they form a continuation of a note by Chastellux or by Grieve.

PART II

Introduction

Interlude between Journeys, January 1781–March 1782

1. Washington to Chastellux, New Windsor, Jan. 28, 1781, Fitzpatrick, ed., *Writings of Washington*, XXI, 149-50.

2. Washington to Chastellux, New Windsor, Mar. 31, 1781, *ibid.*, 347-49.

3. Washington to Tallmadge, New Windsor, Apr. 8, 1781, *ibid.*, 435.

4. On Chastellux's illness see: Washington to Rochambeau (expressing his concern), Mar. 31, 1781, Washington to Chastellux (congratulations on his recovery), May 7, 1781, *ibid.*, XXI, 397, XXII, 54-55; Chastellux to Franklin, Marly-le-Roi, May 30, 1783, Franklin Papers, XXVIII, 127, Amer. Phil. Soc. In this letter to Franklin, recommending Dr. Jean-François Coste, Chastellux mentions that the doctor had saved his life during his illness in America.

5. Washington to Chastellux, New Windsor, May, 7, 1781, Fitzpatrick, ed., *Writings of Washington*, XXII, 54-55.

6. Crofut, *Guide*, I, 345-47. The Webb House, still standing at 211 Main St. in Wethersfield (next door to the Silas Deane House), is open to the public under the auspices of the Connecticut Society of Colonial Dames. Extracts from Trumbull's diary are in Worthington C. Ford, ed., *Correspondence and Journals of Samuel Blachley Webb*, 3 vols. (N.Y., 1893), II, 340-41. Before reaching Wethersfield Chastellux sent ahead to Washington a confidential and rather scheming letter indicating the substance of a plan likely to be discussed at the conference; the letter, dated "White Tavern," May 21, 1781, is in Washington Papers, Lib. Cong.; on White's Tavern, see below, Pt. III, chap. 3, n. 4.

7. Washington to Chastellux, New Windsor, June 13, 1781 (in reply to Chastellux's letter of June 9), Fitzpatrick, ed., *Writings of Washington*, XXII, 204-5.

8. Rochambeau, *Mémoires*, I, 273-75. What appear to be copies of Chastellux's letter to La Luzerne (dated May 28, 1781), made by the British before conveying the original to Rochambeau, have survived in the Sir Henry Clinton Papers and the Earl of Shelburne Papers, William L. Clements Lib.; see Randolph G. Adams, *The Burned Letter of Chastellux* (N.Y., 1935; reprinted from *Légion d'Honneur, Quarterly of the American Society of the French Legion of Honor*). Adams reproduces portions of the two

copies of the letter and prints the translation of it made by the English. See also Freeman, *Washington*, V, 313, n. 84.

9. Sources for the story of the French army during the campaign of 1781, drawn upon here, include: Fitzpatrick, ed., *Writings of Washington;* Fitzpatrick, ed., *The Diaries of George Washington, 1748-1799,* 4 vols. (Boston and N.Y., 1925); "Correspondance du Comte de Rochambeau depuis le début de son commandement aux Etats-Unis, jusqu'à la fin de la campagne de Virginie," Doniol, *Histoire,* V, 309-590; Rochambeau, *Mémoires;* Louis-Alexandre Berthier, *Journal de la Campagne d'Amérique, 10 Mai 1780-26 Août 1781,* ed. Gilbert Chinard (Washington, 1951), and maps in Princeton Univ. Lib.; Blanchard, *Journal;* Dumas, *Memoirs;* Acomb, ed., *Von Closen Journal;* Count William de Deux-Ponts, *My Campaigns in America: A Journal kept... 1780-1781,* ed. Samuel Abbott Green (Boston, 1868); Baron Cromot du Bourg, "Diary of a French Officer, 1781," *Mag. of Amer. Hist.,* 4 (1880), 205-14, 293-308, 376-85, 441-52 (original now in Hist. Soc. of Pa.); Brisout de Barneville, "Journal de Guerre, Mai 1780-Octobre 1781," ed. Gilbert Chinard, *French Amer. Rev.,* 3 (1950), 217-78; etc. Among the secondary accounts: Freeman, *Washington,* V; Stone, *French Allies;* John Austin Stevens, "The French in Rhode Island," *Mag. of Amer. Hist.,* 3 (1879), 385-436, "The Operations of the Allied Armies before New York," *ibid.,* 4 (1880), 1-45, "The Route of the Allies from King's Ferry to the Head of Elk," *ibid.,* 5 (1880), 1-20; Vicomte de Noailles, *Marins et Soldats Français en Amérique pendant la Guerre de l'Indépendance des Etats-Unis (1776-1783),* (Paris, 1903); DeB. Randolph Keim, *Rochambeau, A Commemoration by the Congress of the United States of America of the Services of the French Auxiliary Forces in the War of Independence* (Wash., 1907); James Breck Perkins, *France in the American Revolution* (Boston, 1911); Forbes and Cadman, *France and New England,* I, 131-89; Allan Forbes, "Marches and Camp Sites of the French Army Beyond New England during the Revolutionary War," Mass. Hist. Soc., *Proceedings,* 67 (1945), 152-67; Stephen Bonsal, *When the French were Here, A Narrative of the Sojourn of the French Forces in America....* (Garden City, N.Y., 1945).

10. The map of the Phillipsburg camp in Cromot du Bourg's *Journal* (original, Hist. Soc. of Pa.; reproduction, *Mag. of Amer. Hist.,* 4 [1880], 296-97) designates the headquarters of the different generals, including Chastellux. The site of Washington's headquarters corresponds to present Ardsley High School; Rochambeau was at the Odell farm, still standing on Ridge Road between Hartsdale and Ardsley; Chastellux was adjacent to the artillery park about three-quarters of a mile south of Rochambeau, on what is now Healy Avenue South, Scarsdale, N.Y., on the eastern border of Sunningdale Country Club. The property (within the limits of the town of Greenburgh, Westchester Co.), which belonged in Chastellux's day to a Tory absentee, Frederick Philipse, was sold in 1786 to John Tompkins. The tract, known in more recent times as "May to October Farm," has now been subdivided. The house occupied by Chastellux is still standing, privately owned. I am greatly indebted to Mr. Richard G. Lucid, of Katonah, N.Y., for his report on a reconnaissance of the Phillipsburg Camp made in Oct. 1961. See also Charles A. Campbell, "Rochambeau's Headquarters in Westchester County, N.Y., 1781," *Mag of Amer. Hist.,* 4 (1880), 46-48, map and illus.

11. Chastellux to Washington, "Camp," July 18, 1781, Washington Papers, Lib. Cong.

12. Washington to Chastellux, Head Quarters, July 19, 1781, Fitzpatrick, ed., *Writings of Washington*, XXII, 394-95.

13. See "Instructions for Reconnoitering the Enemy's Posts at the North End of York Island" (the reconnaissance was originally scheduled to begin on July 13, but because of bad weather was postponed until July 21) Fitzpatrick, ed., *Writings of Washington*, XXII, 370-72; Washington, *Diary*, II, 241-45; Deux-Ponts, *My Campaigns*, 119-21; Blanchard, *Journal*, 123; Berthier, *Journal*, 69-72; Acomb, ed., *Von Closen Journal*, 97-101. Several of the maps made at this time by the French are extant. See, for example, "Isle de Newyork, Reconnaissance des ouvrages du nord de l'isle de Newyork faite en présence des Généraux Wasington et Rochambeau soutenue par un corps de 5000 hommes détaché de l'armée combinée de France et d'Amérique campée à Phillipsburg, dont les principaux points ont été déterminés géométriquement le 22 et 23 juillet 1781," by Edouard Colbert, Comte de Maulevrier, in W. L. Clements Lib.: see Brun, *Guide to the Manuscript Maps in the W.L. Clements Library*, No. 359. Similar maps, by Desandrouins, the Berthier brothers, and others, are among the "Karpinski photocopies" from originals in French archives; others in Rochambeau Papers, Lib. Cong.

14. Washington to Congress, Oct. 12, 1781, Fitzpatrick, ed., *Writings of Washington*, XXIII, 213.

15. Washington to De Grasse, Oct. 28, 1781, *ibid.*, 285.

16. "Journal des opérations du corps français depuis le 15 août 1781," Doniol, *Histoire*, V, 573 ff. This official account was copied out, with slight variations, by many of the French officers in their own journals.

17. Fitzpatrick, ed., *Writings of Washington*, XXIII, 245-47.

18. Chastellux to Philip Schuyler, Williamsburg, Feb. 18, 1782, original in French, Schuyler Papers, N.Y. Pub. Lib.; see below, Pt. IV, n. 2.

19. Washington to Gov. Thomas Nelson, Oct. 27, 1781, Fitzpatrick, ed., *Writings of Washington*, XXIII, 271.

20. I am indebted to Miss Jane Carson for searching the files of Colonial Williamsburg, Inc., in an attempt to elucidate this point.

Chapter 1

Williamsburg to the Piedmont

1. Chastellux's text contains veiled allusions intended for his Parisian readers, which Grieve skillfully circumvented: "il est plus aisé de deviner," Chastellux wrote, "ce que sera Madame de S.m.n. à l'âge de 80 ans, que ce qu'a été Madame du D.F.n. à celui de Madame de S.m.n." (it is easier to imagine what Madame de S.m.n. will look like at the age of eighty, than it is to imagine what Madame du D.F.n. was like when she was Madame de S.m.n.'s age). The pleasantry, no doubt obvious to Parisians of the 1780's, refers perhaps to Madame de Simiane, a fashionable young beauty of the day, sister of the Comte de Damas [see above, Pt. I, chap. 1, n. 90] and friend of Lafayette; and to the Marquise du Deffand (Horace Walpole's

correspondent) who presided over a famous *salon* and died in 1780 at the age of eighty-three.

2. *Ch.* Baron de Montesquieu had returned to Europe after the siege of York. He returned only in the month of September following [1782].

Ed. Montesquieu and Lynch had accompanied Chastellux in his first journey, Nov. 1780-Jan. 1781; see above, Pt. I, chap. 1, n. 8. Frank (or Franck)-Théobald Dillon, Chastellux's second aide-de-camp during this Virginia journey, was a lieutenant (subsequently captain) in Lauzun's Hussars. His portrait in the uniform of this corps (painted by Bellier, owned by descendants) is reproduced in Contenson, *Cincinnati*, fig. 60, p. 172; also in catalogue of *Exposition rétrospective des Colonies françaises de l'Amérique du Nord* (Paris, 1929), 188, no. 96 and plate 121. One of Dillon's older brothers, Robert-Guillaume Dillon (1754-1837), also served in America as *colonel en second* in Lauzun's Legion. His cousin, Comte Arthur Dillon (1750-94), Colonel of the Dillon Regiment, was with D'Estaing at Savannah in 1779 and with Saint-Simon at Yorktown in 1781. Members of the Dillon family, of Irish origin, served the King of France throughout the 18th century; the Dillon Regiment, a proprietary regiment which had been recruited in Ireland for service under James II, passed in 1690 into the service of France; it was commanded successively by a member of the Dillon family until 1794; see "Historique sommaire du Régiment de Dillon," in Marquise de La Tour du Pin (*née* Henriette Dillon, daughter of Count Arthur Dillon), *Journal d'une Femme de Cinquante Ans* (Paris, 1913), I, 13-18. Frank Dillon again accompanied Chastellux during the latter part of his third journey, as noted below, Pt. III, chap. 3, Dec. 2, 1782.

The Chevalier d'Oyré (François-Ignace) had played a distinguished role at Yorktown, having commanded the French engineers who advanced the second siege line to permit capture of Redoubt 9 during the night of October 14.

3. Byrd's Tavern, known also as Doncastle's Ordinary, was on the old road from Williamsburg to New Kent Courthouse, about four miles north of Toano and two miles from present Barhamsville. It survived into the late 19th century, but nothing remains of it today; there is no marker to indicate the site of this once important stopping place. Information from John M. Jennings; see Erskine-Dewitt map No. 124-T, N.-Y. Hist. Soc., showing the area "From near Rawson's Ordinary past Duncastle, alias Birds Ordinary, to near Allen's Ordinary," and also Colles, *A Survey of the Roads of the U.S.*, ed. Ristow, plate 77.

4. New Kent Courthouse still retains a distinctly rural appearance. The courthouse itself is a modern structure; an older building across the road from it, if not the actual tavern where Chastellux stayed, is probably on the same site. State Historical Marker WO-16 recalls that "Washington, Rochambeau and Chastellux, on their way to Yorktown [i.e., Williamsburg], September 14, 1781" were here, but does not mention Chastellux's later visit, when he ate shad and listened to the mockingbird. The landlord of the tavern was perhaps James Warren; see exchange of letters with him, Mar.-Apr. 1782, concerning the lodging of French army messengers, Berthier Papers, Nos. 36-37, Princeton Univ. Lib.

5. This was in June 1781, during the Cornwallis-Lafayette hare-and-hounds chase which preceded and led up to the siege of Yorktown. The incidents relating to this campaign, reported by Chastellux here and subse-

quently, had taken place a bit less than a year earlier, and were thus fresh in the minds of those who related them to him. Contemporary British maps of the Virginia campaign, showing many of the localities mentioned by Chastellux in the course of his journey, are found in Sir Banastre Tarleton's *A History of the Campaigns of 1780 and 1781 in the Southern Provinces of North America* (London, 1787), and Simcoe's *Military Journal* (Exeter, 1787; rep., N.Y., 1844). A manuscript map of the "Campagne en Virginie du Major Général Mis. de La Fayette, où se trouvent les Camps et Marches, ainsy que ceux du Lieutenant Général L^d. Cornwallis, en 1781," drawn by Lafayette's aide-de-camp, Major Michel Capitaine du Chesnoy, is reproduced from the original owned by Colonial Williamsburg in Gottschalk, *Lafayette and the Close of the Amer. Rev.*, between pp. 238-39; a reproduction of Capitaine's map, from another copy in the Yale Maps Collection, was published by the Yale Univ. Lib., 1960. A convenient schematic map of "The Virginia Campaign of 1781" is in Charles E. Hatch, Jr., *Yorktown and the Siege of 1781* (Nat. Park Serv., *Hist. Handbook*, 14 [Wash., 1957]), 5.

6. *Gr.* It is with great reluctance that truth compels me to confirm the horrid depredations committed by the English army in their progress through many parts of America. Much has been said on this subject, both in and out of Parliament, but I am sorry to say, that future historians of this unhappy war, will find the fact too well established to refuse a decisive verdict. Happy if *the result* may tend henceforth to alleviate the miseries of mankind, and mitigate the horrors of a civil contest. The wife of an Englishman, one of the principal merchants of Philadelphia, having retired with her family to the neighbourhood of Mount Holly in the Jerseys, assured me, that she found the country in general well affected to the English, until the arrival of their army, whose indiscriminate and wanton enormities soon alienated their most zealous friends, for even the officers were contaminated with the insatiable spirit of revenge and plunder. Among various anecdotes, she related to me the circumstance of the cruel treatment of a lady of her acquaintance, who was devoted to the British interest, and gave up her house with exultation to some officers of Clinton's army in their retreat from Philadelphia. But not only was her zeal repaid with insult and her own house plundered; she had the mortification to see it made the receptacle of the pillage of her poorer neighbours. Observing some of the officers make frequent excursions, and return, followed by soldiers, laden with various articles, she had at length the curiosity to pass into the garden, and looking through the window, saw four of them, and *the Chaplain*, emptying a sack containing stockings, shirts, shifts, counterpanes, sheets, spoons, and women's trinkets. The booty was regularly shared, and the distributor of these unhallowed spoils, to her utter astonishment and horror, was no other than the minister of virtue and religion. The detail of this war is a history of such iniquity: was it possible, therefore, to expect a more favourable termination of it, either on the principle of a Divine Providence, or of human conduct?

7. *Gr.* The Loyalists, no doubt, no more merit indiscriminate censure than any other body of men; the Translator, who thinks he understands the true principles of liberty, for which he has ever been a zealous and unshaken advocate, admits, however, and admires the virtue, honour, and steadfast attachment of many illustrious individuals to a cause, directly

destructive of his own wishes; but with every fair allowance for the violence inseparable from civil contests, he cannot help bearing his testimony to the wanton outrages committed by an unprincipled banditti who attached themselves to the royal cause, and branded it with ruin and disgrace. The root of this evil originated in the *Board of Loyalists* established by Lord George Germain at the instigation of skulking refugees, who flying themselves, from the scene of danger, took up their residence in London, and were in the incessant pursuit of personal and interested vengeance. He does not assert that their councils lost America, but it is now past doubt, that they formed a strong secondary cause of precipitating that event, and of embittering the separation. General Clinton, the whole army at New York, can witness the insolence and indirect menaces of this incorporated rabble of marauders, in the affair of Captain Huddy [see above, Pt. I, chap. 4, n. 1], and the subsequent claim of the Congress. Had the war continued, this *imperium in imperio* must have been attended with the most fatal consequences; this illiberal narrow minded set of men, became the spies and censors of British policy, and British conduct, and the commander-in-chief himself, was struck with horror at their unenlightened, blood-thirsty tribunal.

8. This was the place known as Spencer's Ordinary, which was about five or six miles south of Lightfoot; it was very near the site of Governor Berkeley's 17-century residence "Greenspring." See State Historical Marker W-35, on the present Williamsburg-Toano road.

9. Chastellux's evocation of the encounter at Spencer's Ordinary, June 25, 1781, between Lafayette's American cavalry and the Queen's Rangers under Lt. Col. John Graves Simcoe, prompted Simcoe to write a lengthy open letter to Chastellux, printed in the *Gentleman's Magazine*, 57 (1787), 36-39, soon after the appearance of Chastellux's book in English translation. To correct what he termed Chastellux's misrepresentations, Simcoe submitted an extract from his own journals describing the engagement. See also Simcoe's *Military Journal*, 227-37, map. Gottschalk discusses the conflicting claims in his *Lafayette and Close of Amer. Rev.*, 259-60.

10. *Gr.* The same who afterwards shot himself at Philadelphia. See previous notes [above, Pt. I, chap. 2, n. 7].

11. For other comments by Chastellux on the mockingbird, see above, Pt. I, chap. 2, Nov. 28, 1780, and n. 42.

12. *Ch.* Or rather the "painted plover," which is the lapwing of America. It differs from ours by its plumage, mixed with gray, white, and golden yellow; it differs also a little in its song, but it has the same shape and habits, and is absolutely the same species.

13. Newcastle was situated a mile or so east of the present bridge over the Pamunkey on the Richmond-Tappahanock road (U.S. Route 360). See State Historical Marker O-15, which recalls Patrick Henry's "call to arms" at Newcastle. Nothing remains of Newcastle today. Benson J. Lossing, who visited it in Dec. 1848, described it as "once a flourishing village, but now a desolation, only one house remaining upon its site"; *Field-Book*, II, 225. Chastellux was at Newcastle again on July 5-6, 1782, when in command of the French army on its northward march from Virginia; see map of the encampment at Newcastle by Louis-Alexandre Berthier, Berthier Papers, no. 39-6, Princeton Univ. Lib. A letter from Chastellux to Governor Har-

rison, dated from Newcastle, July 6, 1782, is printed in Stone, *French Allies*, 503.

14. *Ch.* The Author has since had an opportunity to see this garden, which answers the description given him of it, and is really most agreeable.

Gr. The gardens I have hitherto seen in France professedly laid out on the English model, are with great deference to the Author, but very *unsuccessful imitations* of the English style; those of the Comte d'Artois at Bagatelle, and of the Duke of Orleans at Mousseaux [Monceau] near Paris, are indeed no imperfect imitations of Mr. Sterling's in the comedy of the Clandestine Marriage, of the Spaniard's at Hampstead, of Bagnigge-wells, or a Common Councilman's retreat upon the Wandsworth road. They present a fantastic, and a crowded group of Chinese pagodas, gothic ruins, immoveable windmills, molehill-mounts, thirsty grass patches, dry bridges, pigmy serpentines, cockleshell cascades, and stagnant duck-pools. The gardens of the Tuileries and Marly, with all their undisguised, artificial labours, are at least noble, magnificent, and useful; their terraces are grand, and their lofty *berceaux* beautiful, and well adapted to the climate.

Ed. Chastellux's subsequent visit to Mr. Jones's garden was presumably in early July 1782, when the French army, under his command on its way northward, camped at Newcastle on July 5-6, 1782 and at Hanovertown (like Newcastle, now extinct) on July 8.

Mr. Jones was Thomas Jones (1726-86), whose estate called "Spring Garden" was located on the banks of the Pamunkey River, along present State Road 605, about two miles or so west of U.S. Route 360. The estate passed to Jones's son, Meriwether Jones, later to Judge Spencer Roane, and then to Judge John A. Meredith. After the latter's death it was cut up into a number of small properties. Judge Leon M. Bazile, of Ashland, Virginia, has kindly informed me that although the old brick house and barn have long since disappeared, there are remains of the terraces and that it has been reported to him that bulbs from the old gardens still bloom there in spring. *Virginia Magazine of History and Biography*, 5 (1898), 192-93; L. H. Jones, *Captain Roger Jones of London and Virginia* (Albany, 1891), 40-41; Rosewell Page, *Hanover County* ... (Richmond, 1926), 140; Robert B. Lancaster, *A Sketch of the Early History of Hanover County, Virginia* (Ashland, 1957), 5. Thus, little remains of this "garden laid out in the English style," except for Chastellux's passing reference to it. He of course uses the term English garden (*jardin anglais*), as his French contemporaries did, to describe the informal, naturalistic, artificially artless garden then in vogue in France, as distinguished from the traditional formal French garden exemplified in the creations of Le Nôtre at Versailles and elsewhere. Chastellux's mention of Mr. Jones's garden is of some interest as a record of a very early example of the "English garden" in America, and appears to have escaped the notice of the historians of early American gardens. Jefferson applied similar ideas (derived from his reading of Thomas Whately, *Observations on Modern Gardening* [London, 1770], and other theoreticians of the landscape style) in his early plans for Monticello; see Marie Kimball, *Jefferson, The Road to Glory, 1743 to 1776* (N.Y., 1943), 160-65.

15. Both the Hanover Courthouse—a notable example of 18th-century brick architecture, built in 1733—and the Hanover Tavern, across the road from it, survive today. The tavern is now used as a theater. Benson J. Lossing, who was here in 1848, mentions that he slept in the tavern de-

scribed by Chastellux and that "under shelter of the 'covered portico' mentioned by the marquis, I sketched the court-house"; *Field-Book*, II, 223, illus.

16. *Ch.* Lord Cornwallis was unquestionably the English general whose courage, talents, and activity, occasioned the greatest loss to the Americans; it is not astonishing therefore that he should not have inspired them with sentiments similar to those of his own troops, whose attachment, and admiration of his character, were unbounded. Yet they never accused him of rapine, nor even of interested views, and the complaints of Mr. Thilman only prove the sad consequences of war, in the course of which the English suffered more from want, in the midst of their success, than in their disaster; the former carrying them far from the fleet, and the latter obliging them to approach it. But the most painful of these consequences was the necessity which compelled a man of my Lord Cornwallis's birth and character, to conduct, rather than command, a numerous band of traitors and robbers, which English policy decorated with the name of *Loyalists.* This rabble preceded the troops in plunder, taking special care never to follow them in danger. Their progress was marked by fire, devastation, and outrages of every kind; they ravaged some part of America it is true, but ruined England, by inspiring her enemies with an irreconcilable hatred.

17. *Gr.* Colonel ["Light-Horse"] Harry Lee is a smart, active young man, first cousin to Mr. Arthur Lee, and Mr. William Lee, late alderman of London. He rendered very essential services to his country, particularly in the southern war. His corps was mounted on remarkably fine, high-priced horses, mostly half blood English stallions, and officered principally by his own family and relations. Had the war continued, there is every reason to believe that the American cavalry would have taken some consistence, and have become very formidable in the field; Mr. Tarleton received many severe checks in his exploits from the corps under Colonel [William] Washington, and that of Colonel Harry Lee. Towards the close of the war, he had to encounter an enemy very different from flying militia, and scattered bodies of broken, half disciplined infantry, of whom slaughter *may* be service, but conquest no honour.

18. See State Historical Marker E-18, on U.S. Route 1, which recalls that "Lafayette ... crossed the river west of this point, on May 29, 1781, while retreating before Cornwallis, who moved a few miles to the east."

19. "Offley" or "Offley House" (from a family surname) was situated in the "upper end" of Hanover Co. on Nelson family lands which lay between the Newfound and Little Rivers, tributaries respectively of the South Anna and the North Anna, which in turn join to form the Pamunkey. Nothing remains of Offley today, not even the "one gaunt chimney" mentioned in the Federal Writers' Program *Virginia Guide* (New York, 1940), 354. The site is to the west of County Road 601, leading from Coatesville to Hewlett, a mile or so before it descends to cross the Little River, where a mill attached to the Nelson plantation was once located. The locality is still designated as "Offley Mill" (erroneously given as "Ottley Mill" on some maps), although the mill itself, described as still in operation in 1926 (Page, *Hanover County*, 11), is today in ruins. Later generations of the Nelson family lived at "Oakland" some miles to the south of Offley—among them the writer Thomas Nelson Page, some of whose stories are laid in this region.

In his biography of his brother (*Thomas Nelson Page, A Memoir of a Virginia Gentleman*, [N. Y., 1923], 11), Rosewell Page related that certain of the luxuriantly-blooming roses at "Oakland" were known in the family as "Offley roses." See also Robert A. Lancaster, Jr., *Historic Virginia Homes and Churches* (Phila., 1915), 279-81.

20. *Ch.* To "press" horses, wagons, even men, is to order them for some service, instead of requesting them by mutual agreement. "Pressing" sailors, for example, is familiar to all.

21. Thomas Nelson, Jr. (1738-87), signer of the Declaration of Independence, had succeeded Thomas Jefferson as wartime governor of Virginia; he remained in office only from June to Nov. 1781. Nelson was followed by Benjamin Harrison, whom Chastellux met during the present journey, at Richmond, Apr. 26, 1782.

22. *Rose et Colas* was an operetta by Michel-Jean Sedaine, with music by Pierre-Alexandre Monsigny, first performed in Paris in 1764; in it Rose desperately tries to send her obdurate father, Mathurin, on imaginary errands, so that Colas, her young lover, may visit her.

23. Thomas Nelson's house in Yorktown, still standing in the center of the town, is one of the notable landmarks of the place. For a description and photographs see Thomas Waterman, *The Mansions of Virginia, 1706-1776* (Chapel Hill, 1946).

24. The "degrees of relationship" may be found in Richard C. M. Page, *Genealogy of the Page Family in Virginia, Also a condensed account of the Nelson ... Families*, 2d ed. (N. Y., 1893).

25. The father of the Taliaferro [pronounced Tolliver, as Chastellux wrote it] girls was Col. Richard Taliaferro, whose house, "Powhatan," was situated about four miles southwest of Williamsburg, near Five Forks, James City Co. The house, although gutted by fire during the Civil War and subsequently rebuilt within the old walls, is still standing. It was built about 1730-50 by this Richard Taliaferro's father, another Richard Taliaferro (1705-79), who was also architect and builder of the house in Williamsburg known as the "George Wythe House," from the name of Taliaferro's son-in-law who later occupied it. Waterman, *Virginia Mansions*, 202, 217, 222, 420. The younger Richard Taliaferro's daughter Mary married Judge William Nelson (1754-1813).

26. "Secretary" Thomas Nelson (*ca.* 1716-82), was the uncle of General and Governor Thomas Nelson, Jr., owner of "Offley."

27. Secretary Nelson's house—not to be confused with that of his nephew (see above, n. 23)—was on the eastern edge of the town, close to the battle-field. It is no longer standing; a marker indicates the site. See map, "Old Houses and Other Places of Interest in the 'Town of York,'" in Hatch, Jr., *Yorktown*, 46.

28. *Ch.* "Flag," *pavillon* in French, applies strictly speaking to flags of truce and cartel-ships sent at sea, but in English it means a drum, bugle, or anything else used to request a truce.

29. *Gr.* This calculation is much below that given by other writers, and I have reason to believe that it is considerably below the mark.

Ed. See Jefferson's *Notes on the State of Virginia*, Query VIII, "Population."

30. "Willis's Ordinary," according to Chastellux's distances, would have been somewhere on the eastern confines of Louisa Co., perhaps about where Bumpass or Buckner is situated today.

31. *Gr.* The prodigious quantity of French money brought into America by their fleets and armies, and the loans made to Congress, together with the vast return of dollars from the Havana, and the Spanish, Portuguese, and English gold which found its way into the country from the British lines, rendered specie very plentiful towards the conclusion of the war; and the arrival of the army of the Comte de Rochambeau was particularly opportune, as it happened at the very distressing crisis of the death of the paper currency. The French money alone in circulation in the United States, in the year 1782 was estimated, after very accurate calculations, at thirty-five millions of *livres*, or near a million and a half sterling. Although it is impossible to ascertain with any degree of precision the quantity of British money circulating in the revolted part of the continent, under the forms of Spanish, Portuguese, and English coin, yet some general idea may be entertained that the quantity was very considerable, from the following extract from the *seventh report of the commissioners of public accounts*, "We obtained by requisition from the office of the Paymaster-General of the forces, an account of the money issued to Messrs. Hartley & Drummond, pursuant to his Majesty's warrants, for the *extraordinary* services of his Majesty's forces serving in North America *from the* 1st of January, *1776, to the 31st of December, 1781.* This sum amounts to 10,083,863 *l.* 2*s.* 6*d.* There are two ways by which this money goes from these remitters into the hands of their agents: the one is by bills drawn by them on the remitters, which bills they receive the value for in America, and the remitters discharge when presented to them in London; the other is by sending out *actual cash*, whenever it becomes necessary to support the exchange, by increasing the quantity of current cash in the hands of the agents."

Now the votes of Parliament will show the reader, the vast sums *annually* granted to Messrs. Hartley & Drummond, for the specific purpose of purchasing Spanish and Portuguese gold alone, to supply "this quantity of current cash." Besides the vast exportation of English guineas; nor is it to be doubted that a great proportion of this supply found its way into the heart of the United States, in return for provisions, in payment of their captive armies, etc. etc. The British navy too is not included in this estimate. Great sums, it is true, returned to Britain directly or indirectly for goods, etc., but much specie remained incontestably in the country. With respect to the Spanish dollars from the Havana and the West Indies, no just calculation can be formed, but the amount must have been very considerable, as they appeared to me to circulate in the proportion of at least *three* or *four* to *one* of all the other coined specie.

When the Translator added this note, he had not seen *Lord Sheffield's* observations on the subject [*Observations on the Commerce of the American States* (London, 1783; Sabin, No. 32361)]. In these, however, he thinks his lordship discovers *deep prejudices*, mixed with much excellent reasoning and a great deal of truth.

32. General Rochambeau's journey was made in Feb. 1782, in the company of his son, the Vicomte de Rochambeau, of Victor Collot, and of Ludwig von Closen, one of his aides-de-camp. A record of the journey is preserved in the journal of Von Closen, who makes this comment on Johnson's public

house: "In the evening [Feb. 20, 1782] we slept at Louisa Courthouse, 30 miles from Offley, in the house of a certain Johnston, a former major in the militia. I can truthfully say that I had never seen a dirtier, more shocking, and more stinking barracks than that of this major, who, himself, was the greatest pig that the earth has produced, and lived with a wretched woman who wasted his property and left him to die of uncleanliness and misery. Not one of us could shut an eye throughout the night. The general, who alone could have a bed, was eaten by vermin, and we, who slept on straw, had our ears tickled by rats! Consequently, we decamped the next day, the 21st, at dawn." Acomb, ed., *Von Closen Journal*, 181-82.

33. The landlord of the tavern at Louisa Courthouse is identified as one Thomas Johnson (died *ca.* 1802-3) by Malcom H. Harris, *History of Louisa County, Virginia* (Richmond, 1936), 136-37. According to a petition of 1787, cited by Harris, there was then an attempt made to remove the courthouse to another location in the county; one of the arguments used by the opponents of the change was that Mr. Johnson would be unable to attend to his duties as justice of the peace elsewhere because he was too fat to travel. The court has since remained in the same locality, although the courthouse itself is now a modern structure erected in 1904-5. Mr. Johnson's tavern has fortunately not survived.

34. Chastellux is recalling (a bit inaccurately) the 17th chapter of Rabelais' Fifth Book, *Le Cinquième et dernier livre des faits et dits héroïques du bon Pantagruel*, where the country of "*Outre*" is described: "The people of the country, who by their looks seemed to be jolly fellows and boon companions, were all of them bloated and puffed up with fat.... Near the harbor there was a tavern, fine and stately in appearance, towards which people of all ages, sexes, and conditions were hastening, so that we thought some notable feast or banquet was under way. But we were told that they were invited to the bursting (*crevailles*) of mine host."

35. Boswell's Tavern (no longer an inn) is still standing near the junction of Routes U.S. 15 and State 22, Louisa Co., and the name still serves to designate this locality on the map. State Historical Marker W-207.

Chapter 2

Visit to Mr. Jefferson at Monticello

1. *Gr.* The difficulty of finding the road in many parts of America is not to be conceived except by those strangers who have travelled in that country. The roads, which are through the woods, not being kept in repair, as soon as one is in bad order, another is made in the same manner, that is, merely by felling the trees, and the whole interior parts are so covered, that without a compass it is impossible to have the least idea of the course you are steering. The distances too are so uncertain, as in every country where they are not measured, that no two accounts resemble each other. In the back parts of Pennsylvania, Maryland, and Virginia, I have frequently travelled thirty miles for ten, though frequently set right by passengers and negroes; but the great communications between the large towns, through all the well inhabited parts of the continent, are as practicable and easy as in Europe.

2. *Gr.* An Irishman, the instant he sets foot on American ground becomes, *ipso facto,* an American; this was uniformly the case during the whole of the late war. Whilst Englishmen and Scotsmen were regarded with jealousy and distrust, even with the best recommendations, of zeal and attachment to their cause, a native of Ireland stood in need of no other certificate than his dialect; his sincerity was never called in question, he was supposed to have a sympathy of suffering, and every voice decided as it were intuitively, in his favour. Indeed their conduct in the late revolution amply justified this favourable opinion; for whilst the Irish emigrant was fighting the battles of America by sea and land, the Irish merchants, particularly at Charleston, Baltimore, and Philadelphia, laboured with indefatigable zeal, and at all hazards, to promote the spirit of enterprise, to increase the wealth, and maintain the credit of the country; their purses were always open, and their persons devoted to the common cause. On more than one imminent occasion, Congress owed their existence, and America possibly her preservation to the fidelity and firmness of the Irish. I had the honor of dining with the Irish Society, composed of the steadiest whigs upon the continent, at the City Tavern in Philadelphia, on St. Patrick's day; the members wear a medallion suspended by a riband, with a very significant device, which has escaped my memory, but was so applicable to the American revolution, that until I was assured that it subsisted prior to that event, and had a reference only to the oppression of Ireland by her powerful sister, I concluded it to be a temporary illusion. General Washington, Mr. [John] Dickinson, and other leading characters are adopted members of this society, having been initiated by the ceremony of an exterior application of a whole bottle of claret poured upon the head, and a generous libation to liberty and good living, of as many as the votary could carry off.

Ed. The Irish Society mentioned by the Translator was the "Friendly Sons of St. Patrick," founded at Philadelphia in 1772; Stephen Moylan (who served as Chastellux's guide from Preakness to Trenton, above, Pt. I, chap. 2, Nov. 27, 1780, and n. 34) was the first president. The society's gold "medal," adopted in 1772, which members were required to purchase for three guineas and wear at meetings under penalty of a fine, was struck in London. The obverse depicts: Liberty in the center, joining the hands of Hibernia ("the usual figure of a female supported by a harp") and America ("an Indian with his quiver on his back and his bow slung"), with the motto "Unite." On the reverse: St. Patrick trampling on a snake, a cross in his hand, and dressed in his pontifical robes, with the motto "Hier" [Eire]. John H. Campbell, *History of the Friendly Sons of St. Patrick;* a continuation of the *History,* by Daniel J. Dougherty (Phila., 1952). Both works reproduce as a frontispiece the gold medal mentioned above by Grieve.

3. *Gr.* Considerable quantities of peltry are likewise brought from the back parts of North Carolina; and I have met with strings of horses laden with that article passing through Virginia to Philadelphia from the distance of six hundred miles.

4. *"elle brille seule en ces retraites,"* in Chastellux's French text—presumably a quotation or reminiscence of some poem.

5. Jefferson began building Monticello, on lands inherited from his father (Peter Jefferson, 1707/8-57), in 1767-70, but the house was not completed, in the form that the visitor sees today, until 1809. Chastellux's description, although brief, provides an important record of the progress made at the

date of his visit. It will be noted that several of his statements are in the future tense, indicating things planned but not completed, and suggesting that Jefferson not only described his intentions but probably showed some of his drawings to his guest. The "two porticoes" mentioned by Chastellux (*"un gros pavillon carré, dans lequel on entre par deux portiques, ornés de colonnes"*) might refer to one at the west (garden) entrance and to another at the east entrance, or again, to the two shown, one above the other, in several of Jefferson's extant early drawings of the west front. There is, however, some reason to believe that these drawings represent a plan that was never carried out—in which case the first interpretation would be the correct one. Frederick D. Nichols, *Thomas Jefferson's Architectural Drawings*, rev. ed. (Charlottesville, 1961), cover and figs. 1-4, check list nos. 47, 48, 49, 56, 57; James A. Bear, Jr., *Old Pictures of Monticello, An Essay in Historical Iconography* (Charlottesville, 1957), 5-7; Kimball, *Jefferson, The Road to Glory*, chap. 8.

6. Chastellux's mentions of her are among the comparatively few surviving glimpses of Jefferson's beloved wife, Martha Wayles Skelton Jefferson (born 1748), who died Sept. 6, 1782, a few months after Chastellux's visit. One of Jefferson's rare references to his bereavement is in his letter of Nov. 26, 1782, to Chastellux—"your friendly letters...found me a little emerging from that stupor of mind which had rendered me as dead to the world as she was whose loss occasioned it." Boyd *et al.*, eds., *Jefferson Papers*, VI, 203-4. The "charming children" whom Chastellux saw at Monticello were Martha ("Patsy"), then aged nine, who later married Thomas Mann Randolph, Jr.; and Mary ("Polly"), then three, who became Mrs. John Wayles Eppes. Lucy Elizabeth, born on May 8, 1782, lived only until Oct. 1784.

7. *Ch.* Mr. Jefferson having since had the misfortune of losing his wife, has at last yielded to the entreaties of his country, and accepted the place of Minister Plenipotentiary at the Court of France, and is now in Paris.

Ed. Jefferson had declined an appointment as commissioner to the French Court (with Franklin and Silas Deane), offered him by a resolution of the Continental Congress, Sept. 26, 1776; see his letter to J. Hancock, President of Congress, declining the post, Oct. 11, 1776, Boyd *et al.*, eds., *Jefferson Papers*, I, 524. He again declined a Congressional appointment (June 14, 1781) as peace commissioner; letter to Thomas McKean, President of Congress, Aug. 4, 1781, *ibid.*, VI, 113-14. On Nov. 26, 1782, Jefferson accepted another appointment (Nov. 12) as peace commissioner, and reached Philadelphia in late December, expecting to sail thence for France, perhaps on a French vessel in the company of Chastellux and Rochambeau (*ibid.*, VI, 210-18); however, news of the successfully negotiated peace treaty in turn led to a suspension of this appointment. Finally, on May 7, 1784, Jefferson was named (with Franklin and John Adams) one of the ministers to negotiate treaties of commerce with the European powers, left Boston in early July, and reached Paris early in August. He remained in Paris in this capacity until the following year, when he became Minister Plenipotentiary to the Court of France, a post that he held until the autumn of 1789.

8. Jefferson's early enthusiasm for the poetry of Ossian ("the rude bard of the North, the greatest poet that has ever existed") is reflected in a letter that he wrote, Feb. 25, 1773, to Charles Macpherson, an Edinburgh merchant, asking help in obtaining copies of the Gaelic originals of the poems. In reply

Macpherson transmitted to the young Virginian an ingeniously evasive reply from James Macpherson, the "translator" of the Gaelic bard. Boyd *et al.*, eds., *Jefferson Papers*, I, 96, 100-102. Concerning the far-reaching popularity and influence of Macpherson's fabrications throughout Europe, see Paul Van Tieghem, "Ossian et l'Ossianisme au XVIIIe siècle," *Le Préromantisme, Etudes d'histoire littéraire européenne*, 3 vols. (Paris, 1948), I, 195-287, 295-98. When Horace Walpole saw Chastellux at Baron d'Holbach's dinner table in Paris, Oct. 6, 1765, there was a "dispute on Richardson, Marivaux and Ossian"; see above, Vol. I, Introduction, n. 27.

9. Above, Pt. I, chap. 3, Nov. 30, 1780, and n. 10.

10. Several letters from Colonel Armand to the Governor of Virginia and others, extending from Nov. 1781 to Sept. 1782, are printed by W. P. Palmer, ed., *Calendar of Virginia State Papers...*, 11 vols. (Richmond, 1875-93), II and III. In a letter to Col. William Davies, from Charlottesville, Dec. 11, 1781, Armand mentions Dr. George Gilmer as one of those who has aided him in obtaining forage, and adds: "I and my family, which is pretty large, are quartered at his house, it being impossible to have lodging enough to divide much the officers." Dr. Gilmer at this time had a house in the village of Charlottesville; he subsequently resided at the estate known as "Pen Park," across the Rivanna from Monticello. From Armand's correspondence it may be surmised that one of the subjects of conversation at the dinner for Chastellux was—in addition to wolves—"the perpetual hindrance which the military encounter with from the civil authority" and the imminent transfer of the legion to Staunton, where better forage for the horses would be available; see also Jefferson's letter to Governor Benjamin Harrison, Apr. 13, 1782, Boyd *et al.*, eds., *Jefferson Papers*, VI, 175-76.

11. Chastellux apparently showed this description of the Charlottesville wolf to Buffon before he published his book, for we have Buffon's letter of Aug. 20, 1784, addressed to Chastellux from Montbard (his little mountain in Burgundy): "The description that you have sent me is indeed sufficient to suppose that the young animal in question comes from a dog and a she-wolf, and I shall mention it when I publish my little history of these dogs, or mongrel wolves, of which I have followed four successive generations over a period of fifteen years. I admire and respect wholeheartedly the unflagging zeal with which you pursue so discerningly the advancement of our knowledge and all that can do good of any kind." Lanessan, ed., *Oeuvres de Buffon*, XIV, 246-48.

12. *Ch.* I have recently been assured that when these animals grow old their horns are as large as those of the *cerf*, but their flesh certainly has the same taste as that of the *daim* in England.

Ed. The animal that Chastellux saw at Monticello was the Virginia or white-tailed deer (*Odocoileus virginianus*), the species common throughout the eastern United States. It is related to, but not the same as the various European *Cervidae* with which he was comparing it: the *daim* (fallow deer, *Dama dama*), the *chevreuil* (roe deer, *Capreolus capreolus*), and the *cerf* (red deer, hart, or stag, *Cervus elaphus*).

13. *Gr.* The rapid changes of the temperature of the air in America, and particularly to the southward, are apt to destroy the best European constitutions. In the middle of the hottest day in July and August, when the heat was so intolerable as almost to prevent respiration, I have frequently known the wind shift suddenly round to the northwest, attended with a blast,

so cold and humid, as to make it immediately necessary to shut all the doors and windows, and light large fires. It is impossible to conceive anything more trying for the human body, relaxed and open at every pore, from a continuance of burning heat, than this raw, piercing wind which blows over such immense boundless tracts of lakes and forests; but the melioration of the climate, even from the partial and comparatively inconsiderable destruction of the woods in many parts of the continent, is so rapid as to be strikingly perceptible even in the course of a very few years; and its salubrity in proportion to the progress of these improvements, will probably approach much nearer to those of Europe under the same latitudes.

Ed. Eighteenth-century thinking and theories on the relationship between climate and deforestation are surveyed by Gilbert Chinard in "The American Philosophical Society and the Early History of Forestry in America," *Amer. Phil. Soc., Proceedings*, 89 (1945), 444-88; the French version of the same essay is in his *L'Homme contre la Nature, Essais sur l'Histoire de l'Amérique* (Paris, 1949). Further remarks on the subject are in Dr. Coste's Williamsburg oration (see Pt. II, chap. 5, n. 17).

14. This passage concerning the prevailing winds at Williamsburg and at Monticello, and their modification due to the advance of settlement, attracted the attention of Jean-Baptiste Le Roy (1720-1800), member of the French Academy of Sciences and friend of Franklin, who wrote to Jefferson for further information. Le Roy's queries in turn called forth from Jefferson a detailed reply, which constitutes a substantial "scientific paper"—and incidentally, a footnote to this page of Chastellux's *Travels*. Le Roy's letter (Paris, Sept. 28, 1786) and Jefferson's reply (Paris, Nov. 13, 1786) are printed in Boyd *et al.*, eds., *Jefferson Papers*, X, 410-11, 524-30. See also Jefferson's *Notes on the State of Virginia*, Query VII, "Climate," which includes a table of the prevailing winds at Monticello and Williamsburg.

15. *Ch.* This discovery is owed to Dr. Franklin.

Ed. See Franklin to Joseph Priestley, on the effect of vegetation on noxious air, first printed in the latter's *Experiments on Air;* Smyth, ed., *Writings of Franklin*, I, 125-27, V, 551-52.

16. See above, this chap., n. 6.

17. Chastellux and Jefferson were to meet again: very briefly, in Philadelphia, in late Dec. 1782 and early Jan. 1783, on the eve of Chastellux's departure for France; and again, when Jefferson arrived in Paris in Aug. 1784. One of the first services that Chastellux rendered his American friend was to put him in touch with the Abbaye de Pentemont, the fashionable convent school where Jefferson's daughter Martha (and later, his other daughter, Mary) was a boarder during her sojourn in France. The correspondence between the two men, which continued until not long before Chastellux's death in 1788, is printed in Boyd *et al.*, eds., *Jefferson Papers*, VI-XI. Before he published the account of his journey in Virginia, Chastellux submitted the manuscript to Jefferson, who corrected a few errors in name or fact (which Chastellux incorporated into his final text), expressed his general approbation, but protested: "From this general approbation however you must allow me to except about a dozen pages in the earlier part of the book which I read with a continued blush from beginning to end, as it presented me a lively picture of what I wish to be, but am not. No, my dear Sir, the thousand millionth part of what you there say, is more than I deserve. It might perhaps have passed in Europe at the time you wrote it.

and the exaggeration might not have been detected. But consider that the animal is now brought there, and that every one will take his dimensions for himself. The friendly complexion of your mind has betrayed you into a partiality of which the European spectator will be divested. Respect to yourself therefore will require indispensably that you expunge the whole of those pages except your own judicious observations interspersed among them on Animal and physical subjects." (Jefferson to Chastellux, Paris, Sept. 2, 1785.) The protest went unheeded, merely eliciting the reply that Jefferson's protest itself deserved being printed as further evidence of the justice of Chastellux's portrayal of him! (Chastellux to Jefferson, Paris, Sept. 3, 1785).

A year or so later, when preparing during his walks in the Bois de Boulogne an essay called "Thoughts on English Prosody," which he apparently intended to present to Chastellux, Jefferson recalled that "among the topics of conversation which stole off like so many minutes the few hours I had the happiness of possessing you at Monticello, the Measure of English verse was one . . . we have again discussed on this side the Atlantic, a subject which had occupied us during some pleasing moments on the other." *Ibid.*, X, 498-99. After Chastellux's death and after Jefferson had returned to America, the latter received several communications from Chastellux's widow (*née* Plunkett). In 1795 (May 6), for example, she wrote of her reverse in fortunes due to the French Revolution and asked Jefferson to be "advocate and intercessor" with Congress for her son Alfred. In a reply written from Monticello, July 10, 1796, Jefferson explained that his friends in Congress assured him that no aid could be expected from that source, but added: "It would have given me great pleasure to have been able to obtain for the family of my deceased friend, General Chastellux, the aids which unexpected events have occasioned them to want. But I have not been fortunate enough to succeed in my wishes. I had for him a very sincere esteem, which had commenced with our acquaintance here, and had grown under a very intimate intercourse with him in France. His loss was one of the events which the most sensibly afflicted me while there: and his memory continues very dear to me." Madame Chastellux wrote again in 1803 (June 5, June 30) outlining her plan of assigning to her son her own personal claim, "as a direct and legal descendant of Lord Baltimore," for indemnification from the state of Maryland; but this further plea appears to have been unanswered. Jefferson noted in the margin of a letter received from Lafayette enclosing Madame Chastellux's communications: "Alfred Chastellux, son to General Chastellux and his only child in right of his mother Mary Plunkett, great granddaughter to Miss Talbot, Lord Baltimore second daughter direct, and legitimate descendant of Lord Baltimore; is he not entitled in *justice* to claim an indemnification as the legal heir of him who laid the foundations of the state of Maryland." Lafayette to Jefferson, June 4, 1803, Gilbert Chinard, ed., *The Letters of Lafayette and Jefferson* (Baltimore and Paris, 1929), 222-23.

Chapter 3

Across the Mountains to the Natural Bridge; and the Journey back to Powhatan Courthouse

1. These observations provoked Brissot de Warville's ire, and form the basis for his claim, outlined in his *Examen critique*, 102 ff., that Chastellux had insulted the "dignity of man."

2. *Gr.* The Marquis de Chastellux has distinguished himself very honorably in the literary world by several productions, but particularly by his treatise *De la Félicité Publique*, wherein he breathes the generous, enlightened language of philanthropy and freedom. He was chosen a member of the French Academy at a very early age, by dint of his own merit, and not by a court mandate, or intrigue, and was, *if I mistake not*, when very young, in correspondence with, and a favorite of, the illustrious Pope Ganganelli. He has lately translated into French, Colonel Humphreys' poem, *The Campaign*, mentioned in the notes to the first part of this work [above, Pt. I, chap. 4, n. 12].

Ed. Giovanni Vincenzo Ganganelli (1705-74) was Pope, under the name of Clement XIV, from 1769 to 1774. He enjoyed considerable prestige among the philosophers for his abolition of the Jesuit order. Chastellux may have seen him during his Italian journey in 1773.

3. *Ch.* The riflemen are a Virginia militia, composed of the inhabitants of the mountains, who are all expert hunters, and make use of rifle guns (*carabines rayées*). Towards the end of the war little use was made of them, as it was found that the difficulty of reloading the rifles more than offset the advantages derived from their accurate aim.

Gr. The Americans [in 1777] had great numbers of riflemen in small detachments on the flank of General Burgoyne's army, many of whom took post on high trees *in the rear of their own line*, and there was seldom a minute's interval of smoke without officers being taken off by a single shot. Captain Green of the 31st regiment, aide-de-camp to General Phillips, was shot through the arm by one of those marksmen as he was delivering a message to General Burgoyne. After the Convention, the commanding officer of the riflemen informed General Burgoyne that the shot was meant for him; and as Captain Green was seen to fall from his horse, it was for some hours believed in the American army that General Burgoyne was killed. His escape was owing to the captain's having laced furniture to his saddle, which made him to be mistaken for the General. General Burgoyne says, in his narrative, that not an Indian could be brought within sound of a rifle shot.

4. *Gr.* Lord Cornwallis, in his answer to Sir Henry Clinton's narrative [*An Answer to that Part of the Narrative of Lieutenant-General Sir Henry Clinton, K.B. which relates to the conduct of Lieutenant-General Earl Cornwallis, during the Campaign in North-America, in the Year 1781* (London, 1783; Sabin, No. 16811)], gives the following state of his army before the defeat of Tarleton, and subsequent to that event, from which we may authenticate the loss of men, and deduce the importance of Morgan's victory to America. . . . [Statistical tables copied from Cornwallis's *Answer*, p. 53, according to which the total rank and file of his army was on Jan. 15, 1781, before the battle of the Cowpens, 3224; and on Feb. 1, 1781, i.e., after Tarle-

ton's defeat, 2440.] Total loss with the detachment of artillery 800 out of 1050 men, the real number of Tarleton's force.

The names of the regiments that have no numbers annexed to them in the last column are those which were totally destroyed, that is, killed, wounded, or taken, in the battle of Cowpens, on the 17th of January, between Morgan and Tarleton. Lord Cornwallis in his Gazette account, immediately after the affair, stated the loss only at 400, but the truth at length appears, when the purposes of misrepresentation are at an end, and the detail becomes necessary to the general's own honor.

Lord Cornwallis in his account of Tarleton's defeat, mentions a very honorable circumstance for the corps of artillery, but which was by no means unexamined by this brave body of men, in several actions in America: he says, "In justice to the detachment of the royal artillery, I must here observe that no terror could induce them to abandon their guns, and they were *all* either killed or wounded in the defence of them." [*Answer*, 3-4.]

5. Morgan's report on the Battle of the Cowpens (South Carolina, Jan. 17, 1781), addressed to General Nathanael Greene and dated from "Camp near Cain Creek," Jan. 19, 1781, is reprinted in James Graham, *The Life of General Daniel Morgan* ... (N. Y. and Cincinnati, 1856), Appendix C, 467-70, and elsewhere. It was widely circulated at the time and reached the French army in its winter quarters at Newport as soon as Feb. 20. Under this date, Lt. Louis-Alexandre Berthier (one of Rochambeau's aides) noted in his journal the arrival of the report, which he translated and transcribed *in extenso;* Berthier, *Journal,* 44-47. Chastellux's interest in the affair at the Cowpens thus dated from that time, and it must have been a frequent subject of professional discussion among the French tacticians. The evidence that Chastellux later collected from the rifleman, while riding towards Rockfish Gap (subsequently verified in a conversation with Morgan, n. 6, below), concerning the unpremeditated character of the "retrograde movement" in the battle, is in itself a significant historical contribution to the story of the Cowpens (although generally overlooked by historians). The keen interest aroused by the Cowpens affair as a feat of military prowess is further reflected in the action of the Continental Congress in voting special medals, commemorating their respective shares in the victory, to Gen. Daniel Morgan, Col. William Washington, and Col. John Eager Howard. The three Cowpens medals were executed in Paris, the one for Morgan by Augustin Dupré, the two others by Benjamin Duvivier; "Notes on American Medals Struck in France," Boyd *et al.,* eds., *Jefferson Papers,* XVI, 53-79 and illus., v-vi, viii-xvii. A recent recapitulation of Morgan's career, including a study of the Cowpens, is available in Don Higginbotham, *Daniel Morgan, Revolutionary Rifleman* (Chapel Hill, 1961). Higginbotham does not cite Chastellux in his discussion of the "retrograde movement," 139-40, but definitely recognizes its spur-of-the-moment character.

6. *Ch.* Since this journal was written, the author has had occasion to see General Morgan. He is a man of about fifty, tall, and of truly martial mien. The services he rendered during the war were very numerous, so that he made his way very rapidly. It was claimed that he had been a wagoner and indeed, this same ignorance of customs and language has caused it to be said that another general had been a farmer because he was engaged in agriculture before the war; and another a butcher, because he was in the cattle trade. General Morgan's business was cartage: he was engaged in the

transport of goods which were carted in wagons overland, and he often headed these little convoys himself. The first time I had an opportunity of seeing him, I was commanding the French troops (in the absence of General Rochambeau, who had gone ahead to Philadelphia) during their march from Williamsburg to Baltimore. I was then at Colchester [Va., July 16, 1782], where the first division of the troops had just arrived, after having crossed in boats a small river [Occoquan Creek] that flows near this town. The baggage train and the artillery had taken another route to reach a rather difficult ford. General Morgan met the baggage train when it was engaged in a narrow gorge, and finding that the wagoners were not managing very well, he stopped and showed them how they should drive their wagons. After having put everything in order, he called at my quarters and had dinner with me. The simplicity of his bearing and the nobility of his manners reminded me of those ancient Gallic or Germanic chiefs, who, when at peace with the Romans, came to visit them and offer assistance. He expressed great attachment to the French nation, and great admiration for the fine appearance of our troops; he kept looking at them, and frequently repeated that he would be happy to serve his whole life in brilliant and numerous armies. It can easily be imagined that his host asked him many questions, particularly concerning the affair at the Cowpens. His reply confirmed the account of my rifleman; but he candidly admitted that the retrograde movement he had made had not in any way been premeditated: his troops had been intimidated when the English, with less order than confidence, had advanced to attack them; seeing that they had not broken ranks, he let them retreat a hundred paces, and then commanded them to halt and face the enemy, just as if he had himself previously ordered this retrograde movement.

Although these more recent and more authoritative notions might render the comments found in the above text superfluous, it has seemed appropriate to keep them there, because, on the one hand, they are not uninteresting to the Soldier, and on the other, because they can teach Philosophers and Critics to mistrust those who have written history—especially those who, like Livy, Dionysius of Halicarnassus, and all such eloquent and discursive historians, delight in multiplying and varying their descriptions of battles, or what is still worse, when, like Frontinus, Pollio, and the other compilers, they borrow from the Historians the deeds and stratagems of war which they are striving to collect.

General Morgan had not served since the affair at the Cowpens; he was residing in Fairfax [Frederick] County, and was living on lands which he had acquired or increased, while awaiting the occasion that would give him some command.

Gr. General Morgan by thus dexterously availing himself of the circumstances of his very critical position, has perhaps more real merit, than if he had really preconceived the manoeuvre which has given him so much fame; a manoeuvre, from which, unless justified by a necessity such as his, he had no right to expect success, in the face of a *skilful* enemy; but Tarleton never was a *commander*.

7. *Ch.* Colonel Tarleton has given so many proofs not only of courage but of boldness and intrepidity, that all military men must applaud the praise bestowed upon his valor. It were only to be wished that he had always made good use of those qualities, and that he had shown himself as humane and sensitive, as he was brave and determined. The design of these reflec-

tions is then to show how much the English, in this war, have been obliged to swell their successes and diminish their defeats: the more rare the successes became, the more they were disposed to solemnize them. Howe and Burgoyne were disgraced for not conquering America, while others have been promoted for gaining some trifling advantages.

8. *Gr.* Earl Cornwallis in his letter in the London Gazette of March 31st, 1781, says that Morgan had with him, "By the best accounts he could get, about 500 men, Continental and Virginia state troops, 103 cavalry under Colonel Washington, and 6 or 700 militia; but that body is so fluctuating, that it is impossible to ascertain its number *within some hundreds,* for three days following." This account seems to have been intended to qualify the defeat of Tarleton, who was a great favorite; but the fact is nearly as the Marquis de Chastellux states it, for Morgan had very few continentals with him, and his whole body did not exceed 800 men.

9. *Gr.* The *returns* of Lord Cornwallis' army taken a fortnight before the battle, were 2213; the returns seventeen days after it, 1723; his loss consequently may be stated at about the difference, 490. Several attempts have been likewise made to prove that General Greene had with him at Guilford an army of 9 or 10,000 men, but Lord Cornwallis himself, in his letter to Lord Rawdon, dated Camp at Guilford, March 17, 1781, and published in the London Gazette of May 10, 1781, expressly says, "General Greene having been *very considerably* reinforced from Virginia by *eight months' men and militia,* and having collected *all the militia of this province,* advanced with an army of *about* 5 or 6000 men, and 4 six pounders, to this place." From this *unexpected* account we may collect pretty clearly the indifferent composition of General Greene's force, and must render justice to the fairness of the French General's detail which calls them 5000 men, *half* militia, *half* continentals; and states the conquering army *only* at 1800 men. The Translator hopes the reader will not find these comparisons superfluous, as such scrutinies tend to elucidate the interesting events of an ever memorable revolution, and to enlighten history. General [Horatio] Gates showed me, at his house in Virginia, a letter from General [Nathanael] Greene, wherein he took occasion in the most liberal manner to reconcile him to the unfortunate affair of *Camden,* by a detail of the bad conduct of *the same militia,* at the battle of *Guilford,* the *Eutaws,* etc. He touched upon the matter with a delicacy and candor which did equal honor to his sensibility and judgment. Such a tribute of justice from the officer who had superseded him in his command could not but be highly grateful to General Gates, possessing as he does, in the most eminent degree, the warlike virtues, a pure disinterested attachment to the cause of freedom, and all the general susceptibility of an amiable private gentleman. Whilst under a cloud himself, I heard him with admiration uniformly expatiate with all the distressed warmth of public virtue on the successes of other generals, and instead of jealous repining and disgust, pay his tribute of applause to the merits even of those he could not love, and prognosticate, with confidence, the final success of America. It was with real joy therefore, that I saw his honor vindicated by the deliberate voice of Congress, himself restored to his former rank, and that harmony which never should have been disturbed, renewed between this true patriot and General Washington, under whom I left him second in command at the camp at Verplanck's on the North River in October, 1782.

Ed. For other details about Grieve's visit to the American army at

Verplanck's Point, on the Hudson, in Oct. 1782, see above, Pt. I, chap. 2, n. 23; and below, Pt. III, chap. 1, n. 1. Concerning General Horatio Gates (with whom Grieve appears to have been on friendly terms, as he was with the other ousted generals), see Pt. I, chap. 1, nn. 63 and 65.

10. Chastellux's bird seems to be the ruffed grouse (*Bonasa umbellus*), which is still called a "pheasant" in some parts of the South, and a "partridge" in the North.

11. Chastellux is here fording the South River, a tributary of South Fork of the Shenandoah, which in turn flows into the Potomac.

Gr. In travelling from Fredericktown to Leesburgh, in a single-horse chaise for one person, called in America a *sulky*, the shafts of my carriage broke about a mile from the Potomac, on the Maryland side, and I was reduced to the necessity, having no servant, of leaving it with all my papers, money, fire-arms, etc. and of mounting my horse in search of assistance. Night was coming on in a most difficult country, to which I was an utter stranger, and not even a negro hut was to be met with. In these circumstances I approached the Potomac, on the other side of which I discovered a smoke in the woods, which gave me hopes of its proceeding from a house, but the river was near a mile broad, and my horse barely fourteen hands high. Whilst I was thus standing in suspense, two travellers arrive on horseback and push into the river, a little higher up. I flew to follow them, but scarcely had they advanced one hundred yards before they returned, declaring it not fordable, and, to add to my distress, they assured me that I was at a great distance from any house on that side, but, on the other, I should find an ordinary kept by a Scotsman. They excused themselves from assisting me on the plea of urgent business, and left me with the consoling assurance that the river might possibly be fordable, though they who were inhabitants of the country, did not choose to venture it. Perceiving the bottom of a good gravel, and free from rocks, I attempted the passage as soon as they left me, and in about twenty dangerous and irksome minutes reached the other side, where I obtained the cheerful aid of two native negroes at the Scotsman's hut, for it was no better, and recrossing the river, went in search of my broken carriage, which we found in security. It was ten o'clock before I passed the river a third time, always up to my waist, and reached my quarters for the night, where at least I met with as hospitable a reception as the house afforded; but the consequence of this adventure, wherein I was successively wet and dry three times, in the hot month of July, was a fever and ague which tormented me for five months.

At Alexandria, about fifty miles lower down, the Potomac rolls its majestic stream with sublimity and grandeur, sixty-gun ships may lie before the town, which stands upon its lofty banks, commanding, to a great extent, the flatter shore of Maryland. This town, which stands above 200 miles from the sea, is rapidly on the increase, and from the lavish prodigality of nature, cannot fail of becoming one of the first cities of the new world.

12. Mrs. Teaze's inn was in the hamlet which eventually grew into the city of Waynesboro.

13. *Gr.* The Marquis' distress on this occasion, reminds me naturally of a similar, but still worse situation in which I found myself on my return from America towards the end of the war, with four officers of the army of the Comte de Rochambeau. Our captain being obliged suddenly to take advantage of one of those violent north-westers which blow in December,

to get clear of the coast, beset with New-York Privateers, forgot all his crockery ware, so that in default of plates, mugs, etc. we were obliged, during a winter's voyage of seven weeks, to apply two tin jugs we had purchased to drink our cider, to every use; and, in spite of my representations, even to some purposes I am unwilling to repeat; for in bad weather, these excellent *land-officers* could not be prevailed upon to look on deck.

14. Mr. Smith's was in Greenville, Augusta Co.; a brick structure known as Smith's Tavern, presumably of a slightly later date, is one of the landmarks of the town. Federal Writers' Program, *Virginia Guide*, 427.

15. The mill was on Marl Creek, which forms part of the boundary between Augusta and Rockbridge Cos.; the miller's name is still applied to the locality, which is now known as Steeles Tavern (post office in Augusta Co., U.S. Route 11).

16. Lubin is the hero of "Annette et Lubin," one of the *Contes Moraux* (1761) by Chastellux's brother Academician, Jean-François Marmontel. This once immensely popular tale of an innocent shepherd and shepherdess gained still further fame as an operetta, in a succession of musical versions by J. B. Laborde, Benoît Blaise, Charles Dibdin, and others.

17. Gianbattista Guarini (1538-1612), *Il Pastor Fido* (1590), Act II, Scene 5. Richard Fanshawe's translation (*The Faithfull Shepherd*, 1647): "One fountain is her looking-glasse, her drink/ Her bath; and if she's pleas'd, what others think/ It matters not; she heeds not blazing starres/ That threaten mighty ones: warres or no warres,/ It is all one to her; her battlement/ And shield is that she's poor: *Poor, but content!*"

18. It is a bit difficult at this point to determine exactly Chastellux's itinerary, part of which he covered after dark. The map appended to the 1786 edition of his *Travels*, though somewhat sketchy, nevertheless provides some essential indications. The following hypothesis has been proposed by William H. Gaines, Jr.: The mileage given here by Chastellux—38 miles from Steeles Tavern to "some houses," thence 6 more to Paxton's, or a total of 44 miles—indicates that he must have traveled well beyond Lexington and that Paxton's was in the vicinity of present Buchanan. His description of the topography near Paxton's sounds like the James at Buchanan: "a very high mountain" could be Purgatory Mountain in that vicinity, and the "very steep banks" also fit here. Chastellux was presumably mistaken, however, when he said he crossed the James to Paxton's; he probably crossed Purgatory Creek, a large stream which flows into the James near Buchanan. The "Great Road" or "Philadelphia Road" (see map in F. B. Kegley, *Kegley's Virginia Frontier* [Roanoke, Va., 1938], 138) passed several miles to the west of Natural Bridge, and not directly over it as does present U.S. Route 11; thus, as shown on his map, Chastellux would have made a jog back to Natural Bridge when he went there next day. Finally, it may be pointed out that a settlement called Pattonsburg, of which Joseph Paxton and Joseph Paxton, Jr. were among the trustees, was legally established in 1788 along the Great Road at the point where it crossed the James, i.e., in the vicinity of present Buchanan; William Waller Hening, *The Statutes at Large ... of Virginia*, 13 vols. (Richmond, N. Y., Phila., 1809-23), XII, 673-74. Nine Paxtons are listed as taxpayers of this region in 1782; Oren F. Morton, *A History of Rockbridge County, Virginia* (Staunton, 1920), 269, 348-49, 362, 368, 375, 518-21.

19. *Gr.* It was a singular sight for an European to behold the situation of the negroes in the southern provinces during the war, when clothing was extremely scarce. I have frequently seen in Virginia, on visits to gentlemen's houses, young negroes and negresses running about or basking in the courtyard naked as they came into the world, with well characterized marks of perfect puberty; and young negroes from sixteen to twenty years old, with not an article of clothing, but a loose shirt, descending half way down their thighs, waiting at table where were ladies, without any apparent embarrassment on one side, or the slightest attempt at concealment on the other.

20. *Gr.* The South Carolina gentlemen with whom I was acquainted, assured me, that the inhabitants of the back parts of that state, which is one of the most unhealthy on the continent, are a vigorous and beautiful race of people, and possess all that hale ruddiness which characterizes the natives of northern climates.

21. *Gr.* Great attention is paid to the breed of blood horses to the southward, and particularly in Virginia, and many second rate race horses are annually sent from England to serve as stallions. There were two or three in the stables of one [Jacob] Bates, near Philadelphia, which I had seen win plates in England. This Bates is a native of Morpeth in Northumberland, and went to America before the war to display feats of horsemanship, but he had the good fortune to marry a widow possessed of five hundred pounds a year, and is now master of a most beautiful villa on the banks of the Delaware, four or five miles from Philadelphia, still following, however, the occupation of breeding and selling horses, and keeping stallions, for there are no resources for idleness in that country.

Ed. Jacob Bates married Hannah Hopkins at Christ Church in Philadelphia, Feb. 3, 1781; she inherited from her father, Robert Hopkins, a portion of his estate in the Richmond District, then outside the city limits. A Hopkins house in "Point No Point or Richmond," not far from the mouth of Frankford Creek, is shown on the 1750 Scull and Heap map of Philadelphia and vicinity. Bates had traveled widely in the colonies prior to the Revolution (Boston, New York, Philadelphia, Charleston, etc.); advertisements for his "feats of horsemanship" appear in the newspapers of the time. An account of his visit to New York in 1773 is reprinted in George C. D. Odell, *Annals of the New York Stage* (N. Y., 1927), I, 175-76. The Editor is indebted to Mrs. F. S. Roach and to Mr. J. L. Lemay for information about Jacob Bates.

22. *Gr.* Virginia currency. About fifteen shillings sterling. The difference of currency is one of the most puzzling and disagreeable circumstances for a stranger in America, the value of *the pound* varying in every state; an inconvenience which existed under the British government, and I am afraid, is still likely to subsist.

23. *Gr.* Stopping one day at a smith's shop near Winchester, in the interior of Virginia, I found one of the workmen to be a Scotch Highlander in his Gaelic dress, and soon saw several more returning from harvest; these men had been soldiers, and were then prisoners, but they were all peaceable industrious laborers, and I could not find that any of them thought of returning to the barren hills of Caledonia. General Gates had several of them in his employ [at "Traveller's Rest"], and they were dispersed over the whole country, where they appeared completely naturalized and happy. I afterwards saw many of them working at mills, and as quarry-men on the

picturesque banks of that sublime river the Susquehanna, a circumstance which transported my imagination to the well known borders of the Tay, and of Loch Lomond.

24. *Gr.* I am apt to think that the experience of every person who has visited North America, as well as my own country, will rise in judgment against this observation of the author; for my part, were I searching for a general characteristic of that part of the Continent, I should not scruple to distinguish it, κατ' εξοχήν, by the name of *the country of the curious.* Wherever you bend your course, to whomsoever you address yourself, you are indispensably subject to a good humored, inoffensive, but *mighty* troublesome inquisition. Do you inquire the road? You are answered by a question, "I suppose you come from the eastward, don't you?" Oppressed with fatigue, hunger, and thirst, and drenched perhaps with rain, you answer shortly in the affirmative, and repeat your inquiry.

"Methinks you are in a mighty haste—What news is there to the east-ward?" The only satisfaction you can obtain till you have opened your real, or pretended budget of news, and gratified the demander's curiosity. At an inn, the scrutiny is more minute; your name, quality, the place of your departure, and object of your journey, must all be declared to the good family in some way or other (for their credulity is equal to their curiosity), before you can sit down in comfort to the necessary refresh-ment. This curious spirit is intolerable in the eastern states, and I have heard Dr. Franklin, who is himself a Bostonian, frequently relate with great pleasantry, that in travelling when he was young, the first step he took for his tranquillity, and to obtain immediate attention at the inns, was to antici-pate inquiry, by saying, "My name is Benjamin Franklin, I was born at Boston, am a printer by profession, am travelling to Philadelphia, shall return at such a time, and have no news—Now what can you give me for dinner?" The only cause which can be assigned for the Author's error in this respect, is the state in which he travelled, his being a foreigner, and the facility of obtaining information from the persons of his retinue.

Ch. (note added to 2d ed., 1788). The English Translator, who has resided several years [!] in North America and knows it very well indeed, here makes a remark with which the Author must disagree. He asserts that the Americans are the most curious people he has ever seen.... [Chastellux summarizes Grieve's note and his anecdote about Franklin] The Author of these Travels had also heard this jest in America, but as it concerned only the inhabitants of Connecticut, he did not conclude from it that curiosity was the failing of all Americans. The fact of the matter is that he in general found them much more indifferent than curious; which only goes to show that an observation made by one traveler can be missed by another, no matter how attentive. As for the negligence and carelessness of the Vir-ginians—a characteristic quite the opposite of curiosity—a very convincing example of it can be given here. It happened several times during the sojourn of the French army at Williamsburg that important letters from the north or south addressed to M. de Rochambeau were entrusted to travelers, as the post was not yet regularly established and the Americans very often lacked the money necessary to pay couriers. The travelers who were not going specifically to Williamsburg usually left these letters in some inn situated at a crossroad, requesting that they be forwarded to their destination at the first opportunity. But it often happened that the letters remained whole months on the mantelpiece, without anyone thinking of sending them along, even though there had been frequent opportunities. Finally some honest traveler noticed them and took charge of them out of pure kindness and without being asked to do so. Consequently, after having several times had proofs of this negligence, M. de Rochambeau adopted the course of dispatching express riders whenever he had important letters to send.

25. Although Chastellux here appears to accept the theory that the Natural Bridge had been "rent" asunder by some sort of earthquake or "convulsion" (a theory that he must have discussed with Jefferson at Monticello a few days earlier), and to reject the hypothesis of erosion by the action of the waters, he later reached the conclusion that this natural wonder could only be attributed to "the action of the waters." His revised ideas are outlined hereinafter, Pt. II, Appendix A, "Description of the Natural Bridge."

26. *Ch.* See the description and plans at the end of this Journal [Pt. II, Appendix A, below, and illustrations in this volume].

27. Chastellux's text reads "Grisby," but Grigsby must be the correct form of the name. His guide and host was perhaps James Grigsby, who bought land on Buffalo Creek in 1779, who held a tavern license at this time, and who is listed as a taxpayer in Rockbridge Co. in 1782. Morton, *History of Rockbridge County,* 256, 372, 463, 465, 489.

28. *Gr.* The quality of the American oak is found by repeated experience to be by no means equal to, or so durable as that of Britain. A general survey of the American woods was taken by order of the government of England, previous to the war, and the different qualities ascertained by the surveyors, who, on their general report, gave the preference to the southern oak on the Appalachians, and in the interior of Georgia and Florida; but in the English yards, even the Dantzig plank, which grows in Silesia, and that of Stettin, is still preferred to the American.

29. *Gr.* Conflagrations which take their rise in this manner, sometimes spread to a prodigious extent in America, in the morasses, as well as in the woods; in travelling from Easton on the Delaware over the Musconetcong Mountains in the Upper Jersey, in 1782, I saw immense tracts of country lying in ashes from one of these accidental fires; and, during the same summer, Philadelphia was sometimes covered with smoke, from a vast morass which had taken fire in the Jerseys, and kept burning to a great depth from the surface, and for an extent of many miles around, for several months; the progress of which could not be stopped by the large trenches dug by the labor of the whole country, nor until it was extinguished by the autumnal rains.

30. *Gr.* The Author means the soldiers who served in Canada against the French in the war before the last [i.e., the Seven Years' War]. Kentucky is at present peopled by above fifty thousand settlers, and is on the point of being admitted into the union, as an independent state. Kentucky is a settlement on the creek, or rather river of that name, which falls into the Ohio, and is 627¾ miles distant from Fort Pitt; but is extending in every direction over a tract of the finest and most fertile country in the world; and as it is from the interior settlements of this vast country, that America will derive her future greatness, and establish new empires to rival, and perhaps

outdo the ancient world, I hope I shall be pardoned for transcribing the following short but interesting account of the banks of the Ohio from Captain Hutchins' Topographical Description of that country, accompanying his maps. . . .

Ed. Grieve here gives a fairly extensive quotation from Thomas Hutchins, *A Topographical Description of Virginia, Pennsylvania, Maryland, and North Carolina comprehending the Rivers Ohio, Kenhawa* . . . (London, 1778; Sabin, No. 34054), 7-8, 12-18; pp. 78-79, 84-90 in Frederick C. Hicks's well-annotated reprint (Cleveland, 1904). Included in the quotation from Hutchins are Hutchins's own quotations from Lewis Evans, Capt. Henry Gordon, and an anonymous correspondent of the Earl of Hillsborough (who was actually Benjamin Franklin). At the end of the long quotation—well-chosen to depict the attractions of Kentucky lands—Grieve adds by way of conclusion his own remark: "Here surely is a rational and ample field for the well regulated imagination of the philosopher and politician!!!"

31. *Gr.* Twelve or thirteen shillings, Virginia currency: 8¼ shillings, English.

32. Members of the Greenlee family figure among the early settlers of this region. The owner of the ferry was perhaps John Greenlee. Morton, *History of Rockbridge County*, 254-56, 352, 366, 372, 489. The name still designates the village and post office of Greenlee, Rockbridge Co., situated on the James River along State Route 130, about half way between Natural Bridge and Glasgow, and not far from Natural Bridge Station.

33. Chastellux's route over the mountains presumably went by Petit's or "Poteet's" Gap. This is several miles south of the river passage at Balcony Falls (U.S. Route 501) and well to the north of the present Buchanan-Bedford crossing (State Route 43); there is no through road here today, the area being part of the Jefferson National Forest. Jefferson went over Petit's Gap when he traveled from Poplar Forest to the Natural Bridge in 1815; Edward Dumbauld, *Thomas Jefferson, American Tourist* (Norman, Okla., 1946), 194.

34. Chastellux's map also shows three Peaks of Otter, although there are in fact only two (Sharp [or Round] Top and Flat Top). He was perhaps led in error, retrospectively, by the Joshua Fry and Peter Jefferson Map of Virginia, etc. (1754 and subsequent editions), which likewise shows three peaks. Thomas Jefferson (Peter Jefferson's son) apparently did not spot the error when he re-read Chastellux's manuscript in Paris in the autumn of 1785 (Boyd *et al.*, eds., *Jefferson Papers*, VIII, 467-70), although the facts are correct in his own *Notes on the State of Virginia* and in his revised map of Virginia appended thereto. Much later, in 1815, Jefferson measured geometrically "with a Ramsden's theodolite" the height of the two peaks above the level of the Otter River, which he found to be 2946½ and 3103½ feet; Thomas Jefferson, *Notes on the State of Virginia*, William Peden, ed. (Chapel Hill, 1955), 262, n. 7.

35. Chastellux's description seems to be the only surviving description of the octogenarian Mr. Lambert. His son, a captain in the Virginia Line, must have been Captain George Lambert; Francis B. Heitman, ed., *Historical Register of Officers of the Continental Army during the War of the Revolution* . . . (Wash., 1893), 255; John H. Gwathmey, *Historical Register of Virginians in the Revolution* . . . (Richmond, 1938), 455. He was cash-

iered in 1778; the record of his court-martial (for having stolen a hat from a brother officer at Valley Forge) is in Fitzpatrick, ed., *Writings of Washington*, X, 314.

36. Captain Muller and his house have not been further identified. He evidently lived in the vicinity of present Bedford.

37. *Gr.* The rage for dress among the women in America, in the very height of the miseries of war, was beyond all bounds; nor was it confined to the great towns, it prevailed equally on the sea-coasts, and in the woods and solitudes of the vast extent of country, from Florida to New Hampshire. In travelling into the interior parts of Virginia I spent a delicious day at an inn, at the ferry of Shenandoah, or the Catacton [Catoctin] Mountains, with the most enchanting, accomplished and voluptuous girls, the daughters of the landlord, a native of Boston, transplanted thither; who, with all the gifts of nature, possessed the art of dress not unworthy of Parisian milliners, and went regularly three times a week to the distance of seven miles, to attend the lessons of one *de Grace*, a French dancing-master, who was making a fortune in the country. In one of my journeys, too, I met with a young Frenchman, who was travelling on the business of the celebrated M. de Beaumarchais, and was uncommonly successful in his amours, of which I speak from personal knowledge. On my inquiring the secret of his success, he assured me, and put it beyond a doubt, that his *passe-partout*, or master-key, consisted in a fashionable assortment of ribands, and other small articles contained in a little box, from which, in difficult cases he opened an irresistible and never-failing battery.

38. Although he does not mention it and was probably unaware of it, Chastellux, before reaching New London, passed very near "Poplar Forest," a plantation belonging to his friend Thomas Jefferson, where the latter had retired the previous summer to work on his *Notes on the State of Virginia*. Later on, in 1806, Jefferson built there a house of his own design (still standing, privately owned), where he habitually spent some time each year to enjoy greater seclusion than was possible at Monticello.

39. New London was then the county seat of Bedford Co. and the most flourishing settlement in the region, but it subsequently fell into decline when Campbell Co. was formed from a portion of Bedford and the county seat of the latter was moved westward to Liberty (later Bedford City, now Bedford). New London, now called Bedford Springs, is near the western boundary of Campbell Co. It has been completely overshadowed in importance by the city of Lynchburg, a few miles to the north, which was only a handful of houses at Lynch's Ferry across the James when Chastellux was in this neighborhood. State Historical Marker K-139.

40. According to the distances given by Chastellux these four houses, which have not been further identified, would have been in present Campbell, Appomattox, and Buckingham Co., along the old road from New London to Cumberland Courthouse.

41. Neither the courthouse nor the tavern visited by Chastellux is extant. The present Cumberland Courthouse (U.S. Route 60), on the site of the older structure, was built in 1818; the Effingham Tavern survived until 1933. Federal Writers Program, *Virginia Guide*, 490.

42. *Gr.* The reader will here, doubtless, be apt to picture to himself the Author as a grey-headed worn out veteran, or an unimpassioned, stoical

member of the French Academy, barely remembering "the days when he was young;" but it is my duty to undeceive him: the Marquis de Chastellux is a well made, handsome man, of about four and forty [born May 5, 1734], with eyes full of intelligence and fire, the carriage and deportment of a man of rank, and with a disposition extremely remote from an indifference to beauty.

43. *Gr.* It is certain that population is not the main object of marriage in France among the higher classes. Among the nobility, in particular, the parties are generally contracted, when very young, by their respective parents, who bring them together to make an heir, or two, for the family; which object, once completed, they part with as little affection as when they met, but with less passion, and pass the remainder of their lives in perfect freedom. Whilst family duty is performing for family purposes, their conduct is dictated, in general, by the nicest honour, and their noble blood is transmitted tolerably pure and free from contamination; but "unrestrained fecundity," as it is checked by some on principles of economy and prudence, is deemed *vulgar* and *barbarous* by all, except the lower classes, who are strangers to this system of refinement.

44. Powhatan Courthouse is still a somewhat "rustic settlement," just off the main highway (U.S. Route 60); the present courthouse was built only in the 19th century, but an 18th-century brick house adjacent to the courthouse green, said to be a tavern dating from Revolutionary times, is presumably the "public house" where Chastellux stayed. State Historical Marker O-32.

Chapter 4

Petersburg, Richmond, Westover, and back to Williamsburg

1. The raid on Chesterfield Courthouse had taken place Apr. 27, 1781 soon after General Phillips had begun the invasion up the James River from the English bridgehead at Portsmouth.

2. The settlement of Pocahontas, with Blandford and Ravenscroft, was to be joined to the town of Petersburg in 1784. The Pocahontas Bridge had been destroyed during the English invasion earlier in the war, hence the ferry used by Chastellux. For a commentary on several of the places visited in the course of his walks in Petersburg, see Edward A. Wyatt, IV, *Along Petersburg Streets, Historic Sites and Buildings of Petersburg, Virginia* (Richmond, 1943).

3. *Gr.* £800 sterling.

4. "Bollingbrook," the residence of Mrs. Bolling, was on East Hill; it is no longer standing, but see sketch by Benson J. Lossing, *Field-Book*, II, 339. See also C[harles]. C[ampbell]., "Reminiscences of the British at Bollingbrook," *Southern Literary Messenger*, 6 (1840), 85-88. Chastellux's hostess was presumably Mary Marshall Tabb Bolling, second wife and widow of Robert Bolling (1730-75), whom she had married in 1758. Her son, another Robert Bolling (b. 1759, later of "Center Hill"), had married, Nov. 4, 1781, a cousin, Mary Burton Bolling (who died in 1787). "Miss Bolling" was perhaps Anne Bolling, born in 1765, or her sister Frances. Although the elder Mrs. Bolling could not claim descent from Pocahontas, Chastellux's usual

chivalry perhaps failed him when he attributed this illustrious ancestry only to the daughter-in-law; the daughter and son, it would seem, were also among the descendants of the Indian Princess. See genealogy of the Bolling family in Philip Slaughter, *A History of Bristol Parish, Va. with Genealogies of Families connected therewith...*, 2d ed. (Richmond, 1879), 140-47; Wyndham Robertson, *Pocahontas, alias Matoaka, and Her Descendants...* (Richmond, 1887).

5. *Gr.* Dr. [William] Robertson, Mr. [James] Adair, and a number of writers have given an account of the cruel mode by which the Indians torture their prisoners of war, before they put them to death. During my residence near Alexandria, in Virginia, in 1782, I had the following relation of their barbarous treatment, from a gentleman who had just escaped out of the hands of these infernal furies. Colonel [William] Crawford, and his son, two great land surveyors, and most respectable planters in Virginia, in heading a party against the Indians and Tories, aided by some light horse from the British frontiers, who had spread horror and devastation through the infant back settlements of the United States, were defeated and made prisoners. The gentleman, from whom I had this account, was surgeon to the party, and was conducted with Mr. Crawford and his son, to be sacrificed in his turn, at one of the Indian villages, to the manes of their people slain in battle. The bloody business commenced with Mr. Crawford, the father, who was delivered over to *the women*, and being fastened to a stake, in the centre of a circle formed by the savages *and their allies*, the female furies, after the preamble of a war song, began by tearing out the nails of his toes and fingers, then proceeded, at considerable intervals, to cut off his nose and ears; after which they stuck his lacerated body full of pitch pines, large pieces of which they inserted, horrid to relate! into his private parts; to all of which they set fire, and which continued burning, amidst the inconceivable tortures of the unhappy man, for a considerable time. After thus glutting their revenge, by arts of barbarity, the success of which was repeatedly applauded by the surrounding demons, they cut off his genitals, and rushing in upon him, finished his misery with their tomahawks, and hacked his body limb from limb. This dreadful scene passed in the presence of the son of the unhappy sufferer, and the surgeon, who were to be conveyed to different villages to undergo the same fate. The next day, accordingly, young Crawford was sacrificed with the same circumstances of horror; after which, the surgeon, being entrusted to the care of four of the savages, who fortunately got drunk with some rum, given them as a recompense by their European friends, escaped from them in the woods, and, bound as he was, wandered for four or five and twenty days, subsisting on leaves and berries, before he reached the neighbourhood of Winchester, whence he got down to Alexandria. Among these wretches was one Simon Girty, a native of Virginia, who was formerly well acquainted with Colonel Crawford, and had been employed by the assembly of Virginia to conciliate the savages, and obtain their neutrality; but who having been detected by the Governor in some malversations of the public money entrusted to him, and his duplicity discovered, went over to the British and became more merciless than the worst of these infernal hell-hounds. Mr. Crawford, in the midst of his tremendous sufferings, seeing Girty standing in the circle, with a gun, called to him by his name, and implored him as an old friend, a Christian, and a countryman, to shoot him, and by that act of mercy relieve

him from his misery; but the inhuman monster tauntingly replied, "No, Crawford, I have got *no powder*, your assembly did not choose to trust me, and you must now pay for it," and continued to feast his eyes with the bloody sacrifice.

Ed. The death by torture of Col. William Crawford took place on June 11, 1782, at a spot near what is now Crawfordsville, Wyandot Co., Ohio, following the unsuccessful expedition against the Indian settlements on the headwaters of the Sandusky. Accounts by two of the survivors, Dr. John Knight and John Slover, were forwarded by Hugh H. Brackenridge from Pittsburgh (Aug. 3, 1782) to the Philadelphia publisher Francis Bailey, who published them in the *Freeman's Journal* (Apr.-May 1783) and subsequently as a pamphlet: *Narrative of a Late Expedition against the Indians, with an Account of the Barbarous Execution of Col. Crawford and the Wonderful Escape of Dr. Knight and John Slover, from Captivity in 1782* (Phila., 1783; Evans, No. 17993). For a later account, based on the *Narrative* and other sources, see C. W. Butterfield, *An Historical Account of the Expedition against Sandusky under Col. William Crawford in 1782* ... (Cincinnati, 1873); for further references, see Edmund K. Alden in *DAB* s.v. "Crawford, William," and W. J. Ghent in *DAB* s.v. "Girty, Simon." Grieve's statement that Crawford's son also perished reflects an erroneous belief prevalent at the time; John Crawford the younger escaped, although a nephew, William Crawford, was among the victims. Grieve's further statement that he had the account of Crawford's death, at Alexandria, from the surgeon of the party (i.e., Dr. John Knight) is open to question, since other sources state that the doctor reached Pittsburgh on July 4, 1782, and do not mention his being at Alexandria that year. It seems more likely that Grieve, although he no doubt heard of the incident at Alexandria, used the published *Narrative* to refresh his memory when he wrote up his footnote a few years later. For an account of the Gnadenhutten massacre, which had taken place in Mar. 1782 and probably contributed to Crawford's disastrous death, see below, Pt. II, chap. 5, n. 1.

6. See n. 4, above.

7. *Ed.* For a description of "Battersea," John Banister's house—still standing near the Appomattox River within the city limits of Petersburg—see Waterman, *Virginia Mansions*, 373-79, 413, illus. Waterman suggests that Thomas Jefferson, who was related to Mrs. John (Mary Bland) Banister, may have been the designer of this residence in the Palladian villa style, but there appears to be no documentary evidence to confirm this supposition.

Gr. The Italian architecture, that of porticos in particular, is admirably adapted to all hot climates, and of course to the southern states of America. The same motives, therefore, which induced the invention of this mode of building in ancient Greece and Rome, and in general throughout the Eastern world, would naturally give rise to the same inventions of convenience in similar climates; and, in fact, though the richer and more polished descendants of Britain, in the New World, may be supposed to adopt these porticos from Italy, as the cultivated mind of the author imagines, the very poorest settler, nay even the native Indian, invariably attempts some kind of substitute for this necessary protection from the sun and weather. Every tavern or inn is provided with a covered portico for the convenience of its guests, and this evidently from the necessity of the case. We have only to examine the resources of the savage islander in the Pacific ocean, and recur to the origin of all architecture, from the fluted Corinthian in the hall of empire, to the rustic prop of the thatched roof, to discover the natural progress of the human mind, and the similarity of human genius.

8. "Tuckahoe," the Randolph estate where Thomas Jefferson spent part of his childhood, still stands on the north bank of the James, some fifteen miles west of Richmond (privately owned). See Waterman, *Virginia Mansions*, 85-92, illus.

9. *Gr.* I have already said [above, Pt. I, chap. 3, n. 106; see also below, Pt. III, chap. 4, n. 30], that I had the happiness of a particular acquaintance with many of the principal gentlemen of South Carolina. The reflection on the pleasing hours I passed with them in their exiled situation at Philadelphia, and the warm friendship with which they honored me, whilst it reconciles me to the world, and soothes the memory of past sufferings, touches the tenderest affections of a sensible and grateful heart. My bosom beat high with genuine ardor in the cause for which they sacrificed every personal consideration, but I had frequently the opportunity of appreciating that sacrifice. Seeing what I saw, I want no instances of Greek or Roman virtue to stimulate my feelings, or excite my emulation; and it will ever be matter of congratulation with me, to have witnessed in the principal inhabitants of Carolina, all the blandishments of civilized society, the love of life and all its blessings, a humanity void of reproach, an hospitality not exceeded in the patriarchal ages, contrary to the paradoxes of systematic writers, blended with the inflexible virtue which distinguished the best and purest ages of the world. From the number, I shall only select the brilliant examples of Major Pierce Butler, and Mr. Arthur Middleton. Wealth, honor, interest, domestic happiness, their children, were nothing in the eyes of such men, though calculated to enjoy, and to communicate happiness in every sphere, when put in competition with the great objects of universal public happiness, and sacred Freedom's holy cause. How painful is it to be compelled to add, that such was the cold, selfish spirit of too many of the inhabitants of Philadelphia towards their Carolina brethren, who had every claim upon their sympathy and good offices, as to merit the indignation of every feeling mind, and to fix an indelible stain upon their character as men and citizens.

10. Warwick, another vanished town, which has been absorbed by the city of Richmond. It was located on the James near the present southeastern city limits, a site now occupied by the Dupont de Nemours Manufacturing Co. See Francis Earle Lutz, *Chesterfield, an Old Virginia County* (Richmond, 1954), 47.

11. *Gr.* This is the gentleman whose fine mills were burnt by Arnold, as mentioned in the London Gazette.
Ed. "Ampthill," Col. Archibald Cary's house, was removed from its original site here and rebuilt in 1929 in the west end of Richmond. Waterman, *Virginia Mansions*, 212-14, illus.

12. "Wilton," the Randolph house, has also been removed and rebuilt (1934) in Richmond—still overlooking the James—where it is maintained by the Virginia Society of Colonial Dames as an historic house open to the public. *Ibid.*, 203-12, illus.

13. Concerning the Randolph family and its ramifications see, for example, H. J. Eckenrode, *The Randolphs: the Story of a Virginia Family* (Indianapolis and N.Y., 1946).

14. According to information assembled by Edward Dumbauld (*Thomas Jefferson, American Tourist*, 46n) Serafino Formicola kept a tavern, in 1783, in a house belonging to the estate of Joshua Storrs on the south side of Main St. between 15th St. and Shockoe Creek (17th St.) so that it seems probable that he was already at this location when Chastellux was his guest. At a later date Formicola kept the Eagle Tavern at the southeast corner of Main and 12th Sts. Other references to Formicola may be traced through E. G. Swem, *Virginia Historical Index*, 2 vols. (Roanoke, Va., 1934-36).

15. The house on Shockoe Hill where Chastellux visited Benjamin Harrison (Governor of Virginia, succeeding Thomas Nelson, from Nov. 1781 to 1784) was on approximately the same site as the present Governor's Mansion, which was built only in 1811-12. Mary Wingfield Scott, *Houses of Old Richmond* (Richmond, 1941), 96-99; Edward Dumbauld, "Jefferson's Residence in Richmond," in his *Thomas Jefferson, American Tourist*, App. II, 220-27; *The Executive Mansion*, illustrated booklet prepared by Virginia State Library (Richmond, 1961). The Virginia Capitol was not built until 1785-88; although Chastellux thus never saw it, he did perhaps, after his return to France, see the plans and the plaster model for it that Jefferson had prepared in Paris with the assistance of the French architect Clérisseau.

16. *Gr*. I cannot here resist transcribing a passage from Mr. Paine's celebrated letter to the Abbé Raynal, which merits preservation, and may serve to illustrate the ideas of America respecting the general views of Britain, in hopes that every reflecting Englishman is at length dispassionate enough to bear the observation. "I shall now take my leave of this passage of the Abbé, with an observation, which, until something unfolds itself to convince me otherwise, I cannot avoid believing to be true; which is, that it was the fixed determination of the British cabinet to quarrel with America at all events. They (the members who compose the cabinet), had no doubt of success, if they could once bring it to the issue of a battle; and they expected from a conquest, what they could neither propose with decency, nor hope for by negotiation. The charters and constitutions of the colonies were become to them matters of offence, and their rapid progress in property and population were beheld with disgust, as the growing and natural means of independence. They saw no way to retain them long, but by reducing them in time. A conquest would at once have made them lords and landlords; and put them in possession both of the revenue and the rental. The whole trouble of government would have ceased in a victory, and a final end been put to remonstrance and debate. The experience of the stamp act had taught them how to quarrel, with advantages of cover and convenience, and they had nothing to do but to renew the scene, and put contention into motion. They hoped for a rebellion, and they made one. They expected a declaration of independence, and they were not disappointed. But after this, they looked for victory, and they obtained a defeat. If this be taken as the generating cause of the contest, then is every part of the conduct of the British ministry consistent from the commencement of the dispute, until the signing the treaty of Paris [the American and French alliance], after which, conquest becoming doubtful, they retreated to negotiation, and were again defeated.... If we take a review of what part Britain has acted, we

shall find everything which ought to make a nation blush—the most vulgar abuse, accompanied by that species of haughtiness which distinguishes the hero of a mob from the character of a gentleman. It was equally as much from her *manners,* as from her injustice, that she lost the colonies. By the latter she provoked their principles, by the former she wore out their temper; and it ought to be held out as an example to the world, to show how necessary it is to conduct the business of government with civility."

Ed. See Thomas Paine, *Letter to the Abbé Raynal on the Affairs of North America* (1782).

17. *Gr.* The same ingenious author of *Common Sense,* makes another observation, in his answer to the very ignorant, or very prejudiced work of the Abbé Raynal on the revolution of America, to which, however it may militate against the utility of the present publication, or the notes of the Translator, he cannot avoid perfectly subscribing, viz.: "I never yet saw an European description of America that was true, neither can any person gain a just idea of it, but by coming to it."

18. *Gr.* The illustrious and amiable character of Dr. Franklin is far beyond my praise. To have known him; to have been a frequent witness to the distinguished acts of his great mind; to have been in a situation to learn, and to admire his comprehensive views, and benevolent motives; to have heard the profound maxims of wise philosophy and sound politics, drop from his lips with all the unaffected simplicity of the most indifferent conversation; to have heard him deviate from the depths of reason, and adopt his instructive discourse to the capacity and temper of the young and the gay; to have enjoyed in short, the varied luxuries of his delightful society, is a subject of triumph and consolation, of which nothing can deprive me. He too as well as the envious and interested enemies of his transcendent merit, must drop from off the scene, but his name, *aere perennius,* is inscribed in indelible characters on the immortal roll of philosophy and freedom, for the *ardentia verba* of the most honest advocate of freedom, of the present age, the late Serjeant Glynn, on a great occasion, the action against Lord Halifax for the false imprisonment of Mr. Wilkes, may with peculiar justice be applied to this great man: "Few men in whole revolving ages can be found, who dare oppose themselves to the force of tyranny, and whose single breasts contain the spirit of nations."

19. *Ed.* "Westover"—the best known of the surviving James River plantations—has been frequently described and pictured; see, for example, Waterman, *Virginia Mansions,* 146-63, 423, illus.

Gr. The most perfect ease and comfort characterize the mode of receiving strangers in Virginia, but no where are these circumstances more conspicuous than at the house of General Washington. Your apartments are your home, the servants of the house are yours, and whilst every inducement is held out to bring you into the general society in the drawing-room, or at the table, it rests with yourself to be served or not with every thing in your own chamber. In short, nothing can more resemble the easy reception of guests at the country residence of the late Sir Charles Turner in Yorkshire, where hospitality perhaps was strained farther than consisted with a proper assortment of company, or even with safety.

20. A full discussion of this episode, with supporting documents, will be found in Boyd *et al.,* eds., *Jefferson Papers,* V, 671-705, App. I. Chastellux's summary account—considered by the editors "on the whole so accurate

that one is tempted to believe TJ may have furnished some information when Chastellux visited him at Monticello"—serves as a starting point for the discussion.

21. The daughters were Maria Horsmanden Byrd (b. 1761) and Anne Willing Byrd (b. 1763). Two letters from the Chevalier Duplessis-Mauduit (see above, Pt. I, chap. 1, n. 90) addressed to Mrs. Byrd, Jan. 26, 1782, and Dec. 21, 1782, are printed in "Letters of the Byrd Family, II," *Va. Mag. of Hist. and Biog.*, 2d Ser., 38 (1930). They indicate that he was one of the French officers who had been charmed by the young Misses Byrd during the army's winter quarters at Williamsburg.

Gr. The prudent conduct of the French officers, and the strict discipline of their troops in a country with different manners, language, and religion, full of inveterate prejudices, and wherein they had very lately been regarded as natural enemies, must ever be considered as an epocha and a phenomenon, in the history of policy and subordination. Whilst all ranks of officers were making it their study successfully to conciliate the good opinion of the higher classes, nothing could exceed the probity, and urbanity of the common soldiers; not only did they live with the American troops in a harmony, hitherto unknown to allied armies, even of kindred language, interest, and religion, but their conduct was irreproachable, and even delicate to the inhabitants of the country. They who predicted discord on the introduction of a French army, had reason and experience on their side, but the spirit of policy and wisdom which presided in the French councils had gone forth, and diffusing itself through every subordinate class of men, persuaded even the meanest actors in the war, and baffled foresight. Nor was this one of the least extraordinary circumstances of this wonderful revolution.

22. David Meade's plantation, on the south bank of the James (Prince George Co.) was called "Maycox" or "Maycock's," from the name of an earlier owner. It is situated about five miles northwest of Burrowsville (State Route 10); Virginia State Historical Marker K-213. The 18th-century house has been replaced by a modern structure, and little, if anything, remains of Meade's gardens. An early description of Meade's "pleasure ground" is given in John Jones Spooner's "A Topographical Description of Prince George County," Mass. Hist. Soc., *Proceedings*, 3 (1794), 85-93; reprinted in *Tyler's Quarterly Historical and Genealogical Magazine*, 5 (1923), 1-11.

23. *Gr.* Whilst the Translator was employed in this passage [1786], he read in the public prints, the exultation of a friend to his fellow-creatures, that a Mr. Pleasants, a Quaker on James River in Virginia, had liberated his slaves, and made a sacrifice of 3000£ sterling to this noble act of humanity. The Translator knows the country too well not to feel the force of the Author's subsequent reasoning on the difficulty and danger of a general emancipation of the negroes, nor after mature reflection now, and on the spot, is he able to overcome his objections. But God, in his divine providence, forbid that so splendid an example of active virtue, should clash with the unavoidable policy, or the necessary welfare of society!

Ed. The Quaker gentleman was Robert Pleasants of Curles' Neck, Henrico Co. Thomas Edward Drake, *Quakers and Slavery in America* (New

Haven, 1950), 83; Adair P. Archer, "The Quaker's Attitude Towards the Revolution," *Wm. and Mary College Qtly.*, 2d Ser., 1 (1921), 168.

24. *Gr.* From General Washington's house, which stands on the lofty banks of the Potomac, in a situation more magnificent than I can paint to an European imagination, I have seen for several hours together, in a summer's evening, hundreds, perhaps I might say thousands of sturgeon, at a great height from the water at the same instant, so that the quantity in the river must have been inconceivably great; but notwithstanding the rivers of Virginia abound with fish, they are by no means plentiful at table, such is the indolence of the inhabitants! Mr. Lund Washington, a relation of the General's, and who managed all his affairs during his *nine years'* absence with the army, informed me that an English frigate having come up the Potomac, a party was landed who set fire to and destroyed some gentlemen's houses on the Maryland side in sight of Mount Vernon, the General's house; after which the Captain (I think Captain [Richard] Graves of the Actaeon [*Savage*]) sent a boat on shore to the General's, demanding a large supply of provisions, etc. with a menace of burning it likewise in case of a refusal. To this message Mr. Lund Washington replied, "that when the General engaged in the contest he had put all to stake, and was well aware of the exposed situation of his house and property, in consequence of which he had given him orders by no means to comply with any such demands, for that he would make no unworthy compromise with the enemy, and was ready to meet the fate of his neighbors." The Captain was highly incensed on receiving this answer, and removed his frigate to the Virginia shore; but before he commenced his operations, he sent another message to the same purport, offering likewise a passport to Mr. Washington to come on board: he returned accordingly in the boat, carrying with him a small present of poultry, of which he begged the Captain's acceptance. His presence produced the best effect, he was hospitably received notwithstanding he repeated the same sentiments with the same firmness. The Captain expressed his personal respect for the character of the General, commending the conduct of Mr. Lund Washington, and assured him nothing but his having misconceived the terms of the first answer could have induced him for a moment to entertain the idea of taking the smallest measure offensive to so illustrious a character as the General, explaining at the same time the real or supposed provocations which had compelled his severity on the other side of the river. Mr. Washington, after spending some time in perfect harmony on board, returned, and instantly despatched sheep, hogs, and an abundant supply of other articles as a present to the English frigate. The Translator hopes that in the *present state* of men and measures in England, Mr. Graves, or whoever the Captain of that frigate was, will neither be offended at this anecdote, nor be afraid to own himself the actor in this generous transaction. Henry IV supplied Paris with provisions whilst he was blockading it!

Ed. The incident related by Grieve—which omits the fact that Lund Washington was attempting to obtain the return of some Negro slaves who had fled to the English (and thus to freedom)—was viewed in a less rosy light at the time it took place, in Apr. 1781. For example, Lafayette, who was then in Virginia, wrote of it in a confidential letter to Washington, complaining that Lund Washington's conduct was in contrast to the courageous attitude of other neighbors who had lost their property in consequence. Lafayette to Washington, Alexandria, Apr. 23, 1781, Gottschalk, ed., *Letters of Lafayette to Washington*, 187-88; Lafayette, *Mémoires*, I, 428-29. Washington himself sent a stiff rebuke to his overseer: "to go on board their vessels; carry them refreshments; commune with a parcel of plundering scoundrels, and request a favor by asking the surrender of my Negroes, was exceedingly ill-judged, and 'tis to be feared, will be unhappy in its consequences, as it will be a precedent for others, and may become a subject of animadversion." Washington to Lund Washington, New Windsor, Apr. 30, 1781, Fitzpatrick, ed., *Writings of Washington*, XXII, 14-15. See also Freeman's discussion of the incident in his *Washington*, V, 282-83.

25. The notion that the hummingbird expressed its naturally irascible temperament by spitefully tearing apart the flowers that yielded no nectar was a venerable traveler's tale repeated in many 18th-century books on America. Chastellux may have had in mind, for example, the Abbé Raynal's *Histoire philosophique* ([Amsterdam, 1770], VI, Book 17), where the credulous compiler dwelt at length upon *"la fureur de ces oiseaux"* when lacerating flowers. The same theme was picked up by St. John de Crèvecoeur in his *Letters from an American Farmer* ([London, 1782], Letter X, "On Snakes; and on the Humming Bird")—although Chastellux was of course not acquainted with this work when he was writing up his journal at Williamsburg.

Chapter 5

Notes on the State of Virginia

1. *Gr.* The employing the Indians, independent of the measure, it is now pretty generally admitted, produced consequences directly opposite to the interest of Great Britain; uniting the inhabitants of all the countries liable to their incursions as one man against them and their allies, and producing such bloody scenes of inveterate animosity and vengeance as make human nature shudder. The following narrative will prove how far men of all casts, colors, and religions, resemble each other in similar situations, and to what lengths even the Christians of an enlightened age can go, when compelled to act under the guidance of the worst passions. The inhabitants of the back frontiers of Pennsylvania, goaded to fury by the ravages committed on them by the Indians, and by the murder of their families and kindred, collected the militia in the beginning of 1782, and took the field against their savage intruders. In one of their excursions they fell in with a small tribe of Christian Indians, called the *Muskingums*, who being suspected of attachment to the Americans, had been for some time confined at Detroit, and were released only on condition of observing a strict neutrality, since they could not be persuaded to take arms. These unhappy wretches, to the number of about two hundred, returning to their habitations, were employed in putting their seed-corn into the ground, when they were surprised by the American militia. In vain did they urge their situation, and their sufferings from the British; they were *Indians*, and their captors, men who had lost sons, brothers, fathers, wives, or children in this horrid war; no other plea was necessary to palliate their meditated vengeance. The Indians were shut up in a barn, and ordered to prepare for death, but with this barbarous consolation, that, as they were Christian converts, they should be allowed a respite till the next morning. The innocent victims

spent the night in singing Moravian hymns, and in other acts of Christian devotion; and in the morning, men, women, and children, were led to the slaughter, and butchered by their fellow worshippers of the meek Jesus! The Moravians at Bethlehem and Nazareth, whose missionaries [John Heckewelder, David Zeisberger, *et al.*] had converted them, made strong representations to Congress on the subject. I was at Philadelphia when the news arrived; and it is but justice to say, that horror was painted on every countenance, and every mind was at work to devise expedients for avenging this atrocious murder; but after various efforts, both Congress and the Assembly of the State were found unequal to the punishment of these assassins, who were armed, distant from the seat of government, the only safeguard and protection of the frontiers, and from their own savage nature alone fit to cope with the dreadful enemy brought into action by the British.

Ed. The massacre of the Christian Indians at Gnadenhutten (on the Tuscarawas River, a tributary of the Muskingum, in present state of Ohio) in Mar. 1782 by Pennsylvania militia under Col. David Williamson is one of the more sinister incidents of border warfare during the Revolution. It has been frequently discussed by Moravian historians and others, and it forms the subject of one of the essays comprising William Dean Howells' *Three Villages* (Boston, 1884). This punitive expedition against the Muskingum towns was followed in June by the Sandusky expedition, which resulted in the death and torture of its leader, Col. William Crawford; also mentioned by Grieve above, Pt. II, chap. 4, n. 5.

2. *Gr.* The murder committed on Mrs. Maxwell [Caldwell], the wife of a respectable and popular clergyman in the Jerseys, and afterwards on himself, with similar acts of cruelty perpetrated by a licentious soldiery, and unprincipled refugees, inflamed the minds of a great body of the inhabitants, particularly of the Dutch and their descendants, who, as the Marquis observes, were certainly disposed at least to a neutrality.

Ed. Mrs. Hannah Ogden Caldwell was killed during the British raid on Connecticut Farms (now Union), N.J., in June 1780. Her husband, the Reverend James Caldwell, pastor of the First Presbyterian Church at Elizabethtown, was killed by a shot from a sentinel at Elizabethtown Point in Nov. 1781. In 1784 Lafayette took the Caldwells' orphan son, John Edwards Caldwell, to France to complete his education there; Louis Gottschalk, *Lafayette between the American and the French Revolution (1783-1789)* (Chicago, 1950), 142, 162.

3. *Gr.* The Irish and the Germans form the most numerous part of the inhabitants of Pennsylvania. The latter, if I am not mistaken, constitutes a fifth, if not a fourth, of the whole number, and are a most useful, industrious body of men, well versed in the mechanic arts and agriculture. I have travelled several days in the interior parts of that state, and heard scarcely any other language than German. The acts of Congress, and the State, are promulgated in that language, German Gazettes are published at Philadelphia, and in general they proved themselves true friends to the revolution. Congress availing themselves of this circumstance, very politically encamped the Brunswick, and other German troops taken with Burgoyne, near the town of Reading, where I saw them. The neighborhood abounding with their countrymen, the men had permission to work at harvest, and other trades, and soon formed connexions with the females of the country.

Calculating their market price, and the obligation they lay under to restore them or their prime cost, they [the British authorities in New York] took every measure to prevent them from remaining in the country; for which purpose, they transmitted but small sums at a time by their commissaries from New York, taking care to keep large arrears in their hands, as a temptation for their return. But all the precautions were, as may naturally be imagined, but of a partial effect, with men habituated to a country of freedom, wherein they felt themselves restored to their natural rights, and animated by the example of their countrymen, enjoying the full comforts of their honest industry; contrasted too with the degraded state of a wretched mercenary, held up to sale by his arbitrary master.

4. *Gr.* It is true that a great number of Scotsmen are settled in North Carolina, but that they were not even the majority of the inhabitants, is very apparent from the events of the late revolution; for the Scots, though loyalist nearly to a man, were repeatedly defeated, and finally crushed by the militia of the country. Notwithstanding her efforts appeared less con-centered, and more vaguely directed, owing to the local circumstances of the province, and the dispersed state of the inhabitants, rather than disin-clination to the cause, North Carolina rendered most essential services, by her exertions in the field, and the delegates she sent to Congress. Her constitution of government, contracted as it is, is not perhaps inferior to many in the confederacy, and bespeaks the wisdom of "the enlightened few," to which the Marquis attributes the wise councils of Virginia. It was the North Carolina militia which gave the first turn to the ruined affairs of America to the southward, by their spirited attack and defeat of Colonel [Patrick] Ferguson at King's Mountain [7 October 1780]. The Translator, who was then in England, received, by a private channel, the first intelli-gence of that important event, which he communicated to the public; but the circumstances of the surprise of a large body of British troops, flushed with the capture of Charleston, and the victory at Camden, by a body of 1600 *horsemen*, from the back country of North Carolina, appeared so extraordinary, that he could not obtain credit for the fact, either with the friends to America, or the ministerial party in that country. The Ministers had no intelligence of the matter, and the easterly winds then happening to prevail for a period of six weeks, it was treated as a fiction, both in and out of Parliament, and the Translator as an enthusiast or a fabricator of false news. Time, however, verified the fact, which he knew to be authentic, to its full extent, viz. that Colonel Ferguson, with eight hundred British troops, had been surprised; himself slain, and his whole force defeated by sixteen hundred Carolina militia, mounted on horseback, hastily collected, and commanded by a few militia Colonels! This spirited and successful enterprise, with its consequences, merits certainly a conspicuous place in the history of this great revolution; for, like the surprise at Trenton, it changed the whole face of affairs, and restored energy to the friends of America in that important seat of war. North Carolina is a very fine country, beautifully diversified with pleasant hills, large valleys, and noble rivers, though none of them is navigable for vessels above 80 tons, except the rivers Fear and Clarendon; yet as they intersect the country in every direction, they are admirably calculated for inland navigation. There are, for this reason, no large towns; but, from the various produce of this state, and the rapid increase of population, the white inhabitants, now amounting

to near two hundred thousand, there is every reason to believe that it will become not one of the least considerable on the continent, nor will the philosopher view the circumstances which forbid the formation of large towns as an evil, either in this country or in Virginia.

5. *Gr.* The author here refers to the former situation of the province; but as I have already mentioned [above, Pt. II, chap. 3, n. 20], the interior of this extensive state is daily peopling with a race of healthy, industrious planters, and is highly susceptible of every species of improvement. As for sea-ports, there are none worth mentioning but Charleston; and as for Georgia, its position is in every respect similar to that of South Carolina.

6. *Gr.* The lands, *within the mountains,* in the hitherto settled parts of North America, are not in general very good, and it is of these only that the Marquis speaks; but as the authors of the *Nouvelle Encyclopédie* observe, in their *new article* of the *United States,* this must have been the case in almost every new country, the soil of Europe having been meliorated by the progress of population, the quantity of manure, and the means by which the earth is protected from the effects of heavy rains, etc. by care and cultivation. Abbé Raynal's remarks on this subject, in his last work, called the Revolution of America [*Révolution de l'Amérique* (1781)], discover so much ignorance as scarcely to merit the elaborate discussion bestowed on them by the ingenious authors of the *Encyclopédie,* who have likewise transcribed from him several important passages, which have been ably and fully refuted by Mr. Paine [*Letter to the Abbé Raynal on the Affairs of North America* (1782)].

Ed. Grieve is here referring to the *Encyclopédie Méthodique,* a publication launched in 1782 by the Parisian publisher Panckouke. This "new" Encyclopedia differed from its illustrious predecessor, the *Encyclopédie ou Dictionnaire raisonné des Sciences, des Arts, et des Métiers* (edited by D'Alembert and Diderot [1750-80])—in which the articles were arranged in a single alphabetical sequence—by being arranged "methodically" in sections of several volumes devoted to different fields of knowledge. The four volumes (Paris, 1784-88) comprising the section "Economie Politique et Diplomatique," edited by Jean-Nicolas Démeunier, included his separate articles on the different states of America, as well as a comprehensive article on the United States (II [1786], 345-433). Démeunier's article "Etats-Unis" was also issued separately in 1786 under the title *Essai sur les Etats-Unis* (Sabin, No. 19477; Sowerby, *Jefferson Library,* No. 2950). See "The Article on the United States in the *Encyclopédie Méthodique,*" Boyd *et al.,* eds., *Jefferson Papers,* X, 3-65.

7. *Gr.* The indolence and dissipation of the middling and lower classes of white inhabitants of Virginia, are such as to give pain to every reflecting mind. Horse-racing, cock-fighting, and boxing-matches, are standing amusements, for which they neglect all business; and in the latter of which they conduct themselves with a barbarity worthy of their savage neighbors. The ferocious practice of stage-boxing in England, is urbanity, compared with the Virginian mode of fighting. In their combats, unless specially precluded, they are admitted (to use their own terms), "to bite, b-ll--ck, and goudge," which operations, when the first onset with fists is over, consists in fastening on the nose or ears of their adversaries with their teeth, seizing him by the genitals, and dexterously scooping out an eye; on which account it is no uncommon circumstance to meet men in the prime of youth, de-

prived of one of those organs. This is no traveller's exaggeration, I speak from knowledge and observation. In the summer months it is very common to make a party on horseback to a limestone spring, near which there is usually some little hut with spirituous liquors, if the party are not themselves provided, where their debauch frequently terminates in a boxing-match, a horse-race, or perhaps both. During a day's residence at Leesburgh, I was myself accidently drawn into one of these parties, where I soon experienced the strength of the liquor, which was concealed by the refreshing coolness of the water. While we were seated round the spring, at the edge of a delightful wood, four or five countrymen arrived, headed by a veteran cyclops, the terror of the neighborhood, ready on every occasion to risk his remaining eye. We soon found ourselves under the necessity of relinquishing our posts, and making our escape from these fellows, who evidently sought to provoke a quarrel. On our return home, whilst I was rejoicing at our good fortune, and admiring the moderation of my company, we arrived at a plain spot of ground by a wood side, on which my horse no sooner set foot, than taking the bit between his teeth, off he went at full speed, attended by the whoops and hallooing of my companions. An Englishman is not easily thrown off his guard on horseback; but at the end of half a mile my horse stopped short, as if he had been shot, and threw me with considerable violence over his head; my buckle, for I was without boots, entangled me in the stirrup, but fortunately broke into twenty pieces. The company rode up, delighted with the adventure; and it was then, for the first time, I discovered that I had been purposely induced, by one of my *friends,* to change horses with him for the afternoon; that his horse had been accustomed to similar exploits on the same *race ground;* that the whole of the business was neither more nor less than a Virginian piece of pleasantry; and that my friends thought they had exhibited great moderation in not exposing me, at the spring, to the effects of "*biting, b-ll--cking, and goudging.*"

8. Chastellux's remarks on the Negroes in Virginia were violently attacked by Brissot de Warville in his *Examen critique,* 82-102.

9. *Gr.* During the Translator's residence in the West Indies, he took considerable pains to inform himself of the different modes of treatment of the negroes, by the principal European nations, possessing colonies in that quarter of the globe, the result of which was, that the Dutch are the most cruel; the British more humane; the French still more so; and the Spaniards the most indulgent masters. He was greatly struck with this gradation, the truth of which seemed to be confirmed by his own observations; but he leaves it to others to decide what influence the various forms of government, and the religious principles or prejudices of each of these nations, may have in the operation of this seeming paradox. A lover of truth will never shrink from the discussion of any question interesting to humanity, whatever be his political or religious bias. The Translator, from impulse, and from reason, is a strenuous assertor of the rights and original equality of mankind; but it is an old remark, that republicans are the worst masters, a position which pursued through the above succession, seems in some measure to receive a confirmation; yet to him appears unaccountable from any given principles, unless it be the aristocratic principles, which, to the misfortune of mankind, have hitherto uniformly taken possession of all the republican governments, and baffled the foresight of the virtuous and good.

But there is reason to hope that the democracies of America will form a brilliant and consoling exception to the triumphant reproaches of the idolators of regal power.

10. *Gr.* The truth is, that the prevalent religion of the principal inhabitants in America, and particularly to the Southward, is *pure deism,* called by the name of Philosophy in Europe, a spirit which has contributed in no small degree to the revolution, and produced their unfettered constitutions of freedom and toleration.

11. *Gr.* Throughout America, in private houses, as well as in the inns, several people are crowded together in the same room; and in the latter it very commonly happens, that after you have been some time in bed, a stranger of any condition (for there is little distinction), comes into the room, pulls off his clothes, and places himself, without ceremony, between your sheets.

12. *Gr.* I have already spoken of horse-races, but it is with regret I add, that the general spirit of gaming is prevalent in this as well as in all the United States, but more particularly throughout the southern ones, which has already been attended with suicide, and all its baneful consequences.

13. *Gr.* I confess myself at a loss to discover from what source of observation the Author has derived the fact on which he reasons so ingeniously. Perhaps it is the secret spirit of national prejudice that has led me, who was born an Englishman, to reverse the remark, as applied to the two countries of France and England; but I leave the fact and the discussion to more acute observers.

14. Before publishing his account of the Virginians, Chastellux, with some misgivings, submitted it to Jefferson for comment. He was certainly reassured—and perhaps a bit surprised—when Jefferson wrote to him, after perusing the account: "With respect to my countrymen there is surely nothing which can render them uneasy, in the observations made on them. They know that they are not perfect, and will be sensible that you have viewed them with a philanthropic eye. You say much good of them, and less ill than they are conscious may be said with truth. I have studied their character with attention. I have thought them, as you found them, aristocratical, pompous, clannish, indolent, hospitable, and I should have added, disinterested, but you say attached to their interest. This is the only trait in their character wherein our observations differ. I have always thought them so careless of their interests, so thoughtless in their expences and in all their transactions of business that I had placed it among the vices of their character, as indeed most virtues when carried beyond certain bounds degenerate into vices. I had even ascribed this to it's cause, to that warmth of climate which unnerves and unmans both body and mind." Jefferson to Chastellux, Paris, Sept. 2, 1785; Chastellux to Jefferson, Paris, Sept. 3, 1785; Boyd *et al.,* eds., *Jefferson Papers,* VIII, 467-72. A somewhat less commendatory opinion was recorded by the Rev. James Madison, who wrote from Virginia to Jefferson, *ca.* Mar. 28, 1787: "I have just been honoured by Genl. Chastellux with a copy of his Travels in N. America. I find it is but little relished by most here." *Ibid.,* XI, 252-53.

15. *Gr.* During the war there was a great scarcity of ministers of the Episcopal church, on account of the numbers of that body who attached themselves to England, which was pretty generally the case; but after the

peace, many young Americans, distinguished for the gown, finding a repugnance on the part of the English bishops, got ordained by the non-juring bishops in Scotland. An act has at length passed, however, to authorise the ordination of foreign clergy by the English bishops, which is evidently intended to promote the cause of the hierarchy in the United States. I shall here take the opportunity of mentioning, that on account of the great scarcity of Bibles, a new edition was published by one Aiken [Robert Aitken], a printer, of Philadelphia, by order of Congress, under the inspection of the Reverend Mr. White, brother-in-law to Mr. [Robert] Morris, and the other chaplain to that body; but such are ancient prejudices, that very few of the zealous followers either of Luther or of Calvin, could be brought to look upon it as the genuine old book. The wary devotees, dreaded, no doubt, similar errors to that for which the company of station-ers were mulcted in the time of King Charles; the omission of the *negative* in one of the commandments, by printing "Thou *shalt* do murder."

Ed. Robert Aitken's famous Bible–the first complete Bible in English printed in America (Evans, No. 17473)–published at Philadelphia in 1782 in an edition of some 10,000 copies, was not strictly speaking published "by order of Congress," nor did Aitken receive any financial aid from that body. However, in response to his petition for support, Congress, after submitting the work to the scrutiny of its two chaplains (the Rev. William White, an Anglican, and the Rev. George Duffield, a Presbyterian), per-mitted Aitken to include in the Bible its resolution of recommendation. Thomas C. Pears, Jr., "The Story of the Aitken Bible," Department of History . . . of the Presbyterian Church in the U. S. A., *Journal*, 18 (1939), 225-41; Robert R. Dearden, Jr., and Douglas S. Watson, *An Original Leaf from the Bible of the Revolution and an Essay concerning it* (San Fran-cisco, 1930); Carol and Willman Spawn, "R. Aitken, Colonial Printer of Philadelphia," *Graphic Arts Review* (1961).

16. *Gr.* See the constitutions of the different states, republished in Eng-land by the Reverend Mr. [William] Jackson [*The Constitutions of the several Independent States of America* (London, 1782, Sabin, No. 16087)], and the excellent translation from the original, with notes, published in Paris by the Duke de la Rochefoucauld [*Constitutions des treize Etats-Unis de l'Amérique* (Paris, 1783, Sabin, No. 16118)].

Ed. Chastellux is here describing the Constitution adopted by the Virginia Convention in June 1776. In his comments on Chastellux's text, submitted in his letter of Sept. 2, 1785 (Boyd *et al.*, eds., *Jefferson Papers*, VIII, 467-70), Jefferson supplied the following explanation and correc-tions: "The government is divided into three departments, legislative, ex-ecutive, and judiciary. No person can hold an office in any two of them. Consequently all the members in any one department are excluded from both the other. Hence the judges and Attorney general cannot be of the legislature. The clergy are excluded, because, if admitted into the legisla-ture at all, the probability is that they would form it's majority. For they are dispersed through every county in the state, they have influence with the people, and great opportunities of persuading them to elect them into the legislature. This body, tho shattered, is still actuated by the *esprit de corps.* The nature of that spirit has been severly felt by mankind, and has filled the history of ten or twelve centuries with too many atrocities not to merit a proscription from meddling with government. Lawyers, holding no public office, may act in any of the departments. They accordingly constitute the ablest part both of the legislative and executive bodies."

17. It was at their meeting of Mar. 1, 1782, that the president and professors of the College of William and Mary voted to confer upon Chastellux the honorary degree of Doctor of Civil Law. For the Latin text of his diploma, including what would today be described as the "citation," see the "Journal of the President and Masters or Professors of William and Mary College," *Wm. and Mary College Qtly.*, 15 (1907), 264-65. Translation:

"The President and Professors of the University or College of William and Mary in Virginia, to all to whom these presents come, Greeting. Since academic degrees were instituted so that men who have deserved well of the Academic World and of the Republic, whether liberally educated in the bosom of our mother or elsewhere, may be honored by these distinctions; Know that in conferring, gladly as we do, the degree of Doctor of Civil Law upon the CHEVALIER DE CHASTELLUX, we bear witness to our esteem for a man belonging to the armies of His Most Christian Majesty and to the forty associates of the French Academy and to the Philosophical Societies of Philadelphia and of Boston, a man of noble lineage, imbued with profound learning, renowned in both the arts of peace and the deeds of war, defender of our Liberties, who, among other equally distinguished men, has brought strong and also successful assistance. (We hopefully pray that the Muses may frequent these seats dedicated to themselves, long occupied by arms, now at peace, and that the sciences, freely cultivated there and flourishing anew, may be as a Palladium, preserving this place from tyrants, so that ignorance flaunting itself may not be able to intrude again.) Therefore, in solemn convocation held on the first day of March 1782, by unanimous vote, we have created and constituted this honorable and eminent man, the Chevalier DE CHASTELLUX, Doctor of Civil Law; and we bid him by virtue of the present diploma to enjoy the various rights, privileges and honors pertaining thereto. In testimony of which we have caused to be affixed to these presents the great seal of the University. Given at the place of our convocation on the day and month aforesaid."

Chastellux was one of the two visiting Frenchmen singled out by the College of William and Mary for academic honors. The other was Jean-François Coste, first physician of Rochambeau's army, upon whom the degree of Doctor of Physics (or Medicine) was conferred by vote of the president and professors at their meeting of June 12, 1782. The Latin text of Coste's diploma is printed in the *Wm. and Mary College Qtly.*, 15 (1907), 266. Upon this occasion Dr. Coste delivered a Latin oration on the theme of the medical philosophy of the Ancients and its application to the New World, which was afterwards published at Leyden in 1783: *De Antiqua Medico-philosophia orbi novo adaptanda: Oratio habita in capitolio Gulielmopolitano in comitiis Universitatis Virginiae, die xii Junii M.DCC.LXXXII* ... (Sabin, No. 17021); trans. and ed. Anthony Pelzer Wagener in *Journal of the History of Medicine and Allied Sciences*, 7 (1952), 10-67. Coste had also published at Newport, R. I., in 1780 a pharmacopoeia for the use of the French doctors accompanying him to America: *Compendium pharmaceuticum Militaribus Gallorum nosocomiis in orbe novi boreali adscriptum;* Francisco Guerra, *American Medical Bibliography, 1639-1783* (N.Y., 1962), No.

a-665. For further comments on Coste, see above, Pt. I, chap. 3, nn. 56 and 86.

Although Chastellux apparently delivered no oration at Williamsburg upon the occasion of receiving an honorary degree, his "Letter to Mr. Madison on the Progress of the Arts and Sciences in America" (Part IV, below) might be considered a formal acknowledgment of the honor. After his return to France Chastellux was instrumental in obtaining for the college a gift of books, in the name of the King, and a comparable gift for the University of Pennsylvania, which had also conferred a degree upon him; see above, Pt. I, chap. 3, n. 56. The William and Mary books have had a less fortunate history than those at Philadelphia. La Rochefoucauld-Liancourt, who visited Williamsburg in 1796, noted the Royal gift of 200 volumes, but remarked that they had been received in bad condition through the carelessness of a Richmond transfer agent who had let them lie in his cellar among barrels of sugar and oil; *Voyage dans les Etats-Unis d'Amérique* ... (Paris, 1798/9), IV, 291. Other calamities having befallen them, there remain today only two volumes; "Library of the College of William and Mary," *Wm. and Mary College Qtly.*, 19 (1910), 48-51. The survivors are two volumes by the astronomer, Jean Sylvain Bailly: *Lettres sur l'Atlantide de Platon et sur l'Ancienne Histoire de l'Asie* ... (London and Paris, 1779), in the form of letters to Voltaire in reply to criticisms of Bailly's *Histoire de l'Astronomie Ancienne* ... (Paris, 1775). These same volumes are at the University of Pennsylvania, and it is probable that the contents of the two gifts were roughly similar.

Appendix A

Description of the Natural Bridge

1. Further information about Baron de Turpin is meager, although his name is recorded in the military lists of the period. He was presumably trained at the Ecole Royale du Génie at Mézières, where the teaching, under such masters as Gaspard Monge (originator of descriptive geometry, one of the founders of the Ecole Polytechnique), was characterized by a combination of theory and practice. The school at Mézières was liquidated during the French Revolution, but its intellectual tradition and educational principles remained an important influence in the Ecole Polytechnique, created by the National Convention in 1794.

2. *Ch.* So interesting an object could not have escaped the curiosity and observations of Mr. Jefferson. He had measured the height and width of the Natural Bridge, and has mentioned it in an excellent memoir which he composed in 1781, and of which he had several copies printed last year [Paris, 1785] under the modest title of *Notes on the state of Virginia*, or rather with no title, for this work has not been made public. We hope, however, that the precious documents on natural philosophy as well as politics included in this work will not be lost to the public. A well-known man of letters has made use of it,* and we recommend the perusal of a book which is about to appear under the title of *Observations sur la Virginie.***

Gr. *Monsieur De Meunier, in his new article of Etats Unis in the last Livraison of La Nouvelle Encyclopédie. [Jean-Nicolas Démeunier; see

Boyd *et al.*, eds., *Jefferson Papers*, X, 3-65.] **The Abbé Morellet, who is translating them into French. [Abbé André Morellet (1727-1819); his anonymous translation of Jefferson's *Notes* was published in 1786, Paris, under the title *Observations sur la Virginie, par M. J....* A footnote appended by the Abbé Morellet to the description of the Natural Bridge, p. 58, informs his readers that: "This beautiful natural monument has also been described by M. le Marquis de C. in his American Journal, which is now being printed, and his more detailed description will be read with great interest after Mr. J's."]

The following is Mr. Jefferson's account of the Natural Bridge alluded to in this note, which I am happy in being able to lay before the reader:

"The *Natural bridge*, the most sublime of Nature's works,... is on the ascent of a hill, which seems to have been cloven through its length by some great convulsion. The fissure, just at the bridge, is, by some admeasurements, 270 feet deep, by others only 205. It is about 45 feet wide at the bottom, and 90 feet at the top; this of course determines the length of the bridge, and its height from the water. Its breadth in the middle, is about 60 feet, but more at the ends, and the thickness of the mass at the summit of the arch, about 40 feet. A part of this thickness is constituted by a coat of earth, which gives growth to many large trees. The residue, with the hill on both sides, is one solid rock of limestone. The arch approaches the semi-elliptical form; but the larger axis of the ellipsis, which would be the cord of the arch, is many times longer than the transverse. Though the sides of this bridge are provided in some parts with a parapet of fixed rocks, yet few men have resolution to walk to them and look over into the abyss. You involuntarily fall on your hands and feet, creep to the parapet and peep over it. Looking down from this height about a minute, gave me a violent head ach. If the view from the top be painful and intolerable, that from below is delightful in the extreme. It is impossible for the emotions arising from the sublime to be felt beyond what they are here: so beautiful an arch, so elevated, so light, and springing as it were up to heaven, the rapture of the spectator is really indescribable! The fissure continuing narrow, deep, and streight for a considerable distance above and below the bridge, opens a short but very pleasing view of the North mountain on one side, and Blue ridge on the other, at the distance each of them of about five miles. This bridge is in the county of Rockbridge, to which it has given name, and affords a public and commodious passage over a valley, which cannot be crossed elsewhere for a considerable distance. The stream passing under it is called Cedar creek. It is a water of James river, and sufficient in the driest seasons to turn a grist mill, though its fountain is not more than two miles above."

Ed. The passage from Jefferson's *Notes* cited here by Grieve is from the privately-printed 1785 edition, "Query V, Cascades," 38-40. In a manuscript note later added to his personal copy of the *Notes* Jefferson wrote: "This description was written after a lapse of several years from the time of my visit to the bridge, and under an error of recollection which requires apology. For it is from the bridge itself that the mountains are visible both ways, and not from the bottom of the fissure as my impression then was. The statement therefore in the former edition needs the corrections here given to it. Aug. 16, 1817." Jefferson's corrections are incorporated in the Richmond, 1853, edition of the *Notes* and in William Peden's recent edition (Chapel Hill, 1955).

3. *Ch.* Those who wish to form an exact idea of the Natural Bridge should not judge the platform of this Bridge from its appearance in the two engraved views published here [Plates II, III]. The ground over which travelers cross is nearly level, although the sorts of parapets formed along its edges by the rocks are not. The slope is still further exaggerated by an optical illusion, as these views were taken from the banks of the stream and from very close to the Bridge.

Ed. To the best of my knowledge, the engravings from Turpin's "plans" included in Chastellux's book were the first published views of the Natural Bridge. Soon after their publication they were copied by others and thus served as the prototype for many of the later views. The *Columbian Magazine* (1 [1787], 617-18), for example, reproduced Plate III and Turpin's portion of Chastellux's "Description," borrowed without acknowledgment from the English translation of the *Travels* (London, 1787). For a good selection of prints of the Natural Bridge see Robert L. Scribner, "Mr. Jefferson's Rock Bridge," *Virginia Cavalcade*, 4 (1955), 42-47; an excellent series of photographs is in Chester A. Reeds, *The Natural Bridge of Virginia and its Environs* (New York, 1927). A drawing apparently copied from Baron de Turpin's "Bird's-Eye View" (Plate I) is in a group of Jefferson's papers now in the Huntington Library, San Marino, Calif.; see Nichols, *Jefferson's Architectural Drawings*, checklist No. 523.

4. Baron de Turpin's measurements are given in the Ancien Régime *toises* and *pieds:* the *toise* being equivalent to 1.949 m., and the *pied* to 33 cm. Thus the old French *toise* was a bit longer than the English fathom (6 ft.), and the *pied* slightly more than the English foot. According to the measurements taken by Gilmer in 1815, the lower surface of the arch was about 160 feet above the surface of the water—which is not far from Turpin's figure of 150 *pieds*. Gilmer gave the height of the upper surface or top of the arch as 200 feet from the water. Modern descriptions approximate these figures.

5. *Ch.* See following this article the note on martins, which has been found too long to be included here with the text [Appendix B].

6. Chastellux's text reads: "*que c'était au travail seul des eaux qu'on devait la magnifique construction du Pont Naturel.*" Curiously enough, this was rendered by Grieve (or at least, so printed by his publisher) as: "that it was to the labour only of the Creator that we owe the magnificent construction of the Natural Bridge." Thus the key passage in Chastellux's thinking on this subject has long been beclouded for English-speaking readers! *The Story of the Natural Bridge*, a leaflet published by Natural Bridge of Virginia, Inc. (1955), for modern tourists, states (p. 6) under the heading "Frenchmen Came to See": "'It is the work of the Creator,' wrote the French officers in tribute to the mystery of the great rock monument." The leaflet also records that Dr. Norman Vincent Peale, "the magnetic and enthusiastic theologian," when relaxing after a brisk walk beneath the Bridge in 1953, told reporters: "The Bridge is wonderful isn't it, it makes you feel closer to God."

7. *Gr.* Mr. Jefferson, in his excellent *Notes on Virginia*, seems to lean to the system of Buffon, in the following sublime and animated description. . . .

Ed. Grieve here transcribes Jefferson's description of the passage of the Potomac through the Blue Ridge at Harper's Ferry, from "Query IV,

Mountains": "But the course of the great rivers are at right angles with these . . . . Yet here, as in the neighbourhood of the natural bridge, are people who have passed their lives within half a dozen miles, and have never been to survey these monuments of a war between rivers and mountains, which must have shaken the earth itself to its centre." Peden, ed., *Notes on Virginia*, 19-20. Following this passage Grieve then adds Charles Thomson's commentary on it, which had been included by Jefferson in his *Notes:* "The reflections I was led into on viewing this passage of the Patowmac through the Blue ridge were, that this country must have suffered some violent convulsion. . . . But these are only the visions of fancy." *Ibid.*, 197-99. Both passages are cited by Grieve from the 1785 edition of Jefferson's book.

8. John Filson, *The Discovery, Settlement and present State of Kentucke: and An Essay towards the Topography, and Natural History of that important Country* . . . ([Wilmington, Del., 1784]; Sabin, No. 24336), 30; for facsimile reprints, see the edition by Willard Rouse Jillson (Louisville, Kentucky, 1930) and a recent paperback edition by William H. Masterson (N.Y., 1962). A French translation by Parraud was published in Paris in 1785 under the title *Histoire de Kentucke, Nouvelle Colonie à l'Ouest de la Virginia* . . . *Ouvrage pour servir de Suite aux Lettres d'un Cultivateur Américain* (Sabin, No. 24338). Chastellux's quotation was from this French edition; Filson's original English text is used here.

9. The book that Chastellux read at Williamsburg was by Antonio de Ulloa (1716-95), Spanish scientist and traveler: *Noticias Americanas: Entretenimientos Físico—Históricos sobre la América Meridional, y la Septentrional Oriental: Comparacion General de los Territorios, Climas y Producciones en las Tres Especies Vegetal, Animal y Mineral* . . . (Madrid, 1772; Sabin, No. 97687). There was another Spanish edition (Madrid, 1792; Sabin, No. 36806), as well as a German translation (Sabin, No. 97689) and a French translation by J. B. Lefebvre de Villebrune (Paris, 1787; Sabin, No. 36805), but apparently no English translation. Chastellux's quotation is from chap. 2, paragraphs 9-12, "Entretenimiento II, El órden y disposicion en que están los terrenos de las Indias Occidentales, y de la notable variedad que hay en ellos." The English text presented here has been translated directly from the original Spanish; the Editor is indebted to Prof. A. G. Fischer, Department of Geology, Princeton Univ., and to Mrs. Fischer, for helpful suggestions.

10. The localities mentioned by Ulloa are between 12° and 13° South Latitude, in Peru, in the northwestern part of what is now the Department of Huancavelica. According to present administrative divisions, the city of Huancavelica is the capital of the Department of that name, and also designates one of the provinces within the Department. (Angaraes is now one of the other provinces in the Department of Huancavelica.) Conaica is both a small town and the name of one of the eight districts (capital, Izcuchaca) comprising the province of Huancavelica. The small river designated by Ulloa as "Chapllanca" appears to be a tributary of the Rio Mantaro, which flows into other rivers which eventually reach the Amazon. *Mapa Vial de los Departmentos de Huancavelica e Ica*, scale 1:500,000 (Lima, *ca.* 1940), published by Ministerio de Fomento, Direccion de Caminos y Ferrocarrites, Servicio Tecnico de Puentes y Caminos.

11. Jefferson had also pondered the same passage from Ulloa's *Noticias*, but drew conclusions differing from those reached by Chastellux. Whereas Ulloa's description confirmed Chastellux in his belief that the Natural Bridge was the result of the action of the waters, it did not shake Jefferson's theory of a "convulsion." Jefferson's comment (cited by Grieve) is as follows:

"Don Ulloa inclines to the opinion, that this channel has been effected by the wearing of the water which runs through it, rather than that the mountain should have been broken open by any convulsion of nature. But if it had been worn by the running of water, would not the rocks which form the sides, have been worn plane? or if, meeting in some parts with veins of harder stone, the water had left prominences on the one side, would not the same cause have sometimes, or perhaps generally, occasioned prominences on the other side also? Yet Don Ulloa tells us, that on the other side there are always corresponding cavities, and that these tally with the prominences so perfectly, that, were the two sides to come together, they would fit in all their indentures, without leaving any void. I think that this does not resemble the effect of running water, but looks rather as if the two sides had parted asunder. The sides of the break, over which is the Natural bridge of Virginia, consisting of a veiny rock which yields to time, the correspondence between the salient and re-entering inequalities, if it existed at all, has now disappeared. This break has the advantage of the one described by Don Ulloa in its finest circumstance; no portion in that instance having held together, during the separation of the other parts, so as to form a bridge over the Abyss." *Notes on Virginia*, "Query V," ed. Peden, 264.

12. Chastellux's description of the Natural Bridge elicited an interesting comment on the subject from William Carmichael (U.S. Minister in Spain), in a letter to Jefferson, written from Madrid, Oct. 3, 1786: "I have seen the work of the Marquis de Chastellux. I believe I was one of the first who gave a description of the Natural Bridge which excited so strongly his Admiration. In the course of a Voyage which I undertook for my health to the Springs of Augusta County, I was induced to visit that as well as several other Natural Curiosities of the Country. On my return to Maryland I endeavoured to engage Mr. Peale a painter, to make the same tour, with the view of taking views of many remarkable situations which struck me, then in the full enjoyment of a Romantic enthusiasm. I spoke to him so feelingly of this wonderful Bridge that he was induced to ask me a copy of my notes containing the Impression it made on me, assuring me that these only would enable him to sketch the Object. I gave him a very hasty and incorrect copy and I soon after saw it printed in a Philadelphia newspaper. I have still my journal of this voyage. The impressions it made on me are so strong, that if ever I return to America, It is my Intention to sell my little property and to establish myself beyond the Allegany Mountains, where by all forgot I may pass the rest of my days Inoffensively for others, doing all the good in my power and vegetating and decaying like the Trees which surround me, Affording shade in their prime and in their decay manure to the Soil they cover. I think I had the honor to mention this Natural Bridge to the Marquis de Chastellux, then Chevalier, during my residence in Paris in 1776-7." Boyd *et al.*, eds., *Jefferson Papers*, X, 427-29.

Appendix B

Notes on the Purple Martin and other American Birds

13. Mark Catesby, *The Natural History of Carolina, Florida and the Bahama Islands*..., 2 vols. (London, 1731-43), I, 51 and accompanying plate, "Hirundo purpurea/The Purple Martin/ Martinet couleur de pourpre." George Frederick Frick and Raymond Phineas Stearns have recently written a stimulating account of *Mark Catesby: The Colonial Audubon* (Urbana, 1961).

14. *Ch.* Pehr Kalm, Swedish traveler, who has certainly spared no details, speaks only very succinctly of this bird: he does not even note that the female is not of the same color as the male, and he seems to confuse it with the European martin, which he calls the English martin. See Vol. III, 113, German edition.

Ed. Pehr Kalm's work was first published in Stockholm, 1753-61, 3 vols. under the title *En Resa til Norra America;* a German translation was published in 1754-64, and an English translation (from the German) in 1770. An excellent modern edition in English is also available: Adolph B. Benson, ed., *The America of 1750; Peter Kalm's Travels in North America,* 2 vols. (New York, 1937). Kalm's reference to the martins, under date of Apr. 16, 1749 (Raccoon [Swedesboro], N. J.), will be found in the original Swedish edition, III, 88; and in Benson's edition, I, 284.

15. Among the schemes for a French-sponsored scientific expedition to the United States was the "Projet d'un voyage scientifique en Amérique" sent to the French government in Nov. 1784 by Saint-John de Crèvecoeur, "the American Farmer" (then French consul in New York). A copy of this report, addressed to the Duc de La Rochefoucauld-d'Enville, is in the Collection Clerc de Landresse, Bibliothèque Municipale de Mantes (Seine-et-Oise); a summary, in Julia Post Mitchell, *St. Jean de Crèvecoeur* (N. Y., 1916), 102-3. The plan was at least partially realized by the mission of the botanist André Michaux (1746-1802) who came to the United States under French government sponsorship in 1785. Michaux established nurseries for the cultivation and transshipment of American plants to France at Bergen Neck, N. J. and at Charleston, S. C. Through his extensive travels and observations André Michaux—like his son, François-André Michaux (1770-1855), who continued his father's work—had an essential role in the recording and description of the flora of North America. See also Gilbert Chinard, "Les Michaux et leurs précurseurs," in *Les Botanistes Français en Amérique du Nord avant 1850* (Colloques Internationaux du Centre National de la Recherche Scientifique, No. 63 [Paris, 1957]), 263-86.

16. This William Fleming (1736-1824)—not to be confused with others of the same name—was a fellow student of Jefferson at the College of William and Mary prior to the Revolution. An active patriot during the war, he served as a Virginia delegate to the Continental Congress in 1779. In 1780 the Virginia legislature elected him a judge of the General Court; in 1788 he became Judge of the Court of Appeals, of which he was president from 1810 until his death. He had an estate called "Summerfield" in Chesterfield Co. "The Ancestors and Descendants of John Rolfe with Notes on Some Connected Families," *Va. Mag. of Hist. and Biog.,* 24 (1916), 327-33 (with portrait of Judge Fleming).

17. The question of what happened to martins and the other species of swallows during the winter had long puzzled naturalists. Pehr Kalm, for example, noted in his *Travels in North America*, ed. Benson, I, 283: "The people differed here in their opinions about the abode of swallows in winter. A number of the Swedes thought that they lay at the bottom of the sea; others, not only the Swedes and Englishmen but also the French in Canada, thought that they migrated southward in autumn and returned in spring. I have likewise been credibly informed in Albany, that they have been found sleeping in deep holes and clefts of rocks during winter." Samuel Williams in *The Natural and Civil History of Vermont* (Walpole, N.H., 1794), 116-18, reporting "swallow trees" at Middlebury and at Bridport, concluded: "Neither of these accounts, are attended with the highest degree of evidence, which the subject may admit of: But I am led to believe from them, that the house swallow, in this part of America, generally resides during the winter, in the hollow of trees; and that the ground swallows, find security in the mud, at the bottom of lakes, rivers, and ponds." Several decades later DeWitt Clinton alluded to the question in a paper published in the Lyceum of Natural History of New York, *Annals*, I (1824), 158: "The mystery, which has surrounded the brumal retreat of this bird, has also added to its celebrity. Some have assigned to it winter quarters in the moon; others have designated its hybernaculum in invisible satellites closer to the earth. Aristotle and Pliny have placed it in warm and sequestered places. Olaus Magnus and [Athanasius] Kircher have sent it to the bottom of lakes and rivers; and even in our times, reputable men, laboring under optical delusion, have declared that they have witnessed its descent into the Hudson and the pond on Manhattan Island, called the Collect. All these speculations and conjectures have yielded to the doctrine of emigration. Like all other migrating birds, the swallow congregates in flocks at the time of its departure, and probably ascends out of sight on its transit." As a supplement to Clinton's paper this same issue of the *Annals* printed a contribution from John James Audubon (his first published scientific paper) entitled "Facts and Observations connected with the permanent residence of *Swallows* in the United States." By reporting his observations on the winter residence of swallows which had migrated from the north to the lower Mississippi valley Audubon hoped to settle conclusively "the long agitated question, respecting the emigration or supposed torpidity of the Swallow."

Appendix C

The Opossum

18. Buffon's account of "Le Sarigue, ou l'Opossum" first appeared in 1763 in Tome X of his *Histoire naturelle, générale et particulière;* this volume was the seventh in the series devoted to "les Animaux quadrupèdes." There were many subsequent reprintings. Chastellux, upon his return to Paris, no doubt submitted his report on the opossum to Buffon even before he published it in 1786, for it was obviously written with the Master in mind. Although Buffon must therefore have been acquainted with the Chastellux-D'Aboville study before his death in 1788, it was unfortunately never included in any of the supplements or subsequent editions of the

Histoire naturelle published by his disciples. It is mentioned in Thomas Bewick's *A General History of the Quadrupeds* (Newcastle upon Tyne, 1791), 395-97; and by Geoffroy de St.-Hilaire, rather disparagingly, in his "Mémoire sur la génération des Animaux à Bourse et le développement de leur foetus," *Annales des Sciences Naturelles*, 1 (1824), 392-408. But the fact that it failed to be included in Buffon's *Natural History*—which remained the bible of naturalists for many years—probably explains why certain of its valid conclusions were not generally accepted until 1850 or thereabouts.

19. See the correspondence of Peter Collinson of London and John Custis of Williamsburg, Virginia, in E. G. Swem, ed., *Brothers of The Spade...* (Barre, Mass., 1957), 55-56, 59, 169. In his letter of Jan. 25, 1738/9 Collinson writes of the opossum: "I should think that with you a Male & Female might be procur'd and kept in suitable place paled in with high pales and be so Situate as to be Near Dayly Observation & Inspection and soone after Copulation be dayly Examined by some person Skilled in surgery and anatomy and if necessary be Desected and Examined, to see if there was any Ducts or Vessels Lead from the Uterus to the Teats, for it is highly probable they First received their Formation and Vivification in the Womb and in their Minutest State by proper ducts be conveyed to the Teat but all this is conjecture."

20. Fiacre Robillard (b. 1733, St. Rémy-en-l'Eau, near Beauvais), after studies at the Hôtel-Dieu, began his career as army surgeon in 1757 during the Seven Years' War. In 1772 he became *Chirurgien major* at the Hospital in Metz and returned there as *Chirurgien-en-chef* after accompanying Rochambeau's army to America as its chief surgeon. Robillard received the honorary degree of Master of Arts from the University of Pennsylvania in Dec. 1782, at the same time that Chastellux received an LL.D. and Doctors Coste and Borgella doctorates of medicine; the lesser degree given to Robillard emphasizes the distinction maintained in France between surgeons and physicians; see above, Pt. I, chap. 3, n. 56. He was one of the passengers on the *Émeraude*, which took Rochambeau, Chastellux, Dr. Coste, and other officers back to France early in 1783. Rochambeau pays tribute to Robillard's services in his *Mémoires* (I, 296); Coste, the chief physician, has also high praise for him in his brochure, *Du Service des Hôpitaux Militaires rappelé aux vrais principes* (Paris, 1790). Robillard's special care of Charles de Lameth, who was badly wounded at Yorktown, and his decision not to resort to amputation but to trust to natural healing, gained him the gratitude of this young officer's family and friends. During the French Revolution Robillard served as *Chirurgien consultant* with the Armée de la Meuse. Details concerning Robillard and the other medical personnel of the French army will be found in Bouvet, *Service de Santé*. I am indebted to Mr. E. Vialard, of the Archives Historiques du Service de Santé Militaire, Paris, for a transcript of Robillard's *état des services* and for help in collecting other information about him.

21. Louis-Jean-Marie Daubenton (1716-99), one of Buffon's numerous collaborators, supplied many of the anatomical descriptions which were incorporated in the *Histoire naturelle;* his work is specifically mentioned in the article on the opossum, which Chastellux is here referring to. Daubenton was "Garde et Démonstrateur du Cabinet d'Histoire Naturelle" at the Jardin du Roi (of which Buffon was *Intendant* from 1739 until his

death in 1788); and later, after the Jardin du Roi had become the Muséum National d'Histoire Naturelle, professor of mineralogy there. Daubenton's grave is to be seen today on a hillock known as the Labyrinth, within the precincts of the Muséum d'Histoire Naturelle in Paris.

22. The frigate *Hermione*, under the command of Comte de La Touche-Tréville (1745-1804), set sail for France from Yorktown in Virginia on Feb. 2, 1782. Among the passengers was the Baron de Vioménil, who was to return to America the following September. Acomb, ed., *Von Closen Journal*, 173.

23. François-Marie, Chevalier (later Comte) d'Aboville (1730-1817) had only recently been promoted from the rank of colonel to that of *Brigadier*, in recognition of his brilliant role in the siege of Yorktown. D'Aboville was later to play a part in the Battle of Valmy (Sept. 29, 1792), where he commanded the French artillery. Contenson, *Cincinnati*, 128, portrait 2; *Exposition rétrospective des Colonies françaises de l'Amérique du Nord*, 164-65, plate 120. Chastellux saw D'Aboville again at Boston in Nov. 1782 at a farewell banquet in his honor: below, Pt. III, chap. 2, Nov. 21, 1782.

24. "The span of pregnancy in the opossum, based on observed matings and births, was approximated very early. In 1783 [*sic* for 1782] the Count d'Aboville ... determined the period to be fourteen [*sic* for thirteen] days. Dr. Meigs [1847] arrived at the same figure. Dr. Michel [1851] might have corroborated these findings exactly if his medical practice had not prevented his looking for the embryos in the pouch before the sixteenth day after the observed mating. D'Aboville's data were not known to Barton [1806] or to Rengger [1830], whose estimates ranged from twenty-two to twenty-six days." Carl G. Hartman, *Possums* (Austin, Texas, 1952), 73. Hartman himself calculates "the total period of gestation from mating to birth at just about twelve days and eighteen hours."

25. D'Aboville's concluding surmises about the placement of the mother's nipples and their disappearance—which he appears to be reporting from hearsay and not from his own observations—are incorrect. See Hartman, *Possums*, 92.

PART III

Introduction

Interlude between Journeys, May—October 1782

1. Gov. Benjamin Harrison to the Speaker of the House of Delegates, Richmond, May 20, 1782, in *Official Letters of the Governors of the State of Virginia*, 3 vols. (Richmond, 1926-29), III, 237-38.

2. Harrison to Rochambeau, Richmond, June 26, 1782, *ibid.*, 257. See also Harrison's letter to Washington, July 11, 1782, *ibid.*, 265, and for a further discussion of the question, Benjamin Quarles, *The Negro in the American Revolution*, 160-62.

3. Chastellux to Gov. Harrison, Newcastle, July 6, 1782, in Stone, *French Allies*, 503.

4. The story of the claret can be traced in *Official Letters of the Governors of Virginia*, III.

5. Rochambeau to The Gentlemen of the General Assembly of the State of Virginia, Williamsburg, June 28, 1782, Andre deCoppet Collection of American Historical Manuscripts, Princeton Univ. Lib. The letter is in a clerk's hand, signed "le Cte de Rochambeau."

6. For the story of the French army's northward march see sources cited above, Pt. II, Introduction, n. 9. Also: John Austin Stevens, "The Return of the French, 1782-1783," *Mag. of Amer. Hist.*, 7 (1881), 1-35.

7. Rochambeau to Ségur, Minister of War, Baltimore, July 28, 1782, in Vicomte de Noailles, *Marins et Soldats Français*, 313.

8. The adventures of the *Gloire* and the *Aigle*, the ships which brought these men to America (with a shipment of French hard money), and the near-disaster in the Delaware estuary, are vividly related by the Comte de Ségur in his *Mémoires* and by the Prince de Broglie in his "Journal du Voyage...," Société des Bibliophiles Français, *Mélanges* (1903), 13-148.

Chapter 1

Hartford, Connecticut, to Portsmouth, New Hampshire

1. *Gr.* The Translator attended the French army on their march, nearly the whole way, from Alexandria [Virginia] to the North River [Hudson], and was a witness to their strict discipline, and the surprising harmony between them and the people of the country, to whom they gave not the slightest reason of complaint. He insists the more on this fact, as it appears to him no less singular than interesting. On their arrival at their quarters on the march, the whole country came to see them, and it was a general scene of gaiety and good humor. When they encamped at Alexandria, on the ground formerly occupied by Braddock, the most elegant and handsome young ladies of the neighborhood danced with the officers on the turf, in the middle of the camp, to the sound of military music; and (a circumstance which will appear singular to European ideas) the circle was in a great measure composed of soldiers, who, from the heat of the weather, had disengaged themselves from their clothes, retaining not an article of dress except their shirts, which in general were neither extremely long, nor in the best condition; nor did this occasion the least embarrassment to the ladies, many of whom were of highly polished manners, and the most exquisite delicacy; or to their friends or parents; so whimsical and arbitrary are manners.

The French army, at the time the Marquis speaks of, had been for some time encamped at Crompond near Cortland's Manor, a few miles from that of General Washington's and between which there was a daily intercourse. The Translator dined, in October, 1782, in General Washington's tent, with the Marquis de Laval, the Baron de Vioménil, and several French officers, within hearing of the British guns, which were at that period happily become a *brutum fulmen*.

Ed. Grieve records other details of his visit to the American army here, above, Pt. I, chap. 2, n. 23.

2. Lynch had been Chastellux's traveling companion on both his first journey in 1780 (see above, Pt. I, chap. 1, n. 8) and on the Virginia excursion in the spring of 1782 (above, Pt. II, chap. 1, n. 2). Montesquieu, Chastellux's traveling companion on the first journey only, was now back

in America after a leave in France. The "Baron de Talleyrand," who had come to America for the first time in the autumn of 1782, was Jacques Boson (or Bozon) de Talleyrand-Périgord (1764-1830), not to be confused with his older and more famous brother, Charles-Maurice de Talleyrand-Périgord (1754-1838). The elder Talleyrand visited the United States during the French Revolution as an *émigré*, but was not in America during the War of Independence, as some writers have mistakenly concluded from Chastellux's text. The "M. de Vaudreuil" mentioned here was Jean-Louis de Rigaud, *Vicomte* de Vaudreuil (1763-1816), a young cousin of the two other Vaudreuils mentioned subsequently by Chastellux in his narrative: Louis-Philippe de Rigaud, *Marquis* de Vaudreuil (1724-1802), who commanded the French squadron which had come to Boston from the West Indies after De Grasse's defeat in the Battle of the Saints, and which was to transport Rochambeau's army back home; and his brother, Louis de Rigaud, *Comte* de Vaudreuil (1728-1810), also a naval officer, who was at Portsmouth, N. H., with the French ships refitting there. Brief biographies of these three Vaudreuils will be found in Contenson, *Cincinnati*, 276-77.

3. Rochambeau's army had encamped near Bolton meetinghouse in June 1781 on its westward march from Rhode Island to the Hudson; it again camped about 2 miles east of the meetinghouse, as mentioned here, in Nov. 1782, when proceeding eastward to Providence; see MS. maps, Berthier Papers, Nos. 14-4-5, 21-5, 39-46, Princeton Univ. Lib. Bolton meetinghouse—now Bolton Center—is on a hill to the south of the present main roads. The crossroad mentioned by Chastellux is near the present Manchester-Bolton town line. He took the so-called "middle road" to Boston. Chastellux spelled the innkeeper's name "Kindall," which Grieve changed to "Kendall"; but the available evidence points to Kimball as the correct form. Nathaniel Low's *Almanack...for 1777*, as well as Bickerstaff's *Boston Almanack for 1777*, and *for 1778*, in their tabulation of "Roads to the principal Towns on the Continent, &c. from Boston; with the Names of those who keep Houses of Entertainment" give the name of the tavernkeeper at Coventry, along the "Middle Road," as "Kimball." Although there is a gap for the years 1770 through 1784 in the files of tavern licenses for Windham Co., Conn. State Archives, the extant record for 1785 gives the name of Timothy Kimball as tavernkeeper at Coventry. His house was presumably in what is now the village of North Coventry (U.S. Route 44A).

4. Clark's inn at Pompey Hollow, now Warrenville, in the town of Ashford, is still standing as a private residence just to the northeast of the intersection of U.S. Route 44 (the "middle road" to Boston) and State Route 89 (Mount Hope River valley route). The so-called "Pompey Hollow Tavern," still in excellent condition and well cared for, was begun in 1710 by John Mixer; from 1757 to 1799 it was owned and kept as an inn by Benjamin Clark (Chastellux's host), who was in turn succeeded by Joseph Palmer from 1799 to 1825. Information concerning the history of the house and land, collected from the town records by the present (1961) owners, Mr. and Mrs. Robert Haggett, has been made available through their courtesy to the Editor. See also Terry, *Old Inns of Conn.*, 216-19, illus. Chastellux's mention of rivers to the eastward, marked on his map as "Monchoas" and "Bigslack," presents a problem in nomenclature unsolved by the Editor.

5. The meetinghouse that Chastellux saw on Woodstock Hill had been built in 1720-21. It survived until 1821, when it was replaced by the present Congregational Church, located not far from the site of the earlier structure, adjoining the burial ground, on the Main St. of Woodstock Hill. The 18th-century building is described in J. Frederick Kelly, *Early Connecticut Meetinghouses*, 2 vols. (N. Y., 1948), II, 327-31.

6. *Gr.* This is one of the best houses I met with in America.

Ed. Chandler's Tavern was on the northeastern edge of the town of Woodstock, on present Paine District Road, near the point where the road from Woodstock Hill to Fabyan crosses the Woodstock-Thompson town line. Chandler Hill is in the vicinity. The farmhouse known locally as "the old Paine place," although presumably not the original building, is on the site of Chastellux's stopping place. See "Map of Woodstock, Conn.," by John S. Lester, 1883, with topographical and historical names added by George Clinton Williams, 1886; U. S. Geological Survey, Putnam, Conn., quadrangle, 1955. Chastellux's "Mrs. Chandler" was presumably Dorothy Church Chandler, widow of Samuel Chandler, who died Apr. 8, 1781, aged 78; she died Mar. 20, 1793, aged 79; their gravestones, from which these dates have been taken, are in the cemetery on Woodstock Hill. Samuel Chandler had the rank of captain (French and Indian War?); he had a nephew who was also named Samuel (1735-90) and also a captain (Revolutionary War). Portraits of the younger Capt. Samuel Chandler and of his wife Ann Paine Chandler, painted by his brother Winthrop Chandler, are reproduced in Clarence Winthrop Bowen, *The History of Woodstock, Connecticut* (Norwood, Mass., 1926), I, 154, where it is assumed (p. 204) that this younger Capt. Samuel Chandler was a tavernkeeper during the Revolution; however this may be, Chastellux's reference to Widow Chandler would seem to apply to his aunt. See *ibid.*, III, 301-464, genealogy of the Chandler family.

7. The tavern in Oxford, no longer standing, was at the corner of present Main (State Route 12) and Charlton Sts.—still the principal road junction in the center of the town. Dr. Joseph Lord and his wife Lucy kept the tavern for a short period in 1782-83; George F. Daniels, *History of the Town of Oxford, Massachusetts . . .* (Oxford, 1892), 233, 596.

8. Chastellux's host was Lazarus LeBaron (1744-1827), born in Barbados, West Indies, who had come to Sutton from Boston *ca.* 1774 and acquired a house there, which he kept as an inn. His grave and those of three of his wives are in the Sutton cemetery. About 1794 he built on the site of his first Sutton residence a new house, which is still standing in excellent condition and still owned by descendants. It is the second house after the church, on the right (south), just before descending the hill, when proceeding northeast towards Grafton along what is still called the "Boston Road." William A. Benedict and Hiram A. Tracy, comps., *History of the Town of Sutton, Massachusetts, from 1704 to 1876 . . .* (Worcester, 1878), I, 294-95, illus.; Mary LeBaron Stockwell, comp., *Descendants of Francis LeBaron of Plymouth, Mass.* (Boston, 1904), 47-48, and photograph of LeBaron house facing p. 46.

9. The inn kept by Abijah Gale—a citizen of some prominence in the locality—was in the town of Westborough, about two and a half miles beyond the center of the village, on the road to Southborough. The house now on the old site (privately owned), although greatly changed in ex-

ternal appearance, retains some parts of the original structure. It is on East Main St., State Route 30, a half a mile or so from the Westborough-Southborough town line, on the left (west) of this road just before it is crossed by a small brook that loses itself in a swampy meadow and before it is joined by Smith and Walker Sts. H. P. De Forest and E. C. Bates, *The History of Westborough, Massachusetts* (Westborough, 1891); Harriette M. Forbes, ed., *The Diary of Rev. Ebenezer Parkman, of Westborough, Mass.* (Westborough, 1899), 69*n* with photograph of "Gale Tavern"; F. W. Beers, *Atlas of Worcester County, Mass.* (N.Y., 1870), plate 68; U.S. Geological Survey, Marlboro, Mass., quadrangle, 1953. For confirmation of this information I am indebted to Dr. Francis G. Walett, editor of a new edition of Ebenezer Parkman's diary, the first installment of which appeared in the American Antiquarian Society *Proceedings*, 71 (1961), 361-448.

10. *Gr.*–about two pence-halfpenny.

11. *Ch.* It took place on April 19, 1775. General Gage had detached from Boston all his grenadiers, all his light infantry, and some other troops, amounting in all to 900 men, under the orders of Lieutenant Colonel Smith and Major Pitcairn. At Lexington they met a company of militia, whom they found under arms: the English in a haughty tone ordered the Americans to disperse; the latter refused to do so, and while the contestation was still confined to words, the English fired without warning, and by this discharge killed seven or eight Americans, who had not yet taken any measures to defend themselves or take shelter from the fire. They were obliged to give way before greater numbers. The English advanced to Concord, where they paid dearly for their violence and for this first act of hostility, for which they alone were responsible. This day cost them nearly 300 men. Major Pitcairn was killed at the battle of Bunker Hill, a short time after the affair of Concord.

Ed. Chastellux calls the innkeeper Mr. "John," but this was merely his phonetic transcription of Jones. Ephraim Jones's tavern (no longer standing) was on the north side of the road (now Main St.) leading from the South Bridge to Monument Square; it was next to the jail and not far beyond the mill dam. See the reconstructed map of Concord in 1775, and the reproduction of Amos Doolittle's "A View of the Town of Concord," in Allen French, *The Day of Concord and Lexington* (Boston, 1925), 152. Although French does not include Chastellux's account among the sources discussed in his exhaustive study of the events at Concord on April 19, it deserves serious consideration. As the report of a conversation with a witness and participant, only seven and a half years after the event, it is more nearly contemporary evidence than several of the much later depositions and reminiscences cited. In describing Pitcairn's appearance at Jones's tavern, French (pp. 175-76) refers to a "tradition" recorded by Samuel Adams Drake in *Historic Fields and Mansions of Middlesex* (Boston, 1874), 381-82, but he is apparently unaware that Drake's recital of the episode was borrowed almost verbatim from Chastellux. The Chastellux-Jones account is likewise overlooked in the most recent study of the Concord fight, Arthur Bernon Tourtellot's *William Diamond's Drum, The Beginning of the War of the American Revolution* (N. Y., 1959), and in the same author's *A Bibliography of the Battles of Concord and Lexington* (N. Y.,

1959). Tourtellot's map of Concord in 1775 (based on French), facing p. 217, provides a convenient key to Chastellux's narrative.

12. Andover in 1782 consisted of the two towns known today as North Andover and Andover. The earliest settlement was in what is now North Andover, where a church was organized in 1645. In 1709 a South Parish was established with borders similar to the present town of Andover; henceforth the First, or North Parish, became commonly known as North Andover. In 1826 the South Parish was further subdivided by the organization of a West Parish. In 1855 the town was divided, the South and West Parishes retaining the name of plain Andover and the North Parish formally taking the name of North Andover. Chastellux's halt was thus at the locality known today as West Andover, in the town of Andover, although as it was in 1782 part of the South Parish he referred to it, correctly for the time, as South Andover. Captain Asa Foster (who acquired his rank from service in the French and Indian War) kept a public house not far from the crossroads where the present West Parish meetinghouse was built in 1826. See Sarah Loring Bailey, *Historical Sketches of Andover, Mass.* (Boston, 1880), 101, 406–which gives the location of Foster's house as not far from the West Meetinghouse "near the present [i.e., 1880] residence of Mr. Charles Shattuck." Chastellux's road, corresponding to present State Route 133, took him directly from Foster's to North Andover, through today's Shawsheen, and did not pass the South Meetinghouse in what is today Andover.

13. In 1781 Joseph Harrod opened as an inn the house inherited from his father Benjamin Harrod, who died that year. Known as "The Freemasons' Arms," it was located straight up the hill from the ferry on the site now occupied by the City Hall (junction of Mass. State Route 110 and N.H. 125, opposite the Hannah Dustin statue). The Harrod house was torn down in 1847; at the entrance to the present City Hall (built 1859) is a marble tablet, placed there in 1890, recalling that this is the "Site of Harrod's Tavern, 'Freemasons Arms,' Washington's Headquarters November 4-5, 1789 [i.e., during his Presidential tour of that year]." Albert LeRoy Bartlett, The Story of Haverhill in Massachusetts (*ca.* 1925), unpubl. typescript in Haverhill Public Library, 157, 200, 274-75; George Wingate Chase, *The History of Haverhill, Massachusetts* ... (Haverhill, 1861).

14. *Ch.* One should remember that "falls," or rapids, are the places where rivers form cascades, and where navigation is interrupted.

15. The provinces of Bourbonnais and Nivernais are in central France, not far to the south of Chastellux's family estate, the Château de Chastellux in the Morvan hills.

16. There seems to be some confusion, or error, in Chastellux's transcription of this name, which he may have confused with Brewster of Portsmouth. No record of a tavernkeeper with a name resembling "Ruspert" has been found. The chief Exeter tavern at the time was the Raleigh Tavern kept by Col. Samuel Folsom at the corner of Front and Water Sts.; the building was removed from its original site and now stands at the corner of Water and Spring Sts. (owned by the New Hampshire Chapter of the Society of the Cincinnati). Charles H. Bell, *History of the Town of Exeter, New Hampshire* (Exeter, 1888), 95, map of Exeter in 1802, facing p. 317.

17. Colonel William Brewster (1741-1818) was at this time the landlord of the Bell Tavern, located on Market Square in the center of Portsmouth. The tavern, built in 1743, took its name from a blue-painted bell which served as its sign; it was destroyed by fire in 1867. C. S. Gurney, *Portsmouth Historic and Picturesque* (Portsmouth, 1902), 24, 26, with photograph of tavern taken prior to its destruction. Mary Caroline Crawford, *Old New England Inns*, new ed. (Boston, 1924), 304-6.

18. *Gr.* The Marquis de Vaudreuil's squadron was then at Boston, and some of his ships [under the command of his brother, the Comte de Vaudreuil] were refitting, and taking in masts at Portsmouth. M. d'Albert de Rions is the officer who commanded the evolutions of the French squadron, on the late visit of the king to Cherbourg.

Ed. Grieve, in the last sentence, refers to Louis XVI's visit of inspection to the new harbor improvements at Cherbourg in June 1786. The French squadron under the Marquis de Vaudreuil had arrived at Boston, from the West Indies, early in Aug. 1782, and remained there until it set sail for the West Indies again, with Rochambeau's army aboard, on Dec. 24, 1782. From this squadron at Boston several ships were sent to Portsmouth, N. H., among them the *Pluton* and the *Auguste*, which were still there at the time of Chastellux's visit. These two ships did not subsequently sail with the squadron from Boston, as intended, but proceeded separately to Puerto Cabello [Province of Caracas, New Spain, now Venezuela], where they were rejoined by the rest of Vaudreuil's squadron in Feb. 1783; Acomb, ed., *Von Closen Journal*, 294. According to the Comte de Ségur (*Mémoires*, I, 456-60), the delay caused by the Marquis de Vaudreuil's desire to wait just outside Boston harbor for the two ships from Portsmouth nearly resulted in disaster because of a sudden storm that surprised the squadron there. On D'Albert de Rions and his residence, see below, this chap., n. 26.

19. The journal of the Comte de Vaudreuil (younger brother of the Marquis) has recently been published in *Neptunia*, Nos. 45 ff., under the title, "Notes de campagne du Comte Rigaud de Vaudreuil, 1781-1782"; the portions covering the stay at Portsmouth, Aug. 15-Dec. 29, 1782, are in No. 49 (Winter, 1958), 34-41, and No. 50 (Spring, 1958), 29-35. Although this is primarily a naval officer's logbook rather than a discursive personal diary, Vaudreuil gives a few impressions of the town and its inhabitants. Chastellux's visit is not mentioned in Vaudreuil's journal. References to the French hospital and care of sick and wounded at Portsmouth will be found in Bouvet, *Service de Santé*, 102.

20. The Reverend Joseph Buckminster (1751-1812) was pastor of the First (or North) Congregational Church of Portsmouth from 1779 to 1812; the present North Church, on Market Square at the corner of Congress and Pleasant Sts., built in 1854, is on the site of the earlier edifice. A year or so after Chastellux's visit to the church the same young minister, on Dec. 11, 1783, the "Day of the General Thanksgiving throughout the United States after the Ratification of the Treaty of Peace and the Acknowledgement of their Independence," again skillfully introduced politics into his sermon by comparing Louis XVI to the good Samaritan who "rose to our assistance," and, "as a second Cyrus, offered his aid for securing our Liberties" (Evans, No. 18385). Eliza Buckminster Lee, *Memoirs of Rev. Joseph Buckminster, D.D., and of his son, Rev. Joseph Stevens Buckminster* (Boston, 1849).

21. "The little island of Rising Castle" is Badger's Island, where the most important shipyards were located in the 18th century; such vessels as John Paul Jones's *Ranger* were built here. Two manuscript maps of Portsmouth Harbor, roughly contemporary with Chastellux's visit, entitled "Plan de la Rivière de Piscataqua depuis son Embouchure jusqu'à la ville de Portsmouth" (with also, a title in English), are in the French Navy Archives; these are among the "Karpinski photographs" of maps relating to American history in French archives. Both the Portsmouth maps use the name "Rising Castle" to describe Badger's Island; one of them further indicates the "chantier où a été construit l'Ameriqua." A redrawing of this latter map will be found in Samuel Eliot Morison, *John Paul Jones, A Sailor's Biography* (Boston, 1959), 328. The island is today intersected by the Memorial Bridge (U.S. Route 1) leading from Portsmouth to Kittery, Me.

22. *Ed.* The *America*, a 74-gun ship of the line, built for the Continental Navy at Portsmouth, had been presented to France to replace the *Magnifique*, a comparable ship which had been wrecked on Lovell's Island in Boston Harbor when Vaudreuil's squadron arrived there in Aug. 1782; see resolution of Sept. 3, 1782, in Ford *et al.*, eds., *Journals of Cont. Cong.*, XXIII, 543. *America* was finally launched, not without some difficulties, on Nov. 5. The story of this ship is related by Morison in his *John Paul Jones*, 318-30. According to Morison's account (which gives references to pertinent documents in the French National Archives, Marine), the subsequent career of *America* was not a glorious one—despite the assertions of Grieve in his note (below) and of other chroniclers. "When surveyed at Brest in 1786, she was found to be *'entièrement pourri'*—riddled with dry rot, almost every plank and timber rotten, although the finish and joinerwork were still good. The Ministry of Marine condemned her to be broken up."

Gr. This ship was designed for the well known Paul Jones, who by his command of the little squadron on the coasts of England, had acquired the title of commodore and was sighing after that of admiral of America, which Congress, no bad appreciators of merit, thought proper to refuse him. The Translator met him at a public table at Boston [in 1782], on his return from Portsmouth, where he told the company, that notwithstanding the reason he had to be discontented, he had given his advice in the construction and launching of the vessel, in which latter operation, however, the ship struck fast on the slip, but without any material damage. This accident is not intended by any means as an imputation on Mr. Jones, who certainly was fortunate enough, at one time, to render considerable service to America. He is said to have acquired a considerable property by the prizes he made in that cruise, but his officers and crews complain (the Translator does not say with what justice) that there has never been any distribution of the prize money, and that numbers of his maimed and mutilated sailors were reduced to beg for a subsistence in France, and elsewhere, to the discredit of America. Mr. Jones read some pretty enough verses in his own honor to the same company, at Brackett's tavern in Boston, extracted from a London newspaper, and said to be written by Lady Craven. The *America* is now [1786] at Brest, and is esteemed one of the handsomest ships in the French navy.

23. Washington Island is today known as Pierce's Island. Remains of the earthworks of the fort are still in evidence. Concerning the defensive works

built there by the French, at the time an English attack was feared in Oct. 1782, see Vaudreuil, "Notes de campagne," *Neptunia*, No. 50 (Spring, 1958), 30.

24. Chastellux had been colonel of the *Régiment de Guyenne* from 1761 to 1769. The army detachments with the French ships at Portsmouth were from regiments stationed in the West Indies which had come to Boston in 1782 with Vaudreuil's squadron. When it was feared that the English might attack Portsmouth, Rochambeau dispatched Col. de Fleury to confer with the Marquis de Vaudreuil concerning the defenses of Portsmouth and to take command of such troops as might be sent there. The Comte de Vaudreuil writes in his journal: "From intelligence received in Boston that the enemy's naval forces at New York planned some attack on the division we had at Portsmouth, my brother thought it wise to send us a reinforcement of 600 men from the troops with his Squadron. They arrived on the 6th October and were commanded by M. de Fleury, Major of infantry. My brother had come [to Portsmouth] several days earlier with this officer to observe our position and decide upon the defensive measures to be taken in case of attack." *Ibid;* see also Acomb, ed., *Von Closen Journal*, 245-53. The English attack did not materialize; the Comte de Fleury (see above, Pt. I, chap. 1, Nov. 22, 1780, and n. 96) was evidently no longer at Portsmouth when Chastellux was there. In addition to the Viennois Regiment, mentioned by Chastellux, Vaudreuil's journal mentions 300 men from the Armagnac Regiment quartered in Newcastle. A brief account of the Viennois Regiment during the American Revolution will be found in Thomas Balch, *The French in America during the War of Independence of the United States, 1777-83*, 2 vols. (Phila. 1891-95), II, 37-38. The names of nine men from this regiment who died at Portsmouth are recorded in Warrington Dawson, *Les 2112 Français Morts aux Etats-Unis de 1777 à 1783 en combattant pour l'Indépendance Américaine* (Paris, 1936; reprinted from Société des Américanistes, *Journal*, New Ser., 28 [1936]), 74-75.

25. According to the Comte de Vaudreuil's account of the same accident ("Notes de campagne," *Neptunia*, No. 50 [Spring, 1958], 31), the casualties were three men dead and four wounded. He also relates that he sent to Boston for the mast of the wrecked *Magnifique*, which was used to replace the damaged one on the *Auguste*. The names of at least two of the victims have survived in the records of the French navy (Archives Nationales, Paris): Jean-François Goisec, a *bosseman* from Recouvrance, and Pierre Le Men, a sailor from Saint-Brieuc in Brittany. Dawson, *Français Morts*, 89-91.

26. According to Charles W. Brewster, *Rambles about Portsmouth*, 2d Ser. (Portsmouth, 1869), in which Chastellux's account of his visit to the town is discussed, 38-44; "Mr. [d']Albert's abode was probably at Mrs. Richard Shortridge's boarding-house, where some of the officers of the fleet, among them Vaudreuil, boarded. This boarding-house was in Deer Street: the house, remodelled, was long the residence of the late Peter Jenness and his family." Brewster's statement that Vaudreuil also "boarded" here must be taken to mean that he only took his meals at Mrs. Shortridge's, if it is to be reconciled with Chastellux's statement (Nov. 11, 1782) that the Comte de Vaudreuil "lodged" at Mr. Wentworth's. For a brief account of Charles Hector, Comte d'Albert de Rions (1728-1810), see Contenson, *Cincinnati*, 130, portrait fig. 3.

27. In 1782 John Langdon and his wife were living in a house on Pleasant St. (no longer standing, site now occupied by Elks' Home). Construction of the more elaborate house, known as the "Governor John Langdon Mansion Memorial" and now owned by the Society for the Preservation of New England Antiquities, also on Pleasant St., was not begun until late 1783 or 1784. Langdon's role in the history of the state and nation has been treated at length by Lawrence Shaw Mayo in his *John Langdon of New Hampshire* (Concord, N. H., 1937). In attributing the emancipation of a Negro servant to Langdon Chastellux apparently confused the stories he had heard. The incident involved, not John Langdon, but William Whipple and the latter's young slave "Prince Whipple"; Nathaniel Adams, *Annals of Portsmouth* (Portsmouth, 1825), 283.

28. This was Col. Joshua Wentworth (1742-1809), a grandson of Lt. Gov. John Wentworth (1671-1730). Joshua Wentworth's house is still standing at 117-21 Hanover St. (occupied in 1963 by Winebaum's News Service), at the head of Fleet St.; it is not to be confused with several of the more famous Wentworth residences now open to the public as historic houses. C. S. Gurney, *Portsmouth Historic and Picturesque* . . . (Portsmouth, N. H., 1902), 43; Brewster, *Rambles about Portsmouth*, I, 114-16.

29. Chastellux seems to have been mistaken in thinking that Mrs. Whipple was a widow, for both Joseph Whipple (1738-1816) and his brother William Whipple (1730-85)—signer of the Declaration of Independence and Brigadier General of the New Hampshire militia—were living at this time. Joseph Whipple lived at the corner of State and Chestnut Sts. in a house still standing and still known as "The Whipple House"; William Whipple (whose wife was a Moffatt) lived on Market St. in his father-in-law's house, the so-called "Moffatt-Ladd House," which is now maintained by the National Society of the Colonial Dames of America in the State of New Hampshire. It is furthermore probable that the person whom Chastellux visited was actually the *wife* of General William Whipple, and not his sister-in-law; Mrs. William (Catharine Moffatt) Whipple had no children of her own, but her niece, Mary Tufton Moffatt (born 1768)—who subsequently married Dr. Nathaniel Appleton Haven in 1786—was living with her in 1782. If this supposition is correct then the handsome and very well-furnished house which Chastellux visited would have been the "Moffatt-Ladd House" on Market St., and not the "Whipple House" on State St., as it has often been said. Gurney, *Portsmouth Hist. and Pict.*, 128, 32-34.

30. *Gr.* The Marquis de Chastellux, among his various accomplishments, is distinguished not only in the character of an *amateur*, but for his scientific knowledge of music.
Ed. See above, Introduction, nn. 10-13.

31. Dr. Joshua Brackett (1733-1802), a brother-in-law of William Whipple, resided in a house on the north side of State St., no longer standing; the site was occupied in 1961 by the First National Bank. Gurney, *Portsmouth Hist. and Pict.*, 124-25, with photograph of the Brackett house taken prior to its demolition; Adams, *Annals of Portsmouth*, 321-24.

32. Thomas Thompson (1739-1809) commanded the U.S. frigate *Raleigh*, which had been built under his inspection in the shipyards on Badger's Island in Portsmouth. Several of Portsmouth's extant 18th-century houses are

attributed to Thompson, including the "Mark Wentworth House" (179 Pleasant St.).

33. Chastellux's surmise was correct. In 1800 the United States government (which had until that time had several ships built at Portsmouth, without actually owning yards there) acquired Dennett's Island for a U. S. Navy Yard. After the Civil War, Seavey's Island was added. Both islands are in Portsmouth Harbor, but within the boundaries of the town of Kittery, Me. George Henry Preble, *History of the United States Navy Yard, Portsmouth, N. H.* (Wash., 1892).

34. *Gr.* A new form of government has been established since the peace. *Ed.* The temporary New Hampshire constitution of 1776 remained in force until 1784, when a permanent constitution was finally ratified after several proposals had been rejected by the people. The 1784 constitution eliminated the property qualifications.

35. Grieve anglicized the name as "Andrews," but, in view of Chastellux's own expressed uncertainty about the name, it seems probable that he was referring to the Reverend John Murray (1741-1815), the founding father of American Universalism, one of the several groups which were at this time breaking away from traditional New England Congregationalism. Murray, a native of Alton in Hampshire, had come to America in 1770; he first preached at Portsmouth, N. H., in 1773, again in 1775, and, in the words of his biographer, "continued many years an occasional visitor to Portsmouth, where his labors were greatly blessed." Murray later held pastorates at Gloucester, Mass., and at Boston. During the Revolution his appointment as chaplain to the Rhode Island regiments provoked considerable controversy among the orthodox Calvinists. *The Life of Reverend John Murray ... Written by Himself* (Boston, 1816, and several later editions); Clarence R. Skinner and Alfred S. Cole, *Hell's Ramparts Fell, The Life of John Murray* (Boston, 1941). The Universalists, in May 1961, merged with the Unitarians to form the Unitarian and Universalist Association.

36. *Gr.*—about seven shillings and threepence.

37. *Gr.*—twopence halfpenny a pound.

38. *Gr.*—of fifteen shillings [sterling].

Chapter 2

Boston and Vicinity

1. *Ed.* The *Charlestown* was known as the *Boston* before its capture by the British at Charleston, S.C., in May 1780.

Gr. The privateers which so greatly molested the British trade were chiefly from the ports of Newbury, Beverly, and Salem, in which places large fortunes were made by this means: and such must ever be the case in any future war, from the peculiarity of their position, whence they may run out at any season of the year, and commit depredations on any of the maritime powers to which America is hostile, with little fear of retaliation. Newfoundland, Nova Scotia, the Gulfs of St. Lawrence, and of Florida, and the whole trade of the West-Indian Archipelago, are in a manner at their doors. However Great Britain may affect to despise America, she is perhaps, even in her present infant state, from various circumstances, the most formidable enemy she can have to cope with, in case of a rupture; for, as nations ought collectively to be dispassionate, though individuals are not, it behooves her to reflect, where, and in what manner she can return the blow. Mr. Jefferson, the present Minister of the United States at Versailles, amongst other excellent observations on this subject has the following, which I extract with pleasure from his *Notes on Virginia*, a most interesting work, with which I have just privately been favoured. "... the sea is the field on which we should meet an European enemy. On that element it is necessary we should possess some power. To aim at such a navy as the greater nations of Europe possess, would be a foolish and wicked waste of the energies of our countrymen. It would be to pull on our own heads that load of military expence which makes the European labourer go supperless to bed, and moistens his bread with the sweat of his brows. It will be enough if we enable ourselves to prevent insults from those nations of Europe which are weak on the sea, because *circumstances exist which render even the stronger ones weak as to us. Providence has placed their richest and most defenceless possessions at our door; has obliged their most precious commerce to pass as it were in review before us.* To protect this, or to assail us, *a small part* only of their naval force will ever be risqued across the Atlantic. The dangers to which the elements expose them here are too well known, and the greater danger to which they would be exposed at home, were any general calamity to involve their whole fleet. They can attack us by *detachment only;* and it will suffice to make ourselves equal or superior *by the quickness with which any check may be repaired with us,* while losses with them will be irreparable till too late. A small naval force then is sufficient for us, and a small one is necessary. What this should be I will not undertake to say. I will only say it should by no means be so great as we are able to make it. Suppose the million of dollars, or 300,000 pounds, which Virginia could annually spare without distress, to be applied to the creating a navy. A single year's contribution would build, equip, man and send to sea a force which should carry 300 guns. The rest of the confederacy exerting themselves in the same proportion would equip in the same time 1500 guns more. So that one year's contributions would set up a navy of 1800 guns. The British ships of the line average 76 guns; their frigates 38. 1800 guns then would form a fleet of 30 ships, 18 of which might be of the line, and 12 frigates. Allowing 8 men, the British average, for every gun, their annual expence, including subsistence, cloathing, pay, and ordinary repairs, would be about 1280 dollars for every gun, or 2,304,000 dollars for the whole. I state this only as one year's possible exertion, without deciding whether more or less than a year's exertion should be thus applied."

Ed. Jefferson's ideas concerning American naval power, cited here, form part of "Query XXII, Public Revenue and Expences" of his *Notes on the State of Virginia*. A collation of texts indicates that Grieve had access to a copy of the first edition of the book, which Jefferson had had privately printed for distribution among his friends; this edition, printed by P.-D. Pierres in Paris, was ready in the spring of 1785, whereas the first edition in English for general circulation, issued by J. Stockdale of London, was not published until the summer of 1787. The text here quoted by Grieve from the 1785 edition (pp. 320-22) has been corrected from the original by the Editor, but the italics, which are Grieve's, have been retained. Grieve's remark that he had been "privately favoured" with a copy of Jefferson's work might be interpreted to mean that he had himself received it from the author, although it may mean simply that he had had the loan of one of the copies then circulating privately. No copy presented to Grieve is recorded in Coolie Verner, "Mr. Jefferson Distributes His *Notes,* A Preliminary Checklist of the First Edition," *New York Public Library Bulletin,* 56 (1952), 159-86.

2. William Davenport's inn, with a sign depicting General Wolfe, was at the corner of Threadneedle Alley and Fish (now State) St. in Newburyport, and thus not far from the ferry and the waterfront. It was destroyed by fire in the early 19th century; the name "Wolfe Tavern" subsequently designated another inn (recently demolished), corner of State and Harris Sts. Crawford, *New England Inns,* 251-61; Elsie Lathrop, *Early American Inns and Taverns* (N.Y., 1946), 90.

3. John (1753-1815) and Nathaniel (1751-96), sons of Hannah Gookin and Patrick Tracy (1711-89), both had imposing mansions in Newburyport, provided by their father. Nathaniel Tracy's house, State St. and Prince Pl., is now the Public Library of Newburyport. John Tracy's house, where Chastellux spent the evening, is also still standing (privately owned) at 203 High St., near the head of Olive St., next door to the Jackson house, made famous by Lord Timothy Dexter. Tracy's father had acquired the house (built *ca.* 1774) from John Lowell in 1778; it is now generally referred to as the "Lowell-Tracy-Johnson House." John J. Currier, *"Ould Newbury"; Historical and Biographical Sketches* (Boston, 1896), 577-85, illus.; John Mead Howells, *The Architectural Heritage of the Merrimack, Early Houses and Gardens* (N. Y., 1941), 82-84, figs. 88-91.

Mrs. John Tracy was Margaret Laughton. The "Miss Lee," who sang for the guests, was probably a sister of Mrs. Nathaniel Tracy (*née* Mary Lee). Thomas Amory Lee, "The Tracy Family of Newburyport," Essex Institute, *Historical Collections,* 57 (1921), 57-74; Scudder, ed., *Recollections of Samuel Breck,* 25-30. A masterly evocation of the Newburyport that Chastellux visited will be found in John P. Marquand's *Timothy Dexter Revisited* (Boston, 1960), especially chap. 7, which cites Chastellux's description of the evening at John Tracy's house (via Currier), pp. 144-46.

4. The man with the tongue-twisting name was probably Edward Wigglesworth (1741/2-1826), Harvard 1761, colonel of the 13th Massachusetts Continental Regiment, but retired when Chastellux saw him at Newburyport.

5. Chastellux's anecdote has passed into several local histories via Drake, *Historic Fields and Mansions of Middlesex* where it is quoted p. 309.

6. *Gr.*—£120,000 sterling.

7. *Gr.* This observation appears rather forced, as applied generally, the Marquis admitting that these impositions were the result of a critical and immediate want.

Ed. The conflict of interests between the seaboard merchants and the inland farmers of Massachusetts was at the root of Shays's Rebellion, the abortive agrarian revolt that took place only a few years later, in 1786-87. See also, Chastellux's further remarks, below, Nov. 22, 1782.

8. *Gr.* The activity and enterprise of the inhabitants of the eastern states are unremitted. The seaman when on shore immediately applies himself to some handicraft occupation, or to husbandry, and is always ready at a moment's warning to accompany the captain his neighbor, who is likewise frequently a mechanic, to the fisheries. West-India voyages are the most perilous expeditions, so that it is no uncommon circumstance to find in a crew of excellent New England mariners, not a single seaman, so to speak, by profession. Hence arise that zeal, sobriety, industry, economy and attachment for which they are so justly celebrated, and which cannot fail of giving them, sooner or later, a decided superiority at least in the seas of the new world. This education and these manners are the operative causes of that wonderful spirit of enterprise and perseverance, so admirably painted by Mr. Edmund Burke, in his wise, eloquent, and immortal speech of March 22, 1775, on his motion for conciliation with the colonies. "Pray, sir," says he, "what in the world is equal to it? Pass by the other parts (of America), and look at the manner in which the people of New England have of late carried on the whale fishery. Whilst we follow them among the tumbling mountains of ice, and behold them penetrating into the deepest recesses of Hudson's Bay, and Davis's Straits, whilst we are looking for them beneath the arctic circle, we hear that they have pierced into the opposite region of polar cold, that they are at the antipodes, and engaged under the frozen serpent of the south. Falkland Island, which seemed too remote and romantic an object for the grasp of national ambition, is but a stage and resting-place in the progress of their victorious industry. Nor is the equinoctial heat more discouraging to them than the accumulated winter of both the poles. We know that whilst some of them draw the line, and strike the harpoon on the coast of Africa, others run the longitude, and pursue their gigantic game along the coast of Brazil. No sea but what is vexed by their fisheries. No climate that is not witness to their toils. Neither the perseverance of Holland, nor the activity of France, nor the dexterous and firm sagacity of English enterprise, ever carried this most perilous mode of hardy industry to the extent to which it has been pushed by this recent people; a people who are still, as it were, but in the gristle, and not yet hardened into the bone of manhood."

9. *Gr.* The town of Beverly began to flourish greatly towards the conclusion of the war by the extraordinary spirit of enterprise, and great success of the Messieurs Cobbets [John and Andrew Cabot], gentlemen of strong understanding and the most liberal minds, well adapted to the most enlarged commercial undertakings, and the business of government. Two of their privateers had the good fortune to capture in the European seas, a few weeks previous to the peace, several West-Indiamen to the value of at least £100,000 sterling.

Ed. See L. Vernon Briggs, *History and Genealogy of the Cabot Family* (Boston, 1927), I, 66-107.

10. *Ch.* "*Neck*" in English literally means *col,* but it does not have the same meaning here as in French: we call *col* the place where you climb over mountains that cannot be circumvented, such as the Col de Tende and the Col de Mont Cenis [Alpine passes]. The English call "neck" any strip of land that serves as a communication between areas that would otherwise be totally separated and thus form islands.

11. William Goodhue, who had kept the tavern since 1774, leased it in 1782 to Samuel Robinson, Chastellux's host. This was the Sun Tavern on Essex St. at the head of Central St.; the property was acquired *ca.* 1800 by the great Salem merchant William Gray, who built a brick mansion on the site; Gray's mansion subsequently became the Essex House; the Sun Tavern continued, but at another location. Thus, Chastellux's stopping place was in the heart of Salem, on the north side of Essex St. (near corner of St. Peter St., across the street from the present Peabody Museum). Joseph B. Felt, *Annals of Salem*, 2d ed., 2 vols. (Salem and Boston, 1845-49), I, 423; James Duncan Phillips, *Salem and the Indies, The Story of the Great Commercial Era of the City* (Boston, 1947), 26; Essex Institute, *Visitor's Guide to Salem*, rev. ed. (Salem, 1953), 164-65.

12. *Gr.* The Translator, who was residing at this time at Salem, regretted exceedingly his accidental absence on the day the Marquis spent there, which he learnt, to his great mortification, on his return to the inn which the Marquis had just quitted.
Ed. Mr. "de la Fille's" name is changed to "de Lafile" in the 2d ed. (1788) of Chastellux's book—suggesting that the name should perhaps be Delafield.

13. *Gr.* Lynn is a very populous little place, and is celebrated for the manufacture of women's shoes, which they send to all parts of the continent. The town is almost wholly inhabited by shoemakers.

14. *Gr.* This is a most excellent inn, and Mr. Brackett a shrewd and active friend to the true principles of the revolution. His sign of Cromwell's head gave great umbrage to the British under General Gage, who would not suffer it to remain. This circumstance alone could have induced Mr. Brackett to restore it after they were expelled the town, as reflection might have convinced him, that in the actual position of America, there was much more to apprehend from a Cromwell than a Charles.
Ed. The Cromwell's Head, kept at this time by Joshua Brackett (1738-94), was near King's Chapel on the north side of School St., on a site corresponding to present No. 19, which is between City Hall and Washington St. The tavern building survived until 1888; the Second Federal Savings and Loan Association occupied the site in 1962. Samuel Adams Drake, *Old Boston Taverns*, new illustrated edition by Walter K. Watkins (Boston, 1917), 43-45, 62, 106. Paul Revere engraved a pictorial bill-head for the Cromwell's Head *ca.* 1770 and Joseph Callender later copied it; Clarence S. Brigham, *Paul Revere's Engravings* (Worcester, 1954), 116-17 and plate 54.

15. Although Chastellux used the English words "Main Street" in his French text, there was actually no street of this name in Boston, then or subsequently. The main thoroughfare by which one entered Boston over the Neck from Roxbury—present Washington St.—changed names every few blocks. Adam Colson (1738-98), leather-dresser, lived on the part of this street then known as Marlborough St., which corresponds to that portion of present Washington St. lying between Summer and School Sts. Colson is included in the list of innholders approved by the Selectmen of Boston at their meeting of Aug. 28, 1782; "Selectmen's Minutes, 1776-1786," Record Commissioners of the City of Boston, *Twenty-Fifth Report* (1894), 173, 190. The 1789 Boston directory lists Colson as a leather-dresser in Marlborough St.; the 1796 directory describes him as a shopkeeper at No. 50 Marlborough St. The starting point of Chastellux's successive rounds of

calls, described in the following pages, can thus be imagined with some degree of accuracy.

16. The *Marquis* de Vaudreuil, commander of the French squadron at Boston. Not to be confused with his brother the *Comte* de Vaudreuil, whom Chastellux had left at Portsmouth, N. H., or with his young cousin the *Vicomte* de Vaudreuil, Chastellux's aide-de-camp and traveling companion. See above, Pt. III, chap. 1, n. 2.

17. Dr. Samuel Cooper (1725-83) was pastor of the Brattle Square Church (Fourth Congregational). A new church building, for which John Hancock made a substantial contribution, had been completed in 1773; this stone structure served the Society until 1871, when the Brattle Square site was abandoned for the Back Bay district (Clarendon St. and Commonwealth Ave.) and a new church building designed by Henry Hobson Richardson. Dr. Cooper lived near his church, in the parsonage in Court St. that had been willed to the church in 1778 by Lydia Hancock. E. L. Motte *et al.*, eds., *Records of the Church in Brattle Square Boston, 1699-1872* (Boston, 1902), frontispiece (church), plate opp. p. 70 (parsonage). Cooper's features have been preserved for posterity in two notable portraits painted *ca.* 1769 by John Singleton Copley: one in the Lawrence Art Museum, Williams College (formerly collection of Charles M. Davenport), and the other in the Ralph Waldo Emerson House, Concord, Mass. Several copies or replicas are also extant; see Barbara N. Parker and Anne B. Wheeler, *John Singleton Copley, American Portraits...* (Boston, 1938), 61-63, plates 93A and 93B.

18. *Gr.* The reader will observe that the author in speaking of this lady, of Mr. [James] Bowdoin, her father, and the rest of the family, disdains to mention her husband, Mr. John Temple, so celebrated for political duplicity on both sides of the water. This gentleman was, however, at this very time at Boston, abusing Gov. [John] Hancock, Dr. [Samuel] Cooper, and the most tried friends to America, in the public prints, and endeavouring to sow dissensions among the people. Every newspaper into which he could obtain admission, was stuffed with disgusting encomiums on Mr. John Temple, whom Mr. John Temple himself held forth as the paragon of American patriotism, as the most active and inveterate enemy to England, and a victim to British vengeance, which he endeavoured to prove by instances taken from the English prints, of his treachery to England, and by boasting of his dexterity in outwitting the ministry of that country. Yet no sooner did peace take place, than to the astonishment of every sensible and honest man in Europe and America, this very person, equally detested by, and obnoxious to, both countries, was despatched as the sole representative of England to that country, of which he is also a sworn citizen, and whose father-in-law is the present [1785-87] Governor of Massachusetts. It is impossible to add to the folly and infamy of such a nomination. The choice of an Ambassador to Congress would have fallen with more propriety on Arnold. His was a bold and single act of treachery; the whole *political* life of Mr. Temple has been one continued violation of good faith. For further particulars of this gentleman's conduct, see the *Political Magazine* for 1780, p. 691, and 740; but volumes might be written on this subject. The Translator is sorry to add, that whilst he lives and flourishes, the virtuous, the amiable Dr. Cooper [†1783] is in his grave, and Mr. Hancock, that illustrious citizen, he fears, not far removed from it.

Ed. Grieve alludes to the fact that John Temple (later Sir John) was in 1785 appointed British consul general to the United States—the first official representative from the mother country following the peace settlement. Letters of Temple are included in the *Bowdoin and Temple Papers* (Mass. Hist. Soc., *Collections*, 6th Ser., 9 [1897]; *ibid.*, 7th Ser., 6 [1907]), I, II.

19. Louis Froger, Chevalier de L'Eguille, was *"major"* of the squadron at Boston (as well as commander of the *Néréide*), and thus the naval officer principally concerned with arrangements for embarking the land forces. Laurent-François-Jean, Comte Truguet (1752-1839) was a *lieutenant de vaisseau* who had served aboard the *Languedoc* in the Battle of the Saints. Contenson, *Cincinnati*, 213, 275; Vaudreuil, "Notes de Campagne," *Neptunia*, No. 50 (Spring, 1958); M. Dumas, *Mémoires.*

20. *Gr.* The Translator was present at this assembly at Boston, which was truly elegant, where he saw Mr. J. Temple standing behind the crowd, eyeing, like Milton's devil, the perfect harmony and good humour subsisting between the French officers and the inhabitants, not as a friend to Britain, for that would have been pardonable, but to discord, for he was at this very instant boasting of his inveteracy to Britain.

Ed. The fortnightly assemblies probably took place in the Concert Hall, in Hanover St., built by the musician Stephen Deblois in 1756. Caleb H. Snow, *History of Boston...*, 2d ed. (Boston 1828), 333. *The Motley Assembly* (1779; Evans, No. 16668), a play attributed to Mercy Warren, satirizes one of these gatherings: "Here friends to freedom, vile apostates meet,/ And here unblushing can each other greet;/ In mix'd assembly." See also Charles Warren, "Samuel Adams and the Sans Souci Club in 1785," Mass. Hist. Soc., *Proceedings*, 60 (1927), 318.

21. Philippe-André-Joseph de Létombe (b. at Condé, 1738) was French consul at Boston (succeeding Joseph de Valnais) from 1779 to 1793. His consular dispatches (unpublished) in the Archives Nationales, Paris (Aff. étr. B¹ 209, 210), provide further details on the stay of Vaudreuil's squadron in 1782, as well as a good commentary on commercial affairs at Boston during the whole period of his incumbency. Upon his recall to France he had printed a 12-page pamphlet, *Recueil de Diverses Pièces en faveur du Citoyen Létombe* (Paris, 1793), which included testimonial letters from Samuel Adams, John Hancock, and several Boston merchants. Copies of this pamphlet are in Corr. consulaire, Boston, III, fol. 148, Arch. Aff. Etr., Paris; in the same volume, fol. 66 ff., is a report and biographical sketch of Létombe. He returned to the United States as consul general in 1795. Ironically, it was another Bostonian, John Adams, who dismissed Létombe (Presidential proclamation, July 13, 1798) at the time of the XYZ affair. See below, Pt. IV, Editor's Introduction and n. 3.

22. *Ch.* I had seen Mr. Hancock eighteen months before, on my first journey to Boston [spring, 1781]. I then had a long conversation with him, in which I easily discovered that energy of character which had enabled him to act so distinguished a part in the present revolution. He formerly possessed a large fortune, which he has almost entirely sacrificed in the defense of his country, and which contributed not a little to maintain its credit. Though yet a young man, for he is not yet fifty, he is unfortunately very subject to the gout, and is sometimes, for whole months, unable to see company.

Ed. Governor Hancock was forty-five, when Chastellux tried to visit him in 1782; he died in 1793. He lived in a house built *ca.* 1737 by his uncle Thomas Hancock, on Beacon Hill, facing the Common. The mansion, which figures prominently in several of the surviving 18th-century views of Boston, was on a site close to the west wing of the present State House; a bronze tablet on the grounds marks the spot. Allen Chamberlain, *Beacon Hill, Its Ancient Pastures and Early Mansions* (Boston, 1925), 146-159, illus.

23. The residence of James Bowdoin (1726-90) was on a site corresponding to the eastern corner of present Beacon and Bowdoin Sts.; the gardens extended back up over the hill as far as Ashburton Pl. Bowdoin's estate was on the part of the "Trimountain" that was graded down in the 1830's. The Bellevue Hotel is now on the site. Chamberlain, *Beacon Hill,* 19-20. The residence of Lt. Governor Thomas Cushing (1724/5-88) was in Bromfield St.; C. K. Shipton, *Biographical Sketches of Those Who Attended Harvard College* (Cambridge, Mass., 1933———), XI, 377. For Samuel Breck's house, see below, this chap., n. 25.

24. Chastellux had apparently made a brief visit to Boston in the spring of 1781, while he was still stationed with the army at Newport. See this chap., Nov. 18, 1782, and nn. 22, 36. "The younger Mrs. Bowdoin" was the wife of James Bowdoin, Jr. (1752-1811).

25. Breck's son, another Samuel Breck (1771-1862), describes his father's Boston residence in his *Recollections* (ed. Scudder, 37-38):

In 1780 my father purchased a house for twelve hundred guineas in gold. It was greatly out of repair, having been occupied, as I have often heard, by Lord Percy ... during the siege under Gage. My father put it in excellent repair, and adorned the extensive gardens in the midst of which it stood. For a city residence it was remarkably fine, being situate at the corner of Winter and Common streets (now Winter and Tremont, Common having been supplanted by Tremont), with an acre of ground around the house divided into a flower and kitchen garden. The property was sold to my uncle Andrew, when we removed in 1792 to Philadelphia .... The house has since been pulled down and the whole ground built upon. The gardens when in our possession were kept in very neat order, and being exposed to view through a palisade of great beauty were the admiration of every one. In these gardens my father gave a grand fête on the birth of the dauphin. Drink was distributed from hogsheads, and the whole town was made welcome to the plentiful tables within doors.

In his *Recollections* Samuel Breck, Jr., also recalls his father's work as business agent for the French Navy, as a result of which he himself, then a boy of eleven, went to France under the Marquis de Vaudreuil's auspices in order to learn French. Young Breck remained in France from 1783 to 1787, chiefly at the Collège de Sorèze in Languedoc, which was not far from the Vaudreuil family estate. Further recollections of Samuel Breck, not included in the volume edited by Scudder, have been published, from the manuscript in the American Philosophical Society, by Gilbert Chinard, "Samuel Breck's 'Recollections,'" *French-American Review,* 1 (1948), 110-30, 273-89. These include a passage concerning Chastellux (p. 286) based, however, not on personal recollections (Breck wrote these pages just before his death in 1862 at the age of ninety-two!), but on a re-perusal of Chastellux's book: "The travels of this amiable gentleman are green spots;—an Oasis, in the Wilderness of barren, unfertile and unprofitable false predictions of croakers who have dipped their pens in gall, when writing about our Country."

26. *Gr.* This is a very amiable young gentleman, and his father a great connoisseur in prints and paintings. He was happy to have the opportunity of purchasing a complete collection of Hogarth's prints from the Translator, then on his return to Europe.

Ed. The amiable young gentleman was presumably Joseph Barrell, Jr. (Harvard A.B., 1783; died 1801). His father was Joseph Barrell (1740-1804), a Boston merchant who resided at this time in Summer St. Charles Bulfinch, later famous as an architect, recalls that after his graduation from Harvard in 1781 he was "placed in the counting room of Joseph Barrell, Esq., an intimate friend and esteemed a correct merchant; but unfortunately the unsettled state of the times prevented Mr. Barrell from engaging in any active business, so that for except about three months of hurried employment, when he was engaged in victualing a French fleet in our harbour, my time passed very idly and I was at leisure to cultivate a taste for Architecture, which was encouraged by attending to Mr. Barrell's improvement of his estate and [the improvements] on our dwelling house and the houses of some friends, all of which had become exceedingly dilapidated during the war." Ellen Susan Bulfinch, *The Life and Letters of Charles Bulfinch, Architect* ... (Boston, 1896), 41. Barrell's house faced on Summer St.; the gardens, built on swampy ground which he had drained, extended back to include a tract now covered by upper Milk, Hawley, Arch, and Franklin Sts. After his return from a European trip in 1785-87 Charles Bulfinch designed for this area the Tontine Crescent in Franklin Street (demolished 1858). Walter Muir Whitehill, *Boston, A Topographical History* (Cambridge, Mass., 1959), 52-55, illus. Bulfinch also designed (1792) a new house for Joseph Barrell overlooking the Charles River in Charlestown (later Somerville); this tasteful Barrell country house became in 1818 the nucleus of the McLean Insane Asylum, which was in turn demolished in 1896; the site, opposite the North Station, is now covered by Boston & Maine Railroad yards. "The 'Barrell Farm' or Garden, near Milk, Summer and Franklin Streets," *Old-Time New England*, 37 (1947), 69-71; Frank Chouteau Brown, "The Joseph Barrell Estate, Somerville, Massachusetts, Charles Bulfinch's First Country House," *ibid.*, 38 (1948), 53-62, illus.

27. Chastellux's mention of a proposal to make Hebrew the national language, for which there seems to be no contemporary corroboration, was evidently the source of several subsequent references to it. The anti-American editor of the *Quarterly Review* (January 1814), for example, remarked that "one person indeed had recommended the adoption of Hebrew, as being ready made to their hands, and considering the Americans, no doubt, as the 'chosen people' of the new world"; Timothy Dwight in turn denied that any such proposal had ever been made. See H. L. Mencken, *The American Language, Supplement I* (New York, 1945), 136-38.

28. For William Tudor, see below, note 50.

29. This was the artillery corps of Rochambeau's army, which had left Providence on Nov. 17. Acomb, ed., *Von Closen Journal*, 269. The commanding officer was the Chevalier d'Aboville. It was D'Aboville who supplied Chastellux with his observations on the opossum; see Part II, Appendix C, n. 23.

30. There are numerous 18th-century maps of Boston and vicinity to illustrate Chastellux's description; see, for example, Henry Pelham's "A Plan of Boston in New England with its Environs... with the Military Works Constructed in those Places in the Years 1775 and 1776," engraved by Francis Jukes (London, 1777; facsimile, W. A. Butterfield, Boston, 1907). Subsequent changes may be traced with the aid of Walter Muir Whitehill's excellent *Boston, A Topographical History*.

31. *Gr*. Bunker's hill is an eminence neither more steep, nor more difficult of access than Primrose hill near Hampstead, in the neighborhood of London.

32. *Gr*. A bridge of 1503 feet in length, and 42 in breadth, is just completed (in 1786) between Boston and Charlestown, well lighted at night with 40 lamps. This important work was executed by subscription. The greatest depth of the water is 46 feet nine inches, and the least is 14 feet.

Ed. See Whitehill, *Boston*, 48-50, with reproduction of an engraved "View of the Bridge over Charles River" from the *Massachusetts Magazine* (Sept. 1789).

33. *Gr*. This attack on Bunker's hill took place in the time of the hay harvest, and much execution was done among the British by some field-pieces, and musketry concealed behind the cocks of hay.

34. See Pelham's "Plan of Boston." The localities are now engulfed by the cities of Cambridge and Somerville. There is a granite marker (erected 1890) indicating the site of the Winter Hill fort in a minuscule triangular grassplot, called "Paul Revere Park," at the intersection of Broadway (the Concord road) and Main St. (the Medford road) in Somerville; this fort was at the northern end of the line of defense. Farther south, a similar marker identifies the site of the "citadel" on Prospect Hill at the intersection of Munroe Street and Prospect Hill Avenue, also in Somerville; a conspicuous pseudo-medieval memorial tower, surrounded by a small park, now crowns this eminence, which provides a good vantage point from which to survey the "positions" described by Chastellux. Concerning the progressive obliteration of the remains of the fortifications see: "Account of the Forts erected during the Siege," reprinted from *Silliman's Journal* (1822) in Richard Frothingham, Jr., *History of the Siege of Boston* (Boston, 1849), 409-14; Lossing, *Field-Book*, I, 566, 591-92; Justin Winsor, ed., *Memorial History of Boston*, 4 vols. (Boston, 1880-81), III, 104-17.

35. *Gr*. Surely good policy had some share in the alacrity of these proffered succours, nor does this supposition, whilst it does credit to the discernment, derogate from the generosity of the Virginians. *Tua res agitur, paries cum proximus ardet!*

36. See above, this chap., Nov. 15, 1782, and n. 24.

37. Chastellux is referring to Harvard Hall, which had been built to replace an earlier edifice destroyed by fire in 1764. His otherwise inexplicable remark that it was "not completely finished" may perhaps refer to the repair of damage done during the war, when it was occupied for a time by the American army. Harvard Hall still stands, though both its interior and exterior have been considerably modified by 19th-century changes. Other Harvard buildings of the time—which Chastellux does not mention—included Massachusetts Hall (1720), Hollis Hall (1763), and Holden Chapel (1744); "Old Stoughton" (which appears in earlier views

of Harvard such as the Paul Revere engraving of 1767) had been demolished during the year prior to Chastellux's visit. He probably did not think of these other buildings as being " the university," as he understood the term, since they were used mainly as "colleges" or dormitories. For a well-documented history of the early Harvard buildings see Hamilton Vaughan Bail, *Views of Harvard, A Pictorial Record to 1860* (Cambridge, Mass., 1949); Plate 15, the "Griffin Westerly View *ca.* 1783-84," comes the closest to showing Harvard as it looked in Nov. 1782; Plate 18, the *"Massachusetts Magazine* View 1790," also approximates its appearance at the time of Chastellux's visit. A "Plan of Harvard Hall," by P. E. DuSimitière (original, Library Co. of Phila.; reprint in *Old-Time New England,* 37 [1936], 64), shows the location of the library, etc., as described by Chastellux.

38. *Gr.*—£500 sterling.

39. *Gr.* The Translator is happy in being able to supply this deficiency, by recording the respected name of the late Thomas Hollis, Esq.; a truly eminent citizen of England, who, in every act of his public and private life, did honor to his illustrious name, to his country, and to human nature. One of his ancestors too, of the same name, founded, in this same college, a professorship for the mathematics and natural philosophy, and ten scholarships for students in these and other sciences, with other benefactions, to the amount of little less than £5000 sterling. Public virtue, and private accomplishments seem to be hereditary in this family; Mr. Thomas Brand Hollis, the inheritor of this fortune, pursuing the footsteps of his excellent predecessors—*passibus aequis.*

Ed. Prompted no doubt by Grieve's note, Chastellux inserted Hollis's name in the 2d ed. of his book (1788). Thomas Hollis (1720-74) and his benefactions have been the subject of considerable interest in recent years. See, for example, Caroline Robbins, "The Strenuous Whig, Thomas Hollis of Lincoln's Inn," *Wm. and Mary Qtly.,* 3d Ser., 7 (1950), 406-53, and the pertinent chapters in her book *The Eighteenth-Century Commonwealthman: Studies in the Transmission, Development and Circumstances of English Liberal Thought from the Restoration of Charles II until the War with the Thirteen Colonies* (Cambridge, Mass., 1959). A good summary of Hollis's significance, with references to other sources of information, is also found in James Holly Hanford's article, " 'Ut Spargam,' Thomas Hollis Books at Princeton," *Princeton Univ. Lib. Chronicle,* 20 (1959), 165-74, illus.

40. The Rev. Joseph Willard (1738-1804) had assumed the presidency of Harvard College on Dec. 19, 1781, a year before Chastellux's visit. He lived in the "President's House," built in 1726, now known as Wadsworth House from the name of its first occupant, and still standing in the southwestern part of the Yard, facing Massachusetts Ave.; see Bail, *Views of Harvard,* 67-69 and Plates 12, 15.

The American Academy of Arts and Sciences in Boston (founded 1780) elected Chastellux a Foreign Honorary Member on Aug. 22, 1781. The Academy's minutes for that date describe him simply as "Chevalier de Chattelux, a general officer in the French Army at Rhode Island"; Mr. Walter Muir Whitehill, who has kindly consulted the Academy's archives for me, reports that there are no letters from Chastellux there. Ezra Stiles, who had met Chastellux at Newport, noted in his diary, Nov. 3, 1780, that he sent that day to Mr. Gannett of Cambridge, Secretary of the Academy of Sciences "a recommendation of Jno. Francis Chevalier de Chatellux, Major General of the French Army for an Enrollment into the Massachusetts Academy of Sciences"; Dexter, ed., *Literary Diary of Stiles*, II, 476.

41. Samuel Cooper's sermon survives in published form: *A Sermon preached before His Excellency John Hancock, Esq; Governor, the Honourable the Senate, and House of Representatives of the Commonwealth of Massachusetts, October 25, 1780. Being the Day of the Commencement of the Constitution, and the Inauguration of the New Government* (Boston, 1780; Evans, No. 16753). As far as the Editor has been able to determine, no French translation of the sermon was published separately, but it may have appeared in some periodical. A Dutch translation of it (by Francis Adriaan Van der Kemp) was included in the collection of American documents issued at Leyden in 1781 under the pseudonym of Junius Brutus, *Verzameling van Stukken tot de Dertien Vereenigde Staeten van Noord-America betrekkelijk*, 238-300 (Sabin, No. 98478).

Mathieu Dumas, then senior quartermaster of the French army in Boston, gives another glimpse of Cooper in his *Memoirs*, I, 61-62: Speaking to a group of French officers (no doubt at a gathering like the one described by Chastellux), Cooper praised their enthusiasm in the cause of liberty, but warned: "Take care, take care, young men, lest the triumph of the cause on this virgin soil, should too much inflame your hopes. You will carry away with you the germs of these generous sentiments; but if ever you attempt to propagate them on your native soil, after so many ages of corruption, you will have to surmount far other obstacles. It has cost us much blood to conquer liberty, but you will have to shed it in torrents before you can establish it in Europe." Writing his memoirs in the 1830's, Dumas added: "How many times since then, during our political storm—during our fatal days, I have called to mind the prophetic warnings of Dr. Cooper; but the inestimable prize which the Americans obtained by their sacrifice was always present to my mind."

42. Cooper's residence; see above, this chap., n. 17. Samuel Cooper (b. 1725) died in Dec. 1783, a year after Chastellux's visit to Boston.

43. *Gr.* Mr. John Temple finding himself detected, and ill received at Boston, was the undoubted author of these calumnies against Doctor Cooper, who had nobly dared to warn his countrymen against his insidious attempts to disunite the friends to liberty, under the mask of zeal and attachment to America. He dared, contrary to the decisive evidence of a long series of pure disinterested public conduct in the hour of danger, when Mr. Temple was a skulking, pensioned refugee in England, more than to insinuate, that Doctor Cooper, and Mr. Hancock, that martyr to the public cause, were actually in pay of the French court; but if ever there could be a doubt entertained of such characters, founded on the assertions of such a man, his subsequent conduct has irrefragably proved, that as the calumny was propagated by him, so the suggestion must have originated in his own heart. Let not the Anglo-American Consul-General to the United States complain. Historical justice will overtake both him and Arnold. It is a condition in the indenture of their bargain.

Ed. Historical justice obliges the Editor to add that Samuel Cooper did in fact receive money from the French Legation in Philadelphia (as Chastellux must have known)—as did also Thomas Paine and others. The dispatch of the French Minister Gérard (La Luzerne's predecessor) to Vergennes,

Jan. 17, 1779, leaves no doubt about the matter: Cooper accepted a proposal of £200 sterling a year "as compensation for what he has lost and
suffered for the common cause and in order to pay a vicar whom he wants
to hire so that he can devote himself entirely to the work he has undertaken." The dispatch is printed, from the original in the French Foreign
Office Archives, in John J. Meng, ed., *Despatches and Instructions of
Conrad Alexandre Gérard, 1778-1780* ... (Baltimore, 1939), 480-82. Whether
or not the acceptance of such a "grant in aid" was reprehensible and justified
the "insinuations" mentioned by Grieve is a matter of interpretation.
Gérard, in any case, bluntly told his superior that he thought that a man of
Cooper's standing "was worth buying, even at this price."

44. *Gr.* The Translator had the pleasure of being acquainted with the
son of Mr. Russell [Thomas Walley Russell, son of Thomas Russell] and
his friend [Thomas Lindall] Winthrop, in France and Holland. He had the
good fortune likewise to meet with the latter at Boston. He takes pride in
mentioning these amiable young men, as they cannot fail of becoming
valuable members of a rising country, which attracts the attention of the
world.

Ed. In spite of the war, Tom Winthrop (Harvard 1780) and his class-
mate Tom Russell made a trip to Europe in 1781-82; their ship was captured by the British, but they somehow escaped internment and were able
to visit London as well as the Continent. Thomas L. Winthrop (1760-1841)
fulfilled Grieve's prophecy and became indeed "a valuable member of a
rising country"; see the sketch of his life in Lawrence Shaw Mayo, *The
Winthrop Family in America* (Boston, 1948), 209-19, with reproduction
of his portrait by Thomas Sully (1831). Winthrop was Lt. Governor of
Massachusetts in 1826-32; among his many other distinctions was that of
holding simultaneously, from 1835 until 1841, the presidencies of both the
Massachusetts Historical Society and the American Antiquarian Society!

45. Probably Samuel Broome, who had acquired in 1780 from the con-
fiscated Loyalist estates then being sold by the state a dwelling house in
Milk Street (formerly the property of James Boutineau), as well as the
former estate of Gov. Thomas Hutchinson at Milton. Mass. Hist. Soc., *Proceedings*, 2d Ser., 10 (1895), 168-69, 178-79.

46. For Cushing's residence, see above, this chap., n. 23.

47. The angelic Miss Temple (Elizabeth Bowdoin Temple), granddaughter of James Bowdoin the elder, was married in 1786 to the amiable
Tom Winthrop, mentioned above by Grieve, n. 44.

48. *Gr.* It is with real concern the Translator adds, that gaming is a vice
but too prevalent in all the great towns, and which has been already
attended with the most fatal consequences, and with frequent suicide.
Ed. See above, Pt. II, chap. 5, n. 12.

49. See above, this chap., n. 29.

50. *Gr.* Mr. [William] Tudor [1750-1819] is the gentleman who has so
frequently distinguished himself by animated orations on the annual commemoration of some of the leading events of this civil war.
Ed. For example: *An Oration, delivered March 5th 1779 ... to commemorate the Bloody Tragedy of the Fifth of March, 1770* (Boston, 1779; Evans,
No. 16550). See also, "Memoir of Hon. William Tudor," Mass. Hist. Soc.,

Collections, 2d Ser., 8 (1826), 285-325. Mrs. Tudor's maiden name was Delia Jarvis.

51. Recalling his sojourn in Boston at this same time and the charming ladies he met there, the Comte de Ségur wrote in his *Mémoires*, I, 452: "Mrs. Tudor, who has since been seen in France [i.e., in 1807-8], was well known for her very witty writings, one of which was addressed to the Queen of France and taken to that princess by M. de Chastellux." The Prince de Broglie also mentions Mrs. Tudor's verses and says that Chastellux was their bearer to the Queen; *Journal*, 77. The editor must regretfully add that he has found no trace of Mrs. Tudor's masterpiece.

52. The Comte d'Estaing's fleet had come to Boston for repairs at the end of Aug. 1778 after being damaged in a storm off Rhode Island and after the unsuccessful attempt at a combined operation there with the American land forces; the fleet sailed for the West Indies in Nov. 1778. This first meeting between French sailors and the Bostonians was not entirely happy and was not marked by the same spirit of goodwill that seems to have surrounded the visit of Vaudreuil's ships in 1782: on the earlier occasion there were indeed gala dinners, but there were also regrettable incidents, such as the death of the Chevalier de Saint Sauveur when he was attempting to quell a riot between French sailors and "certain riotous persons unknown." Fitz-Henry Smith, Jr., "The French at Boston during the Revolution," Bostonian Society, *Publications*, 10 (1913), 9-75. The era of good feeling that marked the visit of Vaudreuil's squadron in 1782 will appear perhaps the more remarkable, when it is recalled that the name "Vaudreuil" had sinister connotations for most adult New Englanders. Several generations of this family had been officials in Canada during the whole period of the French and Indian wars: the last French governor of Canada was another Marquis de Vaudreuil (Pierre de Rigaud-Cavagnal, 1704-78), an uncle of the admiral who received the homage of Boston two decades later. Details concerning French hospitals and the care of their sick and wounded at Boston (including mention of arrangements made with Dr. Charles Jarvis in 1778) will be found in Bouvet, *Service de Santé*, 11-18, 100-2.

53. *Gr.* During my stay at Boston, a young Chevalier de Malte, Monsieur de l'Epine, belonging to Mr. de Vaudreuil's squadron, died, and I was present at his funeral. He was buried with the forms of the Catholic Church, by the first Chaplain to the fleet, and his remains were attended to the place of interment, besides his brother officers, etc. by the members of the senate and assembly, the principal inhabitants of the town, and the ministers of *every sect of religion* in Boston. The holy candles, and all the Catholic ceremonies were used on the occasion, in a town too, where, a few years before, the hierarchical pomp even of the church of England barely met with toleration; an useful lesson this to Machiavelian rulers, whose strength consists in the silly discord and divisions of their fellow creatures. The Translator contemplated this interesting scene with a complacent curiosity, which was only interrupted by the solitary dissatisfaction of Mr. John Temple, who, as well as his honest coadjutor, the *pious* Arnold, "was shocked at seeing his countrymen participating in the rites of a church, against whose *antichristian* corruptions your pious ancestors would have witnessed with their blood." *See* this zealous *protestant*'s proclamation,

after selling himself to England, for £7000 3 per cents. and sacrificing the amiable, unhappy Major André.

Ed. This note was entirely omitted by the publisher of the New York 1827 edition of the *Travels*. Monsieur de L'Epine, an *enseigne de vaisseau* on the frigate *Amazone*, died in Boston, Oct. 31, 1782; Dawson, *Français Morts*, 80. Grieve's sarcastic reference to Benedict Arnold is to the latter's *A Proclamation To the Officers and Soldiers of the Continental Army who have the real Interest of their Country at Heart, and who are determined to be no longer the Tools and Dupes of Congress, or of France* ... (N. Y., Oct. 20, 1780; Evans, No. 16789), printed by James Rivington as a broadside, and in the Loyalist press: "Do you know," Arnold wrote, "that the Eye which guides this pen lately saw your mean and profligate Congress at Mass for the soul of a Roman Catholic in purgatory, and participating in the rites of a church against whose Anti-christian Corruptions your pious Ancestors would have witnessed with their Blood." The allusion is to the Catholic ceremonies in Philadelphia following the death of the first Spanish minister to the U.S., Don Juan Miralles, at Morristown in Apr. 1780.

54. See above, this chap., Nov. 12, 1782, and n. 7, on Tracy's complaints. As for Samuel Breck, his son relates in his *Recollections*, 186-87, how his father, outraged by the iniquitous system of taxation practiced in Boston, moved in 1792 to Philadelphia "where taxation was equal and where nothing but real estate was assessed.... The whole of our taxes in Philadelphia were fifty-five dollars, being just about the amount of the Boston collector's commission on my father's taxes in that town."

Chapter 3

Providence, across Connecticut, and the Farewell to Washington at Newburgh

1. The French troops, which had reached Providence Nov. 10-11, left there Dec. 1-4, marching to Boston via Wrentham and Dedham. By Dec. 7 they were embarked on the ships of Vaudreuil's squadron, but did not finally sail from Boston for the West Indies until Dec. 24, 1782. Acomb, ed., *Von Closen Journal*, 271-77. The Baron de Vioménil was in command of the departing army. General Rochambeau, who was to return to France with Chastellux and other officers, left Providence on Dec. 1; he took much the same route to Philadelphia that Chastellux did, but followed after him at an interval of a day or more (below, this chap., Dec. 6, 1782). The Comte de Ségur, who was at this time quartered in the vicinity of Providence, wrote a few days later to his wife in France: "On the 30th of November the Chevalier de Chastellux, who was to have dined at my house before leaving, eluded me and left without wanting to say farewell; he perhaps did well for we would have been needlessly affected, but I nevertheless find it hard to forgive him for having deprived me of the happiness of embracing him once again. Am I not right in loving him: he is the best general, the best friend, the best man, the best writer that I know of.... The day after his departure the army set out for Boston." Letter from Boston, Dec. 6, 1782, in "Extraits de lettres écrites d'Amérique par le Comte de Ségur, Colonel en second du Régiment de Soissonnais, à la Comtesse de Ségur, Dame de

Madame Victoire, 1782-1783," ed. Duc de Broglie, in Société des Biblio-philes Français, *Mélanges*, Pt. 2 (Paris, 1903), 178. Ségur, who had come to America only in Sept. 1782, also pays tribute to Chastellux in his retrospective memoirs published many years later, referring to him as "an intimate friend of my father's and my close relative"; *Mémoires*, I, 409-11.

2. On Voluntown and Chastellux's observations during an earlier visit there in 1780-81, see above, Pt. I, chap. 1, Nov. 13-14, 1780; chap. 6, Jan. 7, 1781. It was apparently during the present visit that he found Miss Dorrance happily married, as explained in the conclusion of his long footnote appended to the description of the first visit; see above, Pt. I, chap. 1, n. 23.

3. *Ch.* M. Lynch, who was *aide-major-général* and appointed to be employed under the orders of the Baron de Vioménil, embarked with the troops. M. de Talleyrand was determined to follow them as a simple volunteer, and assuming the uniform of a soldier in the Soissonnais Regiment, he marched into Boston in the ranks of the company of *Chasseurs*. This company was to embark on the same vessel with the Comte de Ségur, then *Colonel en Second* of the Soissonnais; M. de Talleyrand remained attached to it, and did not leave it until after his return to Europe.

Ed. The Comte de Ségur, in his *Mémoires*, I, 448-51, relates how Chastel-lux wanted to take Boson de Talleyrand back to France with him, because the young man's parents had entrusted him to his care and he did not want to be responsible for accidents that might result from a change in destination. Boson, however, conspired with Ségur, who gave him "a grenadier's bonnet and the name of *Va-de-bon-coeur.*" Everyone was in on the secret: Rochambeau indulgently closed his eyes—as Chastellux presumably did, too. Boson gained much favorable notoriety by his ruse, although he saw no military action on his circuitous return trip with the army, as he had hoped. Ségur also relates (I, 508-12) some of the further adventures of Lynch, including his narrow escape from detention as a prisoner when he almost revealed his London birth to the captain of an English frigate—Captain Nelson (later famous as Lord Nelson)—who had hailed some French officers who were sight-seeing off the Venezuelan coast.

4. Grieve expanded Chastellux's words to read "at White's Tavern *at Andover*, near Bolton." Assuming that his interpolation is correct, then White's Tavern—not recorded in Crofut, Terry, *et al.*—was presumably along the Hop River Valley road (now U.S. Route 6), perhaps in the village of Andover, or at some point farther along, before the road took the traveler sharp left up over the hill to Bolton meetinghouse (see above, Pt. III, chap. 1, Nov. 4, 1782, and n. 3). Andover, adjoining the town of Bolton on the east, was not incorporated as a separate town until 1848; it was then formed from parts of the towns of Coventry and Hebron. Because of such changes in town and county boundaries, it is difficult to confirm the exact location of Chastellux's stopping place. He had already stopped here on May 21, 1781, on his way to the Wethersfield Conference (see above, Pt. II, Introduction, n. 6).

5. Concerning Frank Dillon, who had been with Chastellux on his excursion in Virginia, see above, Pt. II, chap. 1, n. 2. For the remainder of the present journey Chastellux was thus accompanied by Dillon, Montesquieu, and the Vicomte de Vaudreuil.

6. On Oct. 28, 1782, on the way eastward from Crompond to Hartford, where Chastellux relinquished his command of the first division of Rocham-

beau's army, and set out on the present journey. The recently enlarged house, kept as an inn by Asahel Wadsworth (1743-1817), was on the east side of Farmington Main St., north of the cemetery; it is still standing at present No. 109 Main St. Gay, *Farmington Papers*, 88, 102-3, 120-21; "Farmington Houses and Farmington Owners file, 1662-1950," in Farmington Village Lib.

7. Chastellux had lodged at Phinehas Lewis's on his first visit to Farmington; see above, Pt. I, chap. 1, Nov. 17, 1780, and n. 49. In a postscript to a letter written to Col. Jeremiah Wadsworth after his return to France (Paris, May 31, 1783; above, Pt. I, chap. 1, n. 42) Chastellux sent "my best respects to Mrs. Wadsworth, your charming children, Mrs. Lewis, etc."

8. In June 1781, during the army's westward march from Newport. The Rev. Timothy Pitkin (1729-1812), pastor of the Congregational [not Presbyterian!] Church of Farmington, was famous for his patriotic sermons; he was the son of William Pitkin (1694-1769), who had been Governor of Connecticut from 1766 to 1769. The house occupied by Timothy Pitkin in 1782, on the west side of Main St. (site corresponding to present No. 90), was among those destroyed by fire in 1864. Gay, *Farmington Papers*, 93-94, 117-18.

9. Sheldon's Tavern, one of the notable old houses of Litchfield—"where Washington slept"—is located on the west side of North St. The house was built *ca.* 1760 by Elisha Sheldon, whose son, Samuel Sheldon, inherited it in 1779, using it as an inn for a few years before selling it to Dr. Lemuel Hopkins. Crofut, *Guide*, I, 396-97, illus.; Terry, *Old Inns of Conn.*, 83-84, illus.; *Some Historic Sites of Litchfield, Conn.*, 3.

10. The two mills were probably at Bantam Falls, in the town of Litchfield, and on the Shepaug River at Woodville, on the edge of the town of Washington.

11. Gideon Morgan was licensed as a tavernkeeper in the town of Washington, Litchfield Co., in 1781. Another tavern—perhaps the one where Chastellux stopped—was kept by William Cogswell; this house still stands, marked with a D.A.R. tablet, a short distance to the east of the present main road (State Road 25) from Woodville to New Preston, before reaching the latter village. Crofut, *Guide,* I, 61, 442, 444-45, illus. Terry, *Old Inns of Conn.*, 194-97, illus.

12. See above, Pt. I, chap. 1, Nov. 19, 1780.

13. *Ibid.*, and n. 62.

14. *Ibid.*, Nov. 20, 1780, and n. 68.

15. Washington's headquarters at Newburgh, from Apr. 1, 1782 to Aug. 19, 1783, was in the Jonathan Hasbrouck house, built in 1750 and still standing. The house commands a splendid situation overlooking the Hudson and (together with an adjacent historical museum) is maintained as an historic site by the state of New York, which acquired the property in 1850. Chastellux's account is the classic description of the house, including its dining room with "seven doors and only one window." The little parlor, which served as an improvised bedroom for Chastellux, is believed to be the room at the northwest corner of the house, on the left of the west entrance hall. Amos Elwood Corning, *The Story of Hasbrouck House, Washington's Headquarters, Newburgh, New York* ([Newburgh], 1950).

16. See above, this chap., n. 1.

17. *Ch.* "Landing," place of debarking. This word comes from the verb "to land," to debark, to touch land.

Ed. It refers here to Fishkill Landing, now Beacon, on the east bank of the Hudson, opposite Newburgh.

18. Washington's letter to Chastellux, dated Newburgh, Dec. 14, 1782, Fitzpatrick, ed., *Writings of Washington*, XXV, 428-29, leaves no doubt about the sincerity of his feelings:

My dear Chevr: I felt too much to express anything, the day I parted with you; A Sense of your public Services to this Country, and gratitude for your private friendship, quite overcame me at the moment of our seperation. But I should be wanting to the feelings of my heart, and should do violence to my inclination, was I to suffer you to leave this Country, without the warmest assurances of an affectionate regard for your person and character.

Our good friend the Marqs. de la Fayette prepared me (long before I had the honor to see you) for those Impressions of esteem which oppertunities, and your own benevolent Mind has since improved into a deep, and lasting friendship, a friendship which neither time nor distance can ever eradicate.

I can truly say, that never in my life did I part with a Man to whom my Soul clave more sincerely than it did to you. My warmest wishes will attend you in your voyage across the Atlantic; to the rewards of a generous Prince, the Arms of Affectionate friends, and be assured that it will be one of my highest gratifications to keep up a regular intercourse with you by Letter.

I regret exceedingly, that our circumstances should withdraw you from this Country before the final accomplishment of that Independence and Peace which the Arms of our good Ally has assisted in placing before us in so agreeable a point of view. Nothing would give me more pleasure than to accompany you in a tour through the Continent of North America at the close of the War, in search of the National curiosities with which it abounds, and to view the foundation of a rising Empire. I have the honr etc.

Washington's farewell letter to Rochambeau, of the same date (*ibid.*, 427-28), is couched in far more formal language. In a letter to Lafayette (then in France), mentioning the departure of the French officers, Washington singled out Chastellux for special mention: "I could not have bid a Brother farewell with more regret than I did the Chevr. Chastellux, than whom no Man stands higher in my estimation." *Ibid.*, 434.

19. The quarters occupied by the army during the winter of 1782-83 ("the last cantonment of the main Continental Army") were situated two or three miles west of the Hudson within the present limits of the town of New Windsor. A contemporary map, drawn by the U.S. "geographer" Simeon Dewitt, successor to Robert Erskine, entitled "The Winter-Cantonment of the American Army and its Vicinity for 1783" (original in N. Y. Hist. Soc., Erskine-Dewitt map No. I reproduced in *Mag. Amer. Hist.*, 10 [1883], 365, and elsewhere), shows the disposition of the campground as well as its relationship to such other sites as Washington's headquarters at Newburgh, the Ellison House occupied by Gen. Gates, etc. The present Temple Hill Monument, marking the presumed site of the so-called "temple," or meeting place used by the army, is owned by the state of New York, while some of the surrounding area has been acquired by the

National Temple Hill Association, with a view to reconstruction of the campground.

20. The house which had been occupied by General Knox in 1780, when Chastellux visited Washington at New Windsor (see above, Pt. I, chap. 4, Dec. 20, 1780) and now, in 1782, by General Horatio Gates, is still standing. The fieldstone house, known as "Knox Headquarters," originally built for John Ellison by William Bull in 1754, is southwest of New Windsor near present Vails Gate (off Quassaick Avenue, State Route 94), and is maintained as an historic site under the supervision of the New York State Education Department. The main road formerly passed in front of the house.

21. The stream is called "Moodna Creek" on modern maps. Benson J. Lossing, in *The Hudson, from the Wilderness to the Sea* (Troy, 1866), attributes the change in name to the writer, Nathaniel Parker Willis, a resident of the region. For the sake of poetry and romance, as well as of propriety, Willis pretended that "Murderer" (traditionally associated with an Indian massacre) was merely a corruption of "Moodna," a euphonious Indian word (of his own imagining)!

22. See above, Pt. I, chap. 1, Nov. 22, 1780, and n. 103. Francis Baird is listed as one of the more substantial property owners in Warwick on the 1775 Assessment Roll; E. M. Ruttenber and L. H. Clark, *History of Orange County, N.Y.* ... (Phila., 1881), 566, 572, 577. The house rented by Mr. Smith from Mr. Baird is still standing in Warwick, on the west side of Maple Ave., at the point where the road from Chester (King's Highway, Colonial Avenue) meets Maple Ave. (State Route 94), opposite the fountain and Frank Forrester memorial. It is a stone house (privately owned), and although somewhat modified in appearance by subsequent additions, the shell is evidently that of the original house. One of the stones on the rear wall is inscribed "F. Baird 1766."

Chapter 4

The Moravian Settlements at Hope and at Bethlehem;
Return to Philadelphia

1. See above, Pt. III, chap. 3, Dec. 7, 1782, and n. 22.

2. *Humane Prudence, or the Art By which a Man may Raise Himself and Fortune to Grandeur,* by William De Britaine. First published, London, 1680, and frequently reprinted during the next century or so. It was translated into French, and there was even a "first American edition" published at Dedham, Mass., in 1806. "This Little Manual," according to the author's dedicatory epistle, "if you please to read it soberly, and practise the principles contained in it, (though you have erected a fair structure of knowledge to yourself, yet) I dare say it will build you a story higher. The conversation of men, is a good expedient to cultivate and improve your parts. Reading of books may make you learned, but it is conversation and business that makes men wise."

3. This is not the present town of Sussex, but the old Sussex County Courthouse, now called Newton, Sussex Co., N. J. "Jonathan Willis was

one of the early settlers. He was also one of the pioneer tavernkeepers, and as a public official his name is of frequent occurrence in the records of Sussex County. He was appointed judge in 1794." James P. Snell *et al.*, eds., *History of Sussex and Warren Counties, New Jersey* ... (Phila., 1881), 249, 258, 259. The Rev. Manasseh Cutler, who traveled along the road from Warwick, N. Y., to Easton, Pa., less than six years after Chastellux did, noted in his journal, under date of July 30, 1788, that at Sussex Courthouse he "breakfasted at a tavern just above the Court-house, kept by Jona. Willis." William Parker and Julia Perkins Cutler, eds., *Life, Journals and Correspondence of the Rev. Manasseh Cutler, LL.D.*, 2 vols. (Cincinnati, 1888), I, 395-96. The present courthouse is presumably on the site of the original building, destroyed by fire in 1849.

4. In Chastellux's text the name is printed throughout as "Poops," an error also followed by Grieve.

5. *Ch.* Bethlehem is a sort of colony founded by the Moravian Brothers, often called Herrenhutter [Herrnhutter]. It was to see this establishment, and at the same time the town of Easton and the Upper Delaware, that I had left the ordinary route leading from New Windsor to Philadelphia.

Ed. The Moravian settlement at Bethlehem, founded in 1741, played a considerable role during the Revolution. A military hospital was located there, and Congressmen and army officers from Philadelphia frequently visited it. Chastellux's brother officers in Rochambeau's army, the Marquis de Laval and the Count de Custine, had stopped there in Jan. 1781 (see above, Pt. I, chap. 3, Dec. 12, 1780). Chastellux had had many opportunities to hear about Bethlehem from his acquaintances, and it was thus a sight that he himself had to see. John W. Jordan, "Bethlehem during the Revolution. Extracts from the Diaries in the Moravian Archives at Bethlehem," *Pa. Mag. of Hist. and Biog.*, 12 (1888), 385-406; 13 (1889), 71-89. On the Moravian settlements in general, see Moravian Historical Society, *Transactions* (1859———), *passim*; Joseph M. Levering, *A History of Bethlehem, Pennsylvania, 1741-1892* ... (Bethlehem, 1903).

Gr. [Several of Grieve's general notes, interpolated at different points in the text, are grouped here]. The Moravian sect is pretty generally known in Europe. They are the followers of the famous Count Zinzendorf, whose picture they have at Bethlehem; they have several establishments in Europe, similar to those the Marquis [Chastellux] is about to speak of, one of which I have seen at Ziest, near Utrecht, where Louis XIVth took up his quarters, but America seems to be the promised land of sectaries. Even the despised, ill-treated Jews, are well received in the United States, and begin to be very numerous; many of them were excellent citizens during the severe trial of the war, and some even lost their lives as soldiers, gallantly fighting for the liberties of their country. One family, in particular, I believe of the name of Salvador, at Rhode-Island, was most eminently distinguished. What a glorious field is this for unprejudiced philanthropic speculation! The following account of the Moravians is taken from a translation from the German [by David Cranz], of an account of that body, by the Reverend B.[enjamin] La Trobe:

"The sect of the *Unitas fratrum*, more commonly known by the names of Herrnhuters and Moravians, was at first formed by Nicholas Lewis, Count of Zinzendorf, at Berthelsdorf in Upper Lusatia, in the year 1722. Finding his followers increase, particularly from Moravia, he built a house in a wood near Berthelsdorf for their public meetings; and, before the end of the year 1732, this place grew into a village, which was called Herrnhut, and contained about six hundred inhabitants, all of them following Zinzendorf, and leading a kind of monastic life. From this time the sect has spread its branches from Germany, through all the Protestant states in Europe, made considerable establishments on the continent of America, and Western Isles, and extended itself to the East-Indies, and into Africa. In England, Moravian congregations are formed at London, Bedford, Oakbrook near Derby, Pudsey near Leeds, Dunkerfield in Cheshire, Leominster, Haverford West, Bristol, Kingswood, Bath and Tetherton."

Their settlements are becoming very numerous too, but not their population, in all the different states in the American union. It is remarked, that on the lands within reach of the Moravian settlements, the cultivation is superior, and every branch of husbandry is better carried on, first, from the emulation excited by these industrious people, and secondly, from the supply the countryman procures from them of every necessary implement of husbandry, etc. fabricated in these settlements. Besides those the Marquis [Chastellux] speaks of, I visited some others, not far from Bethlehem, at one of which, called Nazareth, is a famous gunsmith [William Henry], from whom my friend Major Pierce Butler, bought a pair of pistols, many of which I saw there of the most perfect workmanship. Nothing can be more enchanting than these establishments; out of the sequestered wilderness they have formed well built towns, vast edifices all of stone, large orchards, beautiful and regular shaded walks in the European fashion, and seem to combine with the most complete separation from the world, all the comforts and even many of the luxuries of polished life. At one of their cleared-out settlements, in the midst of a forest, between Bethlehem and Nazareth, possessing all the advantages of mills and manufactures, I was astonished with the delicious sounds of an Italian concerto, but my surprise was still greater on entering a room where the performers turned out to be common workmen of different trades, playing for their amusement. At each of these places, the brethren have a common room, where violins and other instruments are suspended, and always at the service of such as choose to relax themselves, by playing singly, or taking a part in a concert.

The Moravians appear to me to be a sect between the Methodists and the Catholics; at Nazareth, I met with an old Gloucestershire man, who came to America with the late Mr. [George] Whitefield, with whom I had much conversation, and who told me that that gentleman was much respected, both living and dead, by the Moravians; but, indeed, besides that, their hymns resemble much those of our Methodists, by spiritualizing even the grossest *carnal* transactions; I found that they all spoke of him as one of their own sect, but utterly disclaimed Mr. Wesley. They are very fond of pictures representing *the passion*, to which they pay a respect little short, if at all, of idolatry. Their carnal allusions are fully verified in the following hymn taken from one of their books in the Moravian chapel at Pudsey in England, in 1773, an allusion than which nothing can be more infamous and shocking:

> And she so blessed is,
> She gives him many a kiss:
> Fix'd are her eyes on him;
> Thence moves her every limb;

And since she him so loves,
She only with him moves:
His matters and his blood
Appear her only good.

Ed. The American editor of the 1827 edition of Chastellux's Travels adds this further note: "The Moravians are a sect of Christians, so distinguished by the purity of their manners, the scrupulous morality of their principles, and the virtuous and benevolent effects of their doctrine and examples, that the children of the most rigid of other denominations are sent to them for education. If sectarians are driven by the violence of despotic governments into extreme fanaticism, it is not so in a country, where 'error of opinion may be safely tolerated, when reason is left free to combat it.' In the United States, where no separate church or denomination is established by law, many of the singularities and asperities of the most heterodox persuasions or sects, have vanished before the liberty of discussion, the friendly interchange of sentiment, and the harmony of social intercourse. Many of the rites and practices formerly imputed to the strange schismatics which sprung up in every country where they are permitted to exist, are now matters of recollection only, and no part of present faith or practice."

For a discussion of this aspect of Moravianism by a modern scholar see Jacob John Sessler, *Communal Pietism among Early American Moravians* (N. Y., 1933), 156-81. According to Sessler, p. 163, "this extravagant fanaticism was never characteristic of Moravianism at its best, and although a residium of it remained for many years, the frequent revision of the liturgies and hymnals deleted more and more of the sensual imagery."

6. *Ch.* The Moravian Mill is a property they have purchased in the neighborhood of Bethlehem.
Ed. At Hope, N. J. Chastellux's text places it "*à quatre milles au-delà de Sussex*," probably an error for *quatorze* milles, which is closer to the actual distance of about sixteen miles.

7. Moravian Mill was at Hope, N. J., a settlement begun in 1769 by Moravians from Bethlehem, Pa., on land acquired from Samuel Green, Jr. First called Greenland, it was named Hope in 1775 at the time that a regularly organized community was established. The Brethren finally gave up their establishment here in 1808. At the time Chastellux stopped, the settlement was in a promising period of growth: a chapel in the newly built *Gemeinhaus* had been dedicated only the month before; the sawmill had been built in 1780, the gristmill a decade earlier. Several of the stone buildings erected by the Moravians are still standing in the Warren Co. town of Hope, which retains the name given it by the Brethren. Charles F. Kluge, "Sketch of the Settlement of Hope, New Jersey," Moravian Hist. Soc., *Transactions*, 1, (1868), 51-56 (substantially the same article is reprinted, without indication of source in *Pa. Mag. of Hist. and Biog.*, 37 [1913], 248-52, under the title "A Forgotten Moravian Settlement in New Jersey"); Hope Historical Society, *The Moravian Contribution to the Town of Hope, New Jersey* (Hope, N.J., 1955).

The innkeeper who served as Chastellux's guide was Ephraim Culver, Jr. (not "Calver," as printed in the original text and translation of the *Voyages*), who was the second son of Ephraim and Hannah Culver. Ephraim Sr. was a gristmill operator and innkeeper who came from Lebanon, Conn., as did, presumably, his son. The latter married Magdalene Lanius from Catores Township (York), Pa., at Bethlehem, Aug. 16, 1770. Information from the Moravian Archives, Bethlehem, Pa., where the name is sometimes spelled "Colver."

8. *Gr.* Six shillings, Pennsylvania currency—about three shillings and four pence sterling.

9. *Gr.* One farthing.

10. The sawmill is no longer standing.

11. This millrace, still in existence, is described by Harry B. Weiss and Robert J. Sim in *The Early Grist and Flouring Mills of New Jersey* (Trenton, N.J., 1956), 126, as "750 feet long, cut through Martinsburg Shale Formation which is a shaly to slatey decomposition product, the black being more slatey than the lighter colored rock. At one place where the race was cut through the side of a hill, it is 22 feet deep." The large stone gristmill (or flouring mill)—privately owned and no longer in use as a mill—is today one of the landmarks of Hope. It was planned by Christian Christianson, who had designed the waterworks at Bethlehem; the master mason was Philip Maixel, the master carpenter, Joseph Grotz. Chastellux's text places the gristmill *"à une portée de fusil au dessus du premier,"* i.e., *above* the sawmill; but it is actually *below*, or downstream, from the site of the sawmill.

12. In Virginia. See above, Pt. II, chap. 4, Apr. 25, 1782.

13. This building, in which the chapel was located, was the *Gemeinhaus,* or Community House; the cornerstone was laid by Bishop J. F. Reichel, Apr. 1781; the chapel was formally dedicated by Bishop John Ettwein, Nov. 8, 1782. It is still one of the notable stone houses of Hope; one side of it is now occupied by the local bank; a tablet recalls its original use.

14. The religious paintings (*tableaux de piété*) which Chastellux saw here in the Moravian chapel at Hope, and in Bethlehem were the work of John Valentine Haidt (1700-1780), a native of Danzig, who learned painting in Berlin where his father was court goldsmith to the King of Prussia, and who came to Bethlehem in 1754. Haidt painted both portraits of his fellow Moravians and religious pictures for their chapels. Examples of his work may be seen at the Archives of the Moravian Church in Bethlehem and at Whitefield House, the Moravian Hist. Soc. museum in Nazareth. Garth A. Howland, "John Valentine Haidt, A Little Known Eighteenth Century Painter," *Pennsylvania History,* 8 (1941), 304-13 (no illus.); Art Institute of Chicago catalogue, *From Colony to Nation, An Exhibition of American Painting, Silver and Architecture from 1650 to the War of 1812*... (Chicago, 1949), 46-47, Nos. 63-66 (reproductions of Haidt's "Crucifixion" and "Christ before Pilate"); *Lenten Exhibit of Paintings by John Valentine Haidt,* leaflet for exhibition at Moravian College, Bethlehem, Mar. 1956. Haidt was neither a "primitive" nor a "folk artist," but a trained craftsman of considerable skill and originality, working in an established tradition. In his day he apparently was little known outside the Moravian settlements, but in recent years he has been "rediscovered" by historians of American art of the colonial period.

15. Major Robert Hoops's house was at Belvidere, N. J. He had come to this region about 1770 and became one of the largest landowners in the place. Snell *et al.,* eds., *History of Sussex and Warren Counties, New Jersey,* 533-34.

16. *Ch.* At this mill one pays 35 shillings to have one hundred bushels of wheat ground; which comes to 20 or 22 *sols* a *setier*, about the same price paid in France.

17. *Gr.* Thirty-six shillings sterling.

18. The French text reads: "*car en Amérique les Avocats sont en même tems Procureurs et Notaires.*" This distinction between American and French practice still holds good today.

19. *Gr.* The Gazettes have just announced [1786] the death of General Greene. In him America has lost one of her best citizens, and most able soldiers. It is his greatest eulogium to say, that he stood high with General Washington, who recommended him to Congress, and that he amply justified the opinion entertained of him by that great, good man.

20. Chastellux uses the English word, adding in a note: "*Exertions* is a much used term in English, and also very expressive; it signifies the industry and activity that are applied to all difficult things."

21. The name appears as "Fims" in Chastellux's text. The colonel was John Syme, of Hanover Co., whose second wife was Sarah Hoops (sister of Chastellux's host Robert Hoops), and one of whose daughters by a first marriage married one of the brothers (David, or Adam, Jr.?) of Chastellux's host. For the interrelationship of Hoopses and Symes, see *Va. Mag. of Hist. and Biog.*, 32 (1924), 396-97; *Pa. Mag. of Hist. and Biog.*, 35 (1911), 512.

22. The height with a view is on the Belvidere-Easton road at Harmony, N. J.

23. *Gr.* These are called the Kittatinny mountains. For an account of this *hiatus*, or gap, see Mr. Charles Thomson's Observations on Mr. Jefferson's Notes on Virginia, under the account of the Natural Bridge.

Ed. Thomson's observations on the Delaware Water Gap, referred to by Grieve, are not strictly speaking part of Jefferson's account of the Natural Bridge, but are appended to his description of the passage of the Potomac through the Blue Ridge (at Harper's Ferry), where the Shenandoah and Potomac "rush together against the mountain, render it asunder, and pass off to the sea." Jefferson, *Notes on Virginia*, Query IV, "A notice of its Mountains." Like Chastellux, both Jefferson and Thomson were familiar with Buffon's *Théorie de la Terre*, which had undoubtedly stimulated their own interest in "these monuments of a war between rivers and mountains, which must have shaken the earth itself to its center."

24. The Delaware Water Gap, and the Wind Gap.

25. *Ch.* See the first part of this journal [Pt. I, chap. 5, Dec. 26, 1780] where the author gives an account of his conversations with General Schuyler. In whatever manner this expedition was set on foot, which took place in 1779, after the evacuation of Philadelphia and the diversion made by the Count d'Estaing's squadron, the greatest difficulty to overcome was a long march that had to be made through woods, swamps, and wilderness, transporting all supplies on beasts of burden, and being continually exposed to attacks from the Indians. The instructions given by General Sullivan to his officers, the order of march he prescribed to the troops, and the discipline he succeeded in maintaining, would have done honor to the most experienced among the ancient or modern generals. It may safely be asserted that the Journal of this expedition would lose nothing in comparison with the

famous Retreat of the Ten Thousand, which it would resemble very much, if it were possible to compare maneuvers, the object of which is attack, with those which have no other aim than the preservation of a forsaken army. General Sullivan, after more than a month's march, arrived without any setbacks at the entrenched camp which was the last refuge of the savages; here he attacked them and was met with great courage: the victory would even have remained indecisive, had not the Indians lost many of their chiefs in battle, which never fails to intimidate them, and retreated during the night. The General destroyed their houses and plantations, since which they have never shown themselves. However slight and insufficient the idea that I have given of this campaign, it may, nevertheless, astonish our European military men to learn that General Sullivan was in 1775 a lawyer, and that in the year 1780 he left the army to resume his profession. He is now Governor of New Hampshire.

Ed. Col. Simcoe, in his anonymous *Remarks on the Travels of the Marquis de Chastellux,* treats this comment on Sullivan's expedition with particular scorn: "Unhappy Greeks, had you been conquered you would have suffered less disgrace! Unfortunate Xenophon! your talents, your courage, are so miserably degraded, that even the mild philosophy of Socrates would become indignant, could he but know that his illustrious disciple was compared to an attorney of New Hampshire! . . . European military men, I am apt to believe, will think that the whole expedition savours more of the lawyer than of the soldier; the delay of process, minute account of the premises, and of the apple-trees which were enumerated in the American papers as destroyed, the indecision of the action, and the costs of suit, reminded Congress of the general termination of a lawsuit; for they were to pay the bill."

26. The "eastern branch of the Delaware," now referred to simply as the Delaware; the Lehigh, which joins it here at Easton, was in Chastellux's day often called the "west branch" of the Delaware. The site of Easton was known as "The Forks of the Delaware."

27. An interesting reconstructed plan of Easton *ca.* 1776, as it was a few years before Chastellux's visit, is in A. D. Chidsey, Jr., *A Frontier Village, Pre-Revolutionary Easton* (Easton, Pa., 1940). Mr. Smith was apparently a very recent arrival; his name does not appear on the list of taxable inhabitants for 1780 published in Uzal W. Condit, *History of Easton, Penn'a. . . . , 1739-1885* (Easton, Pa., 1889); nor is he mentioned at all under those categories dear to the antiquarian, "Bench and Bar," and "Tavernkeepers and Hotels." Smith seems to have made more of an impression on Chastellux than on the local historians.

28. *Gr.* In travelling over this hill, the Translator stopped near an hour to view this noble and enchanting prospect, with which it is impossible to satiate the eye. Nothing can be more delightful than the town and neighborhood of Easton.

29. *Gr.* The first time I visited Bethlehem was from Philadelphia, and after travelling two days through a country alternately diversified with savage scenes and cultivated spots, on issuing out of the woods at the close of the evening, in the month of May [1782], found myself on a beautiful extensive plain, with the vast eastern branch of the Delaware on the right, richly interspersed with wooded islands, and at the distance of a mile in the front of the town of Bethlehem, rearing its large stone edifices out of a

forest, situated on a majestic, but gradually rising eminence, the background formed by the setting sun. So novel and unexpected a transition filled the mind with a thousand singular and sublime ideas, and made an impression on me, never to be effaced. The romantic and picturesque effect of this glorious display of natural beauties, gave way to the still more noble and interesting sensations, arising from a reflection on the progress of the arts and sciences, and the sublime anticipation of the "populous cities," and "busy hum of men," which are one day to occupy, and to civilize the vast wilderness of the New World.

Ed. The traveler approaching Bethlehem from the south is today greeted by the busy hum of the Bethlehem Steel Corporation plants.

30. *Ed.* The "Sun Inn" is still standing (although somewhat changed in appearance by subsequent alterations) at 560-64 Main St. in Bethlehem; its former glory has departed—*caveat peregrinus!* When Chastellux stopped there the innkeeper was John Christian Ebert, who had succeeded Jost Jansen in 1781. Levering, *History of Bethlehem*, 514.

Gr. This inn, for its external appearance, and its interior accommodations, is not inferior to the best of the large inns in England, which, indeed, it very much resembles in every respect. The first time I was in Bethlehem, in company with my friends Major Pierce Butler, Mr. Thomas Elliot, and Mr. Charles Pinkney, Carolina gentlemen, we remained here two or three days, and were constantly supplied with venison, moor game, the most delicious red and yellow bellied trout, the highest flavored wild strawberries, the most luxuriant asparagus, and the best vegetables, in short, I ever saw; and notwithstanding the difficulty of procuring good wine and spirits at that period, throughout the continent, we were here regaled with rum and brandy of the best quality, and exquisite old Port and Madeira. It was to this house that the Marquis de la Fayette retired, to be cured of the first wound he received in fighting for America [at the Battle of Brandywine, Sept. 1777]; an accident, which I am well assured gave this gallant young nobleman more pleasure than most of our European *petits maîtres* would receive from the most flattering proofs of the favor of a mistress. Mr. Charles Pinkney, whom I have above mentioned, is a young gentleman at present in Congress for South Carolina, and who, from the intimate knowledge I have of his excellent education and strong talents, will, I venture to predict, whenever he pleases to exert them, stand forth among the most eminent citizens of the new confederation of Republics. It is my boast and pride to have co-operated with him, when he was only at the age of twenty, in the defence of the true principles of liberty, and to have seen productions from his pen, which, in point of composition, and of argument, would have done honor to the head and heart of the most experienced and most virtuous politician. Should the present work ever fall into his hands, let him recognize in this just tribute to his worth, an affectionate friend, who, knowing his abilities, wishes to excite him to exertion, in the noble, but arduous field before him.

31. *Gr.* This bird must be what we call the black or grey game, and not what is known by the name of *growse* in England.

Ed. Presumably Chastellux is describing the ruffed grouse (*Bonasa umbellus*), often called a "partridge" in the northeastern United States. "The races of the Ruffed Grouse are still subject to much discussion," according to R. T. Peterson, *A Field Guide to the Birds* (Boston, 1958), 271.

32. *Gr.* Our company was much more fortunate, Major Butler having obtained letters from Philadelphia to Mr. Van Vleck, a man of property, living here, but formerly of New York.

Ed. Grieve presumably refers to Hendrick Van Vleck (1722-85), a New York merchant who joined the Brethren in 1748, became their agent, and moved with his family to Bethlehem in 1774. He was the father of Jacob Van Vleck, whom Chastellux met (see below, n. 40). W. C. Reichel, "A Register of Members of the Moravian Church, and of persons attached to said Church in this country and abroad, between 1727 and 1754," Moravian Hist. Soc., *Transactions*, 1 (1873), 422.

33. *Ed.* The retired seaman and drawing master who served as Chastellux's guide was Nicholas Garrison, Jr., the son of Nicholas Garrison (1701-81), also a seaman and prominent Moravian. The elder Garrison had commanded several ships for the Brethren, including "The Little Strength" which brought "the Second Sea Congregation" to America in 1743. Nicholas, Jr., did a view of Philadelphia which was engraved by J. Hulett in 1767 (I. N. Phelps Stokes and D. C. Haskell, *American Historical Prints...* [N.Y., 1932], 22 [*c.* 1767-B-67]), as well as views of Bethlehem and Nazareth. His view of Bethlehem in 1784 (with Oerter, engraved by J. Spilsbury) shows the town almost exactly as it was at the time of Chastellux's visit. Moravian Hist. Soc., *Transactions*, 1 (1873), 337-38; Levering, *History of Bethlehem*, 519; George C. Groce and David H. Wallace, *The New-York Historical Society's Dictionary of Artists in America* (New Haven, 1957), 250-51. Concerning Nicholas Garrison, III, the son of Chastellux's guide, Grieve adds the following footnote:

Gr. It is remarkable enough, that the son of this Moravian, whose name is Garrison, should have served on board a vessel with me, and was, without exception, the most worthless profligate fellow we had in a mixed crew of English, Scotch, Irish, and Americans, to all of whom his education had been infinitely superior. Neither bolts nor bars could prevent, nor any chastisement correct, his pilfering disposition. In a long winter's voyage of *thirteen* weeks, with only provisions and water for *five*, this fellow was the bane and pest of officers, passengers, and seamen. Whilst every other man in the ship, even the most licentious in prosperity, submitted to regulations laid down to alleviate our dreadful sufferings, and preserve our lives, this hardened, unreflecting wretch, ignorant of every feeling of sympathy and human nature, seemed to take a savage delight in diffusing misery around him, and adding to the distresses of his fellow sufferers. He had been well educated in the humane principles of the Moravians, but he truly verified the just adage of *Corruptio optimi pessima.*

34. The "Sisters' House," still standing, is one of the group of 18th-century Moravian buildings on West Church St. in Bethlehem. Concerning this and the other buildings mentioned by Chastellux see: Kenneth G. Hamilton, *Church Street in Old Bethlehem* (Bethlehem, 1942); Garth A. Howland, "Reconstructural Problems associated with the Moravian Buildings in Bethlehem," Moravian Hist. Soc., *Transactions*, 13 (1944), 174-280, illus.; Joseph A. Maurer and Hans-Karl Schuchard, "Moravian Buildings in Bethlehem," *Archeology*, 3 (1950), 226-32, illus.

35. *Ed.* Chastellux writes "Madame de Gastorff." This was Susanna Charlotte von Gersdorf, born Feb. 23, 1731, in Werda, Upper Lusatia, who was received as a deaconess in Herrnhut on Jan. 19, 1761. After serving as

a laboress among the younger maidens at Herrnhaag, then among the single sisters at Niesky and Herrnhut, she came to Bethlehem in 1763 as laboress in the Single Sisters' choir there. She returned to Europe in 1787. Susanna von Gersdorf was presumably related—distantly at least—to the mother and aunt of Count Zinzendorf, who bore the name of von Gersdorf and played an important role in the organization of the resuscitated Moravian Church at Herrnhut in the 1720's. Levering, *History of Bethlehem*, 401, 487, 579, 536; Elizabeth Lehman Myers, *A Century of Moravian Sisters* (N. Y., 1918), 61-71; other details from the Archives of the Moravian Church, Bethlehem.

Gr. When the Translator visited Bethlehem, the superintendent, or at least her deputy, was a Mrs. Langley, a very mild pretty behaved English woman, who had been a follower of George Whitefield.

36. *Gr.* The Americans in general are remarkably fond of very large soft feather beds, even in the hottest climates, and we suffered greatly in this particular, at the inn in Bethlehem.

37. This church, not to be confused with the larger "Central Moravian Church" built in 1803-6, is now known as the "Old Chapel."

38. The pictures by John Valentine Haidt no longer hang in the Old Chapel; but see above, this chap., n. 14.

39. The Brothers', or Single Brethren's House, now "Colonial Hall," of Moravian College Women's Campus, on the south side of West Church St.

40. This man whose name Chastellux had forgotten was Jacob Van Vleck (1751-1831), the son of Hendrick Van Vleck (see above, this chap., n. 32.). Jacob studied at the school in Nazareth and then at the Moravian theological seminary at Barby in Saxony, whence he returned in 1778 to become assistant pastor of the Bethlehem congregation. From 1790 to 1800 he was inspector of the Young Ladies Seminary, and still later occupied other important positions among the Moravians. Jacob Van Vleck was one of the first American-born Moravians to compose music. "The musical activities of this brilliant man were restricted by the sum of his other activities. Only four of his compositions are preserved. Two of these are mentioned in the earliest Bethlehem catalogue, together with a *Duetto Ich freue mich in dem Herrn*, and another piece *Der dich gemacht hat*, which are lost. The quality of the compositions preserved proves that Van Vleck was a fine musician. Till asserts that Van Vleck played an important part in the improvement of music at Bethlehem. Eventually he cooperated with Nitschmann, his brother-in-law, by writing out organ parts to sets of parts copied by Nitschmann." Albert G. Rau and Hans T. David, *A Catalogue of Music by American Moravians, 1742-1842, From the Archives of the Moravian Church at Bethlehem* (Bethlehem, 1938), 53 ff.

Rau and David describe four compositions of Van Vleck: two anthems, an arietta in the style of a chorale, and a composition intended for a child's funeral; they also reproduce (plate X) a drawing done by girls of the Seminary in 1795, showing Van Vleck standing in front of his harpsichord "singing and playing." On Van Vleck and on Moravian music in general see also: Hans T. David, "Background for Bethlehem: Moravian Music in Pennsylvania," *Magazine of Art*, 32 (1939), 222-25, 254 (valuable also for its reproductions of early views of Bethlehem and Nazareth); Hans T. David, "Musical Life in the Pennsylvania Settlements of the *Unitas Fratrum*," Moravian Hist. Soc., *Transactions*, 13 (1942), 19-58 (reprinted, with foreword, addenda and corrigenda by Donald M. McCorkle, in Moravian Music Foundation, *Publications*, 6 [1959]).

41. *Gr.* The Moravians maintain a constant intercourse with Germany in particular, of which country those in America are chiefly natives, and think nothing of a voyage to Europe. Governor Joseph Reed, of Philadelphia, had a son here, learning the German language, when I was at Bethlehem [in 1782].

42. *Gr.* I do not speak with confidence, but am inclined to think that they have bishops, at least a person was pointed out to us at Bethlehem, under that denomination.

Ed. Grieve is correct, and Chastellux wrong: the United Brethren had, and still have, bishops in their church organization.

43. *Gr.*—after consulting with the superintendent of the women—.

44. As part of their discipline and tradition the Moravians kept systematic records of their activities; copies of their "diaries," or chronicles, were sent to Herrnhut in Germany, where they were in turn abstracted and redistributed to the other Moravian communities in various parts of the world. Thus the Archives of the Moravian Church at Bethlehem provide today an exceptionally complete record of the Moravian settlements of the "Northern Province" (with a counterpart, for the "Southern Province" at Winston-Salem, N. C.). For example, both the so-called "Bethlehem Diary" (the general community chronicle) and the ancillary Brethren's House Diary record Chastellux's visit; there is, however, no mention of him in the Sisters' House Diary. The entry in the Bethlehem Diary, Dec. 11, 1782, reads: "Ein französicher General de Chateloux nebst seinem Gefolge liess sich im Orte herumführen u. befragte sich sehr genau nach unserem Plan und Einrichtungen"—"A French General de Chateloux with his retinue was taken around the town and he inquired in detail about our organization and institutions." The Brethren's House Diary, Dec. 11, 1782, states: "d. 11ten hatten wir Besuch von einem Französichen General mit S[eine]r Suite"— "on the 11th we had a visit from a French General with his suite." Information supplied through the courtesy of the Archives of the Moravian Church, Bethlehem.

45. *Gr.* From this Belvedere the view is beautifully romantic, and among other objects on the eastern side of the Delaware [Lehigh], you see a cultivated farm formed out of an immense wood and near the summit of a lofty mountain, which I likewise visited, and every step of which gives you the idea of enchanted ground. Besides the particular gardens to each private house, there is a large public walk belonging to the community, nay, the church-yard itself is a gay scene of beauty and regularity, the verdant turf being clad in summer with strawberries and flowers.

46. Chastellux's text is: "*C'est que les moeurs des Moraves sont encore tudesques comme leur langage.*" To enlightened and polished 18th-century European cosmopolitans like Chastellux, the word *tudesque* (literally, Teutonic) implied a certain lack of polish and refinement. Germany was thought of as an underdeveloped or underprivileged country, which had not yet fully emerged from the dark ages. German culture and the German language had not yet been rediscovered, and had not yet found their propagandist in Madame de Staël. A free translation of Chastellux's remark might be: "for the ways of the Moravians, like their language, are still a bit

uncouth." In any case, it is a rather mild jibe, and Grieve seriously distorted its meaning and implications when he rendered it as, "because the Moravians are still more barbarous than their language."

47. *Gr.* The eastern [western] branch of the Delaware which passes by Bethlehem, and forms a junction with the western [eastern] at Easton, is here called the Lecha [Lehigh]. There is an excellent ferry over this rapid stream, of which I have spoken in the first volume [Pt. I, chap. 1, n. 36]. The Moravians among an infinity of other ingenious inventions, have a large hydraulic machine in the middle of the town which is at a great height from the river for raising the water to supply the inhabitants.

PART IV

Epilogue

Letter to Mr. Madison on the Progress of the Arts and Sciences in America

1. *Ed.* The Rev. James Madison (1749-1812), president of the College of William and Mary from 1777, first Bishop of the Protestant Episcopal Church in Virginia from 1790, is not to be confused with his cousin James Madison (1751-1836), fourth President of the United States. Concerning the latter Grieve adds this note:

Gr. Mr. Madison's son [cousin] is a member of the Assembly, and has served in Congress for Virginia. This young man, who at the age of 30 astonishes the new Republics by his eloquence, his wisdom, and his genius, has had the humanity and the *courage* (for such a proposition requires no small share of courage), to propose a general emancipation of the slaves, at the beginning of this year, 1786: Mr. Jefferson's absence at Paris, and the situation of Mr. Wythe, as one of the judges of the state, which prevented them from lending their powerful support, occasioned it to miscarry for the moment, but there is every reason to suppose that the proposition will be successfully renewed. As it is, the [Virginia] assembly have passed a law declaring that there shall be no more slaves in the Republic but those existing the first day of the session of 1785-86, and the descendants of female slaves.

Ed. Grieve's sanguine expectation that the proposal for general emancipation of slaves in Virginia would be "successfully renewed" proved to be wrong. When reviewing the matter some 35 years later, Thomas Jefferson wrote in his *Autobiography* (1821) that "the public mind would not yet bear the proposition, nor will it bear it even at this day. Yet the day is not distant when it must bear and adopt it, or worse will follow." Concerning Madison's proposal and its relationship to the "Bill concerning Slaves" (enacted into law, Dec. 1785), see Boyd *et al.*, eds., *Jefferson Papers*, II, 470-73.

2. Chastellux's letter (in French) to Schuyler, Williamsburg, Feb. 18, 1782, is in Schuyler Papers, MSS. Div., N. Y. Pub. Lib.

3. Chastellux's letter (in French) to De Létombe, Williamsburg, June 5, 1782, transcribed in De Létombe's hand, is written on blank leaves of what was apparently once De Létombe's copy of Chastellux's *Voyages* (Paris, 1786). A photostat of the transcript was made available to the Editor by

the late Stuart Jackson when the book was in his possession; it is now in the University of Virginia Library (McGregor).

4. Jefferson to Chastellux, Paris, Dec. 24, 1784, Boyd *et al.*, eds., *Jefferson Papers*, VII, 580-81.

5. Chastellux to Jefferson (in French), Dec. 27, 1784, *ibid.*, 584-85.

6. *Ch*. In my book, *De la Félicité Publique*.

7. *Gr*. There are various opinions in America on the subject of encouraging emigration. Mr. Jefferson, for example, a man of profound thought, and great penetration, is of opinion that emigrants from Europe are not desirable, lest the emigrants bringing with them not only the vices, but the corrupt prejudices of their respective ancient governments, may be unable to relish that bold universal system of freedom and toleration which is a novelty to the old world [See *Notes on the State of Virginia*, Query VIII, "Population"]; but I venture to think, and trust, that such emigrations will be attended with no bad consequences; for who will be the emigrants to a country where there are neither gold nor silver mines, and where subsistence is alone to be obtained by industry? Men of small, or no fortunes, who cannot live with comfort, nor bring up a family in Europe; laborers and artisans of every kind; men of modesty and genius, who are cramped by insurmountable obstacles in countries governed by cabal and interest; virtuous citizens compelled to groan in silence under the effects of arbitrary power; philosophers who pant after the liberty of thinking for themselves, and of giving vent, without danger, to those generous maxims which burst from their hearts, and of contributing their mite to the general stock of enlightened knowledge; religious men, depressed by the hierarchical establishments of every country in Europe; the friends to freedom; in short, the liberal, generous, and active spirits of the whole world. To America, then, I say with fervency, in the glowing words of Mr. Paine, who is himself an English emigrant: "O! receive the fugitives and prepare in time an asylum for mankind." [Thomas Paine, *Common Sense*, 3, "Thoughts on the Present State of American Affairs," last sentence.] The history of the late Revolution, too, may justify our hopes, for it is an observation, for the truth of which I appeal to fact, that the Europeans settled in America were possessed of *at least as much energy*, and served that country with as much zeal and enthusiasm in the cabinet, and in the field, as the native Americans, and to speak with the late Lord Chatham, who said many absurd, but more wise things than most statesmen, "they infused a portion of new health into the constitution."

8. *Ch*. Mr. [Jonathan] Trumbull, Governor of Connecticut, lives in the town of Lebanon, which extends over a league of the country, but where there are not six houses less than a quarter-league distant from each other. [See above, Pt. I, chap. 1, Nov. 16, 1780; chap. 6, Jan. 6, 1781.]

9. *Gr*. I cannot here omit an anecdote which places, in a strong point of view, the distinction between *individual* and *public liberty*, made by the mere merchant. In the early part of life I spent some years in the compting-house of one of the most considerable merchants of the city of London, a native of Switzerland, for the moderate premium of *one thousand guineas*. This happening to be the period of the violent unconstitutional proceedings against Mr. Wilkes, the foreign merchant differing from the English apprentice, entered with zeal into all the measures of the then administration,

which, though a republican by birth, he maintained with all the virulence of the tools of despotism. The American war followed, and this gentleman was no less active with offers of his life and fortune, from his compting-house in the city, in support of the arbitrary views of the same set of men, accompanied on all occasions with positions destructive of every idea of *public charity*. But mark the difference, when *individual liberty* was in question. Happening to dine with Mr. John Pringle, of Philadelphia, in 1782, the conversation fell on this merchant, who is at present one of the first in the world, and some questions were asked me respecting his politics; my answers corresponded with what I have above said of him; but judge of my astonishment, when Mr. Pringle assured me, smiling, and gave me *ocular* demonstrations of the fact, that America had not a better friend; producing, at the same time, an invoice of a cargo of *gunpowder* shipped by his order on *joint account*, for the *Rebels* of America, at L'Orient, by which this Mr. ———[Peter Thellusson?], of London, cleared nearly £10,000 sterling!!

10. *Gr.* America, in her infant state, has already burst forth into the full splendor of maturity in the immortal paintings of a [John Singleton] Copley and a [Benjamin] West. Further glory still attends her early progress even in the present day, in a [Gilbert] Stuart, a [John] Trumbull, and a [Mather] Brown; nor is [Charles Willson] Peale unworthy of ranking with many modern painters of no inconsiderable fame; ages may possibly not elapse before posterity may apply to America, what Mr. Tickell has said, so happily heretofore of the mother country,

> See on her Titian's and her Guido's urns,
> Her fallen arts forlorn Hesperia mourns:
> While Britain wins each garland from her brow,
> Her *wit* and *freedom* first, her *painting* now.

For *wit*, let me refer the reader of taste to the poem of *M'Fingal* [1782], written by another [John] Trumbull of Connecticut, who is justly styled the American Hudibras. *Qualis ab incepto processerit, ac sibi constet.*

11. *Gr.* The Academy of Inscriptions and Belles Lettres [in Paris] have composed medals for the Generals Washington, Greene, Gates, Morgan, etc. The State of Virginia also sent for Monsieur [Jean-Antoine] Houdon, the statuary, from Paris to America since the war expressly to take a model, in order to form the statue of General Washington; an example, however, which Congress do not think proper to follow, *during the lifetime* of the General, for reasons which may possibly not be disapproved of, by the Marquis de Chastellux, even in so unexceptionable an instance.

Ed. Concerning the medals executed for Congress in Paris—designed by such artists as Augustin Dupré, Benjamin Duvivier, and Nicolas-Marie Gatteaux, and for which the Académie des Inscriptions et Belles Lettres provided inscriptions—see J. F. Loubat, *The Medallic History of the United States of America, 1776-1876* (N. Y., 1878); and also, "Notes on American Medals Struck in France," Boyd *et al.*, eds., *Jefferson Papers*, XVI, 53-79, illus. On Houdon's journey to America in 1785 for the purpose of modeling Washington from life (which resulted in the well-known statue in the Rotunda of the Capitol at Richmond, Virginia) and on his never-realized hope of a commission from the Federal government for an equestrian statue of Washington, see Gilbert Chinard, *Houdon in America* ... (Baltimore, 1930).

12. *Gr. Eripuit cælo fulmen, sceptrumque tyrannis.* This verse is of that virtuous politician and good man, Mr. Turgot. The Translator has inserted it here, as it seems by the author's omitting it, to be of too high a flavor for the French *censure* [censorship].

13. *Gr.* Although it be highly proper to insist upon this sort of recompense it may not be amiss that the world should know that Congress, as far as opportunity would admit, *have not been remiss* in bestowing such honorable rewards, which they have decreed in different forms on every suitable occasion to the Baron de Kalb etc. etc., and a marble monument was voted by that body to the memory of my inestimable friend, [General Richard] Montgomery, soon after his glorious fall [at Quebec, Dec. 31, 1775], in the following words:

Extract from the Journals of Congress

Thursday, January 25, 1776

The committee appointed to consider a proper method of paying a just tribute of gratitude to the memory of General Montgomery, brought in their report, which was as follows:

It is being not only a tribute of gratitude justly due to the memory of those who have peculiarly distinguished themselves in the glorious cause of liberty, to perpetuate their names by the most durable monuments erected to their honour, but also greatly conducive to inspire posterity with emulation of their illustrious actions:

Resolved, That to express the veneration of the United Colonies for their late general, Richard Montgomery, and the deep sense they entertain of the many signal and important services of that gallant officer, who, after a series of successes, amidst the most discouraging difficulties, fell at length in a gallant attack upon Quebec the capital of Canada; and to transmit to future ages, as examples truly worthy of imitation, his patriotism, conduct, boldness of enterprise, insuperable perseverance, and contempt of danger and death; a monument be procured from Paris, or other part of France, with an inscription sacred to his memory, and expressive of his amiable character, and heroic achievements, and that the continental treasurers be directed to advance a sum not exceeding £300 sterling to Dr. Benjamin Franklin, who is desired to see this resolution properly executed, for defraying the expense thereof.

This resolve was carried into execution at Paris, by that ingenious artist, Mr. Caffieri, sculptor to the King of France, under the direction of Dr. Franklin. The monument is of white marble, of the most beautiful simplicity, and inexpressible elegance, with emblematical devices, and the following truly classical inscription, worthy of the modest, but great mind of a Franklin:—To the glory of Richard Montgomery, Major-General of the Armies of the United States of America, slain at the siege of Quebec, the 31st of December, 1775, aged 38 years.

Over this monument, the Translator who was the intimate friend of this excellent young man, shed an affectionate, tributary tear, when at Paris in the year 1777. He had long known and looked up to him with admiration, for he was deep in the secrets of his head and heart. His attachment to liberty was innate, and matured by a fine education, and a glorious understanding. The Translator, whilst he indulged his private sorrow at the sight of this sad, though noble testimonial of his friend's transcendent virtues, felt his mind awed and overwhelmed with the magnitude of the event which led to this catastrophe, and with reflections on the wonderful revolutions, and extraordinary dispensations of human affairs. But a few months, and he had seen the deceased hero, an officer in the service of England; an officer, too, of the most distinguished merit, who had fought her battles successfully with the immortal Wolfe at Quebec, the very spot on which fighting under the standard of freedom, he was doomed to fall in arms against her; but a few months, and he sees his dead friend the subject of a monument, consecrated to his memory by the united voice of a free people, and his monument, and his fame, as a victim to tyranny, and a champion of freedom, consigned to be celebrated by an enslaved people, against whom he had often fought in defence of the same cause, in which he sacrificed his life. There is a remarkable circumstance connected with his fall, which merits to be recorded. One of General Montgomery's aides-de-camp was Mr. Macpherson, a most promising young man [John Macpherson, Jr. (1754-75)], whose father resided at Philadelphia, and was greatly distinguished in privateering in the war of 1756 [John Macpherson, Sr. (1726-92), owner and builder of "Mount Pleasant," Fairmount Park]. This gentleman had a brother in the 16th regiment in the British service [William Macpherson (1756-1813)], at the time of Montgomery's expedition into Canada, and who was as violent in favor of the English government, as this general's aide-de-camp was enthusiastic in the cause of America; the latter had accompanied his General a day or two previous to the attack in which they both lost their lives, to view and meditate on the spot where Wolfe had fallen; on his return, he found a letter from his brother, the English officer, full of the bitterest reproaches against him for having entered into the American service, and containing a pretty direct wish, that if he would not abandon it, he might meet with the deserved fate of a rebel. The aide-de-camp immediately returned him an answer full of strong reasoning in defence of his conduct, but by no means attempting to shake the opposite principles of his brother, and not only free from acrimony, but full of expressions of tenderness and affection; this letter he dated "from the spot where Wolfe lost his life, in fighting the cause of England, *in friendship with America.*" This letter had scarcely reached the officer at New York, before it was followed by the news of his brother's death. The effect was instantaneous: nature, and perhaps reason prevailed; a thousand not unworthy sentiments rushed upon his distressed mind; he quitted the English service, entered into that of America, and sought every occasion of distinguishing himself in her service.

Ed. Congress on Oct. 14, 1780, voted a monument to Baron de Kalb, who had died on Aug. 19, 1780, from wounds received during the Battle of Camden. The resolution specified the wording of the inscription and decreed that the monument should be erected at Annapolis, Md. (De Kalb having led Maryland and Delaware troops at Camden). This project, however, was never carried out. Ford *et al.*, eds., *Journals of Cont. Cong.*, XVIII, 923. Nearly a half century later a monument was erected over De Kalb's grave in Camden, S. C., by citizens of that city; Lafayette laid the corner-stone in 1825. Lossing, *Field-Book*, II, 462.

The design for the monument to Montgomery by Jean-Jacques Caffieri (1725-92)—among whose better-known works is a bust of Franklin—was shown at the Paris Salon in 1777; an engraving of Caffieri's design, by Augustin de Saint-Aubin, was also published. The completed monument may be seen today under the Broadway portico of St. Paul's Chapel (Trinity Parish), between Fulton and Vesey Sts., New York City. The inscription reads: "This monument is erected by order of Congress 25th. Janry. 1776. to transmit to posterity a grateful remembrance of the patriotism conduct enterprize & perseverance of Major General Richard Montgomery who after a series of successes amidst the most discouraging difficulties fell in the attack on Quebec. 31st. Decbr. 1775. Aged 37 years. Invenit et sculpsit. Parisiis. J. J. Caffieri Sculptor Regius. Anno Domini MDCCLXXVII." Beneath this is a later tablet recording the fact that "the State of New York caused the remains of Maj. Gen. Richard Montgomery to be conveyed from Quebec and deposited beneath this monument the 8th day of July 1818." St. Paul's Chapel—the only remaining colonial church on Manhattan Island—was completed in 1766 by the architect Thomas McBean. Later additions include an altar designed by the Franco-American engineer, Charles-Pierre L'Enfant. The "Glory" of L'Enfant's altar, inside the church, is set back-to-back to the Caffieri monument on the outside.

14. *Gr.* Mr. [John] Trumbull, son to Governor [Jonathan] Trumbull of Connecticut, who was imprisoned in England as a traitor, whilst he was studying painting under Mr. [Benjamin] West, is now at Paris residing with Mr. Jefferson, and has finished two capital pictures of the death of Warren and Montgomery. They are esteemed *chef d'oeuvres* by all the connoisseurs in this sublime art.

Ed. Trumbull's small oil painting of "The Death of Gen. Warren at the Battle of Bunker's Hill," finished at London in March 1786, is now in the Yale University Art Gallery, as is also his small oil of "The Death of Gen. Montgomery in the Attack on Quebec," finished June 1786. Larger, and later, replicas of both paintings are in the Wadsworth Atheneum, Hartford, Conn.; both subjects were frequently engraved. Sizer, *Works of Trumbull*, 71-72, figs. 30-31. Among the works done by Trumbull while residing with Mr. Jefferson in Paris were life portraits of several of the French officers —including the Marquis de Chastellux—who had served in America and who were included in his painting of "The Surrender of Lord Cornwallis at Yorktown"; see reproduction in this book.

15. *Gr.* In answer to a prejudiced remark of the Abbé Raynal, who says, "On doit être étonné que l'Amérique n'ait pas encore produit un bon poète, un habile mathématicien, un homme de génie dans un seul art, ou une seule science" [One must be astonished that America has not yet produced a good poet, a skillful mathematician, a man of genius in a single art or a single science], Mr. Jefferson, amidst abundance of good reasoning, replies: "In war, we have produced a Washington, whose memory will be adorned while liberty shall have votaries, whose name will triumph over time, and will in future ages assume its just station among the most celebrated worthies of the world, when that wretched philosophy shall be forgotten which would have arranged him among the degeneracies of nature. In physics we have produced a Franklin, than whom no one of the present age has made more important discoveries, nor has enriched philosophy with more, or more ingenious solutions of the phænomena of nature. We have supposed Mr. Rittenhouse second to no astronomer living: that in genius he must be the first, because he is self-taught. As an artist he has exhibited as great a proof of mechanical genius as the world has ever produced. He has not indeed made a world; but he has by imitation approached nearer its

Maker than any man who has lived from the creation to this day." "There are various ways," Mr. Jefferson adds, "of keeping truth out of sight. Mr. Rittenhouse's model of the planetary system has the plagiary appelation of an Orrery; and the quadrant invented by Godfrey, an American also, and with the aid of which the European nations traverse the globe, is called Hadley's quadrant." Thus too, the Translator adds, is the great *Columbus* robbed of the honor of giving his name to *America!*

Ed. The passage from Jefferson here quoted occurs in his *Notes on the State of Virginia*, Query VI, "Productions Mineral, Vegetable and Animal," in which he devotes many pages to refuting a theory then current in European scientific circles, propagated by such writers as DePauw and even the great naturalist Buffon, according to which nature degenerated in the climate of the New World. Abbé Raynal had even gone a step further than the others, and applying the theory to human beings as well as animals, had, in his *Histoire philosophique et politique des Etablissemens et du Commerce des Européens dans les Deux Indes* (Book 18), made the remark that in turn prompted Jefferson's fervent protest. The offending sentence is found, however, *only* in the first edition of Raynal's work (Amsterdam, 1770) and in the various reprintings stemming from that edition. Raynal, who revised and enlarged his very successful book several times, not only omitted the sentence in later editions (after he had become imbued with enthusiasm for the cause of the American "insurgents"), but even conceded that the great Franklin had dispelled the unjust prejudice and that North America, at least, could expect to have its own Homers, Theocrituses, and Sophocleses! Thus Raynal had retracted even before Jefferson cited him, but the Virginian had not caught up with him, bibliographically speaking. However, by the time he came to have his *Notes* reprinted by Stockdale in London (1787), Jefferson was aware that Raynal had begun to change his mind. For this edition of his book Jefferson added, it is true, a footnote pointing out that "in a later edition of the Abbé Raynal's work, he has withdrawn this censure from that part of the new world inhabited by the Federo-Americans"—but he did not alter the text of his magniloquent protest!

16. The rest of Chastellux's letter to Madison, from this point on, was entirely omitted in the American edition of the *Travels*, published in New York, 1827—presumably for the reasons set forth in the Preface to that edition (pp. 4-5): "occasionally an observation of the Author is omitted, in a case where he would not, on the same occasion, have offered it to a Protestant Neighbor. Yet when we keep in view his character as a stranger, a Frenchman, and a Roman Catholic [!], we must admit that he displays no common degree of discernment, of frankness, of good sense and liberality, in his discussion of the various topics before him."

17. *Gr.* Whilst I was at Boston, in 1782, there were violent debates in the Assembly, and the Senate, respecting the duration of the Sabbath—one party were for having it consist of *six and thirty* hours, commencing at six o'clock on the Saturday evening, whilst the others insisted on abridging it to *eighteen*, reckoning from the midnight of Saturday, and finishing at six on the Sunday evening; the former proposition passed the Assembly where the country interest prevailed, but was thrown out in the Senate by the predominant interest of the merchants, aided by good sense, and the palpable absurdity of such a regulation in a commercial city abounding

with strangers. Mr. Cobbet [Cabot], a very sensible man, and a rich merchant of Beverly, distinguished himself on this occasion by a speech full of eloquence and wit. As far as my memory serves me, the sabbath is at length wisely limited to eighteen hours, I say wisely, for not even travelling is permitted on a Sunday in the New England States, insomuch that you are at every instant liable to be stopped by force, and carried by the *deacons* before a magistrate, who inflicts a fine, and puts an end to your journey for the day. This ridiculous and unmeaning austerity will probably be some day put an end to, by the fatal exit of one of these bigoted officers of the church tribunal, who may possibly be mistaken by some sturdy traveller, or stranger, by seizing his horse by the bridle, for a *knight of the pad;* for, pleasantry apart, this is by no means an improbable prediction.

18. The *Émeraude* reached Nantes on Feb. 12 after an adventurous midwinter crossing. Shortly before his departure Chastellux addressed the following farewell letter to Washington: "Annapolis, 8 January 1783. Dear General, At the very instant that I embark and leave the American shore, my thoughts, my affections turn backwards and fly towards your excellency. You was my dearest expectation when I landed in this country, you are my last idea, my everlasting regrett when I am going off. Accept, my dear General, my best wishes for your excellency and excuse these few and imperfect lines that I write in a hurry. I arrived here yesterday very late and Count de Rochambeau already is waiting for me upon the frigate. I have scarce time enough to express once more the true respect and tender attachment with which I have the honor to be dear general your most humble and obedient servant, Le Ch. de Chastellux." Washington Papers, Lib. Cong., original in English.

Three months or so after his arrival in France Chastellux referred to the crossing in a letter written from Paris, May 31, 1783, to Col. Jeremiah Wadsworth: "It is true we had a narrow escape, and while we were chaced and pursued so close, by a Sixty four, I comforted myself with the thought that I would see you once more, had I been carried to New York. But two days after a very severe storm came and left no comfort to me, for we had no other resource, but to send you a last farewell by some herring or other fish. Our last misfortune was to be thunderstruck near the coast of France. The bolt having fallen on our foremast, and almost destroyed it. Of all those circumstances you must conclude, my dear Colonel, that I was saved by a peculiar favour from heaven: for God never abandons his servants." Wadsworth Papers, Box 135, Conn. Hist. Soc., original in English.

INDEX

The index covers the introductions, text, and notes. Pages 1-361 are in Volume 1; pages 365-660 are in Volume 2.

A

Abercrombie, Lt. Gen. Robert, 321

Aboville, François-Marie, Chevalier d', 372, 507, 614, 632; observations of opossum, 462-63, 465-68

Academies, role of, 546

Academy of Inscriptions and Belles Lettres, Paris, 655

Academy of Lyons, 18, 240

Academy of Philadelphia. *See* American Philosophical Society

Action of waters theory, 446-47, 455

Act of Attainder and Confiscation, in Pa., 325

Adams, John, 260, 318-19, 339, 340, 341

Adams, Samuel, 142, 160-64, 306, 318-19

Agriculture, 79-81, 340-41, 480-81, 488; in Dutchess Co., N. Y., 192, 194, 340-41; quality of soil, 438, 601. *See also* Settlements

Aguesseau, Henri-François, Chancelier d', 144, 307

Aitken, Robert, 328, 330, 604

Albany, N. Y., 148, 197-200, 202, 207, 209, 221

Albert de Rions, Charles-Hector, Comte d', 484-87, 620

Alembert, Jean Le Rond d', 4, 6, 9

Alexandria, Va., 31, 401, 583, 615

Algarotti, Francesco, 4

Allen, Ethan, 28, 72, 257. *See also* Vermont

Allentown, N. J., 124

Alliance. *See* France, American Alliance with

Almanach Royal, 17

Amboy, N. J., 125

American Academy of Arts and Sciences, Boston, 17, 504, 634-35

American army, provisioning of, 73-74, 77, 84, 103, 203, 285, 416; quartermaster corps, 73-74, 82, 87, 131, 222;

barracks and huts, 86, 87-88, 91, 117, 118, 266, 286, 514; depot at Fishkill, 86-87, 266; medical corps, 87, 265-66, 275; appearance of troops, 88-90, 98, 102, 107-8, 270, 393; prisons, 88; infantry, 89-90, 281; secrecy regarding troop movements, 92; ammunition depots, 94, 414; clothing, 98, 102, 135, 285, 298; light infantry, 102, 276, 280, 378-79; officers, 103, 114, 222, 269; artillery, 107, 282; cavalry, 108, 120, 150-51, 378-79, 393, 570; military police, 108-9, 280; promotions, 113; winter quarters of 1779, 115, 117, 185, 285; equipment from France, 134, 276, 296, 298, 393; discipline, 138, 141, 173; at Germantown, 140, 323; inexperience of, 141, 150, 157; at Brandywine, 149-52 *passim;* riflemen, 150, 213, 398, 579; batteries, 152, 154, 156, 219, 247, 266, 269; militia, 184, 213, 579; mutiny of Pa. Line (Jan. 1781), 185, 270, 336; Canadian Campaign, 203; guns and armament, 209-10, 276, 337, 350; at Saratoga, 218-20; R. I. regiment, 229; Engineer Corps, 266, 268, 566; salutes Chastellux, 267; morale, 270; financial problems, 277; battle plan against Staten Island and N. Y., 281; rendezvous with French army, 368; communications, 374; salute to French, 475-76; at Concord, 481-82; at Bunker's Hill, 500-501; during British occupation of Boston, 501-3; at Cowpens, 579-82. *See also* Hospitals, supplies

American army encampments, at Preakness (1780), 102-4, 281; at Morristown (1779-80), 115, 117, 185, 285; near Germantown, 140; at Middle Brook (1777, 1778-79), 185, 285-86; at Fishkill, 266; at Verplanck's Point (1782),

280-81, 334, 475, 582-83, 615; at White-marsh, 323; at Barren Hill, 325; at Phillipsburg, N. Y. (1781), 368-70, 564; at New Windsor (1782-83), 514-15, 641-42

American customs, manners, 68; hospitality, 76, 79-81, 189, 383, 425, 497, 595; "Shaking hands," 85-86; politeness, 126-27; social attitudes, 147, 164, 227-28, 374-75; sexual attitudes, 288, 358; curiosity, 586-87; Sabbath laws, 659-60. See also Amusements; Toasts

American morale, 184, 352

American navy, 153, 488, 624, 625-26. See also Ships, American

American Philosophical Society, 17, 178-79, 297, 330, 332, 360

American Revolution, causes of, 75, 160-61, 428-30, 435-36, 594-95

American speech. See English language in America

Americans, in Paris, 18-19; characteristics of, 397-98; regional differences, 429-30, 436

Amherst, Gen. Jeffrey, 198

Ampthill, Va., 593

Amusements, dancing, 164, 170, 176-77, 374, 384, 496, 544, 615; cards, 176, 383, 507, 520; gambling, 176, 386, 441, 507, 603, 636; hunting, 194, 230, 353, 374, 384, 400-401, 441; cockfights, 374, 386-87, 636; horse races, 374, 441, 603; of middle and lower classes in Va., 601-2

Andover, Mass., 483, 619

"Andre." See Murray, Rev. John

André, Maj. John, and Arnold treason plan, 98-99, 268, 274; and the Meschianza, 325; Hamilton on, 344

"Andrews." See Murray, Rev. John

Angell, Miss, 66, 251

Angell, Jeremiah, 252

Angell, Thomas, 252

Anglicans, 127, 442, 603-4; description of service, 167-68, 322

Animals, bear, 194; chipmunks, 359; deer, 194, 262, 393-94, 576; fish and fisheries, 67, 70-71, 379, 432, 597, 627; flying squirrels, 359; foxes, 194; horses: Chastellux's travelling horses, 65, 69, 82, 183-84, 377, 410; of Washington, 107, 111; article of trade with West Indies, 194, 341-42; extrication from holes in ice, 210-11; ascent and descent of escarpment, 214, 217; in interstate commerce, 390, 574; crossing swollen streams, 404; breeding stal-lions, 405; training, 441; in Va., 585; Jacob Bates's stables near Philadelphia, 585; opossum, 462-68; rabbits, 409; raccoon, 411; squirrels, 230, 359; wolves, 393, 576; woodchucks, 411. See also Amusements

Anthony's Kill, N. Y., 211

Anthony's Nose (mountain), N. Y., 96

Architecture, Pa. State House, Philadelphia, 143; Chastellux's description of Monticello, 390-91, 574-75; "Battersea" at Petersburg, Va., 425, 592-93; Moravian buildings at Bethlehem, Pa., 522-23. See also "List of Surviving Buildings mentioned by Chastellux," 549-55

Armaments. See American army

Armand, Col. See La Rouërie, Charles-Armand Tuffin, Marquis de

Armstrong, Maj. John, 154, 156, 316

Arnaud, Abbé, 4

Arne, Thomas Augustine, 361

Arnold, Benedict, treason of, 91, 93, 98-99, 267-68, 273-74, 312, 637-38; expedition against Quebec, 91, 184; early life, 194, 341-42; at Saratoga, 212-13; home of, 300; with British army in Va., 366, 421, 425, 431, 593

Arnold, Mrs. Benedict (Peggy Shippen), 147, 276, 312

Arnold, Jacob, 115-16

Arnold, Welcome, 251

Artillery. See American army; French army; Cannon

Arts, in America, 170, 324, 384; and sciences, Chastellux's letter on, 529-48. See also American Academy of Arts and Sciences; Architecture; Engravers; Engravings; Gardens; Medals; Music; Paintings; Sculpture

Asgill, Capt. Charles, 335

Asphyxia, 319-20

Assunpink [Trenton] River, N. J., 123, 124, 126

Audubon, John James, 346, 612

B

Bache, Mrs. Richard (Sarah Franklin), 135, 299-300, 302-3

Badger's Island, N. H., 621

Baird, Francis, 515, 517, 642

Banditti, 275

Banister, John, 425, 592

Banister, Mrs. John (Mary Bland), 592

Banister House. See Battersea

Barbé-Marbois, François, Marquis de, 26, 132, 302, 310; social activities, 19, 134, 143, 297; and American Philosophical Society, 178, 332
Barbeu-Dubourg, Jacques, 312
Barclay, Thomas, 285
Barlow, Joel, xxiv (Vol. 1)
Barracks. See American army
Barras, Jacques-Melchior Saint-Laurent, Comte de, xxi (Vol. 1), 247, 367
Barrell, Joseph, Jr., 497, 632
Barrell, Joseph, Sr., 507, 632
Barren Hill, Pa., affair at (1778), 170-72, 295, 324-25
Barrington River, in R. I., 65
Bartering, in America, 337
Barthélemy, Abbé, 32
Basking Ridge, N. J., 185
Bates, Jacob, 585
Bates, Mrs. Jacob (Hannah Hopkins), 585
Battersea (house), 425, 592
Battles. See name of battle
Bauman, Maj. Sebastian, 91, 95
Bauman, Mrs. Sebastian, 95
"Beam's height." See Bemis Heights, N. Y.
Beard, Mr. See Baird, Francis
Beaumarchais, Pierre-Augustin Caron de, 14, 589
Beaumesnil, Mlle, 28, 131, 295
Beaurain, M. (Parisian bookseller), 62
Bedford Springs, Va., 589
Bee, Thomas, 330
Belinaye, M. de La, 131
Bell, Robert, 337
Bellini, Carlo, 375, 443
Belmont (house), Philadelphia, 326
Bemis Heights, N. Y., 211-12, 221. See also Saratoga, N. Y.
Benezet, Mr. See Bessonet, Charles
Benezet, Anthony, 165, 319-20
Bergasse, Nicolas, 17
Berthier, Lt. Louis-Alexandre, maps drawn by, 252, 274, 336, 565, 568, 616; map of West Point, xxi (Vol. 1), 267, between pp. 72-73; map of Philadelphia, xxii (Vol. 1), 325, between pp. 136-137; journal of, 580
Bessonet, Charles, 127, 292
Bethlehem, Pa., xxvii (Vol. 2), 522-25, 643, 648, between pp. 510-11
Beverly, Mass., 493, 627
Bewick, Thomas, 613
Biheron, Mlle, 146, 312
Billerica, Mass., 483
Billerica River, Mass., 481

Billingsport, N. J., 154, 155
Bingham, William, 18, 144, 276, 307, 308
Bingham, Mrs. William (Anne Willing), 18, 144, 164, 307
Birds, migration of, 461; blue jay, 378, 379; bob white, 353; cardinal, 379; crow, 379; grouse, 582; hummingbird, 432-33, 459, 598; lapwing, 379, 568; mocking bird, 118, 286, 379-80, 409; painted plover, 568; partridge, 217, 353, 400-401; pheasant, 400-401; purple martin, 457-61, 612; quail, 217, 353; red-winged blackbird, 459; ruffed grouse (partridge), 400-401, 522, 649; starling, 459-60; swallows, 457, 612; swallow trees, 460-61, 612; thrush, 409; wild turkey, 408, 412
Biré, Pierre, Chevalier de, 486
Blache, M., 32
Blanchard, Claude, 15, 66, 250-51, 258, 359, 360
Bland, Col. Theodorick, 142, 147, 306
Bland, Mrs. Theodorick (Martha Dangerfield), 28, 306
Blue Ridge Mountains, Va., 411
Board of Associated Loyalists. See Tories
Boerom, Mr., of N. Y., 265, 513
Bolling, Anne, 422, 426, 590
Bolling, Frances, 590
Bolling, Robert, Jr., 422, 590
Bolling, Mrs. Robert, Jr. (Mary Burton), 422, 424, 426, 431, 590
Bolling, Mrs. Robert, Sr. (Mary Marshall), 420, 421, 424, 426, 590
Bollingbrook (house), Petersburg, Va., 421-22, 590
Books, seen by Chastellux on travels, 67-68, 186, 226, 357, 415, 504, 517, 521; at College of N. J., 123, 290; at Pa. State House, 143; at James Wilson's, 144, 176; at Thomas Paine's, 175; at Offley, 383; at Monticello, 392; at Williamsburg, 450; Louis XVI gift to Univ. of Pa., 310-11; peddled by Robert Bell, 337; Hollis gift to Harvard, 504; Louis XVI gift to William and Mary College, 606; Aitken Bible, 604
Borgella, Marie-Bernard, 310, 613
Boston, Mass., 67, 220, 499, 502, 537, 633; siege of, 92, 184, 501-3; view of, xxv, xxvi (Vol. 2), between pp. 510-511
Boswell, Col., of Va., 388, 389, 573
Boucher, Jonathan, 245
Boufflers, Mme de, 21
Bouillé, Marquis de, 144

Bourbon, Duchesse de, 20
Bowdoin, James, 496, 507, 629, 631
Bowdoin, Mrs. James, Jr., 497, 506, 631
Bowen, Col. Ephraim, 66, 251
Bowen, Mrs. Ephraim (Sally Angell),
  251
Bowen, Jabez, 66, 251
Boylan, John, 185, 335-36
Brackett, Joshua, 496, 621, 628
Brackett, Dr. Joshua, of Portsmouth,
  N. H., 487, 623
Braddock, Gen. Edward, 264
Bradford, William, 257
Brandywine, Pa., battle of, 107, 137, 147,
  148-52, 303, 313-14
Brattle Square Church (Fourth Congre-
  gational), Boston, 629
Breck, Samuel, 496, 497, 508, 509, 631,
  638
Breck, Samuel, Jr., 631-32, 638
Brewster, Benjamin, 252
Brewster, Col. William, 489, 620
Brisout de Barneville, Nicolas-François-
  Denis, 564
Brissot de Warville, Jacques-Pierre, 36-
  37, 39, 292, 320, 323, 360, 579, 602
Bristol, Pa., 127, 129
British army, prisoners of war, 88, 269,
  585-86; use of Indians, 88, 353, 355,
  436, 591-92, 598; withdrawal from
  Philadelphia (June-July 1778), 129,
  130, 170, 286, 316, 320, 324, 325, 567;
  encampments, 137-38, 217-18; at Germantown, 140; at Brandywine, 148-
  52; at Schuylkill, 173; attitude towards
  American military knowledge, 173;
  surrender at Saratoga, 219-20; Saratoga Convention army, 220, 287, 355-
  56, 599-600; at Bunker Hill, 262, 500-
  501; raids, 262-63, 287, 419, 422, 567,
  597-98; under Braddock, 264; in Canada, 348; invasion of Va., 366, 378,
  381; at Savannah, 471; at Charleston,
  471, 475; at New York, 471, 475;
  emancipation of American slaves,
  472; at Concord, 481, 482, 483; at
  Boston, 501-3; at Cowpens, 579-82
British navy, 63, 137, 148, 149, 300, 367;
  coastal raids, 262-63. See also Ships
Broglie, Charles-Louis-Victor, Prince
  de, 475
Broome, Betsy, 496
Broome, Samuel, 506, 507, 636
Brown, Mather, 655
Brown University. See Rhode Island,
  College of
Buckminster, Rev. Joseph, 485, 620

Buffon, Georges-Louis Leclerc, Comte
  de, 3, 79, 278, 343, 446, 462, 659; on
  Chastellux, 12, 35; Epoques de la
  Nature, 260-61, 450-51, 612-13, 613-
  14; and "Petrifactions," 309; works
  cited by Chastellux, 459-60, 463, 464;
  American specimens sent by Chastel-
  lux, 465; opinion on Charlottesville
  wolf, 576
Bulfinch, Charles, 632
Bull, David, 229, 359
Bull, Stephen, 425, 426
Bullion, Mr. See Boylan, John
Bull's Bridge, Conn., 84, 263
Bunker Hill, battle of, 500-501, 502-3,
  633, 658; Trumbull's painting of, 658
Burgoyne, Gen. John, 93, 96, 116, 140,
  148, 149, 160; campaign of 1777, 202,
  211-21 passim, 271, 285, 350-56 passim,
  579; artillery, 209. See also British
  army, Saratoga
Burke, Edmund, 627
Burr, Shubael, 65, 249
Butler, Maj. Pierce, 593, 644, 649, 650
Butler, Col. Richard, 379
Butler, Capt. Walter, 353
Butler, Col. William, 110
Butt's Hill, R. I., 65, 249
Byrd, Mr., of Va., 378
Byrd, Anne Willing, 431, 596
Byrd, Maria Horsmanden, 431, 596
Byrd, Col. William III, 299, 430
Byrd, Mrs. William III (Mary Wil-
  ling), 301, 430, 431

                        C

Cabot, John and Andrew, 627, 660
Cadwalader, Gen. John, 39, 174, 328
Cadwalader, Polly, 175
Caffieri, Jean-Jacques, 656, 657-58
Caldwell, Rev. James, 599
Caldwell, Mrs. James (Hannah Ogden),
  599
Caldwell, John Edwards, 599
Caldwell, Mrs. Maxwell, 599
Cambridge, Mass., 501, 503; view of by
  Samuel Griffin, viii-ix (Vol. 2), be-
  tween pp. 510-11
Camden, S. C., battle of, 657
Canaan, Conn., 226, 357
Canada, trade in horses, 194; American
  invasion (1775-76), 91, 97, 184, 206,
  273, 327, 657; Schuyler's plan for at-
  tack (1777), 202-3, 347; abortive ex-
  pedition under Lafayette (1778), 203,

347; Schuyler's plan for expedition (1778-79), 203-5, 347; annexation by U. S. predicted by Grieve and Paine, 348-49

Cannon, captured from Burgoyne, 81, 95-96, 209, 350

Canterbury, Conn., 70-71

Cape Cod, Mass., 67

Capellen, Baron van der, 259

Capitals, non-commercial towns desirable as, for states, 538-39

Caraccioli, Marquis de, 6

Caribaldi, Gioacchino, 118, 286

Carleton, Maj. Christopher, 353

Carleton, Gen. Sir Guy, 202, 334, 335, 348, 472

Carlisle, Abraham, 320-21

Carlisle Commission of 1778, 133, 273, 297

Carmichael, William, 610

Carpenters' Hall, Philadelphia, 332

Carpenter's Mansion, Philadelphia, 293

Carter, Mr. See Church, John

Cary, Col. Archibald, 427, 593

Case, Dudley, 227, 228, 357

Castries, Armand de. See Charlus, Comte de

Castries, Marquis de, 153, 314

Catesby, Mark, 457, 458, 460

Catherine the Great, 3-4, 237, 312

Chabanel, Mrs., 341

Chace, Mr. See Conway, Thomas

Chadd's Ford, Pa., 150, 151, 152

Chandler, Capt. Samuel, 617

Chandler, Mrs. Samuel, wife of Capt. Samuel (Ann Paine), 617

Chandler, Samuel, 617

Chandler, Mrs. Samuel (Dorothy Church), 480, 617

Chandler, Winthrop, 617

Charles River Bridge, Boston, 633

Charleston, S. C., 131, 181, 268, 437, 471, 537

Charleston Library Society, 50, 239

Charlottesville, Va., 393

Charlus, Comte de, 278, 314, 359

Chastellux, Alfred, Comte de, 22, 23, 578

Chastellux, Claire-Thérèse d'Aguesseau, Comtesse de, 2

Chastellux, François-Jean, Chevalier, and after 1784, Marquis de, portraits of, by Mme Vigée-Lebrun, frontispiece and xix (Vol. 1); by Charles Willson Peale, frontispiece and vii (Vol. 2), 424; by John Trumbull, vii (Vol. 2), 373, between pp. 446-447;

childhood and youth, 2-3; military service in Seven Years' War, 3-4; early writings, 4-5; interest in amateur theatricals, 5-6; English friends, 6; man of the *salons*, 6-7; his *De la Félicité Publique*, 8-11, 13, 14, 18, 23, 29, 529; journey to Italy, 10; relations with Voltaire, 10-11, 12-13; election to French Academy, 11-12; military service and travels in America, 14-17, 365-75, 471-76; residence in Paris, 17, 239; post-war writings, 17-18; relationship with Americans in Paris, 18-19; marriage, 19-22; death, 22, 23; biblio-biography of, 25-29, 35-41; arms, 41; check-list of the different editions, 43-52; honorary degree from Univ. of Pa., 310, 613; honorary degree from William and Mary College, 319-20, 375, 444, 605-6; election to American Philosophical Society, 330; the episode of the "burned letter," 367-68; election to American Academy of Arts and Sciences, 634-35; return voyage to France on *Emeraude*, 660

Chastellux, Guillaume-Antoine, Comte de, 2

Chastellux, Marie-Joséphine-Charlotte-Brigitte Plunkett, Marquise de, 20-23 *passim*, 39, 240, 578

Chastellux, Philippe-Louis, 17

Chastellux, Château de (at Chastellux, Yonne), xix (Vol. 1), 2, 242, 619, between pp. 8-9

Chateaubriand, François René, Vicomte de, 296

Chepontuo. See Glens Falls, N. Y.

Cherbourg, France, 620

Chester, N. Y., 515

Chester, Pa., 147, 152, 153

Chesterfield Courthouse, Va., 419, 598

Chevaux de frise, in Delaware River, 154, 156, 157, 315, 316

Chew, Benjamin, house in Germantown, Pa., 138-39, 141, 304; house in Philadelphia, 299, 307

Chickahominy River, Va., 381, 433

Children, American parental indulgence, 221, 442, 507, 543; French, 442

Chovet, Dr. Abraham, 146, 311-12

Christ Church, Philadelphia, 322

Christianson, Christian, 646

Church, John Barker (Mr. Carter), 18, 258, 259, 288-89

Church, Mrs. John (Angelica Schuyler), 18, 120, 197, 288-89, 343, 360

Cincinnati, Society of, badge, 52
Cities, role in development of arts and sciences in America, 537-39
Clark, Benjamin, 479, 616
Clarkson, Maj. Matthew, 276
Classical literature, allusions to Dionysius of Halicarnassus, 581; Frontinus, 581; Homer, 87; Horace, 9, 530; Livy, 581; Pollio, 581; Sallust, 505; Tacitus, 505; Theocritus, 409; Vergil, 157, 318; Xenophon, 648
Claverack, N. Y., 195, 196, 225
Clement XIV, Pope. See Ganganelli, Giovanni Vincenzo
Climate, influence of deforestation on, 395-96, 576-77
Clinton, DeWitt, 612
Clinton, George, 96, 192, 271, 340, 349
Clinton, Gen. Henry, 93, 96, 129, 213, 270, 271, 500
Clinton, Gen. James, 28, 199, 206, 223, 345
Cliveden. See Chew, Benjamin, house at Germantown
Closen, Ludwig, Baron von, 247, 276, 294, 312, 316-18, 572
Cloth, manufacture of, 77
Clove, The, N. Y., 96, 187, 272
Cogswell, William, 640
Cohoes Falls, N. Y., xxiii (Vol. 1), 200-201, 216, 346, 353; between pp. 200-201
Colbert de Maulevrier, 247
Cole, Thomas, 358
College of New Jersey. See New Jersey, College of
College of Rhode Island. See Rhode Island, College of
College of William and Mary. See William and Mary, College of
Collinson, Peter, 613
Collot, Victor, 572
Colson, Adam, 496, 628
Commerce, influence on individual and public liberty, 538-39, 654-55. See also Trade; Privateering; Speculation
Concert Hall, Boston, 630
Concord, Mass., battle of, 481-83, 618-19
Concord River, Mass., 481
Condorcet, Marquis de, 9, 10-11, 24
Congregational Church, service at Portsmouth, N. H., 485
Connecticut, migrations to Vermont, 72, 73, 77, 256
Connecticut River, 76, 87, 203
Conshohocken, Pa., 172
Constitution Island, N. Y., 90, 96

Constitutions, state, 161-62
Continental army. See American army
Continental Congress, First, 429; Second, 73, 93, 257, 297; and Washington, 113; northern members, 141-42; sectionalism, 143, 305; meeting place, 143, 306; and battle of Brandywine, 149; and Billingsport, 155; and conduct of war, 173; southern members, 174, 327; and Sullivan's expedition, 203; and John Church, 288; and paper money, 333
Continental currency. See Money, paper
Convention army. See British army
Convention of New England Commissioners. See Hartford Convention (1780)
Conversation, art of, 230
Conway, Gen. Thomas, 151, 174; and Conway Cabal, 328
Cooper, James Fenimore, 266, 353
Cooper, Dr. Samuel, 496, 505-6, 629, 635-36
Copley, John Singleton, 629, 655
Cormatin, Baron de. See Dezoteux, Pierre-Marie-Félicité
Cornwallis, Gen. Charles, Lord, 107, 119, 287-88, 370; and battle of Princeton, 122; and battle of Trenton, 123-24, 125, 291; and battle of Germantown, 140; and battle of Brandywine, 151, 152; invades Va., 366, 378-79, 381, 383, 385, 421, 586; surrenders at Yorktown, 372; Chastellux's comments on, 570; on the battle of Cowpens, 580, 582
Corny, Dominique-Louis Ethis de, 74, 174, 258
Coste, Dr. Jean-François, 320, 366, 563, 567, 577, 613; honorary degree, from Univ. of Pennsylvania, 310; resuscitation theory of, 319-20; honorary degree from William and Mary, 605-6
County, use of term, 81, 262, 380-81
Courtheath, Mr. See Curtis, Joseph
Court of Claims, in Va., 416
Court of Sessions, in Conn., 81
Cowpens, S. C., battle of, 398-400, 579-82
Craigie, Dr. Andrew, 266
Craik, Dr. James, 87
Crawford, John, 592
Crawford, Col. William, 591-92, 599
Crawford, William (the younger), 592
Creutz, Count de, 7
Crèvecoeur, Frances-America de ("Fanny"), 324

Crèvecoeur, Michel-Guillaume St. John de, 598, 611
Croce, Benedetto, 237
Cromot du Bourg, Baron, xxi (Vol. 1)
Croton Point (Teller's Point), N. Y., 98, 273
Culver, Ephraim, 518, 645
Cumberland Courthouse, Va., 416, 417
Cunningham [Conyngham?], Mrs., of Philadelphia, 167

D

Damas, Charles, Comte de, 270, 345; tours America, 95, 98, 116, 168, 177, 193, 197, 217, 283, 340; in Philadelphia, 144, 147, 164; aide-de-camp to Rochambeau, 270; loses horse, 370
Dangerfield, Col., 306
Dannemours, M. de, 132
Daubenton, Louis-Jean-Marie, 464, 613-14
Deane, Barnabas, 31
Deane, Silas, 14, 30, 31, 312, 329, 331
De Britaine, William, *Humane Prudence*, 517, 642
Deffand, Marquis du, 565
Delafield, Mr., 628
"De la Fille." *See* Delafield, Mr.
Delaware River, 127, 180, 183; Washington's crossing, 123, 125, 291; and British withdrawal from Philadelphia, 129; ferries, 292; branches of, 332, 521, 648, 653. *See also* Brandywine, battle of; Delaware River forts
Delaware River Forts, defending Philadelphia, 155-60, 303, 315-18, 370; Berthier's map of, xxii (Vol. 1), between pp. 136-37
Delaware Water Gap, ix (Vol. 2), between pp. 510-511, 521, 647
Démeunier, Jean-Nicolas, 601, 606-7
Democracy, in America, 535-37
Destouches, Charles-René-Dominique Gochet, Chevalier, xxi (Vol. 1), 247, 366, 367
Deux-Ponts, the Counts, 16, 278
Dewey, Rev. Orville, 356
Dewey, Capt. Stephen, 225-26, 356-57
Dey, Col. Theunis, 275, 278, 282; house at Preakness, N. J., xx (Vol. 1), between pp. 8-9
Dezoteux, Pierre-Marie-Félicité, 28, 56, 242
Dickinson, the Misses, 21
Dickinson, John, 293, 294, 326, 574
Dickinson, Gen. Philemon, 518

Diderot, Denis, 6, 234, 357
Digges, Col. Dudley, 472
Dignity of man, defined by Chastellux, 398
Dillon, Arthur, Comte, 566
Dillon, Franck-Théobald, 24, 377, 415, 510, 512, 566, 639
Dobbs Ferry Conference. *See* Franco-American cooperation
Doctors, status of, 87, 265-66. *See also* American army, medical corps; French army, medical corps
Donop, Col. Carl von, 157, 158-60, 317
Dorrance, John, 68, 254-55
Dorrance, Samuel, 67-69, 231, 252-53, 254
Dorrance, Mrs. Samuel (Margaret Trumbull), 252, 254
Dorrance, Miss [Susanna], 67-68, 231, 252-54, 359, 639
Dorrance family, 28, 67-69, 231, 252-55
Drovers, 84, 264
Drowne, Dr. Solomon, 246
Drowned persons, resuscitation of, 165, 317-20
Duane, James, 142, 164, 306
Du Barry, Mme, 32
"Duck Sider." *See* Tuxedo, N. Y.
Duffield, Rev. George, 604
Dumas, Mathieu, 15, 73, 242, 496, 506; memoirs, 258
Duportail, Gen. Louis Le Bègue de Presle, 91, 156, 173, 270, 316, 317; later years, 24; designer of West Point, 94; biographical sketch of, 268; and Wethersfield Conference, 367; at Dobbs Ferry Conference, 370
Dupré, Augustin, 580, 655
Duras, Duc de, 242
Du Simitière, Pierre Eugène, 145, 309, 324, 634
Dutch, in America, 86, 115, 265, 519, 599; characterized, 185-86, 196, 343, 436; settlements, 196. *See also* Meetinghouse, Dutch Reformed
Dutchess Co., N. Y., 192, 194, 340-41
Duvivier, Benjamin, 272, 580, 655

E

East Aspetuck River, Conn., 83
East Hartford (Manchester), Conn., 12, 76, 256
Easton, Pa., 520, 648
Eating habits of Americans, breakfast, 75, 95, 134-35, 260, 388; dinner, 109,

126-27, 130, 132; biscuits, 185; frequency of meals, 497; supper, 506
Ebeling, Christoph Daniel, 29
Ebert, John Christian, 648, 649
Education, 146, 254-56, 504, 538, 545-46. *See also* Harvard University; New Jersey, College of; Pennsylvania, University of; Plainfield Academy; Rhode Island, College of; William and Mary, College of
Egremont, Mrs., of N. Y., 513
Electrical storms, 293
Elizabethtown (Elizabeth), N. J., 106, 184
Elliot, Thomas, 649
Ellison, Thomas, house at New Windsor, N. Y., xxiii (Vol. 1), 339; between pp. 200-201
Emblems, 126, 291-92; reproduction of, 127
Emigration. *See* Immigration
Encyclopédie, ed. by Diderot *et al.*, 3, 6
Encyclopédie Méthodique, 601, 606
Engineer Corps. *See* American army, engineer corps
English customs, in Virginia, 386
English language, Chastellux's knowledge of, 16, 93, 366; knowledge of among French officers and diplomats, 16, 131, 139, 159, 178, 248, 448, 498; Indian origin of place names, 71, 83, 338, 418; poverty of specific names for birds and trees, 78; use of terms "farmer" and "gentleman," 92; fondness for abridgments, 102; words of Dutch origin, 211, 272; origin of terms "yankee" and "buckskin," 262; use of term "jockey," 351; use of term "flag," 385, 571; taverns called "ordinaries" in Va., 386; use of word "mighty," 413; replacement by Hebrew proposed, 498, 632; meaning of verb "to press," 571; use of word "neck," 627; "exertions" much used term, 647
English literature, allusions to Addison, Joseph, 125; allusions to Ossian, 392, 575-76
Engravers, Aldring, 47; Joseph Callender, 628; Jacques-Joseph Coiny, 47; J. T. Cook, 48; Amos Doolittle, 618; J. Duff, 49; William Faden, 351; Victor J.-B. Petit, xix (Vol. 1), between pp. 8-9; Bénoit-Louis Prévost, 309; Paul Revere, 476, 628, 634; Augustin de Saint-Aubin, 657; Anker Smith, xxiv (Vol. 1), between pp. 200-201;

J. Stilsbury, xxvii (Vol. 2), between pp. 510-511; Paul Studley, xxii (Vol. 1), between pp. 72-73
Engravings, 95, 136, 480; Hogarth prints purchased from Grieve by Joseph Barrell, 632
Epinay, Mme d', 9, 13, 235, 286
Eppes, Mrs. John Wayles (Mary Jefferson), 391, 575, 577
Erskine, Mr., 187, 337
Erskine, Mrs., 187
Estaing, Charles-Hector, Comte d', 14, 249, 637
Ettwein, Bishop John, 646
Ewing, Dr. John, 145, 178, 311, 332
Experiments in international living, 497, 599, 631-32

F

Fairmount Park houses, Philadelphia, 325-26, 657
Falconet, Etienne-Maurice, 358
Farmington, Conn., 76-77
Farmington River, 78, 227-29
Fell, John, 189
Ferguson, Mrs. Elizabeth Graeme, 133
Ferguson, Col. Patrick, 600
Ferries, at Hartford, 73, 248; at Neshaminy Creek, Pa., 129; over Schuylkill River, 147, 312; at Cohoes, N. Y., 201; at Bristol, R. I., 249; over Delaware River, 292; Greenlee's in Va., 411; at Haverhill, Mass., 483; of Shenandoah, Va., 589
Fersen, Axel, 15
Filson, John, 452, 609
Fish, Maj. Nicholas, 91
Fishkill, N. Y., 77, 86-87, 88, 191, 266
Fishkill Landing [Beacon], N. Y., 191, 514, 641
Fishkill River, 87, 317-18
Five Nations. *See* Indians
Flahaut, Mme de, 23
Fleming, William, 460, 611
Fleury, François-Louis Teissèdre de, 97, 173, 272, 315, 316, 622
Flowy, Mr. (Howly, Gov. Richard?), 174, 327
Foacio, Bagneux de, 258
Folsom, Col. Samuel, 619
Folwell, John, 322
Fontenelle, Bernard Le Bovier de, 11
Food, in America, 379, 388, 397
Footman, Elizabeth Julian. *See* Shippen, Mrs. Edward, Jr.
Forest fires, 407-8, 587

Forges. *See* Ironworks

Formicola, Serafino, 428, 594

Forster, Mr. *See* Foster, Capt. Asa

Fortifications, at Newport, R. I., 63, 65, 247-48, 501; at Butt's Hill, 65, 249; at West Point, 89-96 *passim*, 266-72 *passim*, 337; at Stony Point, 96-97, 98; at Verplanck's Point, 97, 98; at Philadelphia (1777-8), xxii (Vol. 1), between pp. 136-137, 130, 147, 173, 292-93; at Billingsport, 154; at Portsmouth, N. H., 622. *See also* Delaware River forts

Forts: Fort Ann, N. Y., 211; Fort Arnold (*see* Fort Clinton); Fort Chastellux, R. I., 247-48; Fort Clinton (first), N. Y., 96, 271; Fort Clinton (formerly Fort Arnold), N. Y., 94, 266, 268, 271; Fort Denham, R. I., 248; Fort Edward, N. Y., 211, 214-16, 352-53; Fort Harrison, R. I., 247; Fort Meigs, N. Y., 269; Fort Mercer (Red Bank), N. J., 156-60, 303, 317, 318; Fort Mifflin, Pa., 155-56, 315-16, 317; Fort Montgomery, N. Y., 271, 272; Fort Prospect Hill, 501; Fort, on Plum Island, Mass., 490; Fort Putnam, N. Y., 93, 269; Fort Schuyler (Fort Stanwix), N. Y., 216; Fort Washington, N. H., 485, 621-22; Fort Webb, N. Y., 269; Fort Wyllis, N. Y., 93-94, 269. *See also* Delaware River, forts

"Fort Wilson." *See* Wilson, James, House

Foster, Capt. Asa, 483, 619

Foster, Mrs. Asa, 483, 619

Fox, George, 322

France, American alliance with (1778), 13, 14, 96, 155, 249, 473

Franco-American cooperation, 249, 329, 368, 473, 508, 596, 615-16; Hartford Conference (Sept. 1780), 63, 247, 268; Newport Conference (Mar. 1781), 366; Wethersfield Conference (May 1781), 247, 268, 284, 367, 368, 369; Dobbs Ferry Conference (July 1781), 369-70; *Ville de Paris* Conference (Sept. 1781), 371

Frankford, Pa., 129-30

Frankfort (Leestown), Kentucky, 452

Franklin, Benjamin, and Chastellux, 7, 13-14, 17, 18, 236, 297, 302-3; opinion of *Travels in America*, 38; and Joseph Reed, 134, 136, 297; and Pa. politics and government, 181, 297, 334; and Comtesse Golowkin, 241; and David S. Franks, 268; and John Dickinson,

294; house in Philadelphia, 299-300; president of American Philosophical Society, 330; and John Holker, 331; and the Indians, 350; Grieve's panegyric of, 586, 595; and Jefferson, 658

Franklin, Gov. William, 335

Franks, Maj. David Salisbury, 18, 91, 268

Fraser, Gen. Simon, 212

Freaks: Pieter Van Winkle, 111-12, 281-82; Mr. Johnson, 387-88, 573; Mr. Pattison, 414-15

Frederick the Great, 3, 4, 9, 190, 236, 305, 340

Frederick, Md., 583

Fredericksburg, Va., 347

Freehold, definition of, 92

Freeman's Farm, N. Y., 212, 213

French Academy, 11, 13, 17, 18, 29

French army, officers, 15, 173-74, 267, 271, 308, 312-13; functions of *intendant* and *munitionnaire* defined, 74; medical corps, 87, 265-66, 310, 613; arrives at Newport, 246, 250, 251, 267; sojourn at Newport (1780-81), 246, 247, 248, 401; operations against New York City, 247, 471; in Providence, 251; march from R. I. to Hudson (1781), xxii (Vol. 1), between pp. 72-73, 251, 252, 255, 258, 368, 511, 616; with American civilians, 265, 413, 472, 473, 596, 615-16; march from Va. to Boston (1782), 281, 473-76, 477, 568, 569, 581, 615, 616; artillery, 282, 632; march from Hudson to Va. (1781), xxii (Vol. 1), between pp. 136-137, 336, 370-71, 566; winter quarters in Va. (1781-82), 353, 373-75, 377, 384, 431, 462, 465, 529, 566, 586-87; encampment at Phillipsburg, N. Y. (1781), 368-70, 564; regiments from West Indies, 371, 485, 622; at Siege of Yorktown (1781), 372-73; encampment at Crompond, N. Y. (1782), 475-76, 615; embarkation at Boston (1782), 499, 510, 638; discipline, 596, 615. *See also* Hospitals; Supplies; Capitaine du Chesnoy; Duportail; Fleury; Galvan; Gimat; Gouvion; Lafayette; La Rouërie; L'Enfant; Mauduit du Plessis; Ternant; Tousard; Tronson du Coudray; Villefranche

French customs, American adoption of, 133; marriage among the higher classes, 590

French diplomacy, Grieve on, 296-97

French language, knowledge of among

German officers, 126, 159; knowledge of among Americans, 207, 209, 479, 497-99; Lamb and Franks, 91; Col. James Livingston, 97; Witherspoon, 122, 289; John Laurens, 131, 294; Bland, 142; Bingham, 144; Benezet, 165; Le Roy, 193; Hughes, 224; Wadsworth, 259; Carter-Church, 259; Hamilton, 344; Mrs. Tudor and Mrs. Morton, 497, 507; S. Breck, Jr., 631

French Legation, in Philadelphia, 19, 26, 293

French literature, allusions to: La Rochefoucauld, 278, 540; Marmontel, 402, 584; Molière, 415; Montaigne, 248; Rabelais, 387-88, 573; Racine, 178-79; Sedaine, 132, 168, 296, 322, 382, 571

French navy, printing press at Newport, R. I., 25-26; De Guichen's squadron expected in R. I., 63-65, 247; influence on trade, 136, 180; D'Estaing's fleet in Boston harbor (1778) depicted by P. Ozanne, xxv-xxvi (Vol. 2), between pp. 510-511; D'Estaing's fleet at Savannah (1779), 249, 637; defeated at Battle of the Saints (1782), 308, 471; Chesapeake expedition under Destouches (Mar. 1781), 366; De Grasse's fleet at Yorktown, 370, 371, 372; De Grasse's fleet sails for West Indies (Nov. 4, 1781), 373; Vaudreuil's squadron at Boston (1782), 471, 475, 495, 508, 620, 621, 637; at Portsmouth, N. H. (1782), 484-86, 620, 622. See also Ships

French Revolution, 15, 23, 24, 32

Friends, Society of. See Quakers

G

Gage, Gen. Thomas, 289, 481

Gale, Abijah, 480-81, 617-18

Galiani, Abbé, 6, 10, 235

"Gallo-Americans," 15, 308

Galloway, Joseph, 298-99, 301, 321, 325

Galvan, François Louis, de Bernoux, 276

Galvan, Maj. William de, 103, 276, 277, 379, 568

Ganganelli, Giovanni Vincenzo (Pope Clement XIV), 579

Gardens, 76, 228, 380, 431, 491, 525, 569

Garrick, David, 5-6, 295

Garrison, Nicholas, Jr., 522, 650; his view of Bethlehem, Pa., xxvii (Vol. 2), between pp. 510-511

Garrison, Nicholas, Sr., 650

Garrison, Nicholas, III, 650

Gates, Gen. Horatio, 31, 264, 265, 338, 515, 582-83; at Saratoga, 212, 218; accepts Burgoyne's surrender, 219-20, 354, 355; and Van Schaick's Island, 345; and Conway Cabal, 347; and Baroness von Riedesel, 355

Gatteaux, Nicolas-Marie, 655

Genlis, Comtesse de, 240, 346

Geoffroy de Saint-Hilaire, 613

Geology, Buffon's theory of the earth, 79, 260-61, 278, 647; observations by Chastellux, 79, 105, 229, 407; speculation by Chastellux, 79, 105, 145, 195, 229, 343, 406-7, 450-56

George II, portrait of in Princeton, 123, 290

George III, 273

Georgia, 111, 437

Gérard, Conrad-Alexandre, 306, 309, 331, 635; portrait by Charles Willson Peale, xxii (Vol. 1)

Germans in America, 121, 193, 289, 420, 599-600. See also Moravians

Germantown, Pa., xxii (Vol. 1), between pp. 136-137, 295, 304; battle of (Oct. 1777), 131, 137-41, 168, 303-5, 323

Gersdorf, Susanna Charlotte von, 522-23, 650

Gibbs, Maj. Caleb, 106

Gibbs, Parnell, 322

Gilbert, John, 227, 357

Gillon, Alexander, 298

Gillon, Mrs. Alexander, 298

Gilmer, Francis William, 446-47

Gilmer, Dr. George, 576

Gilpin, Gideon, house of, 313

Gimat, Col. Jean-Joseph Sourbader de, 102, 108, 126, 129, 141; attends Pa. State Assembly, 144; visits Brandywine, 147, 148, 152; visits British lines at Philadelphia, 172; biographical sketch of, 280, 305; at Barren Hill, 325; at Yorktown, 344

Girondists, 36

Girty, Simon, 591

Glandevès, Jean-Baptiste, Chevalier de, 497, 499

Glass, scarcity of, 87

Glen, Col. John, 207-8

Glens Falls, N. Y., 216, 353

Gléon, Geneviève de Savalette, Marquise de, 5, 17, 240-41

Glover, Gen. John, 110, 111

Gluck, Christoph Willibald, 5, 286

Gnadenhutten, Ohio, massacre, 592, 598-99
Godfrey, Thomas, 659
Goffle Brook, N. J., 101-16 *passim*, 275, 278
Golowkin, Wilhelmina von Mosheim, Comtesse de, 241
Goodhue, William, 495, 628
Gorges, 454
Gotha, Germany, 27, 56, 550
Gouvion, Jean-Baptiste de, 24, 94, 97, 268, 270
Government, American, Chastellux on, 161, 181-82; U. S. state constitutions published in Europe, 604. *See also* Continental Congress; Constitutions, state; and under names of states
Governor's Mansion, Richmond, Va., 594
Governor's Palace, Williamsburg, Va., 375
Graham, Maj. John, 199, 214, 514
Granby, Lord, 92-93
Grant, Gen. James, 171, 172
Grasse, François-Joseph-Paul, Comte de, 308, 366, 367, 371, 373, 471
Graves, Capt. Richard, 597
Gray, Isaac, 330, 332
Great Britain, Parliament of, 303, 314, 318, 323, 351, 354-55; Gov. Trumbull on right to tax, 259; and money sent to America, 333; ceases offensive war, 334. *See also* American Revolution, causes of
"Greeg-Town." *See* Griggstown, N. J.
Green, Capt., 579
Green, William, 252
Greene, Col. Christopher, 66, 156, 157, 249, 359
Greene, Gen. Nathanael, 328; as Quartermaster General, 131, 187, 520; Grieve praises, 283; and battle of Guilford Courthouse, 400, 582; death of, 647
Greene, Mrs. Nathanael, 360
Greenland, N. H., 484
Greenlee, John, 411, 588
"Green Mountain's Boys," 73. *See also* Vermont
Greenspring, Va., 568
Green Woods, Conn., 226, 228
Grenville [Greville?], 269
Grétry, André E. M., 279
Greuze, Jean-Baptiste, xxiv (Vol. 1), painting between pp. 200-201; 225, 231, 357

Grey, Maj. Gen. Sir Charles, 171, 172, 323
Grieve [or Greive], George, biographical sketch of, 29-35, 243, 244; Chastellux's comments on, 254; visits Washington, 280
Grieve, Richard, 30
Griffin, Col. Jacob, 86, 265
Griffin, Samuel, view of Cambridge, Mass., viii-ix (Vol. 2), between pp. 510-511
Griggstown, N. J., 121
Grigsby, James, 405-11, 587
Grimm, F.-N., Baron de, 6-7, 9, 27, 35
Grog, definition of, 85
Grotz, Joseph, 646
Grünewald, Gustavus, view of Hope, N. J., ix (Vol. 2), between pp. 510-511
Guerrilla warfare, 335
Guibert, Jacques A. H., Comte de, 92, 190, 305, 340
Guichen, Comte de, 63-65, 247
Guilford Courthouse, N. C., battle of, 400, 402, 582

H

Haidt, John Valentine, 519, 523, 646
"Haldimand correspondence," on Vt., 257
Half Moon (Waterford), N. Y., 211, 221
Hallidon Hill, 247. *See also* Fort "Chastellux"
Hamilton, Col. Alexander, Chastellux meets, 105, 110, 197, 202, 346; and Society for Useful Manufactures, 277; at Yorktown, 280; and portrait of George II, 290; Chastellux's sketch of, 343-44
Hamilton, Mrs. Alexander (Elizabeth Schuyler), 198, 202, 343, 344, 345, 346
Hamilton, William, 326
Hampton, N. H., 490
Hancock, John, 496, 505, 630, 631, 635
Hand, Gen. Edward, 349, 514
Hanover Courthouse, Va., 380, 569
Harrison, Gov. Benjamin, 327, 429, 430, 472
Harrison, Carter Bassett, 429
Harrison, Col. Charles, 429, 430
Harrod, Benjamin, 619
Harrod, Joseph, 483, 619
Hartford, Conn., 73, 76, 229, 256, 257
Hartford, Conn., townships, comparison of, 76

Hartford Conference. *See* Franco-American cooperation

Hartford Convention (Nov. 1780), 73, 257

Hartford Courthouse, Conn., 72, 76, 256. *See also* Hartford, Conn.

Harvard Hall, 503, 633

Harvard University, view by Samuel Griffin, ix (Vol. 2), between pp. 510-511; 499, 503-4, 633, 634

Harward, Mr. *See* Harrod, Joseph

Harwinton, Conn., 81

Hasbrouck, Jonathan, house at Newburgh, N. Y., xx (Vol. 1), between pp. 8-9; 339, 513, 640

Hasenclever, Baron Peter, 337

Haverhill, Mass., 483

Haverstraw, N. Y., 99, 274. *See also* Kakiat, N. Y.

Haywood, William, 327

Hazard, Ebenezer, 330

Hazen, Gen. Moses, 269

Heard, Capt. John, 120, 121

Heath, Gen. William, 66, 89-96 *passim*, 251, 267, 268-69

Heckewelder, John, 599

Hele, Lt. Christopher, 273

Helvetius, Claude-Adrien, 6, 7, 235

Henry, William, 644

"Hern," Capt. John. *See* Heard, Capt. John

Herrnhutter. *See* Moravians

Hessians, 125-26, 152, 156-58, 213, 218-19, 307

Hill, Mrs. (of Lebanon Crank Tavern), 71, 256

Hizeures, M. d', 486, 487

Hodnett, Mr., 415-16

Hog Island, Pa., 155, 156

Hoid, Mr. *See* Hyer, Col. Jacob

Holbach, Paul-Henri, Baron d', 6, 7, 576

Holker, John, Chevalier, 330-31

Holker, John, Jr., 178, 300, 330-32

Hollis, Thomas, 634

Hollis, Thomas Brand, 634

Honeysuckle, 432

Hooper, Robert Lettis, Jr., 337

Hoops, Maj. Robert, 518-21, 643, 646, 647

Hope, N. J., view by Gustavus Grünewald, ix (Vol. 2), between pp. 510-511. *See also* Moravians

"Hope" [Hop] River, Conn., 72

Hopewell, N. Y., 86

Hopkins, Robert, 585

Hopkinson, Francis, 309

Hopper's Mill, N. J., 275

Horsemanship, 111, 120

Horses. *See* Animals; Amusements

Hospitals, French army, 66, 250, 374, 508, 620, 637; American army, 87, 209-10, 250, 265, 350, 375, 643; Trinity Church, 87, 265; Quaker, 130, 293; British army, 214

Houdon, Jean-Antoine, 655

Housatonic River, Conn., 83-84, 512

"Howard," Mr. *See* Hyer, Col. Jacob

Howard, Col. John Eager, 580

Howe, Gen. Robert, 28, 105, 109, 111, 281

Howe, Gen. William, 148, 149; attempted invasion of N. J. (1777), 117, 120-21; at Brandywine, 150; receives M. de Mauduit, 160; at Whitemarsh, 168-69, 323; attempts to capture Lafayette, 170-72; in Philadelphia, 301; and Parliamentary inquiry into conduct of war, 303, 314, 318, 323; and Quakers, 321; and *Meschianza*, 325; at Bunker's Hill, 500

Howly, Gov. Richard, 147, 327. *See also* Flowy, Mr.

Huancavelica, Peru, 452-55, 609

Huddy, Capt. Joshua, 335, 568

Huddy-Asgill affair, 335

Hudson [North] River, as goal of British, 86; chain across, 96, 272, 337; and Major André, 274; Hudson River, view of, 281. *See also* Fortifications, West Point; Saratoga

Hughes, Col. Hugh, 222, 223, 224, 266

Humane Society of Philadelphia, 319

Hume, David, 6

Humphreys, Col. David, 18, 34, 190, 284, 338, 339, 513

Hunter, Mr., of New London, Va., 414

Hunting. *See* Amusements

Huntington, Gen. Jabez, 230

Huntington, Gen. Jedidiah, 110, 111

Huntington, Samuel, 28, 134, 143, 160, 173, 283, 299

Huntington, Mrs. Samuel, 160

Hussars. *See* Lauzun legion

Hutchins, Thomas, 588

Hyer, Capt., 184

Hyer, Col. Jacob, 184, 335

I

Immigration to America, 534-35, 654

Independence Hall. *See* Pennsylvania State House

Indians, raids by, 88, 194-95, 208-9, 350, 436; at Barren Hill (1778), 170, 171, 325; Schuyler's plan for expedition against (1778), 205-6, 349; Sullivan's expedition against Six Nations (1779), 206, 349, 521, 647-48; displaced Indians at Schenectady, 207-9, 349-50; murder of Jane McCrea, 214-15, 351-52; origin of "Yankee," 262; and Wyoming Massacre, 512-13; in battle, 579; and Crawford's expedition against Sandusky, 591-92; massacred at Gnadenhutten, 598-99; Williamson's expedition against Muskingums (1782), 599. *See also* New York State; and names of specific tribes

Inflation. *See* Money, paper

Ingersoll, Jared, 330

Inns, Chastellux's general comment on, 315; expense of, 428; Jacob Arnold's, Morristown, N. J., 115-16, 285; Benezet's, Bristol, Pa., 127, 292; Blennissens, Albany, N. Y., 200; Brandywine, Pa., 148; David Bull's (Bunch of Grapes), Hartford, Conn., 229, 359; Shubael Burr's, Warren, R. I., 65-66, 249; Dudley Case's, Canton, Conn., 227-28, 357; Benjamin Clark's (Pompey Hollow Tavern), Ashford, Conn., 479, 616; Cromwell's Head (Joshua Brackett's), 476, 496, 628; William Davenport's, Newburyport, Mass., 490, 626; Capt. Stephen Dewey's, Sheffield, Mass., xxiv (Vol. 1), 225-26, 356-57, between pp. 200-201; Mrs. Egremont's (Boerom's Tavern), Fishkill, N. Y., 87, 265, 513; Serafino Formicola's, Richmond, Va., 428, 594; John Gilbert's House, New Hartford, Conn., 227, 357; Harward's (Joseph Harrod, "Freemasons Arms") Tavern, Haverhill, Mass., 483, 619; John's Inn (Ephraim Jones), Concord, Mass., 481-82, 618; Joseph Lord's, Oxford, Mass., 480, 617; Gideon Morgan's, Washington, Conn., 512, 640; Norfolk, Conn., 226; Mrs. People's (Elizabeth Peebles), Half Moon, N. Y., 221; Mr. Smith's, Kakiat and Warwick, N. Y., 99, 274, 515, 642; Mrs. Spencer's, Petersburg, Va., 419-20; Mrs. Teaze's, Waynesboro, Va., 401-2, 583; Jacob Thomas's, Rhinebeck, N. Y., 193, 195, 341; Asahel Wadsworth's, Farmington, Conn., 511, 640; Washington's House, Chester, Pa., 315; William Rensselaer (Royal

Oak), Trenton, N. J., 126, 291; Mrs. Mary Withy's, Chester, Pa., 153-54, 315. *See also* Ordinaries, Taverns

Inoculation, 3

Ipswich, Mass., 493

Irish in America, 67, 115, 336, 389, 397, 517, 599-600; characterized, 82, 574; Friendly Sons of St. Patrick, 284, 574; from North Ireland, 341

Ironworks, 84, 187, 337-38

Italian literature: Ariosto, 167; Guarini, 403, 584; Metastasio, 4, 231, 232, 360

Italians in America, 428

Izard, Ralph, 147, 328, 332

J

James River, Va., 404

Jamestown, Va., 418

Jarvis, Dr. Charles, 508

Jarvis, Mrs. Charles, 496, 507

Jefferies's Ford, Pa., 151

Jefferson, Lucy Elizabeth, 575

Jefferson, Martha. *See* Randolph, Mrs. Thomas Mann

Jefferson, Mary. *See* Eppes, Mrs. John Wayles

Jefferson, Thomas, view of Monticello, xx-xxi (Vol. 1), between pp. 8-9; friendship with Chastellux, 18, 389-96, 531, 577-78; and Thomas Shippen, 19; comments on Chastellux's *Travels*, 26, 28, 38, 302; and Grieve, 30; and John Graves Simcoe, 37; and Hartford Convention (1780), 257; and De Corny, 258; and David Humphreys, 339; and Chastellux's opinion of Mrs. Philip Schuyler, 347; and First Continental Congress, 347; and Natural Bridge, 445, 446, 606-10; and swallow trees, 460; and Monticello, 574-75; appointments to foreign missions, 575; "Popular Forest," plantation of, 589; as architect, 592, 594; childhood residence, 593; on Chastellux's characterization of Virginians, 603; justifies anti-clericalism in Virginia Constitution, 604-5; ideas on American naval power, 625-26; on slavery, 653; on emigration to America, 654; on eminent Americans, 658-59; *Notes on the State of Virginia:* cited by Chastellux, 606; cited by Grieve, 607, 608-9, 610, 647, 654, 658-59; Grieve's copy of first edition, 625-26

Jefferson, Mrs. Thomas (Martha Wayles), 18, 391, 392, 396, 575
Jews in America, 268, 643
Johnson, Mr., of Va., 415
Johnson, Sir John, 353
Johnson, Thomas, 387, 572-73
Johnston, Mr. See Johnson, Thomas
Johnstone, Gov. George, 133
Jones, David, 214, 352
Jones, Ephraim, 481, 618
Jones, Commodore John Paul, 621
Jones, Thomas, 380, 569
Jones's Ford, Pa., 152
Judges, 442

K

Kakiat, N. Y., 274
Kalb, Johann, Baron de, 656, 657
Kalm, Pehr, 611
Kassel, Germany, 27, 56
Keane, Capt., 308
Keese, John, 87, 88, 89, 266
Kemble, Peter, 336
Kent, John, 8, 29, 236
Kent, Conn., 83
Kentucky, 408-9, 587-88
Kimball, Timothy, 479, 616
Kindall, Mr. See Kimball, Timothy
Kinderhook, N. Y., 196
King's Ferry, N. Y., 95, 96, 97
King's Mountain, S. C., battle of, 600
Kingston, N. J., 121-22, 125
Knight, Dr. John, 592
Knox, Gen. Henry, 16, 105, 107, 367, 515; biographical sketch of, 112, 282; HQ at Vails Gate, N. Y., xxiii (Vol. 1), 338, 642
Knox, Mrs. Henry, 28, 112, 190, 282
Knox, Henry Jackson, 112, 282
Knox, Lucy Flucker, 112, 282
Knyphausen, Gen. Wilhelm, 151, 152; corps, 314

L

Lacey, Gen., 321
La Chevrette, 5, 6, 17, 241
Lafayette, Marie Joseph Paul Yves Roch Gilbert du Motier, Marquis de, 74, 157, 190, 267; American tour of 1824-25, 24, 282, 313, 657; and proposed attack on Staten Island, 92, 281; Chastellux visits, 101-11 passim, 153, 275, 278; at meeting of Pa. State Assembly, 144; and Brandywine battlefield, 147-48, 151, 152, 313, 314, 649;

visits Whitemarsh battlefield, 168-69, 323; visits Barren Hill post, 170-72, 325; visits Thomas Paine, 175; election to American Philosophical Society, 178, 330; command of Light Infantry, 276, 280; and abortive Canadian expedition (1778), 203; letters to Guichen, 247; at Griffin's Tavern, 265; Grieve on, 275-76; Va. campaign of 1781, 366, 371, 378-79, 381, 383, 566-67, 568
La Harpe, Jean-François, 9, 35, 37
Lake Champlain, N. Y., 116
La Luzerne, Anne-César, Chevalier de, 27, 75, 103, 247, 259, 367, 475; portrait of by C. W. Peale, xxiii (Vol. 1), between pp. 136-37; entertains Chastellux, 130-37 passim, 141-47 passim, 164, 173-75 passim, 178; Chastellux's tribute to, 179; Grieve's comment on, 296-97; and Battle of the Saints, 308; and Thomas Paine, 329; and Asgill, 335; visits Williamsburg, 375, 377
Lamb, Col. John, 91
Lambert, Mr., of Va., 412, 588
Lambert, Capt. George, 588
Lameth, Charles de, 613
Lancaster, Pa., 129, 269
Langdon, Col. John, 486, 487, 623
Langdon, Mrs. John, 486
Langley, Mrs. of Bethlehem, Pa., 651
Languages, education in, 497-98. See also English language; French language
Lansing, Col. Jacob, 211, 351
La Radière, M., 268
La Rochefoucauld-d'Enville, Duc de, 278
La Rochefoucauld-Liancourt. See Liancourt
La Rouërie, Charles-Armand Tuffin, Marquis de, 28, 131, 295-96; portrait by C. W. Peale, 296; his legion at Charlottesville, 392-93, 576
Laski, Harold, 237
Lathrop, Dr. Daniel, 341
La Touche-Tréville, Comte de, 465, 614
La Tour du Pin, Henriette Dillon, Marquise de, 566
Laumoy, M., French engineer, 268
Laurens, Henry, 131, 199
Laurens, Col. John, 141, 175, 297, 298, 304; biographical sketch of, 131, 134, 294-95; at Chew house, 139
Lauzun, Armand-Louis Gontaut, Duc de, 24, 73, 75; and Chastellux, 71, 229-31; biographical sketch of, 255-56;

HQ at Lebanon, 359; returns to France, 373, 474; returns to America, 475

Lauzun legion, at Windham, Conn., 71; at Lebanon, Conn., 229-30, 255; and Gov. Jonathan Trumbull, 230-31; at Hampton, Va., 374; march to Boston (1782), 473-74

Laval, Marquis de, 16, 173, 271, 278, 475, 648

La Villebrune, Jacques-Aimé Le Saige, Chevalier de, 373-74

Lavoisier, Antoine, 309

Lawrenceville, N. J., 121, 124, 125

Lawyers, 344, 442-43, 520

Leavenworth, Mark, 33

Lebanon, Conn., 229, 230, 231, 255

LeBaron, Lazarus, 480, 617

Lee, Miss, of Mass., 491

Lee, Arthur, 147, 293, 294, 306, 332, 570

Lee, Gen. Charles, 264, 381

Lee, Col. Henry, 108, 381, 570

Lee, Richard Henry, 429

Lee, William, 570

Leesburg, Va., 583

L'Eguille, Louis Groger, Chevalier de, 496, 630

Lehigh River, Pa., 525

Leisure in America, 542-43. *See also* Amusements

L'Enfant, Pierre-Charles, 658

L'Epine, M. de, 245, 637

LePrince, Jean-Baptiste, 172

Le Rouge, M. (Parisian bookseller), 62

Le Roy, Jean-Baptiste, 193, 341, 577

Lespinasse, Mlle de, 11, 286

Létombe, Philippe-André-Joseph de, 496, 505, 530, 630, 653

Lewis, Phinehas, 76, 77, 78, 81, 260, 640

Lewis, Mrs. Phinehas, 78, 260, 511, 640

Lexington, Mass., battle of, 184, 483, 618

Liancourt, La Rochefoucauld, Duc de, 21, 606

Libraries. *See* Books

Library Company of Philadelphia, 332

Lincoln, Gen. Benjamin, 119, 213, 285, 288, 351, 370

Litchfield, Conn., 81, 261

Little Mud Island, Pa., 316

Livingston, Lt. Col. Brockholst, 276

Livingston, Henry Beekman, 324

Livingston, Mrs. Henry Beekman (Nancy Shippen), 19, 147, 164, 170, 323-24

Livingston, Henry Walter, 33

Livingston, Col. James, 97-99

Livingston, Gov. William, 126, 292

Livingston's Manor, N. Y., 195

Locke, John, 530, 532

London Coffee House, Philadelphia, 328

Longevity, of Americans, 412

Long Island, 63, 67; battle of (1776), 75, 77-78, 106, 337

Longwy, France, 16, 17

Lord, Dr. Joseph, 480, 617

Louis XV, 3, 32, 40

Louis XVI, 310, 606

Louveciennes, France, 32

Lowell-Tracy-Johnson House, Newburyport, Mass., 626

Loyalists. *See* Tories

Luxury, Chastellux's definition of, 539

Lyman, Maj. Daniel, 89, 96

Lynch, Lt. Isidore, 24, 73, 175, 223; accompanies Chastellux on tour (Nov. 1780-Jan. 1781), 65, 69, 81, 107, 147, 197-98; biographical sketch, 248; accompanies Chastellux on tour (Ap. 1782), 377, 566; accompanies Chastellux on tour (Nov.-Dec. 1782), 477, 480, 615; leaves Chastellux's tour, 510; narrow escape from capture by British, 639

Lynn, Mass., 495, 628

M

McBean, Thomas, 658

MacCarthy-Martaigue, Jean-Baptiste de, 486

McClenachan, Blair, 304

McCrea, Jane, 214, 351-52, 355; murder depicted by Robert Smirke, xxiv (Vol. 1), between pp. 200-201

McCrea, John, 352

MacDonald [MacDonnell], Mr., of Va., 397-98

McHenry, Dr. James, 87, 103, 104, 105

McKean, Thomas, 310

Mackinson, Mr. *See* Makingston, Mr.

Macpherson, Charles, 575

Macpherson, James, 576

Macpherson, John, Jr., 657

Macpherson, John, Sr., 657

Macpherson, William, 657

Madison, James, 174, 327, 653

Madison, Rev. James, 375, 394-95, 443, 603, 653; letter to, on arts and sciences, 35, 529-48

Magnanville, M. Savalette de, 5, 235

Maidenhead (Lawrenceville), N. J., 121, 124, 125

Maixel, Philip, 646

Makingston, Mr., 225, 356

Malcom, Col. William, 190

Malesherbes, M. de, 10, 12

Manchester, Va., 427

Mandeville, Messrs. 186, 336

Manners, John, Marquis of Granby, 268

Manorial system, in the Hudson Valley, 343

Mansfield, Samuel, 341

Maps consulted by Chastellux: 62, 85; drawn by Dezoteux, 56; of Brandywine, 148, 152, 313; of Mud Island, 156, 316; of Saratoga, 212, 218, 221, 351, 355; of Virginia, 412, 588; of Conn., 479; of Portsmouth, N. H., 486; of Massachusetts coastline, 493. *See also* Berthier; Villefranche

Marlborough, Mass., 481

Marmontel, J. F., 7, 279

Marsh, Daniel, 72, 256

Marsh, Mrs. Daniel, 256

Marsh, James, 256

Marsh, Rev. John, 367

Marteques, M. de. *See* MacCarthy-Martaigue, Jean-Baptiste de

Maryland, historical factors determining character of, 437; government, 489

Marx, Karl, 237-38

Mash, Mr. *See* Marsh, Daniel

Mason, John, 270

Massachusetts, defense of, 70; and Hartford Convention (1780), 73; Council, 75; constitution, 161, 318-19; agriculture, 480-81

Matthews, Gen., 273

Maubois, M. de, boîtes de, 277-78

Mauduit du Plessis, Thomas-Antoine, Chevalier de, 193, 596; travels with Chastellux, 95, 98, 147, 148, 152, 198, 283; exploits at Germantown, 139, 141; at Red Bank, 156-59, 317-18; biographical sketch, 270; death of, 25, 304

Maulevrier, Edouard-Charles-Victurnien Colbert, Comte de, 565

Mawdsley, Capt. John, 246

Mawdsley House, Newport, R. I., 25, 246

Mawhood, Col. Charles, 124

Maycocks, Va., 431, 596

Meade, David, 431, 596

Meade, Mrs. David, 431

Meaux, M. de, 293, 294

Medals, awarded to Fleury by Continental Congress, 272; as rewards for patriotic services, 545; Friendly Sons of St. Patrick, 574; awarded for valor at Cowpens, 580; struck in Paris for Continental Congress, 655

Meetinghouses, as center of town, 70, 83; Claverack, N. Y., 195; Concord, Mass., 481; Dutch Reformed, 104, 274, 277; Farmington, Conn., 77, 260; Kinderhook, N. Y., 196; Lebanon, Conn., 229; Litchfield, Conn., 81, 261; Morristown, N. J., 115; Plainfield, Conn., 70; Quaker, 151, 313, 314, 321, 322; Saratoga, N. Y., 355; Sheffield, Mass., 226; Washington, Conn., 83; Woodstock, Conn., 479, 617

Meigs, Col. Return Jonathan, 269

Mercer, George, 278

Mercer, Gen. Hugh, 124

Meredith, Mrs. Samuel (Margaret Cadwalader), 39, 174, 303, 328

Merrimack River, Mass., 483, 490

Meschianza, the, 170, 325

Mesmerism, 17, 241

Mesnil-Durand, Baron de, 141, 304, 305

Meteorology, 394-95, 577

Michaux, François-André, 611

Middle Brook, N. J., Washington's engagement with Howe, 117, 121, 148-49; Washington's camp, 285-86

Middleton, Arthur, 285, 328, 593

Mifflin, George, 295

Mifflin, Gen. Thomas, 131, 144, 295, 326

Mifflin Island, 156, 316-17

Milford, Conn., 83, 263

Military positions, assessed by Chastellux: Plainfield, Conn., 70, 255; Canterbury, Conn., 71; Middle Brook, N. J., 117; Whitemarsh, Pa., 168-69, 323; Van Schaick's Island, Cohoes, N. Y., 200, 345; Anthony's Kill, N. Y., 211; Saratoga, N. Y., 211-13, 218-19, 351, 355; New London, Va., 414; Bunker Hill, Mass., 500

Military theory, 112, 117, 304-5. *See also* Frederick the Great; Guibert; Mesnil-Durand

Militia, 213, 600; individual officers mentioned, 69; choice of officers, 84; at Cowpens, 398-400

Miller, Mrs., of Philadelphia, 306

Millico, Giuseppe, 118, 286

Mills, 402; flour, 129-30; sawmills at Saratoga, 218; of Mrs. Bolling at Petersburg, Va., 421; Moravian sawmill and gristmill at Hope, N. J., 518-19, 646

Millstone, N. J. *See* Somerset Courthouse

Miralles, Don Juan, 134, 299

Mitchell, Col. John, 177
Mohawk Indians, 209
Mohawk River, N. Y., 200, 210
Monckton, Gen. Robert, 273
Moncrief, Lt. Col. 314
Money, hard, 337; cost of land estimated in French, 72; for French army, 174; value compared with paper, 181; circulated by British troops, 333; French money in Virginia, 387, 472; French money in America, 572, 615
Money, paper, 572; depreciation of, 180-81, 187, 277, 333; Continental bills of credit, 291-92; cost at inns estimated in, 337; in Va., 585, 588, 416; receipts for tobacco, 420
Monmouth, N. J., battle of, 118, 286
Montagu, Mrs., "Queen of the Blues," 7
Montesquieu, Charles de Secondat, Baron de, author of De l'Esprit des Lois, 10, 24, 144, 223-24, 307, 356, 530
Montesquieu, Charles-Louis de Secondat, Baron de, Chastellux's aide-de-camp, accompanies Chastellux on northern journey (1780), 65, 69, 73, 107, 147, 207; biographical sketch of, 248; on John Witherspoon, 289; recommends John Laurens, 294; on Rittenhouse orrery, 311; returns to France (1781), 374, 566; returns to America (1782), 475, 566; accompanies Chastellux on northern journey (1782), 479, 491, 510, 615-16, 639
"Monte Video," Daniel Wadsworth House, 358
Montgomery, Gen. Richard, 97, 206, 273, 327; monument by Caffieri erected by Continental Congress, 656-58; Trumbull's painting of, 658
Montreal, 203
Moodna Creek. See Murderer's Creek
Moore, Elizabeth, 19
Moore, Thomas, 346
Moravians (Unitas Fratrum), settlement at Hope, N. J., 518-19, 645; settlement at Bethlehem, Pa., 522-25; social and economic organization of communities, 523-25; missionaries among Indians, 598-99; history outlined by Grieve, 643-45; settlement at Nazareth, Pa., 644; "Sisters' House," 650; Old Chapel, 651; archives at Bethlehem, Pa., 652; inventions, 653. See also Hope, N. J.; Bethlehem, Pa.; Nazareth, Pa.

Morehouse, Col. Andrew, 84, 264; servants of, 512-13
Morehouse, Mrs. Andrew, 512
Morellet, Abbé, 5, 9, 17, 37, 319, 607
Morgan, Gen. Daniel, 474, 512; strategy at battle of Cowpens, 398-99, 579-82; Chastellux meets, 580-81
Morgan, Gideon, 640
Morris, Gouverneur, 18, 19, 22, 131, 240, 294, 301
Morris, Robert, biographical sketch, 135-36; and Revolutionary finances, 277, 294, 300, 301, 331
Morris, Mrs. Robert, 136, 164, 295, 303
Morristown, N. J., winter quarters of 1779, 115, 117, 185, 285
Morton, John Ludlow, view of Washington's HQ at New Windsor, xxiii (Vol. 1), 339, between pp. 200-201
Morton, Mrs. Perez, 497
Mosley, Comte de. See Otto, Louis-Guillaume
Mountains in Virginia, 389, 452-56
Mount Holly, N. J., 567
Mount Vernon, Va., 21, 34; Grieve visits, 279, 298-99, 371, 595, 597
Moylan, Francis, Bishop of Cork, 115
Moylan, James, 284, 285
Moylan, Jasper, 284, 285
Moylan, John, 284, 285
Moylan, Col. Stephen, 115-18 passim, 120, 123, 126, 127, 340; and Friendly Sons of St. Patrick, 284, 574
Moylan, Mrs. Stephen, 119
Mud Island, 155, 316. See also Fort Mifflin
Muhlenberg, Frederick Augustus, 144
Muller, Capt., of Bedford, Va., 412-13, 589
Muller, Mrs., of Bedford, Va., 413, 414
Murderer's Creek, N. Y., 515, 642
Murray, Rev. John, 489, 624
Museums, Du Simitière's, 144-45, 309; Chovet's, 146, 311-12; Mlle Biheron's, 312
Musgrove, Col. Thomas, 304
Music, Chastellux's writings on, 4-5, 623; Huron march, 107, 279-80; organ, 168; at Mrs. Shippen's, 170, 324; songs by Richard Peters, 176; comic opera, 296; Artaserse, by Metastasio, 360; singing by Miss Taliaferro, 384; by Miss Saunders, 419; by Mr. Victor, 420; descendant of Pocahontas plays her guitar, 426; concert by Viennois regimental band, 487; songs from home, 499; in Moravian settlements,

523, 644-45, 651-52; mentioned, 286, 506, 543, 584, 615
Muskingum Indians, 598
Mutterson, Mr. *See* Madison, James

N

Nails, scarcity of, 390, 514
Napoleon Bonaparte, 23, 24
Naragontad [Still?] River, Conn., 226
Nassau Hall, Princeton, N. J., 122, 124, 289, 290; depicted by C. W. Peale in portrait of Washington, xxiii (Vol. 1), between pp. 136-137
Nations, character of, determined by circumstances of origin, 434, 532-34
Natural Bridge, Va., 28, 226, 396; views of published by Chastellux, viii (Vol. 2), between pp. 446-447; Chastellux's visit (Apr. 19, 1782), 406-7, 587; Chastellux's "description," 445-56, 606-10
Natural philosophy, 290
Natural science. *See* Science, natural
Nazareth, Pa., 644
Necker, Mme, 7
Needlework, 522
Negroes, 67, 82, 388, 404; in American army, 229, 359; condition in Va., 431-32, 438-40, 585; effects of slavery on masters, 435; Chastellux's proposed method of abolishing slavery, 440-41; British emancipation of, 472, 597-98; John Langdon's emancipation of, 486; Robert Pleasants's emancipation of, 596-97; treatment of, in West Indies, 602-3; Madison's proposal for emancipation, 653
Nelson, Mmes, 383
Nelson, Mr., of S. C., 425-26
Nelson, Horatio, Viscount, 639
Nelson, Thomas, Jr., Gov. of Va., 21, 382-83, 571
Nelson, Thomas, "Secretary," 384-86, 571
Nelson, William, 21, 382
Nelson, Mrs. William, 384
Nelson family, 374, 383, 385, 386
Nesbitt, Alexander, 270
Nesbitt, John Maxwell, 270
Neshaminy Creek, Pa., 129
Neville, M., 147
New Brunswick, N. J., 125, 184, 287
Newburgh, N. Y., 513, 640
Newburyport, Mass., 492
Newcastle, Va., 380, 568

New England, 15; settlement of, 160-61, 436, 533; Sunday law, 255; business enterprise of, 627. *See also* Trade
New Hampshire, 73, 84-85, 263, 488-89, 624
New Hartford, Conn., 76, 227
New Haven, Conn., 263
New Jersey, Howe's attempted invasion of (1777), 106-7, 117, 119, 120-21; described, 125, 436; and Gen. Anthony Wayne, 185; communications with N. Y., 187
New Jersey, College of (Princeton Univ.), 122-23, 289, 290
New Kent Courthouse, Va., 378, 566
New London, Va., 414, 589
New Milford, Conn., 263
Newport, R. I., 14, 16, 25, 63; view of, in 1781, xxi (Vol. 1), between pp. 72-73; trade of, 67; Gen. Heath at, 93; French at, 246; hospitals in, 250. *See also* Fortifications; Franco-American cooperation; French army; French navy
New Preston Hill, Conn., 83, 262
New Windsor, N. Y., 113, 189-90
New Year's celebrations, 222-23
New York City, British troop landings at, 63, 102, 116, 537; proposed American attack against (Nov. 1780), 90, 91-92, 107, 110-11, 267, 268, 281; as objective of Franco-American strategy, 96, 247, 367, 370, 471; contraband trade with Pa., 180; Tory raids near, 334-35; Chastellux and Lincoln command reconnaissance of (July 1781), 370-71
New York State, Northern Invasion of 1780, 88, 207-8, 216, 353; communications with N. J., 187; Clinton's expedition up Hudson (1777), 96, 271-72; historical factors determining character of, 436. *See also* Burgoyne's Campaign of 1777
Nichols-Wanton-Hunter House, 26
Nicola, Col. Lewis, 293, 332
Noailles, Louis, Vicomte de, 24-25, 116, 144, 153, 164, 340; tours America (1780), 95, 98, 101, 147, 168, 177, 191; plays violin, 170; and Mr. Le Roy, 193; visits Gen. Schuyler, 197, 200, 201, 209, 217, 222, 346; biographical sketch of, 270; and Lafayette, 278; and Washington, 283, 345
Noble, Robert, 356
Nobletown, N. Y., 225, 356
North Andover, Mass., 483, 619

North Bridge, Concord, Mass., 482
North Carolina, 181, 389-90, 437, 600-601. *See also* Guilford Courthouse
North River. *See* Hudson River

O

Oberkirch, Baronne d', 20
Oblong, The, between Conn. and N. Y., 84, 263-64
Offley, Va., 381-83, 570, 571
Ogden, James, 270
Oneida Indians, 209, 349-50
Opossum, 375, 462-68, 612-14
Ordinaries, Doncastle's (Byrd's Tavern), Va., 566; Willis's, Va., 386, 572. *See also* English language; Inns; Taverns
Orléans, Duchess d', 20, 21, 22, 240
Orrery. *See* Rittenhouse orrery
Osborne, Sir George, 303
Otto, Louis-Guillaume, 19, 170, 297, 324
Otto, Mrs. Louis-Guillaume (Eliza Livingston), 324
Oyré, François-Ignace, Chevalier d', 377, 417, 566
Ozanne, Pierre, view of Boston in 1778, viii (Vol. 2), between pp. 510-511

P

Paine, Thomas, 28, 175, 176, 311, 328, 635; influence of writings assessed by Grieve, 329; *Common Sense*, 175, 329, 654; *The Crisis*, 329; *Letter to the Abbé Raynal*, 311, 348, 595, 601
Paintings, xix, xxiii, xxiv (Vol. 1); vii-ix (Vol. 2), 339, 358, 629; Barrell collection, 632; by Winthrop Chandler, 617; by Du Simitière, 145, 309, 324, 634; portrait of George II in Nassau Hall, 123, 290; Jane McCrea as subject of, xxiv (Vol. 1), 352; Middleton collection of, 327-38; by C. W. Peale, xxii-xxiii (Vol. 1), vii (Vol. 2), 290, 295, 296, 306-7, 324, 474, 655; by Matthew Pratt, 302; of Marquis of Granby, 268; by John Trumbull, xxiii (Vol. 1), vii (Vol. 2), 346, 352, 358, 373, 655, 658; relation to historic deeds and liberty, 545; American artists extolled by Grieve, 655
Paintings, allusions to: Greuze, 225, 231, 357; Jean Baptiste Le Prince, 172; Gaspard Poussin, 226; Raphael, 417; Hubert Robert, 84, 172; Salvator Rosa, 226; Vandyck, 119
Paintings, seen by Chastellux on travels: religious pictures of J. V. Haidt, 519, 523, 646; Peale's portrait of Washington in Pa. State House, xxii-xxiii (Vol. 1), 143, 307; Powell collection, 136
Paramus, N. J., 101, 102
Parkman, Dr. Ebenezer, 618
Parliament. *See* Great Britain
Parois, M. de, 499, 506
Parr, James, 325
Parsons, Gen. Samuel Holden, 28, 75, 260
Passaic Falls. *See* Totowa Falls
Passaic River. *See* Totowa River
Paterson, N. J., 277, 282. *See also* Totowa Falls
Pattison, Mr., of Va., 414
Patton, Col. John, 295
Paxton, Capt., 404-5, 584
Peace negotiations, 474. *See also* Carlisle Commission of 1778
Peaks of Otter, Va., 412, 588
Peale, Charles Willson, 324, 655; portrait of Washington in Pa. State House, xxii-xxiii (Vol. 1), 143, 307, between pp. 136-137; portrait of Washington at Princeton, 290; portrait of La Luzerne, xxiii (Vol. 1), between pp. 136-137; portrait of Ternant, 295; portrait of La Rouërie, 296; view of Pa. State House, xxii (Vol. 1), 306-7, between pp. 136-137; portrait of Chastellux, vii (Vol. 2), frontispiece, 474; prints Carmichael's notes on Natural Bridge, 610
Pearce, Miss, of Voluntown, Conn., 68, 231
Peck, Col. George, 66, 251
Peebles, Mrs. Elizabeth, 221
Pemberton, Joseph, house of, 299
Pendleton, Henry, 131, 164, 165
Penn, Gov. John, 299, 325, 333
Penn, Richard, 300, 301, 332
Penn, Mrs. Richard (Mary Masters), 301
Penn, William, 37, 179, 180, 333
Pennsylvania, 113, 125; government of, 133, 181-82, 297, 334; meeting of Assembly, 144, 308-9; and Billingsport, 154; contraband trade with New York City, 180; Campaign of 1777, 303; historical factors determining character of, 436-37; settlement of, 533; inhabitants of, 599

Pennsylvania, University of, 17, 144, 145, 309-11

Pennsylvania Line, 107, 374; mutiny of, 185, 270

Pennsylvania State House, Philadelphia, xxii (Vol. 1), 143, 144, 293, 306-7, 308, between pp. 136-137

People, Mrs. *See* Peebles, Mrs.

Percy, Hugh, Lord, 483

Peters, Richard, 173, 176, 312-13, 325, 326, 329

Petersburg, Va., 419, 426, 590

Petit's Gap, Va., 411, 588

Philadelphia, Pa., 15, 26, 537, 593; map by L.-A. Berthier, xxii (Vol. 1), between pp. 136-137; British occupation (1777-78), 117, 137, 155, 301, 309, 325; Chastellux visits, 129-78 *passim;* hospital, 130, 293; Chastellux's assessment of military importance, 140; assembly balls, 176-77; merchants of and war, 270; spying in, 273; ladies of, 302; Grieve's description of, 332, 334; Bates's stables, 585. *See also* British army, withdrawal from Philadelphia; Fortifications

Philadelphia Academy. *See* American Philosophical Society

Philips, Mr., of Litchfield, Conn., 81-82, 261

Philipse, Frederick, house of, 369, 564

Phillips, Thomas, 261

Phillips, Gen. William, 93, 355, 366, 421, 425

Phillipsburg, N. Y., 564

Piccinni, Niccolo, 4-5, 235

Pinckney, Charles, 649

Pitcairn, Maj. John, 481, 482, 618

Pitkin, Caleb, 256

Pitkin, Rev. Timothy, 368, 511, 640

Pitkin, William, 640

Plainfield, Conn., 70, 255

Plainfield Academy, 255

Plater, George, 300

Plater, Mrs. George (Elizabeth Rousby), 28, 135, 300

Platter, Mrs. *See* Plater, Mrs. George

Pleasants, Robert, 596-97

Plunkett, Marie D'Alton, Baronne de, 240

Plunkett, Marie-Josephine-Charlotte Brigitte de. *See* Chastellux, Marquise de

Plunkett, Thomas, Baron de, 240

Pocahontas, 422-24

Pocahontas, Va., 419, 426, 590

Pompton, N. J., 101, 185

Ponds, 484

Popham, Maj. William, 199, 210-11, 214

Poplar Forest, Va., 589

Porter, Mr. *See* Potter, Simeon

Porter, Brig. Gen., 65

Port Island, Pa., 316

Porto Rico, 342-43

Portsmouth, N. H., 484, 487, 488, 620, 622, 624. *See also* Congregational Church

Potomac River, 401, 583, 608-9

Potter, James, 170

Potter, Simeon, 249

Poughkeepsie, N. Y., 191

Poussin, Gaspard, 226

Powel, Mrs. Samuel (Elizabeth Willing), 28, 39, 136, 144, 168, 301-8 *passim*

Powel, Samuel, 131, 136, 301, 302, 307

Powhatan, King, 418, 422, 423

Powhatan Courthouse, Va., 418, 590

Pownal, Gov. Thomas, his view of Totowa Falls, xxii (Vol. 1), between pp. 72-73

Pratt, Matthew, 302

Prault, M., Printer to the King, 27, 28, 29

Preakness, N. J., 115, 275, 278, 281, 283

Prescott, Gen. Richard, 254

President's House, Philadelphia, 301

Prevost, Gen. Augustine, 111

Price, James, 174, 327

Price, Richard, 32

Pride, John, 192, 340

Priestley, Joseph, 32, 309

Princeton, N. J., 121, 123, 125, 183; battle of (Jan. 1777), 123, 123-24, 184, 225, 290, 291. *See also* Nassau Hall; New Jersey, College of

Princeton orrery. *See* Rittenhouse orrery

Princeton University. *See* New Jersey, College of

Pringle, John, 655

Prints. *See* Engravings

Prisoners of War. *See* British army, prisoners, and Saratoga Convention army

Privateering, 136, 180, 300, 309, 472-73, 491-92, 624-25, 627

Property, as qualification for citizenship, 535

Providence, R. I., 63, 66, 67, 70, 232, 251, 368. *See also* Rhode Island, College of

Province Island, Pa., 155, 316

Provisioning. *See* American army; Supplies

Public houses, required by law, 82, 357
Public office, not esteemed by Americans, 534
Putnam, Gen. Israel, 93, 265, 269
Putnam, Col. Rufus, 269

Q

Quackenboss, Henry, 222
Quakerbush, Mr. See Quackenboss, Henry
Quakers, 127, 157, 255; and Brissot de Warville, 36, 292, 320; hospitals, 130, 293; characterized, 148, 165-67, 181, 182, 292, 320; Grieve's arraignment of, 320-31; as loyalists, 321
Quartermaster corps. See American army
Quebec, 273, 327, 656-57
Quinebaug River, Conn., 70-71

R

Ramapo Valley, N. Y., 272. See also Clove, the
Ramsay, David, 328
Randolph, Edmund, 593
Randolph, Thomas Mann, 425
Randolph, Mrs. Thomas Mann, Jr. (Martha Jefferson), 391, 575, 577
Randolph family, 374, 427, 593-94
Randolph Mansion, Philadelphia, 325
Raritan River, N. J., 120, 185
Raynal, Guillaume, Abbé, 18, 595, 598, 601, 658, 659
Red Bank (Fort Mercer), N. J., 156; battle of, 157-60, 303, 317, 318
Redoubts, Northern and Southern, of West Point, 89
Redwood, Trumbull house, 359
Reed, Joseph, 133, 136, 144, 153, 178, 325; house of, 134, 298; and Pa. constitution, 297; enemy of Robert Morris, 301; son studies German, 652
Reed, Mrs. Joseph, 325
Refugees. See Tories
Reichel, Bishop J. F., 646
Reid, Lt. Col. George, 514
Religion, sects in America, 167-68; effects of war on, 442; politics in the pulpit, 485, 505, 511, 620, 635, 640; miracle in Boston, 519; tolerance in America, 547; deism prevalent in America, 603. See also specific denominations
Rendón, Don Francisco, 131, 134, 299
Reparations, from French, 472
Rey, Marc-Michel, 8

Rhinebeck, N. Y., 193, 194, 341
Rhode Island, French fleet press at, 55; threatened British attack (1780), 63, 93, 246-47; British abandonment of, 63; trade of, 67; and Hartford Convention (1780), 73; Quakers of, 166; French arrival at, 246; campaign of 1778, 249, 272
Rhode Island, College of (Brown Univ.), 66, 68, 249-50, 255
Riccoboni, Mme, 6
Richmond, Va., 395, 427
Ridge Road, Pa., 170
Riedesel, Gen. Friedrich Adolph von, 220, 287
Riedesel, Baroness von, 220, 287, 355
Ring, Benjamin, 148, 313
Ringwood. See Ironworks
Rittenhouse, David, 28, 145, 291, 311, 658
Rittenhouse orrery, in Philadelphia, 145, 291, 311, 322, 659; in Princeton, 123, 290-91
River forts. See Delaware River forts
Rivers of America, formation, 451-52
Roads, 405, 573
Robert, Hubert, 84, 172
Roberts, John, 321
Robillard, Fiacre, 310, 464, 613
Robinson, Beverly, 273
Robinson, Samuel, 495, 628
Rochambeau, Donatien-Marie-Joseph de Vimeur, Vicomte de, 572
Rochambeau, Jean-Baptiste-Donatien de Vimeur, Comte de, 16, 24, 63; arrives in America, 246; and Washington, 247, 366, 367, 372, 514; visits Gov. Bowen, 251; and De Lauzun, 255; and John Adams, 319; and Asgill affair, 335; and Va. campaign, 370-71, 374, 431, 473; victory dinner and ball, 374; journey in Va., 387, 428, 448, 572-73; and threat against New York, 471; recommends Chastellux, 475; and march from Va. to Boston (1782), 476, 477
Rock or Rocky Bridge. See Natural Bridge
Rocky Hill, Conn., 76
Rocky Hill, N. J., 121
Rodney, Adm. Sir George, 63, 471
Rolfe, John, 424
Roman Catholics, 39, 245, 637-38; observance of Sabbath by, in Europe, 547-48
"Romantic," Chastellux's use of term, 118, 286. See also Scenery

Rosa, Salvator, 226
Rotondo, M., 32
Rousseau, Jean Jacques, 4, 350, 532
Rulhière, Claude-Carloman de, 172
Rumney, Rev. Joseph, 265
Rumney, Dr. William, 265, 266
Rush, Benjamin, 293, 294
Ruspert [?], Mr., of Exeter, N. H., 484, 619
Ruspert, Mr., of Portsmouth, N. H. See Brewster, Col. William
Russell, Joseph, 251, 368
Russell, Thomas Walley, 506, 635
Rutledge, Miss, of Philadelphia, 170
Rutledge, John, 328
Ryerson, John Francis, house, 275

S

Saddle River, N. J., 102
St. Clair, Gen. Arthur, 109, 116, 199, 285
Saint-Germain, Comte de, 159, 303, 314, 318
St. Germain l' Auxerrois, church of, 22
St. John's, Canada, 97
Saint-Maime, Comte de, 16
Saint-Maur, Dupré de, 12
St. Patrick, Friendly Sons of, 284, 574
St. Paul's Chapel, New York City, 658
Saints, Battle of the, 308, 471
Saint-Sauveur, Chevalier de, 637
Saint-Simon, Marquis de, 371, 372
St. Thomas's Church, Pa., 169
Salem, Mass., 493, 495
Sandy Run, Pa., 169
Santo Domingo, 25, 63, 247, 439
Saratoga, N. Y., battles of: Sept. 19, 1777, 212-13, 351; Oct. 7, 1777, 213, 351; Burgoyne's retreat and surrender (Oct. 7-17, 1777), 217-20, 355
Saratoga Convention, 287. See also British army, Saratoga Convention army
Saratoga (Schuylerville), N. Y., 199, 200, 202, 214, 216-18, 350
Saratoga Springs, N. Y., 350
Sartine, Comte de, 314
Sauerland, Germany, 121, 289
Saunders, Miss, of Petersburg, Va., 419, 426
Saut Saint Louis Indians, 208
Savannah, Ga., 249, 471
Scarsdale, N. Y., 564
Scenery, picturesque, Washington, Conn., 83, 511; Bull's Bridge, Conn., 84, 512; Hudson River, 89, 90, 98; Middle Brook, N. J., 117-18; Falls of Schuyl-
kill, 172; Still River Valley, Conn., 226; Talcott Mt., Conn., 229, 358; Natural Bridge, 406; view from Blue Ridge, 411; Salem, Mass., 495; Easton, Pa., 521; Bethlehem, Pa., 648-49. See also Waterfalls
Schenectady, N. Y., 206, 207
Schuyler, Angelica. See Church, Mrs. John
Schuyler, Casparus, 336
Schuyler, Peggy, 28, 198, 345, 347
Schuyler, Gen. Philip, 288; house at Albany, xx (Vol. 1), between pp. 8-9; Chastellux visits, 62, 197-206, 214, 217, 344-45, 346-47; court martial, 199; plan for attack on Canada (1777), 202-3, 347; plan for Canada expedition (1778-79), 203-5, 347; plan for expedition against Indians (1778), 205-6, 347, 349, 647; gout, 209, 345; and Chastellux visit Saratoga battlefields, 210-11, 217-21; house at Saratoga burned, 218, 354-56 passim; and Vermont, 257; and Van Schaick's Island, 345; and treatment of Burgoyne, 356; letter from Chastellux on public happiness, 530, 653
Schuyler, Mrs. Philip (Catherine Van Rensselaer), 28, 202, 220, 223, 346, 355
Schuyler family, 198, 355
Schuylerville. See Saratoga, N. Y.
Schuylkill Falls, 171, 172, 325-26
Schuylkill River, Pa., 137, 138, 140, 149, 173; Lafayette's skirmish on, 170-71; Chastellux describes, 180
Science, natural, 394-95, 546
Scientific expedition, French sponsorship of, proposed by Chastellux, 458, 611
"Scorched earth" policy of Gen. Burgoyne, 354
Scotch in America, 116, 190, 252, 289, 388, 415, 437, 574, 585-86, 600
Scotland, Mr., of N. J., 520
Sculpture, Falconet's Peter the Great, 229, 358; statues at Chew House, Germantown, Pa., 304; commemorative statues and monuments as guardians of patriotism and liberty, 545; Houdon's Washington, 655; DeKalb monument, 656, 657; Richard Montgomery monument by Caffieri, 657-58
Second River. See Totowa River, 102
Ségur, Louis-Philippe, Comte de, 15, 475, 638-39
Seneca Indians, 207-8
"Sentiment," definition of, 110

Settlements in America, 79-81, 189, 262-63, 389-90, 408, 410, 511-12

Seuganick (Shetucket) River, Conn., 71, 72

Seven Years' War, 3, 198, 264, 289

Seymour, Moses, Jr., 81, 261

Seymour, Samuel, 81, 261

Shakers, 322

Shakespeare, William, 5-6

Sharpe, William, 174

Shays's Rebellion, 626

Sheffield, Mass., 225

Sheriff, 81

Shield, Hugh. *See* Shiell, Hugh

Shiell, Dr. Hugh, 270, 330

Shippen, Ann "Nancy" Hume. *See* Livingston, Mrs. Henry Beekman

Shippen, Edward, 147

Shippen, Mrs. Edward, Jr. (Elizabeth Juliana Footman), 177, 329-30

Shippen, Peggy. *See* Arnold, Mrs. Benedict

Shippen, Sally, 276

Shippen, Thomas, 19

Shippen, Dr. William, 147, 323

Shippen, Mrs. William (Alice Lee), 169, 323

Ships, American: *Alliance*, 490; *America*, 621; *Boston* (renamed *Charlestown* after capture by British), 490; *General Galvez*, 31; *Holker*, 308; *Ranger*, 621; *South Carolina*, 298; *William and John*, 472

Ships, British: *Augusta*, 156; *Charlestown* (formerly American *Boston*), 490; *Formidable*, 273; *Fury*, 156; *Hotham*, 273; *Maria*, 472; *Merlin*, 156; *Royal George*, 308; *Savage*, 597; *Vigilant*, 156; *Vulture*, 98

Ships, French: *Aigle*, 615; *Amazone*, 638; *America*, 485, 486, 621; *Auguste*, 485, 486, 620, 622; *Duc de Bourgogne*, 14, 246; *Emeraude*, 15, 548, 613, 660; *Gloire*, 615; *Hercule*, 497; *Hermione*, 258, 465, 614; *Languedoc*, 630; *Magnifique*, 486, 621, 622; *Neptune*, 26; *Néréide*, 630; *Pluton*, 484, 486, 620; *Queen Charlotte*, 371; *Romulus*, xxi (Vol. 1); *Souverain*, 497, 499; *Surveillante*, 373; *Victoire*, 280; *Ville de Paris*, 308, 371

Shoemaker, Samuel, 325, 332

Shoemaker, Mrs. Samuel, 325

Short, William, 18, 21, 35, 38, 443

Shortridge, Mrs. Richard, 622

"Showell." *See* Chovet, Dr.

Siber, M. de, 486

Silver Bullet affair, 271-72

Simcoe, Lt. Col. John Graves, 378; *Remarks on . . . Travels of . . . Chastellux*, 37, 52, 245, 287-88, 314, 568, 648

Simiane, Mme de, 565

Sinclair, Mr., of York, Eng., 306

Six Nations, 349. *See also* Indians

Skippack Creek, Pa., 137

Slaves. *See* Negroes

Slover, John, 592

Smirke, Robert, painting of Jane McCrea, xxiv (Vol. 1), between pp. 200-201

Smith, Mr., of Easton, Pa., 521, 648

Smith, Mr., of Kakiat, later of Warwick, N. Y., 99, 274, 515

Smith, Mr., of N. Y., 189, 338

Smith, Mr., of Va., 402, 584

Smith, Adam, 11

Smith, D. W., 245

Smith, Capt. John, 422-23, 424, 462

Smith, Joshua Hett, 98-99, 274; Treason House, 243, 273, 274

Smith, Rev. William, 309

Smith, Col. William Stephens, 18, 28, 190, 191, 339-40

Smith, Mrs. William Stephens (Abigail Adams), 340

Smith's Store, N. Y., 274

Smuggling, 181

Societé Royale des Sciences et Belles Lettres, Nancy, 239

Society for Useful Manufactures, 277

Society of Fort St. David's, 326

Society of Moravian Brethren. *See* Moravians

Society of the Cincinnati, 319; emblem, 52

Somerset Courthouse, N. J., 117, 120, 121

Sourland Mountains, N. J., 121, 289

South Anna River, Va., 381

South Carolina, displaced persons from, 181, 425-26, 593, 649; John Laurens's death in, 294; delegates to Continental Congress, 327-28; historical factors determining character of, 437, 533

South Kent, Conn., 83

South River, Va., 401

Sparks, Jared, 240

Speculation, 308, 331, 378-79. *See also* Privateering

Spencer, Mrs., of Petersburg, Va., 419-20

Spencer's Ordinary, Va., engagement at (June 1781), 378-79, 568

Staatsburg, N. Y., 193

Staffordshire pottery, 358

Stark, Gen. John, 90, 91, 110, 267, 281
Staten Island, N. Y., attack on, 281
Steel, David, 402, 403
Stephen, Gen. Adam, 265
Sterling Hill. See Voluntown, Conn.
Sterrett, Samuel, 144
Steuben, Baron von, 173, 265, 277, 419
Stewart, Mr., of Boston, 506
Stewart, Archibald, 517
Stewart, Col. Walter, 110
Stiles, Ezra, 16, 38, 261
Stillwater, N. Y., 211, 221
Stirling, Gen. William Alexander, Lord, 106, 142, 151, 279
Stony Point, N. Y., 96, 97, 98, 112, 272, 273
Strasbourg. See Staatsburg, N. Y.
Stuart, Gilbert, 655
Sullivan, Gen. John, 121, 124, 340; at battle of Germantown, 138, 141; at Brandywine, 150, 151, 152, 314; expedition against Six Nations (1778), 205-6, 349, 521, 647-48; and battle of Rhode Island (1778), 249, 272
Sunday, observance of, 255, 547-48, 659-60
Supplies, for American army, 77, 84-85, 180, 194, 257, 277, 382, 416, 501-2, 520; for French army, 74, 174, 250, 257-59, 288, 289, 327, 367
Surveyors, 226
Sutton, Mass., 480
Swan, Mrs. James, 497
Swang, Mr. (Col. Jacob Lansing?), 211
Swede's Ford, Pa., 170
Swords House, N. Y., 351
Syme, Col. John, 520, 647

T

Talcott Mountain, Conn., 229
Taliaferro, the Misses, 374, 384
Taliaferro, Col. Richard, 384, 571
Taliaferro, Richard, Sr., 571
Talleyrand-Perigord, Boson de, 475, 479, 491, 616, 639
Talleyrand-Perigord, Charles-Maurice de, 616
Tallmadge, Maj. Benjamin, 366
Tarlé, M. de, 251
Tarleton, Lt. Col. Banastre, 280, 381, 398, 570, 579, 581-82
Taverns, generalizations by Chastellux, 76, 82, 315, 337, 380-81; hospitality of, 414; generalizations by Grieve, 603; Jeremiah Angell's, Scituate, R. I., 252; Francis Baird's, Warwick, N. Y., 517, 642; Richard Barry's (Withy's Inn),

Chester, Pa., 315; Bell (of Col. William Brewster), Portsmouth, N. H., 484, 620; Boerom's, Fishkill, N. Y., 87, 265, 513; Boswell's, in Va., 388, 573; Buckhouse's [Backus's], Canterbury, Conn., 255; Bullion's (John Boylan), N. J., 185, 335-36; Byrd's (Doncastle's Ordinary), Va., 378, 566; Samuel Chandler's, Woodstock, Conn., 480, 617; City Tavern, Philadelphia, 141, 305; William Cogswell's, New Preston, Conn., 640; Courtheath's (Joseph Curtis), Pompton Lakes, N. J., 186, 336-37; Samuel Dorrance's, Sterling Hill, Conn., 67, 252, 359; Forster's (Asa Forster), South Andover, Mass., 483, 619; Abijah Gale's, Westborough, Mass., 480-81, 617-18; Goodhue's (Sun Tavern), Salem, Mass., 495, 628; Grant's, Baltimore, Md., 337; Col. Jacob Griffin's, N. Y., 86, 265; Hanover (Paul Thilman), Va., 381, 569-70; Hern's, N. Y., 189, 338; Mrs. Hill's (Lebanon Crank), Lebanon, Conn., 71, 256; Col. Jacob Hyer's (Hudibras Tavern), Princeton, N. J., 183-84, 335; Kalf's, Pa., 525; Timothy Kimball's, Coventry, Conn., 479, 616; Lazarus LeBaron's, Sutton, Mass., 480, 617; Louisa Courthouse (Thomas Johnson's), Va., 387, 573; Makingston's, Nobletown, N. Y., 225, 356; Moosehead, Dover, N. Y., 264; Col. Andrew Morehouse's, Dover, N. Y., 86, 264, 512; Paxton's, Va., 403, 404-5, 585; Thomas Phillips', Litchfield, Conn., 81-82, 261; John Pride's, N. Y., 192, 340; Raleigh Tavern, Exeter, N. H., 619; Samuel Sheldon's, Litchfield, Conn., 261, 511, 640; Skillman's, Griggstown, N. J., 121; Smith's, Easton, Pa., 521, 648; Smith's, Greenville, Va., 402, 584; Smith's, N. Y., 189, 338; Stillman's, Wethersfield, Conn., 367; Waterman's, R. I., 252, 368; Whit's (White's), Andover, Conn., 510, 563, 639
Taxes, 492, 509, 638
Taylor, Lt. Daniel, 271
Teaze, Mrs., 402, 583
Teller's Point. See Croton Point, N. Y.
Temple, John, 629-30, 635, 637
Temple, Mrs. John, 496, 507, 629-30, 636
Temple Hill Monument, New Windsor, N. Y., 641-42
Tenducci, Giusto Ferdinando, 118, 286

Tenmile River, N. Y., 84
Tenon, M., and inoculation, 3
Ternant, Jean, Chevalier de, 24, 131, 295
Ternay, Henri d'Arsac, Chevalier de, 14, 63, 246, 247
Tew, Capt. Francis, 272-73
Thacher, Dr. James, 350
Thames River, Conn., 71
Thellusson, Peter, 30, 655
Thilman, Paul, 381
Thomas, Jacob, 194, 341
Thompson, Mr. *See* Thomson, Charles
Thompson, Thomas, 487, 623
Thompson, Mrs. Thomas (Margaret), 487
Thomson, Charles, 142, 306, 332, 647
Tickell, (Thomas?), 655
Ticonderoga, N. Y., 72, 116, 148, 199, 203, 219
Tilghman, Col. Tench, 106, 263, 513, 514
Tioga Indians, 203
Toasts, custom of, 109-10, 132-33, 177, 281
Tobacco, 420-21
Tocqueville, Alexis de, 531
Toiles de Jouy, 5
Tolliver, Miss. *See* Taliaferro, Miss
Tories, 37, 146, 147, 157, 177, 229; prisoners at Fishkill, 88; in New Jersey, 101, 275, 292, 334-35, 520; hanged at Charleston, S. C. (1780), 131; characterized, 181; numerous in N. Y. state, 192; and Indians, 207, 209; in Virginia, 378, 437-38; role of Board of Associated Loyalists, 567-68; used by Lord Cornwallis, 570. *See also* New York State, northern invasion of 1780
Totowa Bridge, N. J., 104, 277
Totowa Falls (Paterson), N. J., 104, 216, 275, 277, 343, 353; view of by Pownal, xxii (Vol. 1), between pp. 72-73
Totowa or Second [Passaic] River, N. J., 102, 275
Tott, Baron de, 32
Touche-Treville, Comte de La, 465, 614
Tousard, Maj. Anne-Louis, 317
Town, Ithiel, 257
Town, use of term, 70, 76, 229, 262
Tracy, John, 490, 491, 509; house of, 626
Tracy, Mrs. John, 491
Tracy, Nathaniel, 491-92; house of, 626
Trade, American, with West Indies, 65, 67, 73, 300-301, 308, 341-42; slave trade, 67, 73. *See also* Bartering, Commerce. Privateering, Speculation

Travelers, treatment in Taverns, 82, 222, 226-27, 337, 573
Treason House, N. Y., 274
Trees, of America, 78, 79-80, 195, 207; Fir, 410; Judas, 410; Oak, 407, 410, 587; Peach, 410; Pine, 407; Spruce, 226, 228
Trenton, N. J., 121, 292; battle of (Dec. 1776), 123-24, 124-26, 291
Trenton River. *See* Assunpink River
Trinity Church, Fishkill, N. Y., 265
Tronchin, Dr. Théodore, 3
Tronson du Coudray, Philippe-Charles-Jean-Baptiste, 112, 147, 312
Troy, N. J., 115
Truguet, Laurent-François-Jean, Comte, 496, 630
Trumbull, David, 359
Trumbull, J. Hammond, 29-30, 243
Trumbull, John, view of Cohoes Falls, N. Y., xxiii (Vol. 1), 346, beween pp. 200-201; portrait of Chastellux in "Surrender of Cornwallis at York-town," vii (Vol. 2), 373, between pp. 446-447; sketches of, 352; painting of "Monte Video," 358; pictures of Warren and Montgomery, 658
Trumbull, John, author of *M'Fingal,* 655
Trumbull, Gov. Jonathan, 74, 230, 231, 367, 536, 654; projected history of the American Revolution, 75, 259; house of, 359
Tuckahoe plantation, Va., 425, 593
Tudor, William, 499, 636
Tudor, Mrs. William (Delia Jarvis), 497, 506, 507, 637
Turgot, Anne-Robert-Jacques, Baron de l'Aulne, 3, 5, 9, 14, 656
Turpin, Baron de, 28, 445, 606; views of Natural Bridge engraved for Chastellux's *Travels,* viii (Vol. 2), 407, 448, 608, between pp. 446-447; observations of Natural Bridge, 449-50
Tuscarora Indians, 349-50
Tuxedo, N. Y., 189, 338
Tuxedo Lake, N. Y., 189, 338

U

Ulloa, Antonio de, 450, 454-55, 609, 610
Unitas Fratrum. *See* Moravians
"Universal Friend, the." *See* Wilkinson, Jemima
Universalists, 322, 489, 624
University Hall, Brown Univ., 250

University of Pennsylvania. *See* Pennsylvania, University of

Upper Red Hook, N. Y. *See* Rhinebeck, N. Y.

V

Valley Forge, Pa., 170, 172, 323

Valnais, Joseph de, 630

Van Buren, Abraham, 343

Van Buren, Martin, 343

Van Burragh, Mr., of Kinderhook, N. Y., 196

Van Cortlandt, Col. Philip, 337

Van der Kemp, Francis Adriaan, 260

Van Horne, Col. Philip, 118-19, 286-87

Van Horne family, 119-20, 287

Van Horne House, 118-19, 286-87

Van Schaick's Island (Cohoes), N. Y., 200, 345

Van Vleck, Hendrick, 650, 651

Van Vleck, Jacob, 523, 651

Van Winkle, Pieter, 111-12, 281-82

Van Wyck, Cornelius R., house of (Wharton House), 266

Varnum, Brig. Gen. James Mitchell, 251

Varnum, Mrs. James Mitchell (Martha Child), 66, 251

Vaudreuil, Jean-Louis de Rigaud, Vicomte de, 24, 491, 629; accompanies Chastellux on tour (Nov.-Dec. 1782), 475, 479, 490, 510, 639; biographical sketch of, 616

Vaudreuil, Louis de Rigaud, Comte de, 616, 622, 629; Chastellux visits, in Portsmouth, N. H., 485, 487, 490; journal, 620

Vaudreuil, Louis-Philippe de Rigaud, Marquis de, 479, 616, 629; squadron returns to New England (1782), 471, 475, 620, 621; entertains Chastellux in Boston, 496, 479, 499, 506, 507; Chastellux praises conduct of squadron, 508, 637

Vaudreuil, Pierre de Rigaud-Cavagnal, Marquis de, 637

Vergennes, Comte de, 259, 310

Vermont, 72-73, 256-57, 353, 612

Vernet, Claude-Joseph, 84

Verplanck's Point, N. Y., 31, 281, 585-83. *See also* Fortifications, Verplanck's Point

Vico, Giovanni Batista, 237

Victor, Mr., of Va., 420, 421, 425

Vigée-Lebrun, Mme Elisabeth, portrait of Chastellux, xix (Vol. 1), frontispiece

Villefranche, Jean-Louis-Ambroise de Genton, Chevalier de, 89, 317; maps by, 266, 267, 316

Vining, Miss Mary, 28, 39, 177, 330

"Viny," Miss. *See* Vining

Vioménil, Maj. Gen. Antoine-Charles du Houx, Baron de, 16, 24, 246; at Yorktown, 280, 372; returns to France, 374; returns to America, 475; and embarkation of troops from Boston, 476; in command of Rochambeau's army, 477

Vioménil, Maj. Gen. Charles-Joseph-Hyacinthe du Houx, Comte de, 16, 246, 372, 477

Virginia, operation in, discussed at Wethersfield, 247; treatment of French army, 265, 472-73; British invasion (1781) of, 366, 378-79, 381, 383, 419, 421, 422, 425, 431, 566-67, 590, 597-98; Secretary of Council of, 384-85; population of, 386, 571-72; British invasion (1780) of, 391; topography of, 395-96, 412; inhabitants of, 400, 429, 533, 601-3; Chastellux's general view of, 434-44; government of, 442-43, 604-5. *See also* Negroes

Voltaire, F. M. Arouet de, 8, 10-11, 12-13, 23, 237, 279, 305

Voluntown (Sterling Hill), Conn., 67, 231, 251, 252, 254

W

Wadsworth, Asahel, 511, 640

Wadsworth, Daniel, 358

Wadsworth, Jeremiah, 18, 76, 228, 229, 358, 660; house of, 73, 257; as deputy commissary of purchases, 73-74, 258; and Chastellux, 259, 367; and paper money, 277; and John Barker Church, 288-89

Wadsworth, Mrs. Jeremiah, 229, 510

Wadsworth House, Cambridge, Mass., ix (Vol. 2), between pp. 510-511, 634

Wagaraw, N. J. *See* Goffle Brook

Wages, 185

Walker, Maj. Benjamin, 513

Wallace, John, house of, 286

Wallen, Mrs., of Conn., 227

"Wall-nut," 78, 260

Walpole, Horace, 7, 576

Wapping (Wappingers) Creek, N. Y., 191

Wapping (Wappingers) Falls, N. Y., 191

Ward, Gen. Artemas, 164, 306

Warren, James, 566
Warren, Dr. Joseph, 500, 658
Warren, Mercy, 630
Warren, Mass., 65
Warren, R. I., 249
Warwick, N. Y., 515
Warwick, Va., 427, 593
Washington, Gen. George, Hasbrouck House HQ at Newburgh, xx (Vol. 1), 513, 514, 640, between pp. 8-9; portraits by C. W. Peale, xxii-xxiii (Vol. 1), 143, 283, 290, 307, between pp. 136-137; winter quarters at New Windsor (Ellison House), xxiii (Vol. 1), 183, 190, 339, between pp. 200-201; friendship with Chastellux, 16, 62, 197, 267, 284, 345, 365-66, 641, 660; corresponds with Chastellux, 18, 21-22, 284, 365; business transactions with Grieve, 31; Chastellux visits at Mount Vernon, 34; attacked by Simcoe, 37; sent copy of Chastellux's *Travels*, 38, 284; and Hartford Conference, 63; and Jeremiah Wadsworth, 73-74; and Dr. Craik, 87; and Gen. Heath, 91-93; and Fort Clinton, 96; Chastellux's eagerness to meet, 101, 104; official "family," 105-6; at Middlebrook, 107, 117, 121; at Lafayette's camp, 108; hospitality of, 109-10, 595; horsemanship of, 111; personality of, 113, 114; physical description, 114, 278; and battle of Princeton, 122, 124-26, 184; and battle of Trenton, 123-24, 291; and stores and Lancaster, 129; and Joseph Reed, 133-34, 297; and battle of Germantown, 137-41 *passim*; and battle of Brandywine, 148-50, 152, 313; at Whitemarsh, 168-69, 323; at Valley Forge, 170, 172; and Gen. Arthur St. Clair, 199; and Alexander Hamilton, 202, 344; and Schuyler's Canadian expedition plans, 204, 347; and Marquise de Chastellux, 241; and Rochambeau, 247; and Gen. Braddock, 264; and French officers, 267, 278; at Totowa, 275; HQ at Preakness, 275, 278; American attitude toward, 275-76, 279; Grieve's comments on, 278-79; and wines, 280, 369; at Verplanck's Point, 280, 281; and Pieter Van Winkle, 281; HQ at Morristown, 285; and Benjamin Chew House, 299; and death of John Parke Custis, 299; and promotion of Mauduit du Plessis, 318; and Conway Cabal, 328, 347; and exchange of officers, 335; Chastellux informs of De

Grasse's sailing, 366; arrival at Wethersfield, 367; at Dobbs Ferry Conference, 370; and reconnaissance of New York City, 370; route to Williamsburg, 370-71; apprehensions about war after Yorktown, 373; Gen. Nelson assists, 382; review of French troops, 474-75; and incident of slaves with Lund Washington, 597; Jefferson praises, 658
Washington, Mrs. George (Martha), 28, 134, 190, 297-98, 337, 513
Washington, Lund, 597-98
Washington, Col. William, 399, 570, 580
Washington, Conn., 83, 262
Washington Co., Va., 83, 262
Washington family, 298-99
Washington Island (Pierce's Island), 621
Watchung Mountains, N. J., 185, 285, 286
Waterbury (Naugatuck) River, Conn., 81
Waterfalls, 84, 511, 619; Cohoes Falls, N. Y., xiii (Vol. 1), 200-201, 345-46, between pp. 200-201; Glens Falls, N. Y., 216, 353; Haverhill Falls, 483; Falls of Schuylkill, 171, 172, 325-26; Totowa Falls, N. J., xxiii (Vol. 1), 104-5, 277, between pp. 72-73; Wappingers Falls, 191
Waterford, N. Y. *See* Half Moon
Watmough, James, 39
Wayne, Gen. Anthony, 105, 107, 152, 314, 336; at Stony Point, 96-97; Chastellux visits, 111-12, 185
Weather observations, 395-96
Webb, Joseph, 367, 563
Webb, Col. Samuel B., 269
Weld, Isaac, 346
Wentworth, Col. Joshua, 486, 487, 632
West, Benjamin, 655, 658
West Hartford, Conn., 76
West Indies, 30, 67, 73, 247, 471, 475
Westover, Va., 430-33, 595
West Point, N. Y., 353; Berthier's map of, xxi-xxii (Vol. 1), between pp. 72-73. *See also* Arnold, Benedict; Fortifications, West Point
West Point, Va., 374, 395
Wethersfield Conference. *See* Franco-American cooperation
Wharton House, Fishkill, N. Y., 266
Whigs, in Va., 437
Whipple, Mrs., of Portsmouth, N. H., 487, 623; house of, 252, 487, 623
Whipple, Joseph, 623
Whipple, Prince, 623

Whipple, Gen. William, 487, 623
Whiskey, 409
Whitall, James, 157, 159, 317
Whitall, Mrs. James (Ann Cooper), 317
Whitall, Job, 317
White. See Whyte, Robert
White, Rev. William, 131, 295, 322, 604
Whitefield, George, 644, 646, 651
Whitemarsh, Pa., 133, 140, 168-69, 303, 323
White Plains, N. Y., 99, 285
Whitmore, Mrs., of Boston, 496, 506
Whyte, Robert, 316
Wigglesworth, Edward, 626
Wilkes, John, 6, 30, 354, 654
Wilkinson, Col. James, 177
Wilkinson, Jemima, 322
Willard, Rev. Joseph, 499, 504, 634
William and Mary, College of, 17, 374, 443-44; Louis XVI gift of books, 310, 606; honorary degree conferred on Chastellux, 375, 444, 605-6. See also Madison, Rev. James
Williams, Rensselaer, 126, 291
Williams, Samuel, 612
Williamsburg, Va., 420, 433, 450; Chastellux writes Part II at, 26, 471; generals arrive at, 371; French army in, 374; dances at, 384; disadvantages as capital, 427
Williamson, Col. David, 599
Willing, Charles, 299
Willing, Thomas, 301, 307
Willing & Morris, 300
Willis, Jonathan, 517, 518, 642-43
Willis, Nathaniel Parker, 642
Willis, William, 50
Wilmington, Del., 149
Wilson, James, 143, 176, 177, 307, 328, 329
Wilson, Mrs. James, 176
Wind Gap, Pa., 521, 647
Windham, Conn., 71, 255
Wine, 153, 255, 649; Chastellux's supply for journey, 69; Washington prescribes, 280; luxury in America, 315; cask of claret presented by Chastellux to Washington, 369, 472-73; aides-de-camp intoxicated, 491; made from cider, 519. See also Toasts

Winthrop, Gov. John, 75, 259
Winthrop, Thomas Lindall, 636
Wissahickon Creek, Pa., 169
Witherspoon, John, 122, 123, 289, 290
Withy, Mrs. Mary, 315
Women, American: unmarried mothers, 67, 227-28, 231-32, 253-54, 358; characterized, 68, 81, 175, 383, 408-9, 419-22 passim; behavior before and after marriage, 119-20, 441-42; sewing by, 135; dress of, 135, 177, 282, 405, 413-14, 496, 540-41, 589; conversation, 136; status of, 136, 302, 383, 441-42, 524; relationship with French visitors, 177, 276-77, 306, 323-24, 330, 374, 384, 431, 508, 589, 596, 615; early puberty and consequences, 288; physical beauty of, 417-18; British, 417, French: 417-18
Woodlands, the, Pa., 326
Woodruff, Judah, 260
Woodstock, Conn., 479, 617
Wyllis, Col. Samuel, 269
Wyoming, Pa., 512-13
Wyoming Indians, 203
Wythe, George, 375, 443, 653; house at Williamsburg, xx (Vol. 1), 26, 374, 571, between pp. 8-9

Y

Yale College, 263
"Yankee," use of term, 82, 262, 481
Yorktown, Va., Siege of, 1, 371-73, 382; Trumbull's painting of "The Surrender of Cornwallis," vii (Vol. 2), 1, 373, between pp. 446-447; Chastellux's role in, 14, 16, 284, 366, 371-73; Lafayette at, 280; Gimat at, 280, 344; Gen. Henry Knox at, 282; John Laurens at, 294; Hamilton at, 344; Secretary Nelson, besieged by his sons, 385; La Rouërie at, 392-93; Chevalier d'Oyré at, 566; D'Aboville at, 614
Yorktown victory celebrations, 374, 475

Z

Zeisberger, David, 599
Zinzendorf, Count, 643

DATE DUE

3/7/76			
GAYLORD			PRINTED IN U.S.A.